BEDE JARRETT ANTHOLOGY

edited by
JORDAN AUMANN, O.P.

NEW PRIORY PRESS
EXPLORING THE DOMINICAN VISION

Contents

FOREWORD..v
EDITOR'S PREFACE vii

Part One: Dogmatic Principles 1
1 GOD 1
2 THE BLESSED TRINITY... 7
3 JESUS CHRIST...19
4 THE MOTHER OF GOD..52
5 THE MYSTICAL BODY...73
6 THE SACRAMENTS 87

Part Two: God's Handiwork
7 THE CREATIVE WORD 113
8 WHY HAVE WE NO HOM E?..118
9 OUR EYES ARE HOLDEN...126
10 GOD'S PRESENCE IN US...132
11 INDWELLING OF THE TRINITY 141
12 FRUITS OF GOD'S LOVE...150

Part Three: Growth in Holiness
13 THE CULTIVATION OF PERFECTION 167
14 SANCTITY..171
15 FORMATION OF CHARACTER....................................175
16 EMOTIONS AND SENTIMENT 181
17 FREEDOM OF SOUL...185
18 SIN 190
19 CONSCIENCE 200
20 LAW 207
21 OBEDIENCE...212
22 SUFFERING 219
34 COURAGE...230
24 FAITH 236
25 HOPE...245
26 LOVE...254
27 PRAYER 261

Part Four: The Christian Family
28 VOCATION...278
29 VOCATION TO MARRIAGE 280
30 WHAT IS LOVE?..287
31 LOVE'S CHOICE..293
32 MUTUAL LOVE...299
33 LOVE'S EXPRESSION...304
34 LOVE'S RESTRAINT...309
35 TWO IN ONE FLESH...316
36 THE UNBREAKABLE BOND 323
37 THE HOME FIRES..330
38 THROUGH CHRIST TO GOD 337

iv

Part Five: The Last Things
39 WE ARE TRAVELERS..343
40 DEATH...346
41 JUDGMENT..351
42 HELL..353
43 PURGATORY...357
44 HEAVEN..362

Epilogue: Salve Regina
HAIL HOLY QUEEN!..367

APPENDIX: Sources 413

FOREWORD

Father Bede Jarrett, OP (1881-1934), true to the religious vocation given to him by God, was above all a preacher. By reason of his natural gifts, combined with an unlimited capacity for concentrated work, he could have become a notable scholar and a prolific writer. The administrative duties, imposed upon him relatively early in his Dominican life and fulfilled by him with exemplary conscientiousness and abundant fruit until the day of his untimely death, prevented him from developing his gift for scholarship and his capacity for writing. But nothing could prevent him from being a great preacher. To this primary and beloved duty he brought all his outstanding natural gifts of understanding and sympathy, of gentleness and friendliness, of affability and unwearied patience, of personal charm and appealing oratory. But it was not this that made him a great preacher. Much that he was and did might have been purely natural; in actual fact it was not, for it was inspired and illuminated throughout by an intense love of God and of all things, especially of all men, that burned in him as an unquenchable fire. As I have written in another place, 'the keynote of his whole life was that of integrity, an integrity that came of a transcendental vision of truth and goodness and beauty which became clearer and more compelling as the years of his life passed from youth to the fullness of his manhood. . . .He saw the truth of God expressed in terms of goodness and he could see only goodness in the works of the Creator. Out of this came a joyousness of soul that adversity could not diminish, a confidence in his fellow-men that experience could not undermine, a sublime trust in Providence that was abundantly fruitful in its reward.' It was this vision of truth that set him afire with charity, that made him a true son of St Dominic and so worthy a member of his Order of Preachers.

This outstanding aspect of Father Bede Jarrett's life and work is of particular significance in relation to the present anthology, for it is an anthology of the spoken, rather than of the written, word. Notwithstanding the number of published volumes that bear his name, he actually wrote few spiritual treatises. A number of the books from which extracts have been taken are in fact verbatim reports of courses of sermons taken down as he delivered them. This is true of *No Abiding City, House of Gold, Lourdes Interpreted by the Salve Regina*. He was profoundly grateful to those who recorded him in this fashion, but wondered humbly and most sincerely whether the record was worthy of publication. Undoubtedly for us who still hear him in our memories the living word loses something in the coldness of print, but even so the great qualities of the preacher are enshrined in the printed word and will still move the heart while they appeal to the head. The other books quoted in this anthology are sermon records too, though they come directly from Father Bede's own pen. He had a special appeal to youth, as indeed youth had to him For them above all he felt a personal responsibility and for them he marshaled all his natural gifts in the cause of God. For this reason *Living Temples* and *The Space of Life Between* have a quality all their own. But perhaps it is in his *Meditations for Layfolk* that the preacher most clearly shows himself as having become, like St Paul, 'all things to all men'. This book, still in constant demand amongst learned and unlearned alike, as it has been since it first appeared in 1915, is one that will live amongst the spiritual classics, though not for its writing and design as much as for its material content. It is perhaps the only one of his many purely spiritual books that was directly composed for the press; yet it is in no sense contrived and represents Father Bede, possibly best of all his works, as the preacher *par excellence*.

It is easily seen, therefore, that in making this anthology Father Jordan Aumann has chosen his sources well. He could have quoted from Father Bede's notable historical works or from his biographies, for the busy administrator unbelievably found time for these too; but, without any depreciation of the historian and the biographer, he has rightly illustrated the preacher. Within this deliberate limitation he has chosen well; nor has he chosen at random but has used the material at his disposition to develop and illustrate a general plan of his own designing which has a particular merit of its own. His anthology has therefore a dual quality in its own right to recommend it and needs no further recommendation from me. I would add only the expression of my gratitude to Father Aumann for undertaking this labor of *pietas* and for completing it so successfully.

FR HILARY CARPENTER, O.P.
Prior Provincial

EDITOR'S PREFACE

The life of a man is like the passage of a ship across the ocean. As the ship cuts its path through the waters, there is a brief movement of the waters in the wake of the ship, but in a moment the ocean's tide obliterates all the traces of the voyage and no one could know that a vessel had passed that way. So it is with the life and work of the priest. He is called by God, ordained for the ministry, and when his labors are finished he is soon forgotten.

Father Bede Jarrett is one of the few priests whose life and work remain as a tremendous power for good in succeeding generations. Although most of his priestly life was spent in the discharge of the duties of a major religious superior, he yet found the time and opportunity to become an unusually competent preacher, writer, and spiritual director. In every land where the English language is spoken the spiritual writings of Father Bede Jarrett have found a receptive and enthusiastic audience.

The editor of an anthology is often tempted to make an apology for his selection of texts, as if to forestall criticism of his compilation. And yet it is futile to make any apology or defense, for it is unlikely that any two editors would omit the same material or compile the anthology within the same general frame-work. Therefore, as far as this present anthology is concerned, suffice it to say that it was with regret that certain passages were omitted. What was selected, however, was chosen as representative of the doctrine of Father Bede Jarrett and then arranged according to a general plan or theme.

Wherever possible, the particular work by Father Jarrett was presented as a whole. Thus, Part I, which treats of the basic dogmatic principles of the faith, is taken largely from *Meditations for Layfolk*; so also with Part III, which treats of growth in holiness. Part II, which considers man as a creature of God, depends for the most part on *The Abiding Presence of the Holy Ghost*; Part IV, a treatise on the vocation to marriage, is taken from *The House of Gold*; and Part V, the last things, leans heavily on *The Space of Life Between*. The Epilogue, an interpretation of Lourdes by a commentary on the *Salve Regina*, seemed a fitting close to the anthology; first, because the Church celebrates the Lourdes centenary this year, and, secondly, because the *Salve Regina* is a fitting conclusion for the life and work of a Dominican.

The editor expresses his profound gratitude to the Very Reverend

Hilary Carpenter, Provincial of the English Dominican Province, for his kind encouragement and permission to compile the *Bede Jarrett Anthology*. For that which is instructive and inspiring in this volume the reader is indebted to Father Bede Jarrett, for that which is deserving of criticism the editor claims responsibility.

JORDAN AUMANN, O.P.

Feast of the Assumption, 1958

Part One: Dogmatic Principles

1 GOD

THE power of God is beyond the conception of man. Just as the being of God and the life of the Blessed Trinity are known to us only through the light vouchsafed us by revelation, so also are his actions equally impenetrable to our gaze, except for his condescension in telling us about himself. We should really be unable to follow the progress of his power had he not himself assured us of his intervention and his design in the history of the race. Indeed, the unity of God is so straight and close that it is absolutely and logically necessary to admit that in God there is no distinction between his acts and himself. His very being and his acts are one: hence his power is as infinite, as limitless, as is his nature.

For the same reason, too, I can never look for the cause or motive of his action outside himself. If it were possible for him to find the reason of his actions in what I do, then he could not be all-powerful. It is essential that he should do all things for himself alone: for a God who was directed by this or that, by what he saw in his creatures, would be changeable and no longer independent. When, then, I say that God is all-powerful, I mean quite simply that his power is commensurate with every possibility; and I am assured that this is true because I realize that his power is identical with his being; and in consequence, as the one is infinite, the other must be infinite also.

Yet it might seem as though there were things that he could not do, limits that might be set to his power. He could not, it is obvious, make something that should be at once and from the same point of view both round and square. He could not make himself or any other thing three in exactly the same sense as he is one, for that would be a sheer impossibility. He is, indeed, three and one, but one in nature and three in personality; that is, he is not, in the meaning of the word, three and one from the same standpoint. Still, even in cases like these which could be multiplied indefinitely, St Augustine tells us that it is true to say that God can do everything, for he points out that really it would be more correct to express the apparent contradiction in this way: not that God cannot do the thing, but that the thing itself cannot be done, and the reason that he brings forward for this is most interesting. In all these things, he tells us, God is moved by his intelligence, and not by his will; that is to say, there are truths in ethics, in faith, in science, etc., which are true, not because God wants them to be true, but because he knows them to be true. We may put this more clearly perhaps, but less accurately, by saying that some things are wrong not because God has forbidden them, but that he has forbidden them because they are wrong. Thus polygamy is wrong, not in itself, but because it has been forbidden; whereas injustice is wrong in itself and is for that reason forbidden by God. Just, then, as in these moral cases, certain things cannot be allowed, so in those other instances which seem to limit God's power we see really that it is the contradiction which is opposed by the intelligence of God.

God, then, in a certain sense can be said to be at the mercy of truth. And this is truly so, for God is Truth. He is at the mercy of himself. He is all-mighty, but he is also Truth, Mercy, Justice; therefore truth, mercy, justice must prevail. The interplay of these great forces is beyond my reason to discover – I cannot find out the limits of each. Humanly speaking, it is difficult to reconcile justice and mercy, truth and charity, wisdom and love; but with him all these things are one, for they are all himself. He, in the height of his Godhead, includes all these attributes, and with him they are in perfect order. So, too, his power is compatible with truth.

Let me take this to a personal point. The whole series of com-mandments, the articles of faith, are not the choosing of God, but spring from God's own nature. They are all true because God is truth. The faith which, if you will, tyrannizes over me, tyrannizes also over God. I submit to it; and so, if you will, does he, for it is himself. No doubt my ideas of his power are often at fault. I want this done and that, forgetting, it may be, that God cannot act contrary to his own nature. There are, in that inaccurate sense, limits to the power of God – namely, the limits set by his own being. I have grumbled because I did not see that the very truth of his nature forbade what seemed to me to be necessary for myself or another. Let me then, as always, put myself passively into his hands. He is almighty, but there is also the full domain of truth. With him, although not with man, might is right.

God's Presence
We must always begin with God as we must end with him. From him we came and to him we go. This divine ancestry and divine destiny of

ours is none of our doing; it happens to us whether we will or no. But what is to happen in the years between our coming and our going? Here we come on something that does lie with us to settle. We can determine for ourselves whether we keep by him or not. Rather, perhaps, we ought to say, not that we can determine to keep by him, but only that we can determine to open our eyes to his presence, for we are kept by him whether we will or no. He made us and will receive us at the end, and is with us all our lives, so that upon us rests only the choice of determining whether we shall be conscious of that presence or ignore it. It steadily and forever abides, but what shall we do with it?

To answer this we must first note that we have one great desire always, and that is to live. We desire life. Even when, under stress of grief or failure or pain, we cry out for death, it is only because our distress makes us realize how life is denied us by grief or failure or pain. These do not necessarily shorten existence, but if we surrender to them they quench something of the thrill and stir of life. Life is indeed our desire. We turn then, variously, according to our temperament or experience, to what we think will give us life. Under whatever guise or disguise we fancy it to be, we still pursue it. The crowd in the streets, the line of lamps, the wet pavements reflecting the lights, music, the dance, the play, or the sounds and sights of nature in the country, or the companionship of books, or art, or friends – these, according to each one's taste, may seem for the moment to be life's most attractive form, most vital, most energizing. But whichever at any time most appeals to us, does so precisely because it seems most vividly to be filled with life.

Now God is life. He is indeed the Creator of all living things; they are his, and have through him their being and movement. But more than this, mysteriously he shares with them this wonderful life. It is a participation by them in his being, without loss to him, of course, without impinging on his essence, without at all breaking in on his incommunicable divinity. Yet truly he is life; so truly that he gave it as the name by which he should be known to the children of Israel: I AM WHO AM, which is the very fullness of life. Being, existence, crammed to the edge and limit of it with activity, is the nearest we can get – and even then quite inadequately – to our imagination of God. He has no limits; not then as life that is pent and glowing, but as wholly without anything to narrow him, we must conceive of him and try to realize him within us, endlessly, a perpetual source of life.

Because God is life, we are made more alive by being conscious of his presence. We desire life; also we need it. We desire it, and under many forms pursue it, and if we did not we should die. Men do so die, who have deliberately laid aside desire for living. In illness, when it reaches that moment of crisis, whence slopes in either direction life or death, much depends on the desire of the patient for either choice. If he really has no desire for living, gives in, is listless, will not put up a fight for life, his case is already hopeless. It is more often the spirit than the body that decides between living and surrendering life. A man can refuse to surrender himself, make violent efforts against the attacks made on him, and eagerly throw such energies of mind as remain to him into every remedy proposed, contest every failing breath, drive with each heartbeat a fresh supply of blood through all his veins, and fight his way steadily and without recoil back into the paths of health. Even without illness, a man can let himself lose vitality by making no contrary effort. He can acquiesce in and encourage and hasten his end.

Life, therefore, must be fought for. Despite our normal thoughts of it, as something wholly independent of us, it does in some measure fall under our power; so, too, in some measure does God. He too is life, and in that shape lives similarly at our mercy. We can live through him or fail to live at all. His presence is indeed within us, whether we will or not; but we have this left to us, that we can keep conscious of his presence or ignore it. We can refuse to remember that he lies at the center of our soul, or we can have the blessedness of arriving at a state when we know that we walk with God. Nor need that be a mere passing mood; it can be a continuous experience; not exactly that we deliberately and directly think of God the whole time, but that we are never really far from him at any time. Just as sometimes, when we know beforehand that something happy is to come to us during the day, we have a happy feeling in all that we do, without directly remembering what makes us happy, so can the consciousness of God's presence infuse itself into our temper of mind.

Is it possible for the ordinary man to have this consciousness? Would it not destroy the pleasure of exercise, of friendship, of work and amusements? Would we not become too solemn for our part in the world? Not at all. Frequently quite ordinary men of any age have it and are not the less, but the more, happy for having it. It is merely the result of an intense though brief act of the presence of God made in morning prayers, in night prayers, and at midday. Nothing more complicated is needed than that. The consciousness will grow of itself from these three moments and become so habitual as to entwine itself with all our acts and thoughts and give an unconscious refinement to our views and dreams.

The living presence of God that gives us life cannot, however, usually be experienced directly. It is only through faith that we come to a knowledge either of God or of his presence. We cannot prove this presence of God, for the emotions or feelings which we sometimes experience and which seem to convince us of it are not real proofs of it at all. They may be due as much to external circumstances as to our inner spirit, for it is of the very nature of these emotions which seem to give us direct knowledge of God, that they should depend upon conditions of health or weather, or perhaps upon a great trial or a great joy or on the influence of others – upon things, that is, which make the proof no proof at all. We experience God by faith, and by faith only. We have no deeper knowledge of him than that which comes by faith and is illumined by faith.

How do I know God through faith? I know all that I do know about him through the revelation of his Son. It was God the Son, made Man, who came on earth not only to redeem the world, but to give it saving truth. He was the truth and he came to teach truth. Now the truth that he taught was nothing else than the knowledge of God, of God's dealing with man, of God's providence, judgments, rewards, and punishments, and of the way to God. He revealed to us the Father. He revealed to us that this Father had care of the whole world, because he was in the world, present in every part of it. The world is his because he made it; but besides making it, he guides it; and besides guiding it, he is in it. The knowledge then of this presence of God all the world over, shown already, indeed, in the Old Testament, was reinforced by our Lord's doctrine and by his example. Everywhere we find him openly appealing to his Father to support his preaching, to confirm it by signs, because the Father was everywhere present, needing no prayer to make him aware of his Son's travail, constantly beside him. This is the particular revelation of Christ that was fresh to the world: the ubiquity of God, not as a stern judge but as a kind Father.

Very naturally in our Lord's mind it was this teaching which was to be the source of life to all that would hear him: 'He that believeth in me shall not die for ever' (John 2:26). His words were life, and he was himself the life, and in him was life. His flesh and blood were instruments of life, and without these as the food of the soul, it could have no life. The sacrament of initiation into the kingdom was 'a new birth,' because through it a new life was bestowed on the soul. Its waters were 'living waters' because they led to the life-giving doctrine of God's fatherhood and of his benign and eager presence so close to man and so devoted to his interests. Our Lord, therefore, plainly conveyed by his words that the presence of God in the world and our consciousness of it would give us a share in the 'eternal life' of God, not hereafter only, but even here in this passing pilgrimage.

2 THE BLESSED TRINITY

THE mysteries of faith are revealed as truths, but the purpose of their revelation is life. They are received by the intelligence, but they perfect their work in the will. They enlighten the mind, but they inflame the heart. Nothing has been told us by God as a mere matter for remembrance; it is committed to us to be-come a means to achieve the higher life. Even the doctrine of the Trinity comes as an aid in the struggle of my soul to its perfect development, not as a mere puzzle which I have with difficulty to remember in some examination by God or man.

Let me, then, consider the meaning of this mystery as far as the halting and inadequate language of human thought allows me to do so. All the while I must be conscious that I am using human expressions and therefore merely endeavoring to state infinite things in finite categories, to pack divinity into human pigeon-holes. But there can be no harm in my making use of such a method (namely, the attempt to grasp the meaning of mysteries), so long as I realize that any such attempt must be frankly inadequate. The use of this must be fairly admitted since it is something (for which I should be eternally grateful) to have even an incomplete view of God, so long as it is the best view that at the moment is possible to me. The Church has never suggested that with the advance of time she does not obtain a clearer comprehension of the truths of faith: indeed, she has frequently proclaimed by repeated decisions and definitions the gradual unfolding of her sacred deposit.

The Blessed Trinity is, then, the name which we give to that mystery of the divine Persons, who are three yet one, Father and Son and Holy Ghost, constituting in themselves one single God. Of these the Father represents power, for I begin my Creed by professing belief in 'God the Father Almighty, Creator of heaven and earth'. To God in the Person of the Father, therefore, I attribute omnipotence. Of the Son I learn that he is the Word (the Logos as the Greek of the Gospel terms it, making use of the very phrase current among the philosophers of the time) of the Father, that he is the figure of the Father's substance, the brightness of the Father's glory. By all of which I see that the Son is represented as the reflected image of the Father, the idea that the Father has of himself, the knowledge of himself in the mind of the Father, the exact reproduction of himself begotten of his own intelligence. To the Son, therefore, I attribute wisdom. Now God knowing himself must love himself. His own perfections are so lovable that once (if these expressions of time may be used of that which is outside all time) God is known even to himself, he must be loved. Hence the love of the saints towards him is not free, but follows necessarily from the sight of him. Hence also, God's know-ledge of himself must be followed by a second or final act, his love. That love then that proceeds from the Father and the Son (for in love there are always two) is the Holy Ghost. It must not be forgotten that we are trying to put into human language what is above language, but we can in this way obtain some glimpse of the truth.

By my belief, then, in the Holy Trinity I acknowledge in one single God, Power, Wisdom, Love, and I repeat that these three are one. Therefore are these three inseparable. I cannot suppose that one can operate without the other two, since it is part of my belief that they constitute a Trinity. Now surely I do see what an immense effect such a doctrine must have upon life. It is no mere question for theologians, but one that concerns every living soul. Whatever is allowed by God's power must be guided by his wisdom and urged on by his love. All that happens to me in life, the little worries and the great anxieties, the crises and the daily annoyances, the sorrows and joys, the harms that reach me through the sins of others, the great crimes of history, the huge and devastating wars, the partings and loves and whole cycle of human experience, are permitted by power which is itself wise and loving. These three Persons determine my life, and, since I walk by faith, I must surely grow very patient in my attitude to life. For how can I complain or criticize God's providence, since it all comes under that triple influence of Power, Wisdom, Love? Under the guidance, then, of this mystery I can walk through the valley of death or the more perilous borders of sin without loss of courage or hopefulness. Nothing can make me afraid. How these are separate, yet one, I do not know, nor can I reconcile in my concrete experience the claims of each. It is always a mystery, but a mystery in which I believe. Whatever Power allows on earth is designed in Wisdom and attuned by Love.

The Holy Ghost
The Third Person of the Blessed Trinity is the most mysterious; about him we seem to hear least and to understand most vaguely. The work of Father and Son, their place in the economy of the divine plan, is simple and evident, at least in its main lines, but of the Holy Spirit it appears as though his precise purpose had not been sufficiently

described to us. He is the equal of the Father and the Son, of the same nature, power, substance, eternally existent with them, participating in the same divine life, forming with them the ever-blessed Three-in-One. He represents to our human point of view that wonderful mystery, the personified love that proceeds from Father and from Son forever, and by this act completes the perfections of God. We can conceive of no further addition to that being, save power and knowledge and love. Yet we know also that he has his place, not only in the interrelation (if the word may be allowed) of the Godhead, but in the relationship (though this phrase is certainly inaccurate) that exists between God and us. For since God is one and indivisible, his love for us cannot be other than the love that he has for himself. In him there can be no distinction at all. Hence it is that we discover that he loves himself and us in the love of the Holy Ghost. His love we see to be nothing else than himself, unchanging, undying, without shadow of alteration. Sin as we may, we cannot make God love us less. Children though we be of wrath, he cannot help but love us, for the gifts of God, especially the supreme gift of himself, are without repentance.

God cannot cease to love me. That is the most startling fact that our doctrine reveals. Sinner or saint, he loves and cannot well help himself. Magdalen in her sin, Magdalen in her sainthood, was loved by God. The difference between her position made some difference also in the effect of that love on her, but the love was the same, since it was the Holy Spirit who is the love of the Father and the Son. Whatever I do, I am loved. But, then, if I sin am I unworthy of love? Yes, but I am unworthy always. Nor can he love me for what I am, since in that case I should compel his love, force his will by something external to himself. In fact, if I came to consider it, I should find that I was not loved by God because I was good, but that I was good because God loved me. My improvement does not cause God to love me, but is the effect of God having himself loved me. Consequently, even when I am punished by God, he cannot hate me. It is his very love itself that drives him (out of the very nature of its perfection) to punish, so that Dante spoke truly when he imagined over the portals of Hell the inscription: 'To rear me was the work of immortal power and love.' Each of us is, therefore, sure that he is loved eternally, that from God's side that love can suffer no change. How, then, is it that we grow evil or lose the familiar intercourse that we once had with him? It is because he has given us the terrible power of erecting, as it were, a shield between ourselves and his love. He loves forever the same, but it is we who by our sins have the power to shut off that love from effecting anything good in our souls.

Surely there is something overpowering in the concept of this work of God, this unceasing and unchanging love? I talk of fidelity in friendship as being to me the most beautiful thing on earth. The sight of a lover, faithful despite disillusionment to his beloved, is the most wonderful thing in all the world; this loyalty of soul for soul, despite every toil and stress, good repute and evil; beyond all degradation and above all ambition, when soul has been knit to soul.

> Love is not love
> which alters, when it alteration finds
> Or bends with the remover to remove.

Yet this is but a feeble representation of the ineffable union between God and myself. Sinner though I be, he is my lover always. Even my sins cannot break his persistence, can only set a barrier between myself and it, can only by the dangerous gift of my free will prevent its effect from being seen in my soul. But the love of God is with me always, 'in me and within me and around, in million-billowed consentaneousness, the flowing, flowing, flowing' of the Spirit. How can I hold back, howsoever wrongly I have acted, for his love is the same forever? As I was deep in his love when I was a child, so also does he love me now.

The work of the Spirit has been outlined in the Gospels. Our Lord at his Last Supper, when his teaching seems to have expounded in the full splendor and height of its tremendous mysteries and when, if ever, the apostles could truly say that he had passed out of the realm of parable and had come into the deepest ways of truth, said that his going away was necessary for the coming of the Paraclete. He had to die and rise and ascend, and then from the right hand of the Father his own work would continue in a ceaseless intercession for all the children of men. On earth, however, his place would be taken by the Holy Ghost, who should teach the apostles all things and bring back to their minds whatever he had taught to them. In this way was guaranteed the infallibility and growth in doctrine which are the work of the Spirit. Our Lord had certainly to temper his doctrine to the minds of his hearers. He could not from the first reveal to them the full meaning of his words. In the beginning, indeed, the need was simply for the main ideas to sink gradually in; then slowly the other less important though necessary truths could be added. The little that he did teach was not too clearly retained, so that he had frequently to be upbraiding them with not having understood his meaning. The length of his stay with them had not made them always grasp of what spirit they were. What should happen when he was gone? He answers that only his going will set them on their own strength.

As the Church grew in the range and depth of her doctrine, so must she forever grow. The problems that distract her must increase; with each generation they change their expression, for the forms of thought are the most mobile and uncertain of all human construction. A cathedral lasts longer than a philosophy; a haunting song outlives the latest system of metaphysics. Questions are settled only that the restless mind of man may add another difficulty to the solution that allayed its previous doubt. Rapier-like in its power to find the weak joint in the armor, reason, sharpened by scientific criticism, picks here and there at the composition of the Creed. New conditions, new discoveries, new languages, require new attitudes, new difficulties, new adjustments of old principles. Obviously it is not sufficient to know the rules of the art, the great trouble and anxiety comes in their application.

So, too, is it in the faith. The articles of belief seem at times to suggest contradictory answers to the problem that happens at the moment to be perplexing our minds. According to one mystery, one solution; according to a second, another. How to choose and select, to decree without fear or favor, without danger of mistake, is the work of the Church. Not merely in the broad line of the Church, but in the individual soul, the same task must go on – the balance between what has to be discarded as of passing significance and what is of abiding import. I have to discover for myself which is the mere adventitious dressing of some bygone form of thought and which is of enduring truth. Yet not indeed for myself, since in the Church abides forever the indwelling of the Spirit of God.

Thus came the Holy Spirit on the first Whitsunday. He came, we read, in the rush of a great wind and in the form of fire, to typify the illumination of the mind by faith and the impulse given to the will by love. He came to teach all things, to recall to their minds the full doctrine of Christ. At once, after their reception of his grace, the apostles become changed men. No longer timid and frightened followers who fled at the first sight of danger and denied with an oath that they had ever known the name of Christ, they now become glad missionaries, declaring themselves willing to suffer in defense of that name. In council chambers and before kings they announce the Gospel. So, too, when perplexities come as to whether or no they should force on all Christians the ceremonies of the Old Law as being of binding value on the conscience of the New Dispensation, they assemble, discuss, and decree in a phrase that clearly marks their own appreciation of the place they had to take in giving to the world the message of Christ: 'It has seemed good to the Holy Spirit and to us.' They and the Holy Spirit are fellow-workers in the apostolate of Christ. The revelation made to them by their Master was but a grain of mustard-seed compared with the full development that should come after. It should grow from that till it included all truth; but the knowledge of every detail of that truth would not at once be necessary, so the gradual unfolding was left to the work of the Spirit. The work, then, of the Holy Ghost is two-fold: it is to inflame love and to enlighten the mind. Let me wait patiently for this illumination of my spirit by the Holy Spirit, putting no obstacle in the way, praying daily for that illumination which shall light as by a vision my view of life.

The Gifts of the Holy Ghost

The real difficulty experienced by most of us in keeping up our courage in the unceasing battle of life is that we realize how utterly we depend upon ourselves. Of course it is true that the grace of God will be always with us, that it is never withheld, that there is always a sufficiency of it for us to meet and triumph over every assault of the evil one; yet even so, the disquieting thought comes home to us that it is always we ourselves who determine our own actions; so much so, indeed, that if they are worthy of reward, it is we who obtain the reward, but if of punishment, that it is we who suffer. St Thomas says with stimulating paradox: 'Not partly by God and partly by man, but altogether by God and altogether by man.' That is to say, I have to reconcile these two separate truths: I cannot will anything without God's grace helping me to do it; yet God's help does not take away from me my responsibility in the act, for its moral value will be adjudged to my credit or demerit. It is in the second part of the paradox that the difficulty lies. Conscious as I am of my past failure, I can hardly look forward without dismay to future troubles. Consequently, I turn to see if there is anything that the Church teaches that can relieve me from the burden of this discouragement. Is there any doctrine that gives me in any way at all an escape from the terror of my own responsibility?

To this the Church makes answer that her doctrine of the indwelling of the Spirit of God by means of the sevenfold gifts does go a long way to remove the load from my own shoulders, does suggest to me a perfectly true sense in which my soul is ruled not by me but by another. As far, then, as these things can be stated in human language, we may say that the gifts differ from the virtues in this, that the gifts are moved into operation not by me but by God. When I perform an act of virtue it is obvious that (not excluding God's grace) it is I who perform it and acquire merit in consequence; but in the movement of the, gifts it is not I but God who is the mover. He is the sole mover, In the actual movement of the soul under the influence of the gifts I cannot claim any part at all. It is he who has his hand on the tiller, who guides, steers, propels. Hence it is he, not I, who has control of my soul. With the four gifts that perfect my intelligence, he illumines my mind; with the one gift that perfects the will, he inflames my desire; and with the two that perfect the passions, he strengthens with his intimate indwelling my emotions of love and fear. By the instrumentality of the gifts the soul is keyed-up to the level of God, tuned to concert-pitch. Or, to vary the metaphor, the soul is made so responsive to the divine influence that, like some delicate electrical receiver, it registers every passing breath of God. I must remember always that it is his doing, not mine.

Must it therefore be admitted that by the gifts I merit nothing? Surely if this be so it would seem as though I had no need of them. If their influence on my life was only to leave me no better off than before I received them, I might just as well not have had them at all. If in them God is the mover to the exclusion of myself, then it would be absurd for me to expect any reward for what has been absolutely no work of mine. This is true. Yet to this I must also add that I can profit by them. The Holy Spirit lights up my mind and enables me to see, or refines my perception of and responsiveness to his least suggestion. That is his doing so far. Illumination and refinement are entirely his work. But my part comes later, when I act up to these suggestions or in accordance with this vision. Then I am profiting by the gifts. Suggestion and vision alike are from God. He opens my mind and I see him everywhere, in a flower, in trouble, in the soul of a sinner If in consequence of seeing him in the sinner, I turn to that sinner and speak kindly of the love that never fails, or if I help him even by my sympathy, though I speak no word of spiritual significance, then the good that I achieve, or at least the good I am trying to do, becomes my way of profiting by means of the gifts. This indwelling of the Spirit of God, while it takes from me the control of my soul and hands it over for the moment to God, yet gives me something by which I can again love and be rewarded.

Out of these sevenfold gifts there are four that perfect the intellectual side of man. They are wisdom, understanding, knowledge, and counsel. Of these it is obvious that the last is chiefly given me for the benefit of others, the first three for myself. The gift of counsel means quite simply that I receive suggestions from the Holy Spirit what advice I am to give to those who come to consult me. I am made so responsive to the divine wisdom that I at once perceive what is best for others, in a way that without the gifts I should be wholly unable to do. Thus it sometimes happens that I am suddenly conscious of words apparently suggested to me from outside, which are as much a surprise to myself as they are of evident comfort to my hearers. The very phrase for which they have been longing, and which alone seems to have the power to enable them to see straight into the entanglement of their affairs, comes trippingly to my tongue, though I am perhaps unacquainted with their circumstances, except for the little that they have been able to tell me. The gift of knowledge enables me to see God in the natural world of creation, in reason, in the arts and crafts of man, in nature. It is an understanding of God, learnt from the material things of life. On the other hand, the gift of understanding allows me to see him in the supernatural world of faith, in truths and mysteries; while wisdom further acquaints me with the interrelation between faith and reason, nature and supernature.

In these ways God, by means of his gifts, lights up our minds. Under this illumination I now look out upon creation and find it to be alive with the traces of God's presence. Nature becomes at once the very loveliness of his vesture and I say to myself that if I can touch but the hem of it I shall be made whole. Even in the relentless preying of beast on beast I see somehow the wonderful work of God. The machinery of man is no longer a sight of ugliness, but becomes colored by the brightness of his power. It is the child's toy that reproduces on an infinitely smaller scale the creative energy of the Creator. The linked reasoning of philosophy is the imitation of an infinite intelligence. Then I lift my mind higher to the ampler regions of faith. Here surely is the very splendor of God. In the depths of mysteries that my intelligence is too faulty and finite to fathom, lurks the wonder of his truth and the ways of his wisdom. Justice, mercy, loving-kindness, and overpowering majesty are all crowded upon my imagination by the thought of all that he has revealed to me of himself. Here, if anywhere, I can at least understand that God is altogether above me. Then, again, the highest gift of all floods my soul with even clearer light, and I see the interrelation of all things. I see how the death of a sparrow, the sunset, the Incarnation are all parts of a perfect whole. It is not an uplifting of the soul from earth to heaven, but a perception that earth and heaven are themselves the fragments of a larger scheme.

These, indeed, are visions such as the gifts that perfect the intelligence evoke in the mind. But it is our business to see that they do not remain barren visions. Just as faith is allowed us that it may lead to life, and as we shall be the more straitly condemned if we do not carry into practice what faith reveals, so also will our judgment be the more severe if with all the light which is vouchsafed to us we yet prefer to walk unheeding in the midst of this wonderful world. There are many who find life dull and religion a thing that bores them. Perhaps the reason is that they neglect the vision; it is there before their eyes if they would only look. But for me the world must become transfigured. Life then will be found more easy, less vexatious, will lose that dreary outlook which is the most depressing of all temptations, and which makes me consider it not worth living. I shall at least understand that there is a purpose in existence. Evil and suffering are seen to be parts that require to be handled carefully that their places in the design may not be overlooked; not ignored but acknowledged, they are found to be the stepping-stones to greatness. Success and failure have no separate meaning, for the need is for them both. Patience is discovered to be the most perfect virtue to have achieved, patience with others, with oneself, with life, with God. Nor is this state of soul due to a disregard of the circumstances that attend our time on earth, but to a more thorough appreciation of the terms of existence. I see life fuller, enjoy it more. It is the patience not of the wearied voluptuary but of the enraptured lover, who is so sure of his love that he can afford to wait through all time for eternity.

This gift is fortitude, which, as we have already stated in general terms, must be carefully distinguished from the virtue of fortitude. This gift is entirely under the direction of God and excludes altogether on my part any action at all in the operation of the gift. This exclusion of all human co-operation seems harder perhaps to understand when the will is in question, as it is in the gift of fortitude. It seems altogether impossible to imagine that God can direct the will and yet that its act should be voluntary. It is clear, indeed, from the Catholic doctrine of grace, that it is possible for God to move the will so powerfully as to determine not merely that the will shall act, but to determine also that it shall act freely. God is so intimate to the will that he can, so to say, save it from within. But this is different from his control of it in the gift of fortitude. In the intellect a light can be present that is none of our own; but in the will how can there be a force that is not itself of the will?

To grasp the way in which God works, we can describe it only as a sense of firmness imparted to the soul by the perceived presence of God. A comparison, however inadequate, suggests to us in what manner this is effected. The mere presence of others gives us a courage that alone we should probably not have experienced. A child having to undergo some slight operation, some test of pain, is usually willing to bear it patiently if only its mother will hold its hand. It is, of course, not that the pain is in this way rendered any the less, but only that a feeling of bravery is imparted by the mere presence of the mother. So, again, in a still more striking way is it with children in the dark. They are frightened by the loneliness of it; but if another is in the room, though he may not be seen or heard, without any sensible appreciation of the presence and sustained only by the knowledge of the nearness, the child becomes at once reinforced by a courage that springs entirely from the other's proximity. An invalid will grow querulous when he knows that he is alone. The mere presence of an onlooker will nerve us to bravery without a word being spoken or a thing done. In some such sense our soul, by the perceived presence of the Holy Spirit, is encouraged, despite its natural or acquired timidity, to persevere. Thus it will be seen that the paradox has been reconciled. The perception of the presence has not been our own doing, still less has the nearness of God been through any merit of our own. But the mere indwelling of the Holy Ghost has itself refined the perceptive faculties of the will so that they are strengthened by the divine friend.

This, then, is the precise purpose of this particular gift – a perception, apart from all the ordinary methods, of the proximity of God to the soul. Not, indeed, as though it meant nothing more than the appreciation that God is everywhere, but rather just one aspect of the appreciation, namely, such an idea of it as will enable the soul to gain courage. Always the gifts mean, according to the teaching of the Church, such a refinement of spirit as shall enable us to perceive the least passing breath of God. So still has our soul become that the slightest stir ruffles the surface with ripples of a passing presence. So delicate is my soul that instinctively I am conscious of the indwelling of the Spirit of God and nerved in consequence by a corresponding strength which is no result of any determined act of will, but is, as it were, forced on me by the very nature of the case. Neither presence nor strengthening are in any case my doing nor do I participate in either. But when I take the further step and proceed to act in consequence of them, when in virtue of a strength that is not my own, I banish fear and face resolutely the difficulties of the good life; then has the gift led to the virtue, and out of something that was divine has blossomed something that is human Surely it will be of the utmost consequence to me to realize this nearness of God and the courage that its perception will give. In all my trials none is so hard for me to bear as discouragement and depression. How, then, can I now shirk my duty and the disagreeable necessities imposed on me once I have made use of this divine friend whose hand is always locked in mine?

Besides the intelligence and the will there are other faculties which, though they are numerous and diverse, can be grouped under the heading of the emotions. Sometimes they are called passions, in the philosophic meaning of the word; that is to say, the movements of the non-rational portion of our being. Sometimes we speak of them as sentiments, especially when we wish to imply that they are to be considered weak and effeminate. Here, however, we have only to consider them as perfected by two gifts of the Holy Ghost. For this purpose it will be necessary to say that these emotions, though various, can be divided into two main headings, such as fall under the general name of love and anger. Under the first would come joy, desire, etc., namely, all those sentiments that have upon us the effect of drawing us towards something or some person and giving us expansive feelings towards all humanity. The chief result of these, even physically, is that they widen our sympathies. Under the heading of anger we would place fear and the other set of feelings, the effects of which are to chill the soul, to contract the emotions, and to produce upon us the feeling of numbness. Even physically we know from experiments of psychologists that the result is to stifle action. The one set shows that our mind has been attracted, the other that it has been repelled.

Piety, then, is said to perfect the attitude of man to God and to things of God, by giving to his relation to his Maker the appearance of friendship. Fear of the Lord, on the other hand, inclines him rather to look upon God in the character of a judge. The one sanctifies the feeling of love, the other hallows the feeling of fear; and in the life of the soul there is room and need for both. Indeed, it may be said not unjustly that together they produce in the soul that instinct of reverence that is begotten of both. Love that knows no reverence is not love at all, but passion; and fear that cannot revere the object of our fear is altogether inhuman. So, too, from the opposite standpoint it can hardly be questioned that the chief obstacles that get in the way of our perfect service of God are the two characteristics of hardness and independence. We do not respond to his appeals; the Passion and the ever-flowing love leave us cold because our hearts are so hardened by the interests and the cares of our daily life, and that deep respect that we owe to the Master of life becomes too often irritation at the way in which his commands cut across our pleasures. We object to the manner in which through his ministers we are told to do something that altogether revolts us, not because it is something very great, but because of its very pettiness. He treats us, we are often inclined to think, as though we were children. Fear of restraint is a natural instinct in men and animals.

Reverence, then, suggests that there is needed in us somehow a feeling of tenderness towards God, a softening of the hardened edges of the soul, and at the same time a subjection, an avowal of our dependence on him. The Holy Ghost is, then, to be considered as perfecting by means of these gifts even that borderland of man that lies between the purely reasonable and the purely sensual. The vague stretches of man's consciousness are by the indwelling of the Spirit of God made at once responsive to the slightest communication from it. Psychology in our own time has made its greatest progress by exploring all the really unknown lands that are in each of us. The phenomena that are produced by hypnotism and spiritualism are evidence of many other things, which are at present as closed to us as the regions of Tibet. But in this connection they explain to us how whatever lies beyond the influence or direction of reason and will must still be brought into subjection to the standard of Christ. We have, therefore, nothing to fear from the researches of professors, for they are but giving us opportunity for extending in our own souls the territory that must be handed back to him who made it. This communication and susceptibility to the movement of God is his work, not ours. The virtue must be added to the gift, must follow it as man's contribution (not, of course, to the exclusion of God) to the work of his salvation. It is not sufficient for me to feel this presence or to be conscious of the reverence due, but I must further add to it the love and fear of my heart embodied in action; namely, in thought, word, and deed.

3 JESUS CHRIST

THE foundation of the Christian name is belief in the divinity of Christ, that is, a belief that he is God equally with the Father and the Holy Spirit. Without this clear expression of faith there can be no acceptance of the plain meaning of the Gospel. For if he were not God, then he could not even have been a good man, since he certainly claimed to be divine in a sense altogether different from everyone else, and distinct from the vague conceptions that made Buddha and Mahomet the sons of God. Schlegel has crystallized this in a sentence: 'If Christ was not more than a Socrates, then a Socrates he certainly was not.' Lessing turns it another way: 'If Christ is not truly God, then Mohammedanism was an undoubted improvement of the Christian religion. Mahomet on such a supposition would indisputably have been a greater man than Christ, as he would have been far more veracious, more circumspect, and more zealous for the honor of God, since Christ by his expressions would have given dangerous occasions for idolatry; while, on the other hand, not a single expression of the kind can be laid to the charge of Mahomet.'

Our Lord proclaimed himself unique, sinless. Now to do this, and not to be this, is either hypocrisy or madness, for the claim of a man to be God is such an act of assurance as can come only from knowledge or from an unbalanced mind. The whole force of existence is continually teaching us our own littleness by means of the little aches, pains, and disappointments of life, so that for one habited in human flesh to claim immortality, infinity, all-mightiness, and responsibility for all existing beings, requires full deliberation and absolute conviction. Even the Caesars who demanded to be worshipped in their lifetime looked upon themselves merely as symbols of empire and heroes, not as unique in divinity.

Now Christ our Lord did make this absolute claim. In his parables and broken sayings, apart from the definite allusions to his Sonship of God (which might indeed be differently interpreted), he shows us the greatness of his claim. In one place he tells us about a vineyard, to which the king (who is evidently God) sent his messengers to demand the fruit of the vines. These messengers, whose coming was received by the Jewish people with insults, injuries, and persecution, are admitted by all to represent the prophets. Then, the parable continues, the father sent at last his son. This son was of his own nature, sole heir to his possessions, whom at least, he thought, the workers would treat with respect. The prophets were God's messengers, but the new arrival was his Son. Our Lord, therefore, put himself above the prophets as the sole Son of God; we are told expressly that the Pharisees knew that he was speaking of them.

In another place he says that the day of judgment is known neither to the angels nor the Son, but to the Father; here too he places himself above the angels also Finally, he claims the privilege of a unique and mutual relation with the Father: he alone knows the Father, and the Father alone knows him. What is this but the claim of an equality of knowledge with God? To know and be known solely by another is surely to be equal to that other – to be so penetrated with his spirit and so to dominate him with one's own spirit that nothing can in any sense separate one from the other. Nor is there, finally, any passage in the New Testament in which our Lord ever asks for the prayers of others.

Jesus Christ then claims to be God and justifies that claim by miracles and still more by a blameless life. He is not merely one who is conscious of the indwelling of the Spirit of God, not simply divine in the sense in which all are touched by the spark that is of God, but uniquely the only-begotten Son of the Father, full of grace and truth. 'My Lord and my God' was the confession of St Thomas.

O true and perfect God! Like the apostle, I, too, am on my knees before him. I can see in his life signs evident and manifest that he is human. I read of him under the terrors of life and death. Man surely I know him to be, but he is more. 'I know men,' said Napoleon, 'and Jesus Christ was not a man.' My eyes may see only the human form. I see the print of the nails and spear, the marks of scourging and crowning, the linen cloth lying, the very signs of death. Yet all the while I know him to be God as well as man. I profess my belief in his divinity precisely in the same sense in which I profess the divinity of the Father. There is no difference of nature between them, without beginning or end, eternal, yesterday and today and the same for ever, the King of ages, immortal, invisible, the only God. The importance of the revelation is immense. Neither flesh nor blood could reveal it, but the Father only who is in heaven. By his grace it is that I say: 'My Lord and my God.'

The coming of Christ was for a definite purpose: to atone for the sins of the world. Whether he would have come if the world had not fallen into sin, it is impossible to say, though Scripture implies that it was sin alone that made his coming imperative. Even the Church sings in one of her most beautiful hymns° 'Happy fault of Adam that required so worthy a Saviour!' but that is a point apart, and needs no mention here. We know that man sinned. Through the action of Adam the whole race was by the decree of God involved in the loss of original justice and suffered the privation of grace and became children of wrath. Man had sinned, yet he could not make satisfaction for his sin; since a fault is partly to be measured by the dignity of the person against whom it is committed, sin took on something of the infinity of God. Man, therefore, was not able of himself to atone. God alone could do that.

Yet how was God to suffer or make redemption? He is immortal, impassible. The divine wisdom discovered a way, in the person of one who should be at once God and man; man that he might suffer, God that his suffering might have infinite avail. Hence our Blessed Lord was born God and man, as we see to have been rigorously demanded by the circumstances of the case. Before he came as man, he was already a person, the Second Person of the Blessed Trinity. His humanity, therefore, could not add a second personality to him, else the redemption would have been useless, being achieved by one who was man only or God only. Hence the Church, under the impulse of the Holy Spirit, has defined that in Christ there are two natures but one person.

Christ our Lord, therefore, is a true and perfect man. He came into the world through the same portal as all others come, formed out of the flesh and blood of his mother's womb. Slowly he grew to man's estate, increasing in wisdom and grace before God and man, adding to the fruits of his know-ledge by experience, learning language from his mother whom he had created, growing conscious of the outward fabric of the universe which his own hands upheld. Boylike, he strayed away from his parents and was found at that pursuit that has always been the pleasure of all childhood – asking questions that his grown-up hearers could not answer. In the desert, after he had fasted, he was hungry; on the cross he cried aloud that he had thirst. He was weary when he sat down at the well and spoke those revealing words to the woman of Samaria which drew her to faith in his messiahship. As a true patriot, he whose own country was no less than all the world, he wept over the far sight of his own fair city when he saw it in his prophetic vision, overrun and battered by the Roman arms. Hypocrisy and cant were abhorrent to him; he denounced them with all the scorn of which humanity is capable, and in his terrible anger flung the tables of the money-changers down the front steps of the temple and scourged with cords all those that trafficked where had been built a house of prayer. And even as he took upon himself all the weakness of humanity, save that he did not sin, so into his soul crept that great dread of death which is so distinctive of the human heart.

Ah, yes, he came in the winsome garb of childhood, for he came as a brother to save. He is as truly man as I – with all a man's limitations – save that he did not sin. Tempted, he knows our weakness, for he had trial of it in himself. 'He needed not that anyone should show him what was in man,' for he was man. In life and after death he retained his divine powers over all creation. His body had qualities not given to us or to ordinary flesh and blood; none in all the world could convince him of sin. Yet for all that he was truly man:

> Our fellow in the manger lying,
>   Our food within the supper room,
> Our ransom on the Cross, when dying,
>   Our prize in His own kingly home.

I must therefore always be conscious of his humanity. I must realize that my sorrows are akin to his, that my difficulties are such that he will understand, that though his strength is divine and is upheld by all the force of his Godhead, his compassion is thereby not less human, that he is God indeed from all eternity, but man as truly from the moment of the Incarnation. Man to understand by experience, God to help; man to suffer and die, God that death and suffering may have infinite avail. Oh, the dignity of my human nature, that it, too, is clothed about the strength of God! Oh, the real union achieved in the Blessed Sacrament when I am one with Christ! No wonder Lacordaire broke out in accents of human love in his address to his Redeemer: 'O Father, O Master, O Friend, O Jesus!' There is a real relationship of love between me and his humanity.

The Name of Jesus
It is astonishing to note the power that names have over us. At the time of a parliamentary election, it would seem as though the whole purpose of the rival candidates, by posting their names over all public places, was to hypnotize us into thinking all the more of them according to the frequency with which we meet their names when on our walks abroad – the more conspicuous the name, the greater the success. Indeed, the very formation of the name may have its own consequences in the sense that there are certain names which by their

very sound make an appeal. This is not a question of the names which are hallowed by venerable history, or the exploits of past heroes, but the simple sound of the letters. Again, the modern science of advertisement, which struggles to combine startling effects with familiar phrases, insists always on the importance of the name: it must be something that can easily be asked for. A novel will have its sale largely determined by the title with which it goes into life. Revolving lights are brought into requisition, brilliant colors, verses, anything that can stamp a name on the memory. Nor is this unreasonable, since to human fancy the name sums up the man. It awakens unconscious echoes; at the mention of a name our imagination goes dreaming on, of faces, words, deeds, of long ago. In an age of abridgements, a name is the shortest abridgement of human life. There is something touching in the remark of Scripture that God knows each one of us by name. It seems to make him more intimate with us, more familiar.

The use, therefore, of names is a custom of human nature. Now it is noticeable that all human customs have received from God consecration, so that it is not to be wondered at that this custom should also receive from him its hallowing. This comes through that Name which is above all other names, since at its sound every knee in heaven and earth must bow. It towers above every other because it sums up in itself the human life of One who was unique. 'He shall be called Jesus,' said the angel, 'for he shall save his people from their sins.' That work was possible to One only, consequently that one name takes on an importance that is supreme. It is itself the record of a tremendous event, without equal in importance since the world began. The work was unique; then the name which was given to signify the work must also be unique. Throughout Scripture there is continuously the idea that names signify the office given by God, both in the Old and in the New Testaments. Here the holy name Jesus does itself mean Saviour. At the sound of it, therefore, we catch the echoes of power, trust, and mercy. It is like some quickly-drawn sketch that, with its bold strokes, suggests rather than defines a perfect picture. It brings the haunting memories of so many scenes: the calling of Matthew, the forgiveness of the Magdalen, the repentance of Peter, the chosen friendship of the Beloved Disciple, the wonders of his death. About it, too, is the fragrance of the parables, with their repeated tale of infinite compassion, and the miracles worked as the fruit of that compassion. The sacred Name is, indeed, an epitome of the Gospels.

The Holy Name therefore, echoed in Christ, the Anointed of God, has dominated history. By its sound we find that the first miracles were worked, and its power was put forward to the first persecutors by the first apostles. For it many were willing to lay down their lives. Even the crusading wars that seemed to be hostile in their fierceness to the meekness of Christ were defended and preached for the honor of it. The very beggar in the street begged for alms for the love of that sacred sound. To how many, too, in life, has it not come as a spell to be repeated softly to themselves, that the mere echo might ease them in the midst of their troubles, as the lover steels himself to labor in a foreign land or in some distant place by repeating the name of his beloved? And in death's approach it has brought a steadiness to the wayward fear that ebbs and flows in the souls of the dying. For so many of the martyrs it brought strength, for the confessors hope, for the virgins purity. In Catholic days in England, the prayer was familiar 'Jesus, be to me a Jesus.' Richard Rolle says of it: 'It shall be in thy ear joy, in thy mouth honey, in thy heart melody.' Indeed, as we grow older we find that the simpler prayers are the best. We get into the way of repeating prayers we have found to suit us, instead of venturing upon new fields or more complicated emotions. Thus, the short ejaculation of the Holy Name supplies the place of all others; it is the shortest, the simplest, the best. In the busy hours of daylight let it be upon my lips as an unceasing prayer.

The Passion of Christ

The life of Christ was evidently less thought of in the early days of Christianity than his death and its preceding passion. The authors of the Gospels devote to the three last days of his time on earth an amount of space altogether out of proportion to that given to the rest of his three-and-thirty years. St John, for example, out of his twenty-one chapters, allots seven, or exactly one-third, to the events of the passion. Again, in the first and simplest of the Creeds, there is hardly any mention of his life at all; attention passes on at once from the birth to the death: 'Was born of the Virgin Mary, suffered under Pontius Pilate'. The same is true of the whole devotional attitude of the Church: the birth and the passion and death absorb almost the whole attention of her children. In the liturgy, in the artistic tradition, in the ascetic meditations of the Fathers, always it is to the passion that thoughts are turned. It has, indeed, been made a taunt against the Catholic Church that she has made Christianity nothing else than the religion of the crucifix, and in a sense this is perfectly true, for it represents the whole attitude of the followers of the Crucified. Our thoughts move swiftly to the passion because, in a quite definite sense, the passion is of more value in itself and to us than the rest of the crowded moments of his life on earth.

Why do we insist that the value of the passion outweighs the rest of our Lord's days on earth? Just because it is through the passion that we have been redeemed. But surely, we make answer, he could have redeemed us without any of that agony? He had no need to die, since every single action of his life could have made atonement for the sins of all the world. Yes, truly, he had no need to suffer; we could have been saved by the simple decree of his divine will. There is but one answer to all this questioning as to why he died. There is but one word that can explain the tenderness of the Crucified: 'God so loved the world'; 'Christ also hath loved us'; 'having loved his own who were in the world, he loved them to the end'; 'greater love than this no man hath than that he lay down his life for his friend'.

Blessed Juliana of Norwich says in a passage of beautiful phrasing: 'Love is his token. Who told it to you? . . .Love. Where-fore told he it to you? . . .For love.' Yes, love is his token. Love alone supplies the reason for his death willingly suffered, since this is the highest expression of love. Truly when he hung on the Cross he cried out that all was consummated, for even love almighty could no further go. Like the penitent whose sins he forgave so freely, he broke the fair white alabaster box of his own dear body, and the whole world has been filled with the fragrance of it. Thus it is, then, that quite rightly the passion and death of our Blessed Lord do come most powerfully into our lives; since it was by his death that we were redeemed and because his death represents to us the highest achievement that love can offer. Love expresses itself in the broken phrase of sacrifice.

It behooves me, therefore, to keep ever fresh in mind the passion of our Lord. How is this best to be done? By a tender devotion to the Five Wounds of Christ. It is true that devotions are always personal, that the whole value of them depends precisely on their being the spontaneous movement of our own hearts. If they are not of our own choosing, if they are foisted on us by someone else who has found them helpful and who would have us therefore take them up, they may lose all their efficacy. Hence it is quite possible that this particular devotion may have to be replaced by another according to the feelings of each individual; for one perhaps the Sacred Heart, for another the sorrowful mysteries of the Rosary. Christendom is so full of love, yet not of sentiment or gush, is so bracing with its refining fierceness of suffering, that it must find many who would welcome its reappearance in this modern world. It is an old devotion, but it is coming back, just because it does keep alive the memory of Christ's death. No one can be unmanned, made effeminate by the sight of a wound. The sight must steady me, give me the necessary sternness to meet life sturdily, yet it adds to all this strength the tenderness of love. At Communion or when I make my visit, and words and thoughts seem to fail, let me turn to these 'dumb mouths that open their ruby lips to beg the voice and utterance' of my love.

The Problem of Suffering

The one thing that we have always to remember about the sufferings of Christ is that he took sufferings on him by his own free choice. His case was different from everyone else's, because in his case a life of suffering was deliberately chosen before even he came into the world. God from all eternity, man only from the moment of his conception and birth, he chose a life on earth that should be full of discomfort and of suffering. He could have become man under very different conditions. He could have made atonement to the divine justice by an act of infinite love and obedience. The Incarnation by itself could have redeemed man; it could have been accepted as a world's ransom and would have outweighed all man's sins. There was no need for him to have suffered if merely he had wished to satisfy divine justice. Justice would have been content with the least, but generosity wanted to give all. So he chose suffering of his own free will. By that means he taught man a wholly new way of life. For however you read the story of his life and his sayings, and whatever critics and others may say about them, no one can take out of them their note of austerity and suffering. These can never be explained away. The Cross is too prominent in the Gospels to be left out of them. There are too many texts that speak of what his following entails for anyone to suppose that the Christian way of life is possible without suffering. Suffering is the sign of his fellowship according to St Paul. Who should know better than he?

And so it is that God loves us too much to let us escape out of life without suffering, for it is because he loves us that suffering comes. This is a dark saying, but it is of the essence of Christianity that we should believe it. Our attitude to suffering is, therefore, the test of our attitude to the teaching of Christ. Suffering and man's attitude towards it have always been the touchstone of faith. His real difficulty against the existence of God has always been the existence of sin and suffering. If you remember the life of St Augustine, you will remember that this was the precise point on which as a young man he went wrong, for he could not reconcile the world's imperfection with the doctrine of one

Creator who was infinitely perfect. He chose the particular heresy of the Manicheans because, by denying the sole creatorship of God, it allowed another creator to be responsible for the world's evils.

To pass over eight hundred years and come to St Thomas Aquinas is to find the same problem torturing the minds of that age too. Nor is our own age any different. The Christian Science churches are a standing witness of the same confusion wrought on man by the finding of sin and suffering in his world. To what is this religion due but to the wish of man to explain away sorrow, suffering, and sin in the world? These try to answer the problem by denying that it exists; they answer the problem of evil by saying that there is not any. Listen in any public place to those who preach the gospel of Communism, walk through any of the drearier streets of our cities and towns and stop to hear the speaker talking to his mates at night. What is it they discuss so earnestly? They raise the question of religion only to condemn it, because 'if there were a God, would he let man suffer so much wrong?' It is the inevitable problem. Not only in the dreary streets and amongst the workers dwelling there, but everywhere it is the supreme problem.

It is the eternal problem: 'What are you going to do about suffering? How will you place it in your life?'

Into our world came the Son of God. Coming, he chose suffering. Chose it. That is our answer. They say to us that there cannot be a God, for God would not allow suffering. Is it unwise for us to argue with them? Perhaps it is better to go our own way believing. Those who do not accept God have (we hope) some comfort from their denials, for at least the suffering still remains, deny him or no. Suffering indeed will always be there. If by denying God you could shut out of life all sorrow, staunch sorrow's wounds, wipe the tears from sorrow's eyes, it might be worthwhile considering the advantage of a lie, but the whole point is that sorrow still remains and has still to be dealt with. When one denies God, all that has happened, as far as this problem is concerned, is that atheists have taken away not sorrow but the means to bear with sorrow, not the tears of mortal things but the stilling of them. They shall still hear men crying in pain in their streets, still hear the voices of children sobbing in distress. Not only in the streets do we hear this lamentation but in every human experience. We may never guess how deep it lies in this or that one, simply because we cannot see their hearts.

Our Lord came then and chose suffering. That is his answer to the problem of pain. His Gospel is that man can be the greater for suffering. It depends entirely on how he bears it. Love can make suffering wonderful, love of God or love of man. Christ our Lord was on earth as a man, suffering and weighed down with suffering; he came like that because he was in love. Now, we do know that man is at his best in love. Man, woman, and child are at their best, noblest, finest, when they are in love. And the reason is not far to find. It is because then are they most unselfish. Now, love speaks by suffering. It is eager to suffer if only thereby it is able to relieve its beloved of suffering. It is the very prerogative of love to ask that some task be set it to prove itself, that it be given some burden to bear. Love demands stern proving. Protestations it knows are cheap. Love wants to pay its due with coin that shall have cost it dearly. Love therefore wants suffering assigned it that shall enable it to show how greatly it loves. The old romances sang of it. When the knight went tilting to prove his fidelity to his beloved and entered the tournament with his lady's glove on his helmet to challenge all the world that she was the fairest lady, he sought hard blows, peril, uncertain issue; he sought pain. Man is noblest when he is in love. He wishes to be dared a hazard as a proof of his manhood: 'To you it is given not only to believe in Christ but to suffer for him'.

Our Lord came, making choice of suffering. That is the point of his life and its relation to his doctrine. He came choosing suffering, he who was most wise, most sane, most true. No language is so clear as his is, no judgments so even-balanced; no beauty of word can compare with the beauty of his quiet parables as he told them, the perfect poetry of truth told finely, loveliness of thought matched with adequate speech. Sensitive, an artist (much more than that, but still an artist), tender, compassionate, he does not hide his infinite compassion for sinners, for children, for all suffering, for the poor suffering birds. Immensity of compassion is his. No one could call him callous; yet, he is the one who tells us that suffering can make us beautiful, can fashion the soul to beauty, to make it great.

Now, the point is here that in this poor world we must believe somebody. We could believe those speakers who deny the divine existence, these Manichees, Christian Scientists, atheists, or we could believe him. These others cannot prove that God is not. To deny him is to dogmatize. Belief it is in either case.

What does he say? He says that he can deal finely with us and make us of use in his world. After all, that is a great promise! What a little service we are able to give people, do we the best and most we can! When we get towards middle age, how futile so much of our past life seems, how aimless our activities! When we were young, life seemed very full of business We had little time to think, only time to do. But later on this doing hardly seemed to justify itself or redeem itself from mere fussiness. Life grew uninteresting. We grew more comfort-loving, selfish. People seemed less alive. Life's greatness seemed to have evaporated. We settled down to routine work, to keeping friends, to humdrum service. Life dwindled into littleness.

Now indeed there still remains a chance of greatness – not what we once thought of, a greatness of action, but a truer greatness, the greatness of pain well borne. Pain can bring greatness to us. It can make people great. It need not. We have seen it in some of our sick, making them only discontented till they find life terribly wearisome. But this failure to grow great by suffering is not due to suffering but to the soul. This it was that our Lord had as his object when he said: 'Follow Me'. For 'to us it is given not only to believe in him but to suffer for him'. That is, it is given to us to suffer for him out of love. Then only is suffering fine when love is the motive of its acceptance. Then it is borne not only with courage but with content.

Perhaps it is hardly right to speak of our troubles actually as if they were suffering in any real way. Suffering sounds too grand for them. They are rather petty, small. Perhaps our difficulties, if we told them to some outsider, would seem foolish and unreal. There is this person whom we find uninteresting, yet with whom we have to live. We are tired of this person, and all his stories which we have heard over and over again. We are tired of his slackness or domineering habits or secretiveness. All this sounds small enough, tedium rather than suffering. But it is this very same smallness that makes it less easy to bear. What concerns us is that it can be turned to beauty. We can not only believe in our Lord, but suffer whatever comes to us out of love for his blessed will. What we have sent us, at least does not depend upon our choosing. That is as well. We should not choose aright. To us it comes from God unchosen, a gift from on high. That is, we are asked to believe that it is a gift to us. The saints, those masters in the school of suffering, tell us that one day we shall awake to find it indeed a divine gift, experience it as something holy, though not in the years between. At present we have to believe this and live up to it. Then, say they, in God's incredible goodness he will show us the real beauty it has wrought. But for the moment all we can do is to go on believing and trusting in him absolutely – our hands in his hands though they be marked with wounds, our feet in pace with his feet, wounded too. So shall our heart beat beside his heart and feel it shares his sore troubles and the strain of its distress.

Remember that it is possible to suffer and yet be happy. I remember a woman once in a parish where I worked, down in terribly poor streets. I remember her dying of cancer, that type of cancer that is all pain. One day she said to me: 'Need I take morphine? The doctor wants me to. Need I?' 'No,' said I, 'there's no need to; but why not?' 'I think it would be better for me not to. You remember my boy?' Yes, I knew and remembered all about her boy. 'It would be much better for me not to, because then I could offer all my sufferings for him. I'd love to make an offering of them. I can, can't I? That is the teaching of our faith?' What could I answer except that this was indeed our faith. She died in very great agony but wonderfully happy. The worse her pains grew, the happier she became. She thought that she was doing all the more for him.

These things can be. You will have them in your own experience also. The result of suffering depends on the soul. Not indeed entirely on the soul, for Christ must be brought in and God's love also. The remembrance of these does not take away but gives courage to bear pain. Thus, whatever pain is given is seen to be the act, not of God's cruelty, but of his kindness. We must not only believe, but also suffer for him. That is our gain.

He that was man's lover was crucified. He asks us to accept the pain we can neither choose nor lay aside, and bear it, believing that it is able to make us great, as Christ was great, not in the fullness of his Godhead but in the fellowship of his pain.

The Three Hours' Agony

You must hush all chatter if you would hear the drama of Calvary; follow it and understand. You must guard your heart if you would hear the voice of God speaking to you. You can only hear if your heart is really silent and tranquil. Even if you are expecting God's voice, you cannot hear it in storm. So here we begin, then, our contemplation of the drama or tragedy of Calvary, which is the drama of the failure of love: God pursuing man, God appealing to man in the one way that might have been thought to have made the most appeal. He came, the most beautiful of the sons of men, with exquisite external beauty, chastely fashioned in a virgin's womb. He came with beauty, not only without but within – gentle, patient, tender, forgiving, open, fearless, strong, exactly the type of character that you would have thought would have appealed to everyone. He came, he worked his miracles, he spoke his still-living word. Yet he was rejected of men, and he died at last on a cross, lonely, desolate – faithful to him just a handful of women, one rescued from the streets, just that one disciple that was most of all a poet, a dreamer, who years afterwards on an island dreamed his gorgeous dream. Christ alone on his cross, save for the women, a dreamer, the rescued sinner, and his mother, of course. They were under the Cross. He suffered as he had loved, utterly alone. But then, having suffered, he has so much confidence in our fidelity that he turns round to us and says:

'Follow Me,' not blind-eyed, but with eyes open, knowing where the road ends. In his magnificent confidence he thinks each of us to be big enough to walk his way; not of course as well as he went, but the same way he went and in some fashion meeting the same ending. We must be prepared to see our life a failure, to come to its end and find it empty of result. It will seem to us then that there has been so little done; of all our activities so little left us. But out of the things he suffered he learned obedience. Now that is our following of Christ. You will never escape suffering, failure, pain. You will have exactly that measure of them that God, who knows you, knows you are great enough to bear. You will have the chalice measured to your capacity. You are great enough to drink it without bitterness, to receive it, to go on tasting it to the end. The story of love, love's failures, love's tears, and yet of the loyal following of the heart, of the spirit, alone matters. The rest will be absorbed into the glory of God. Lonely and desolate, denied, betrayed, sold, falsely accused, he draws all men's hearts to himself – compassionate, merciful, forgiving, fearless, open, strong.

He asks of us, then, as we contemplate the story of his love's suffering, that we should learn what Scripture tells us he taught, too: the beauty of pain, the beauty of suffering, the beauty of the things that men are irked by and all the world avoids. They have beauty, real exquisite beauty. You will see it unveiled as you watch him die. Never so great as his will be your suffering. More squalid yours will be, more simple, smaller, not on so big a scale. Yet you will be his follower, watching, learning, imitating him. Beauty can be won from the heart of pain; so he who loved and lost his life loving, bids us watch him, with wide-open eyes, knowing the price that we must pay for our faithful following in the way God would have us go. Don't ask for suffering; accept patiently what God gives you. Watch. Love. Learn, if you can, a little of his great love showing on Calvary, manifest to us after the lapse of the forgotten years.

Father, forgive them, for they know not what they do.
As we watch the drama of Calvary, as we listen to the words that come

from his lips, we know, out of his kindness and mercy, what was passing in his heart. And the first word which he spoke is the first rule that all those must learn who would find, if they can, beauty in the pains of life. He began with forgiveness. Had he not intended to forgive mankind, he would never have come. He came to forgive. But it was not merely that he forgave humanity. Almost anyone can forgive. Almost everyone must have often forgiven. There is nothing so wonderful in that. But he said that which shows out of what spirit sprang his forgiveness: 'They know not what they do.' He had had suffering and pain. He had been through the agony of the Garden; he had been beaten to the ground by it. He had been in such dreadful agony that in his human will he would even have avoided death if he could. But after that long wrestle in the Garden, he rose from his knees: 'Not my will, but thine ' His forgiveness saw, behind what was done by the soldiers, the divine will: 'They know not what they do.' He saw not just soldiers driving nails into his hands and feet; he saw them as instruments of the divine love, divine power, divine will.

Can you go as far as that? Can you take your life, whatever it be, its pain that at times seems so wantonly inflicted by others, by their thoughtlessness or their lack of gratitude – what you will – can you take your life as you find it fashioned for you, can you look on it as he looked on his, as the working out of the divine will? He forgave them because he saw behind them power and love, his Father's power and his Father's love. He forgave them because they were but instruments, unknowing, unaware, of some plan designed by love and power divine. It means that in the Garden when he surrendered to the power of his Father he had already faced the whole meaning of the Passion.

He had surrendered to his Father: 'Not my will, but thine.' He had learned obedience; he that was wisdom shows us ever more wisdom. Always he was wise, but his wisdom grew more manifest. He grew in wisdom as he grew in age.

That, then, is the first lesson: that we must surrender to God.

If you have pain and can find no beauty in it, the fault is not because of pain. It is because of you. It is because you have missed, misunderstood, got the lesson awry somehow. You haven't seen the beauty. Somehow, for you it is veiled; it is veiled of course by self. You must surrender to God if you would see as this great Lover saw, behind all his pain, his Father's hands. You must go on surrendering. There is never an end to it. You must give all. This is a command, not something which is merely suggested to you as a higher counsel. It is actually the only command he gave: 'Thou shalt love the Lord, thy God, with thy whole heart, whole soul, whole strength, whole spirit'. You will be unhappy till you do that. You will miss the beauty of life, God's nearness to you. If you have learned that, there is hardly more for you to learn. Till you have learned that, you have missed his following. That is the first step. So while they nailed him and his fingers quivered, while his whole body shuddered in his pain, even so he saw filling his horizon the power and the love of God. 'Father – most tender – Father – merciful, majestic, strong, Father forgive them, they know not what they are about. Thou knowest. Behind them, I see Thee'.

Oh, you who stiffer everywhere, if anything in your life has gone as you would not have it go, learn to see in those human instruments of your pain, those who hurt you, who turn the knife in you that pierces, the awful power that lies behind them. Dare to see behind them the wonderful power of God. If you can do that, you will taste something of Calvary. You will see something of the beauty that he saw. You will make your life beautiful as his was, although it looked squalid, racked by pain. Though the mob jeered, though this Lover was rejected, yet in his own heart was the greatest beauty love could ever give. We too have to see love everywhere in everything. To laugh at it, seeing it play its jests in life, is to see God and to forgive the world, because you know that God is greater than the world. Behind the world always must be God's power and God's love. Forgive whosoever pains you, finding in those that inflict it God himself.

Amen, I say to thee this day thou shalt be with me in Paradise.
His way is not merely the way of forgiveness. He dares even more. It is not merely to see God's power, God's action, God's love behind whatever happens and to forgive the human instruments because they are mere instruments. He goes beyond mere forgiveness of injuries. He welcomes those that have injured him He gives not mercy, but love. So you must not only surrender to God, you must somehow learn how to possess God. You must surrender so absolutely that it is no longer you but he. With our Lord there was that human will of his that shrank and shuddered on the very edge of death. For he was sensitive because so innocent; his body was the most sensitive of any body to every type of pain. He shuddered and surrendered, but God was in him and he possessed God. He didn't just surrender. God was in him God walked with him. There was no will except his will attuned to God's will and God holding all, God possessing him because one with him. He was somehow transfigured and radiant because this thief on the cross penetrated through the uncomeliness that now was on him –

scourged, crowned, spat on, looking dreadful as he hung there – this thief with all his past of sin about him, with all that had gone before, whatever had twisted his life and sent it astray, saying truly: 'King, remember me when thou shalt come into thy kingdom.' Mocked, rejected, ill-used – this thief hailed him as a king. Here was someone hanging neighborly to him, also in dreadful pain, and his eyes pierced through all the uncomeliness that veiled him hideously and he saw love crowned. 'Thy kingdom! Ah, remember me. You, love, you are unforgetting. Me, even me, when you come at last to your crown.'

We must somehow aim at those heights. Not just to forgive people, not just to look out at the world and see it as far as we are concerned as an instrument of God; we must take pain and suffering and death and poverty and disgrace and all those things that in little or great come to us and not merely look behind them and see God's power fashioning our life through them, but we must take all men to our hearts, not by way of forgiveness, merely, but by way of love. It is his way. It is the way he would teach us. To do it especially because God possesses our soul. That is the point: that God should use us as instruments of his love. Here was this most loved Son, whose whole life was obedience, surrender, acceptance. 'Not I. I work no works. The Father worketh in me. I say nothing of myself. I say what I have heard.' He was wisdom, yet he said nothing except what he had been taught. He was the Word; no echo of God, but was possessed by God, radiant with God; he was God. He attracted those about him in whom there was anything Godlike. They came to him. He drew them. 'He that is of God knoweth the works of God; knoweth his word; knoweth his Son.'

We watch the beauty of his suffering, watch how he treated the world, as it dealt with him, for we have here no idle drama. It is nothing that you may watch and then go your way unmoved. It should move your life, or rather your attitude to life. Love will follow if you see it truly as he saw it. Life's beauty depends upon the eye. An artist is just someone who sees. Artistry is not in the hand; it is in the eye. The artist sees beauty where you and I pass it by. He sees things His eyes are open. With us, too, we see truly in proportion to the way God has entered into us; in proportion to the way that we surrender to him; in proportion to the way that he possesses us and our lives.

Now we are none of us great. We are just ordinary people, and our lives are petty and small. Rather they seem so. They are magnificent. God liveth in us. That is a truth of our faith. That is no mere reward hereafter. That is true now. In our heart we carry God. Give yourself to God. Let him govern you. You must know there is a price to pay for this. But it is his way. If you refuse to surrender, if you hold back what you know he now asks of you, self is intruding. God by that much loses his hold on you. Give yourself absolutely to him, with utmost trust and confidence. If you can dare to do so, see him as your king, betrayed and denied as he was, as he still is. See that your faith be unsullied, though its beauty be betrayed by those that should hold it dear. Don't judge the world or the faith by those you see misusing it, for you can't see them properly. You don't see into their souls. You have no right to judge. See God in them, in everyone, bestowing, not forgiveness only, but something finer – love.

God didn't forgive merely, God lifted us, else we should never be here. He passed by. We were wounded. We shall never know till we see him how deep were the wounds we had. He passed by. He stopped and healed us. And when this Good Samaritan poured in the wine that hurt, the oil that healed the pain, he did so because he loved us. Again he lifted us and made us his friends, and he calls us, as he called this robber, this thief hanging by his side, calls us to paradise even in our pain.

That boy, because he saw this was the King, was in paradise. Men have looked on death as something of which they could be proud if they died by the side of a king, if someone was there that led them, someone whom they loved, someone who inspired them, someone who seemed to make all life about them great and big. Ah, you meet them sometimes in a lifetime, and you are glad to be of any service to them, to help them to their dreams. Let him be your king. Know that he is a king, whatever disguise hangs about him He forgave. Now turn, not just be forgiven, you must turn, turn to him with your heart, with your life, with all you have to give. It is little. Ah, no! It is great: it is all you have. 'Others,' he said as he sat and watched those that gave their gifts, 'others give out of their abundance. This woman has given all the living that she had.' Have you given? What have you left? What do you still cling to? What is the will after? Give all you have. Remember he is your King. He will remember. He is unforgetting. You may forget. Pain

Oh, that shouldn't make you forget. That should make you remember. It is his livery; it is his pain. He wore wounds. That is the badge of his fellowship. 'Lord, remember me.' I will not forget. Though a mother forget the child that she bore, I forget never.' Forgive. Let God hold you. Go God's way. Turn to him. You are not merely forgiven; you are lifted into the kingdom of the Son of his love.

Woman, behold thy Son. Behold thy Mother
Under the pressure of the passion, under this suffering, the obedience
of Christ to his own vision, to the purpose of his coming, stands out
clear. 'Art thou a king?' For this was I born. For this came I into the
world,' he told Pilate. He was to be a king, yet it looked as though his
kingship were but a sorry kingship. It looked as though he had failed.
He had preached, he had worked miracles, he had forgiven sin. He had
had a crowd following him, and now he had none – except the robber
and this handful under the Cross. He is king. But of such a tiny
kingdom! A robber, and then the Mother, the Beloved Disciple, and the
rest. Now he looks at this little kingdom. His Mother, of course she
believed in him, and St John, and just those few.

    It made no difference to him, this apparent failure. He saw beyond
down all the world; us he saw. First he lifted men by forgiveness and
then out of forgiveness into a welcome for his kingship, and now he
makes them somehow one with himself. That was his magic; that is
what he came for; that is his kingdom: that he and everyone, somehow,
should be one. So he said to his Mother as she stood by his side,
pointing to St John – ah, not with his poor hands! They couldn't point!
But with his eyes, all that was left, and his lips by which he could speak
to her. He had no gesture, except by his eyes, and the words that fell
from him. He said: 'This is your son. He must take my place. For you, he
is I. Find me in him.' Such a mother! Such a son! Now the Son was
taken, and John was all the world to that Mother of Christ. She had still
years to live after he was gone. After the pain of his parting, she had
still to live, and this was all that was given to her: 'Now, everywhere, in
everyone, find me. You are the mother of all the living, of all the dead.
Gather them. They are yours. Each one of them is me.' So to John he
said: 'This is your mother. You are her son because she is the Mother of
Christ. Look for me in your own heart. Be me to her.' Behind is John's
own mother, the mother of the sons of Zebedee. For her this ended her
motherhood of this son. John was no longer her son. He had been given
to another mother; her heart robbed – ah, not robbed! She, a mother
now, had Christ for her son. That strange paradox spoke he, as he went
out of life, to this little huddled kingdom gathered at his feet. 'Mother,'
he says, 'look for me everywhere.'

    All mothers must find him in all sons. All the world must find him, he
would say to us everywhere. Not she alone but everyone must find him
in everyone, because he is in everyone. That is part of the Incarnation;
that is what we learn from the sacrifice of the Mass and from the whole
story of his Passion. He is mankind, its mystic body. In him we are one.

He on the Cross and we in some fashion with him He is the head. We are one with him. It is this vision of the world that the mystic has bought by his own pain, or bought by the pain of this other, to learn from the discipline of the school of pain, that all the world was Christ, and that he himself somehow had Christ within. All the combat of the saint is to let Christ live in his heart; as though round about this imprisoned God within us were something heavy that impeded his birth within us; as though our will impeded his gesture or his movement, hampered his great possession of our soul. He is within us, and all about us and in our heart and in every soul alive. 'Thou shalt find him in every soul.' He only knows God truly who knows God everywhere. He only really follows this master who has learned that lesson: God in every soul. Everyone is great or near to greatness. 'Behold I stand at the door and knock. If any man open to me. . .'Any man,' just anyone. There is something foolish about love, something that seems ridiculous to those that are not loving. Of course it is foolish. That is love's way. His love was as foolish as the love of others; foolish, that is, unless you happen to be in love yourself and then you see it not foolish, but wise: 'The folly of the Cross.' They said it that knew him. Just folly it seemed, human folly, yet the wisdom was divine.

'Any man, open.' That is what you have to do, all you have to do. Open! He is pathetic; he just stands and knocks. He is not rude, discourteous. He won't break in on you. Don't be afraid. If you shut your door against him, he will stand outside waiting, waiting until you open. That is his foolishness. It is so foolish to have to stand at a doorway if they won't let you in. You see people coming back and forth and looking at you, and you feel so foolish waiting there, as though nobody wanted you. Ah! but you, God is knocking. God stands without, so foolish. You have made him a fool. He loves you. Don't you see that? He is in love with you, any man, whoever you are, he is in love with you. That is the folly of the Cross. That is the ridicule of his love, that he just squanders it, that he throws it away on people who aren't worth while. He is the only one that loves those that are not worth while; and by his love he works on them strange miracles and changes them into himself. Fairy stories are only a dim presage of the greater work he would do, the magic of his way, by which he turned people, not into princes or princesses, but into himself. So Mary is now your Mother because you now are Christ to her. She loves you because she sees in you all that she saw in him. You are her child, because you are the Christ that was begotten of her. You, even you. 'If any man open, I will come in,' he said. 'I will sup with him.' A half-lit room and the door opening, and he enters. Kneel as he passes you by. He will go to the table that is spread. He will share his meal with you: 'My meat to do the will of him that sent me.' It is a price that you must pay, if you will sup with love. Surrender possession to him, accept identification with him. Your love at your table. He eating with you under your roof.

'Lord, I am not worthy.' Nobody ever could be worthy. Because we are all unworthy, that is why he came. He came because mankind was not worthy of God, and he came to make mankind worthy, even of God. 'And God is not ashamed,' says Scripture, 'to be their God.' God not ashamed to be our God! Ours, because of that miracle that, if we will, he works in us. That is all he asks, that we should will it. Do you want him? Do you want to have this Lover? Do you want to share life with him? Do you want really to be his friend and to go his way always, eyes wide open, knowing where the road leads? Now will you have him? Let there be no faltering. 'Lord, that I may love thee always, and then do with me what thou wilt,' so glibly on our tongue. Supposing he took us at our word? 'Lord, that I may love thee always, and then do with me what thou wilt.' You see what love may one day do with you? You see what it did with him? Suffering, loneliness, bought, false accusations, and the rest of it? Here on the cross he speaks and he manifests us great enough to listen and to follow. That is the splendor of his love, that he thinks us great enough to go his way. He thinks us big enough to walk with him on that rugged pathway, to go as he went, with pierced feet, pierced hands, pierced open heart. He thinks us big enough to bear the crown of thorns, to mount the throne with him, to have the agony of parting, to lose all things but him, because we believe, so to say, his faith in us. Ah! big enough if we will. But you must open to him. Open to him! Keep nothing back from him! And as he enters, give him all. 'But I shall lose so much.' Oh, but you have gained so much, more than all the world beside. Once a man sold all his treasures for this hidden treasure. What God hides is indeed well hid. Once someone sold all their pearls for this most precious pearl, out of the treasure of God. At least know the way that he wants you to follow. Have your eyes open to it. Don't complain if he takes you at your word. Leave him or follow him, but if you follow, bear the hurts of love.

My God, My God, why hast thou forsaken me?
In that drama of his sacred Passion he now enters into that portion of it in which he seems most lifted above all men, as though perhaps the mercy of God veiled the world from him. The world seems forgotten and he alone with God. The darkness and the mob blurred by it, and

even those that love him seemingly hid by the darkness from him. Not they are in his thoughts, but God. Thus he turns from the world. Death is always like that, a severance from the world about. Between us and the world we are leaving, an angel with a flaming sword comes, impenetrable, as death gathers its forces. Isolation hems you in, the world about you far off, forgotten. It is a greater business that you must be about. There is something you long to tell those that are about you, but your lips falter and are dumb. You have come out of this little world rounded by sleep; you are getting out of your sleep into waking. It has always been so: that after a long sleep to wake up is agony, almost agony.

He wakes from earth to his Father. The loneliness of dying has come on him and the greater loneliness of love. So strange a thing is it that he should have sought all mankind and loved them, and would have all the world to love him – so strange, to us that are irked by the love of those for whom we hardly care. He wanted all men's love, any man's, so wide, so wonderful, so foolish this strange love of God. No wonder they flung the garment of a fool around him. That is the judgment of man about God. That is what makes faith so hard. God seems so strange. Well, if we only knew what fools we were, it would prove God to be God. If we only knew how blind we were, how small, our very judgment that God seemed foolish would prove him wise. Love is like that because God is love; and God's behavior will seem foolish to you unless you happen to be in love with God. To the saints, to this great Lover it was wonderful, bewildering and yet wonderful, to see the wisdom of the high ways of love. That is the beauty of that cry: 'Why hast thou forsaken me?'

Here is mortal love dying. Above it is immortal love that cannot die. Here is humanity fashioned by God. There is the God that fashioned him. Humanity is climbing higher, leaving all things behind, yet God is hidden from it and veiled. If you would love God, and if you would serve God, and if you would pay the price of your service, notice that this is the way he went; and if you call yourself a follower, this is the way you too will go. If you follow God, you lose the little things. You lose things visible. He dwells in inaccessible light. His light blinds you till you think it darkness. It is not darkness, it is only too strong a light. To us, with eyes that dare not look at the sun, for us to see God in his beauty unveiled, would be, says Scripture, to die. Our sight would be shattered with the glory that we should encounter; our hearts broken by the torrent of love. Men have died through love, human love. Men have died too from the love that is divine. The saints, some of them were shattered by it. They carried the torrent of love in an earthen vessel. With the pressure of the swelling tide of love it broke. It was earthen but what it held, divine. His way is a way in which as he lifts he carries you till the lesser things are left behind. In the valley are the houses and the laughter and the children and human love; in the valley the noise of that traffic, of that commerce. But if you climb, you must go above their roofs, above the little smoke, blue smoke that comes curling up; you must get above that and lose all the beauty of the world – that is, if beauty for you means color or scent. Down below are the flowers, their beauty, their fragrance; you must come up out of these if you would dare the hills. Come up, climb up, out of this color and fragrance and all that men call beauty. Below you are the living things. A few sparse flowers may still follow your footsteps and go for a while ahead of you, and then at last you come to the pines. They are the outposts of life on the hillside. Where they end, all life ends. Below you the birds, the clouds even. You are now above the clouds. If you look to the valley, you long for the valley, and your heart is torn. If you look to the hills, you step out fresh again. That is where you want to be, on the peaks of the hills. You get up out of movement and color, and you stand up high. Rock is about you, bare bleak rock, with hardly a color, and then above that is the width of snow. Silence. . . Stillness. . .Immensity. . .Not hills but the peaks of hills. No valley is in sight. Your valley even is hidden from you, and beyond it never a valley, just hills and the summit of hills, going on to the skyline. No color. This vast spread of the still, silent snow. It sparkles. As it sparkles, it hurts your eyes. But life, you feel life, the live air just lifting you, as though it were life itself. Men can die at a height. You, if you would go with God, you must pay the same great price. You must leave that little valley. Are you prepared? Don't complain about it afterwards. 'Ah! if my prayers were comforting, if I only got some sort of consolation out of them, I shouldn't mind.' Oh, that is cheap. That is not service. At least, it seems that you are looking for pay. There is no love in that. God's way is unselfish. You have surrendered. That is the beginning. Now go up on the hills, and pay the price if you really would serve God. Don't ask consolations.

'Why has thou forsaken?' He wasn't forsaken, he knew, else why did he speak to God? He spoke to God because he knew that God was near him, that God was hearing him. Up on those hills above the skyline when you stand, there is no life about you. Oh, yes, there is life. Where shall I look for it? Shall I look about on the hillside for it? No. Where then? Look within, for you are alive. Don't look for God elsewhere.

Look in your heart. But I don't see him. No, no. You are still thinking of the valley, its color, fragrance, sight. Anybody would serve God if he were always to taste the beauty of God's presence. That would be cheap. That would only attract the crowd. That would not be generous. That is not for the young who love generosity. It is the young for whom he calls; for those at least whose hearts are young, daring, generous, attracted by sacrifice. Those are the ones he wants. 'Why has thou forsaken me?' He never forsakes. He hears. To that height he calls you. That is where he wants you. Perhaps it is where you are, but you don't notice it, it seems so dull. Climbing is tiring. It is wearying, and color and fragrance are no longer with you. They must be left below you if you want to enjoy the hills. And your eyes will be hurt. You are on the summit. This is what God asks you to know. Here you are. Prayer so desolate, but you are trying, and you have turned self aside, and you are holding to the garment of God. That you have climbed at all is only because you have held his hand and he has lifted you. He has been Father and guide to you. Go his way untroubling. Ask no payment, no consolation, no reward. That men should leave you perhaps has never troubled you. That God has, may perhaps once have seemed to shatter your faith in him. Believe, unseeing, unhearing, untasting. If you must cry, cry not to men but to God. Don't look about. Look within. Within is light inaccessible. Only you must serve this love without payment, aloof, remote, intimate, exquisitely near to you. The mysteries of God are in your heart's shrine.

I thirst

This great Lover of God, and because of God, a great Lover of mankind, has reached that bleak place whence all else than God is banished. No consolation is left him, nothing but God. The light inaccessible has been reached at last. Bright clouds distant, as it seems, are intimate, near. And our Lord, who taught obedience by the things that he suffered, here in the darkness, in the desolation, in the utter loneliness, briefly says: 'I thirst.' It is the test of his love that though he has gained nothing, though, despite his continued enjoyment of the beatific vision from birth to death, here he tastes nothing of God's nearness or God's beauty, he still desires. It is always the test. So many come to that part of the road that is bleak and barren, that is empty of anything that would give pleasure to a soul, so many reach that far and are hurt, and turn and go back to the valley. God gives us only what we can bear. God knows our capacity more than we do. What God asks, we can always give. He is just, but he is all-knowing, and he asks only what is within the competence of him from whom he asks. That is God's way. Bleakness, coldness, piety losing its pleasures – sometimes people are hurt by all this.

The young, so full of adventure, and generous, are hurt by that part of the road. They have tried with all their childish enthusiasm and generosity to live up to Christ's idealism and can remember how they have prayed; yet somehow they have failed somewhere on the road. 'I have done everything, and still somehow I don't seem to get anything out of it. I have been to Mass but it seems to mean nothing to me. I have been and received the Sacrament of love and it just makes no difference. It has become a routine. It means no more to me than that, and so, reluctantly, I must let it go.' How blind they are! How much they have misunderstood! How little they know of love's language: for it has none. Silence is its speech. To love and to serve simply because love is pleasant to you, because love gives – that is the beginning. That is not the end. Pain comes, and pain cleanses and purifies and burns out the dross in us: 'Some will be saved yet so as by fire.' If your soul has any greatness, that is its way. Don't be hurt if God seems to leave you. He is testing you. Are you big enough still to desire? Can you still want him, though he means nothing? Is your faith big enough and your hope, your confidence, and your love? Are you shrunken and small, and just out for what you can get from him, and not for what you can give? His way is that way of hard service, testing you, seeing if once you have got to those hills, once you have found everything bleak, once you have left that valley with all its pleasures, such as it has that appeal to you, that please you, that rest you, you will come up to those bleak heights, without feelings, and still hold on, still desire, still long for him. That is the test. It isn't love (though you may have thought it love), it isn't love until it can get to that height, till it can go blind, and yet accept what comes to it, lose all and yet believe in God's love and desire naught but it. To have them removed, one by one, from you, the things on which you had set your heart, and still to say to God, 'I want you, and only you.'

Ah! those others are frightened of God. He is jealous: he says it himself. Whomsoever you work for, remember that man is ungrateful and God is austere. If you work for men, your reward will not be much from them. If you work for God, he is austere. He says it in the Gospels: 'Out of your mouth I will convict you. I am austere.' That is the way of this service. Our Lord wishes that we should come to it open-eyed. Don't complain afterwards. Don't turn round on him. Don't say that he tempted you by any false description of the way. Faith is asked of you and that is what faith means; faith is nothing unless it has love's flame in it. Without love it won't lift. Its wings won't lift. It can't fly. You have to trust God absolutely. Whatever he seems, indeed, whatever he does, you just have to trust him absolutely. Now you can, whatever he does, still want him, though he seems humanly unwantable, something too much for us, too much above us, too austere. There is a type of beauty that almost frightens us. It is not pretty, but it is beautiful. It almost holds us off. That is God. Which of you can live with a consuming fire? God is that. He will burn out all that is little, all that is dross, burn it, and make you what his eyes see you could be.

Will you, dare you, still desire him? Will you dare? Then, if you will, you must indeed want him; you must thirst. His way, you see, is a high way. It is a long way. It is a bleak way. It is lonely. Ah! no, there is God; invisible, intangible, but God. You shall not hear him. Above you he is, but also within you. If you still want God, you also are a lover. His love has lit your flame. While we talk, he is dying. Lesser things don't concern a man in death; realities only matter, nothing then can matter that is less than God. Darkness, desolation troubled him dying, and yet he had a thirst for the strong, living God. To that greatness he calls our little souls. He will help us to reach it. He died to help; not to set an example merely, but to give us help. Divine the love that ran through him dying. He died to be nearer to us. May we be near him then, lonely, not conscious of his presence, yet still believing, hoping, loving, desolate but athirst.

It is consummated

After his desolation he still had his undaunted desire, and beyond desire there comes, now, silence. 'It is finished,' he said. Not finished, really, for what he did is still being done. He ever liveth, to show forth the death of the Lord until at last he come. It is not finished, but all that love could do is done. He has come to the end of it. There at the foot of the Cross are the few that are faithful, and beyond, the great world goes on its own way. Darkness, so near him, and beyond the darkness the souls he came to save. 'I have done everything It is finished,' he said. 'I have finished,' he said in the supper place, 'the work thou gayest me to do. It is finished. I can do no more.' He had given, you see, his body and blood to feed mankind, in the supper place. He had given that. He had done that. Now he has tasted everything• man's ingratitude and the austerity of God. He is still undaunted in his desire. He is still the great Lover, and it is we whom he loved, we and God.

Here and now, at that height, above the desolation, above even desire, he comes into silence, which is love's language. There is nothing that love can say. When it speaks, you know it has not reached its height. When men are so ready to speak, you never believe them. When they pour their compliments out, it does but embarrass your soul. Love has no language but silence, for words are too small for the long thoughts of love. Here he, this Lover with his love incarnate, even he comes at last to silence: 'It is finished.' What love could do is done. Love is always stammering, trembling, tongue-tied, hesitant, because it is trying to say what cannot be said. You cannot convey love by speech. You touch it somehow by silence. In silence souls meet. In silence he saw the God he thirsted for, the God that seemed aloof, desolating, forsaking, and who yet hadn't forsaken, for when he cried with a loud cry that pierced the clouds, God heard. He thirsted for God, and now there is nothing he can say. Now all that is left him is waiting and looking. He has reached contemplation, which is a sight, a looking-out at God, a gazing, nothing to be said, just to look and to see. That is his height of prayer.

You see, all the while we have been describing his prayer on the Cross; the seven words are the words of his prayer; and as you listen to them you see the wings of prayer lifting him. Now he has gone beyond desire. He has gone into that higher silence, where is naught but he and God. He just looks at God: 'It is finished.' Here speech breaks down, even his speech, that was so wise. Just as love that is so bold stops on the edge of speech, after stammering, and can only say: 'But I love,' and beyond that all words are spent; so is he silent, happy. It may have happened that love has silenced you sometimes because love has lifted you where you are with that which you love. The saints have shown us how at times they have reached that wonderful place, and they have felt then – no, not felt, known by faith that God was there, and have just looked for him that haply they might find him. By faith they knew he was present 'and they rested with God'. Our Lord, not by faith but by vision, has reached that point in his prayer which is the death of the soul in love. He has reached the point beyond darkness, beyond desire. He has come into the place of silence.

Some souls, perhaps all souls, he calls to that height. If you have desire in spite of your desolation; if beyond the darkness you can still desire, then this is higher still. If in spite of that lack of sense and consolation, that dryness, that dreariness, that drift of distractions over you that might else discourage you were you not in love, if in spite of that, you still desire God, whatever he costs you, if you still desire, you will come up into this place of silence. Don't look for speech. Seek no more the gates, but enter. You are there. You have reached silence – unutterable silence – this is the inaccessible light. This is where the high souls go. As in the olden Scripture, but once a year the high priest entered within the shrine, the Holy of Holies, and stepped into it alone, so it is still a 'seldom pleasure' to gaze in silence on beauty half unveiled. Yet this is the ultimate place of love. Hands hold on to it, nestling under his wings.

'It is finished;' he said. The hurly-burly's done. All the business, all the action, all the courage, all the infinitude of desire are over. Just silence now. No seeking of words. There are none, merely he is content in silence to be with God. It may be that he has called you to sorrow somewhere. Perhaps, nobody knows, perhaps it is human love that wounds you, your child, someone you love. It may be death that has hurt you. You have looked behind and tried to see in whatever did hurt you the instruments of the divine will, but you cannot bring yourself to speak, to say to him: 'I accept it.' How much pain is there not that you can bear if nobody speaks to you? Sorrow you can hold, however desolating, if nobody speaks to you. If they speak, you break down. You cannot speak. You dread their coming. You say: 'But I couldn't say anything to him. I can take his will, but I can't speak.' Don't. There is no need to speak. This is love. He loves you. He knows you. He understands. Don't speak. Know that he is with you. Beyond desire, comes silence . . .be there with him in the intimate, ultimate silence. That is the speech of love. Don't speak. Look. He is there.

Father, into thy hands I commend my spirit.
And so it is, that by his own deliberate will he dies. He has done all that love could do: 'It is finished.' There follows silence, and then, seeing that all things were accomplished, he cried, gathering his strength in that last cry, still a king, still complete master of himself, of all the world – and then crying with this loud voice he dies. He bows his head. 'Into thy hands, Father, into thy hands I commit my soul.' Acquiescence, in the Father's hands! He had lived through so much. It was so long ago since he had begged forgiveness for the soldiers, so long since he had been spoken to by the robber at his side. He has passed through so much, and all else had been tasted by him. He had taught obedience by what he suffered. Blessed Master, that would teach us his own blessed way, out of pain to teach obedience! Love, else, is but a vain desire. Love that will not obey is self-love. It is the intuition of self clinging to its wings. Love that obeys is real love. Love that holds nothing back, that has no prejudice, no desire of its own,

that desires only what love desires, no more, no less. The infinite Lover loved mankind because he loved God. He comes to the end, and he finishes it with that thought: 'Into thy hands, O Father, I commend my spirit,' and unto God he goes. 'As thou, Father, in me, and I in thee.' Love merging into love.

'Into thy hands ' He sees his Father's hands in all life, in death. They are the hands of God, pure, wise, loving, the delicate hands of an artist fashioning something of beauty; slim, slender, sensitive. These were his Father's hands. Out of pain fashioning beauty; for pain is the price you must pay for beauty. The beauty of an art work depends on the pain of fashioning the material. It must be carved or chiseled or burnt. Or the fingers may be like the fingers of those that fashion machinery. Clever fingers, feeling at once where that machine has faltered, gone wrong. Swift fingers that go to the root of trouble, smeared with the grease of the engine; and yet not slender only, but strong. The hands of God are the hands of an infinite artist, of an artificer working until now: 'Into thy hands, O Father.' He has tasted all our sorrows. He has carried all our griefs. He has gone beyond desire into silence. It is finished, and now death at last, and death is even that. He and the Father held separate, in a sense, by life, are linked now with death. 'Till death do us unite' is the pledge of this sacrament of dying. It has its own ritual and its own way.

Love, our love, must run the way his did, and we must just put ourselves into the divine hands. When he went on earth he touched men, and, touching, healed them. He made clay with his fingers and plastered the wound with the clay, and men were healed because of what he had done. He touched them and life ran through his finger. They were sick; but then they were healed, they said. He had touched them and something had happened. His were healing fingers, fingers that brought peace. The sick were tossing with fever, and he just soothed their tortured, fevered, exaggerated views begotten of fever, and smoothed them away. He healed what he touched, and his fingers thrilled with love. John, who leant back on the bosom of his Master at the supper place, says boldly: 'Our hands have handled the Word made flesh.' Love had awakened in him in his boyhood by the lakeside as he touched hands with Christ. Something happened, some fire broke out and kindled life in him and love ran between. So they that listened knew what the words meant as he spoke them. They, still standing under the Cross, they knew what his hands meant to them. The Mother knew the hands that were her own; she knew the hands that had patted her in his babyhood; that had helped her in eager boyhood; that had waited on her with the energy of youth; the hands that had held her hands as he went out of the supper place into the darkness. She knew what sort of hands were the hands of God. The Son's hands were human. God's would be more wonderful, more full of life, more full of love, more healing, more peace-giving, infinite hands. She knew what he meant when he said that he gave himself into his Father's hands; but we, not knowing, have yet to do as he did and give ourselves into the hands of God.

In those hands we are. Beneath us are the everlasting arms. Go fearlessly the way you know he calls you. Go, he holds you; he will not let you fall Hold his hand. Go his way. Let him deal with you. He surely must have proved to you by this time that he is worthy of trust. This is death, his death. This is the way that we keep to the memory of it. On such a day, you shall not be afraid. Commit your way as he committed his. Silence may lead you there, hold you there by faith and hope and love. We stand in the hands of God, too powerful to be escaped from, to be avoided. If you love the hands, you will go in quietness and peace. Here is this Lover. As he ends, he puts himself into his Father's hands. With all the pain they have given him, he knows them as his Father's. Pain has blossomed into beauty under his hands and all his soul becomes radiant now because he has put himself into his Father's hands. God upholds all souls. Those are happy that go the way God wants them to go. The unhappy are those that seek their will. They shall not find it. He is too powerful, too wise, too much in love.

And now we end the memory of his suffering, his death out of love for us. Let us remember that we must forgive because we see God's will behind all the hurt that is done us, looking behind the instruments to God that wields them in our lives. But we must do more. We must welcome with love all the world to us, robbers, thieves, whomsoever comes to us – at least for forgiveness and love. And we must do it because we see him everywhere. 'My mother, my brethren,' he said pointing with his hand to the crowd. And again we must go often into that way of desolation. That is the way of all souls, who dare hold a love that will not doubt; and beyond that we must still have unbroken desire, in spite of the bleakness of our prayer; and again, beyond desire, we must be glad to rest tranquil in utter silence. 'It is finished,' he said. It is never finished. Dying, and behold! we live. So we ask him, this strong Son of God, that he would lift us to his own blessed heights; that he would help us to see clearly the beauty pain has for those that will look for it, the beauty in the little small disappointments or failures, or whatever goes awry; that he would lift us to that height, and that we should bear whatever comes from our own folly and blindness and our lack of generosity (which lies at the back of so much that we call grandly our pain and our failure) and carry our griefs like men. Shall we ever reach there? Oh, that matters nothing. Go his way.

May he that is our Teacher, our Friend, our Lover, do his work with us in his own blessed way! May he teach us obedience through what he suffered! He that is our Teacher, may he teach us that! He that is our Friend, may he help us to be ourselves, to go the way he would have us go, because we are his friends, because he is neighborly to us! May he that is our Lover burn us, purge us, cleanse us with the flames of his love, for we are poor and small in our souls, yet we wish to be more than that! He will help us. But don't cry out at the way he deals with you. If you love, you must trust, and if you trust, all is well. Lifting us, teaching us, helping us, loving us, may he make us, because we have striven to love him, still, for all our failure, look for beauty in the heart of pain.

Christ's Resurrection

The resurrection of our Blessed Lord has been regarded as the central mystery of the Catholic faith. Certainly from apostolic times it has been held to be the pivot round which revolved and on which depended the arguments of Christian theology. For while the death of Christ might be taken to imply that he was in no way different from other men, his triumph over death could have no other meaning than the significant challenge of his claim to unique divinity. To die in defense of one's belief is evidence, indeed, of sincerity, but it cannot demonstrate the authenticity of that conviction, since men have died for contradictory beliefs. That Christ was sincere cannot be denied; the conclusion that he was therefore divine is also itself paradoxically logical; for one who sincerely believes himself to be God and dies to prove it, must either be hopelessly insane or really divine.

But the final touch is given to the argument, and all the proof rendered irresistible, when to it is added the reappearance of the dead Christ, clothed and habited in a human body. The argument may be put thus: Our Lord claimed to be God, died to attest the sincerity of his claim, was raised up by his own divine power to life again in testimony of the truth of his doctrine. The author of life and death has therefore added his own witness to the witness of Christ. God has sealed by his power the declaration of his Son. If Christ were not God, God himself would have been a party to the deceit.

St Paul is so persuaded of the efficacy of this retort that he seems to be content to base the whole argument of Christianity upon it, for he says expressly that if it be not a fact that Christ has risen from the dead, then is our faith vain. For him it is no question of spiritual experience of a risen master, but he is convinced of the bodily life of the man Christ. He proceeds, in fact, in the epistle to the Corinthians, to arrange with scientific procedure those who had been witnesses of the fact of Christ's reappearance. He puts them in some sort of chronological order. The only two whom he mentions by name, Peter and James, are the very two of whom he tells us in another place that he had personal relations with in Jerusalem. Nor was there evidently any expectation in the minds of those who saw him buried that Christ would break through the portals of the tomb. Looking back, they might remember the hints he had made about a three days' sojourn in the grave, but the holy women set out on the first Easter morning to anoint a body that was presumably dead. The account, too, of the disciples who were on their way to Emmaus when our Lord himself met them, points in the same direction. They were actually going away from Jerusalem, though they had heard the report of the women that an angel had told them of the resurrection of the Master, so unprepared were they for any vision of him Even when the rest had seen him, St Thomas could continue to doubt, confident in the unexpectedness of the event. The resurrection, then, is to be accounted a fact, not of hysteria, but of history.

For me, therefore, the historical side of the mystery must never become obscure. Undoubtedly there is a mystical meaning that lies hid within the truth. The new birth, the rising sap of spring, the feeling of hope that the very season of the year brings with it, are all contained in the notion of Easter and its festive interpretation. But beneath all that, and giving it the value which it bears for me in life, is the underlying occurrence which was witnessed to by so many. 'He rose again according to the Scriptures.' No hallucination will account for it, for they felt his hands and feet, and put their fingers into the print of the nails and into the open wound of the spear. By the lakeside he ate with them. In the room he appeared when not expected, was seen by more than five hundred brethren at once. This shows no sense of visionary excitement, but a fact vouched for by as good evidence as any other fact in history. On this fact our faith rests, in the sense that it testifies to the divinity of Christ. As such the Jews demanded it, the Pharisees understood it and prepared for it, our Lord promised it; and to it the apostles confidently appealed. For me, then, it is the earnest of my own resurrection. It tells me that as he triumphed over death, so must I triumph. It bids me look forward to the new life, not back to the wasted and fallen years. It comes, indeed, as the basis of faith, but also as pointing the lesson of hopefulness, for the actions of Christ are not merely the examples that I must strive to copy, but they are still more importantly the very power by which I get grace to overcome and to attain my final reward.

Christ in Heaven

After asserting our belief in the resurrection of our Lord, we continue in the Creed to profess our belief in his ascension. This doctrine of the Church is clear alike from Scripture and tradition. After the forty days during which he still lingered on the earth, he gathered the apostles around him, upbraided them all with their slowness to accept the fullness of his teaching, commissioned them to go forth to preach and to baptize, and then was with-drawn from their midst. His sacred body, by virtue of his own divine power, was itself transported to heaven, where it takes precedence of all other created nature and exercises forever the atoning purpose for which he came.

In his own human species, that is, in the outward semblance of humanity which had been visible to the apostles and the people of Palestine, he has dwelt at the right hand of the Father, in the possession of his unlimited power over all creation. To him is also committed the judgment of the world. He is present, indeed, on the altars of the Church, body and soul alike – not, as is evident, in the visible form of his manhood, but under the appearance of bread and wine. This bodily presence must be insisted on as part of the Christian faith. There, he is perfectly human, and humanity requires the double existence of soul and body. The Church has always frankly professed this and never allowed the idea that things of corporeal matter are unfitted for the majesty of God. With all her intense asceticism, she has unswervingly taught the doctrine of the 'human form divine'.

His continual work, therefore, of interceding for the children of men goes on unabated, since the marks of the wounds appeal unceasingly to the Father. His power is a power, not of destruction, but of salvation. The older painters, with their high contemplative talent, expressed this in their own picturesque way. Florentine or Fleming or Venetian, they made no effort to suppose that the crucifixion and all that it entailed was some past event. For them it was an eternal act which was as true and as present to their own day as it ever had been. Hence you find that the soldiers are dressed in the garments of the artists' own fashion. The towns and architecture that are at the back of the picture are nearly always the familiar scenes of their life. Nor is it to be thought that the appearance of contemporary modes was due to an ignorance of Palestinian custom; they had, indeed, the unchanging East ready at hand, and with the extensive commercial connection that Venice and the other cities of Italy kept up with the Byzantine Empire, there was plenty of opportunity for them to find out how things were done. As well as we, and better, they could and did know the dress and architecture of the Holy Land. But it was a deliberate attempt to make the life and death of Christ an ever-living event of eternity rather than of time. Hence, too, in the frescoes of Fra Angelico one sees in the corner a saint contemplating some scene of the Gospels, present in spirit at that far-off tragedy. Nor are these things mere whimsical fancies; they are the sober truths of the faith. Christ is always being born, always dying, always at the right hand of the Father.

Let me realize what this means. It forces me to view the life of Christ as unending and unended. It means that Christ our Lord is now in heaven at his Father's side, 'ever living to make intercession for us,' as St Paul expressly notes it. The promise of divine assistance till the end of time, the never-failing springs of grace which the sacraments continually conduct to the soul, and the abiding presence of Christ in the hearts of them that love him, show, indeed, that these events are not far off, but continuous. Just as Mass can never be a repetition, but only a continuation of Calvary, so Calvary itself can never cease, since the risen Saviour, wounded and glorified, is forever before the majesty of the Father. The redemption becomes a fact that is linked, not to a date, but to a Person who is our sole Mediator, since no other can be needed. This mediation was not the work of a time, but of eternity. Christ is risen indeed and is at the right hand of the Father.

Now, it cannot be too often repeated that the main safe-guard to the spiritual life is the constant realization of the living facts of the spiritual world. Never to be blind to the vision is the best possible way of assuring ourselves that we shall not neglect the vision; hence we have to be reminding ourselves unceasingly of the daily meaning of the mysteries of the faith. It is just this memory that the presence of our Lord at the right hand of the Father tends to produce. It makes me see that the work of redemption is still carried on, in that the appeal of the wounds and outpoured blood cries without ceasing to the Father. Let me make myself forever conscious of the eternal value of the facts of the Incarnation.

4 THE MOTHER OF GOD

SINCE the Council of Ephesus, the Church has unhesitatingly proclaimed her faith in the divine maternity of our Lady. There had been much discussion on the point at first, for it was only gradually that the Christian people began to consider how our Lord could be God and man at the same time. Heretics had arisen to assert that he was either one or the other, so that the Church was forced to define precisely what was the true teaching. Then when he had been declared to be God and man – one single Person subsisting in two natures, human and divine – the further point was immediately raised as to whether it was to be judged correct to speak of his Mother as the Mother of God. Only by degrees did this come up for discussion. It was clear, indeed, that our Lady could not be the mother of the Godhead: God, as God, could not have been born of her, since he was of eternity and she but a creature of time. As God, he could not be her son, but as man he was obviously her child. Now did this constitute her his mother in such a way that she could rightly be spoken of as the Mother of God? It was a question, in other words, of precise terminology, for in all these matters it is common knowledge how careful the Church has always been to be perfectly accurate. The position, then, was to discover the tradition of Christian people, and it was in Ephesus that the bishops were gathered together who were to announce what had been the constant teaching of the Church.

It was a coincidence that at Ephesus this decision had to be taken, for it was at Ephesus that our Lady had lived after the apostles had been dispersed. When she had been confided to the care of St John by our Lord on the Cross, this had been interpreted to mean that the young apostle was to have charge of her while she yet remained separate from her Son. When, then, John came himself to settle at Ephesus in the position of bishop or chief of the Christian community there assembled, it was only natural that she should accompany him and live with him. This, at least, is the ordinary account that is given us of the matter, and still at Ephesus is shown 'the Virgin's house'.

The decision of the bishops can be easily guessed. They declared her to be rightly acclaimed the Mother of God, and since that date the title has been unfailingly assigned to her in the official liturgy of the Church. The basis of this claim is the doctrine of the Incarnation. Our Lord came to redeem us, to atone for the sins of the human race. This he could not do unless he was at once God and man – man that he might suffer, God that his sufferings might have infinite avail. Moreover, before he became man he was already a person, being indeed the Second Person of the Holy Trinity: consequently there was no reason why he should take to himself a new personality. The divine personality alone could enable him to fulfill all justice; consequently when he was born, he was born as man, but it was a divine person who was born as man. Man by nature, he still retained his unique divine personality. Our Lady, therefore, is the Mother of him who is God.

The importance of this decision can hardly be overestimated, since on it alone rests the whole reason for our special devotion to our Lady, above the devotion that we show to all the saints. Her position in the Catholic world depends upon the acceptance of this truth: if she was chosen to be his Mother, she must have been fitted for her work. Whoever is singled out by God for a special place on earth is no doubt prepared by every necessary grace for that place. If, then, out of all humanity he fitted our Lady to be his Mother, it is obvious that she must have been made ready by every possible grace for her close relationship to him. To no other was it granted to have such intimate acquaintance with him. For months he abode within her womb; for years he was tended by her alone, left to her sole care and control; surely, then, we have a right to assume that she must have been fitted above all others to sustain so absolute a trust. He would not have permitted one so closely related to his own body to see corruption, for of her very flesh was that body formed. From the moment, then, that she accepted her high destiny from the angel's voice, there shone in her eyes the light of motherhood. Without human intervention or concurrence, by her sole union with the Deity, was born her Son. Surely, then, with truth did the angel hail her as full of grace. Because she is the Mother of God, we draw to her with confidence, assured that from her own humanity will spring her wish to help us, and from her close union with God her power to do so.

Handmaid of the Lord

It is evident that the important attitude of soul on which we have to be insistent is that of confidence in God. If we can achieve that, we shall have the firm foundation that our spiritual life needs. It does need foundations if it is to last. But confidence in God means confidence in whatever he does. It cannot mean that we are confident that we shall have what we wish to have; that would be confidence in our own judgment. Confidence in God means that we are sure that God will look after us, that he knows better than we do what we need, and that he will give us and is now giving us what he sees we require. And if we are truly confident in him, we shall have this confidence not least but most when he seems to us to be doing the very opposite of our desire. Even when he seems not to realize how we have set out to do the best for him, we must still determine with ourselves that his judgment is best.

So often it happened that in the Sacred Scripture, where we have manifested to us the working of God's plans, we are shown how God was securing what he wanted by very circuitous ways. Thus, for instance, when God had promised to Abraham that from his seed should come a great people, he seemed to be doing something that would make that promise of no effect when he bade him sacrifice his only son, through whom alone could that seed be born. Or still more clearly when the promises made to the patriarch Joseph that he should rule his parents and his brethren seemed to be rendered nugatory by his various misfortunes, his sale by his brethren, his being carried to Egypt, his unjust treatment in the house of Potiphar, his imprisonment; and yet it is clear to us, as it was clear later to Joseph, that by those very means that looked so unfavorable was he at last to reach that height which had been foretold. All the while his faith still impelled him to trust in God that all would come right in the end; it did. But had his faith wavered, had he tried to assert himself to come by his own, we can see that he would never have secured the mastership of the wealth of Egypt. Leaving himself in God's hands meant that the best and the promised vocation would be fulfilled

But striking as was the faith of Abraham and Joseph, the faith of our Lady was greater. She was tried even more severely than they. Her confidence in the divine purpose for her must have come early in her life, since it must have been early in her life that she consecrated her virginity to God. Like every Jewish maiden, she must have hoped to be the Mother of the Messiah. That was and is still the hope of the women of Israel. Yet, when the angel came to salute her and offer her that motherhood, she could only reply that it was no longer possible to her, for she had forsworn the company of men. She had made her vow with the clear knowledge that it would apparently put her out from any such choice by God; she had felt the inspiration to take the vow so strongly that she had taken it, aware of what it implied and prevented. Actually it was this very virginity of hers that made it possible for her to become the Mother of God: 'A virgin shall conceive and bring forth a son.' But so convinced was she that all was well after the angel had spoken to her that she did not attempt to speak to St Joseph about it. She was sure that if he needed telling, he would be told by someone from God. Still, her confidence was tested by this doubt of his about her.

Was not Bethlehem also a testing of her faith? Was this child really God? He could not protect himself, it would seem. He was dependent on these two, and without them had little chance to survive his birth. Men talk of the difficulties of believing in the face of what God lets happen. But where in the world was faith tried like hers in all that sadness, poverty, exclusion from the inn? She still had to believe him the very God.

All this had to be faced again when there came the persecution of Herod, for it must have come to her as a temptation that he could not really be God whose only safety lay in escape from his enemy. But even this was easier than what happened at the finding in the temple where she came on him and could not but reproach him for having deliberately made her suffer so much pain. There was no question that it was not done deliberately. He was God. He knew exactly what would happen when he stayed behind, knew all the time that she and St Joseph were looking for him, how they sought him sorrowing; yet he did not let them know where he was. Before he left them, he had only to say where he was going, for them to have trusted him alone. But he did nothing of the kind. He let them suffer and made no sign to them to explain things to them. Even when they did find him, he did not apologize to them (how could he?) nor explain to them; he left them entirely to themselves. Words indeed he spoke, but these she did not understand. She pondered over them; she 'kept all these words in her heart'.

The fruit of this pondering was evidenced at Cana of Galilee, for there too he seemed to repel her, or at least almost to say that he would not do what she hinted to him that he should do. He did not repel her, but he seemed not to give her suggestion any countenance. Now she had learnt her lesson, so that at once she says to the waiters: 'Whatever he shall say to you, do ye.' That was her own attitude to him. She told him her needs and then she left things, perfectly ready to do whatever he told her after that. It did not matter whether it seemed to be the answer that she had expected; she knew that all that was necessary was to do exactly what he said. Thus, she prolonged the same lesson into that period of her life which now followed – her desertion by him as it might have seemed in the village: 'Who is my mother? These are my mother and my brethren.' Still she was now ready to do whatever he asked of her, for she knew that whatever he did was wise. She knew that whatever he did was loving, was done out of love for her. He knew too to what heights of confidence she had risen, so that when the woman lifted up her voice in the crowd and praised his Mother, he gave the real greatness in her that merited all praise: 'Blessed are they that hear the word and keep it.' This is what St Luke had said of her after the finding, that she kept all these words in her heart. Now he too said it of her, and thus canonized her to the world.

What again was Calvary to her but a long agony of pain? She suffered in all his sufferings; every blow of the hammer made her hands, as well as his, contract with pain. Every jeer of the crowd shook her with anguish. Every coarse insult stung her as a whip. She had all the while to know that he was God, all the while to know that the Father watched all things serenely, to be sure that, only because God loved, this awful thing could have been let happen. In our time folk have said that there could not be a God in heaven, else he would have interfered to save the world from war. But she had far more reason to be staggered at the sight of such suffering, since she - knew his innocence and the Father's love. But her faith failed not. Remember that she had nothing else but faith.

Did she know when they laid him in the tomb that he would rise again? Tradition seems to affirm it, but there is no absolute sureness that she did. At least we can say that, if she did not, it would have been consistent with what had happened when he was a boy. Then during the after years, when he had gone and there was nothing for her to do for him or anyone, she must have wondered why she was left. At times she must have wondered at the reason of her being left behind without him, except under the eucharistic veils at the hands of St John. But her wonderment was serene and quiet and untroubled. She knew that all was as the Father willed. But through what strange ways had God led her to this ending! Well, that was his affair. She had nothing to do with understanding why he did things; she had only to do what he arranged. So she was still as she had been in the first scene of her direct and visible contact with divine things. 'Be it done unto me according to thy word.' That was her philosophy. All that was needed was to let God go on with his plan. She had learnt through life, more lovingly with every experience of it (and we know only a little of what she suffered at the hands of God), that sublime lesson of perfect confidence.

How splendidly she comes up to every occasion, this valiant woman to whom all was the outcome of the divine will! That is what made her able to face the apostles after their denials and desertions with gracious welcome; made her forgiving and magnanimous; inspired her with courage when all the rest of them had fled like curs. Thus came her patience, the stead-fastness, the unbroken heroism that allowed her to stand erect under the Cross.

How then about us? The New Testament was written that we might have hope. Through all sorts of ways God guides his people to bring them where he wants them. So Abraham was brought, so Joseph, so the Mother of God. Who then are we to complain if we find that he does unaccountable things, apparently unwise things, in his treatment of us? We have at least the consolation of knowing that the treatment that we receive at the hands of God is easier than that treatment to which our Lady was subjected. She had far harder tests put to her faith than we shall ever have, for each receives only that amount of temptation that he is able to bear. To him that hath, more shall be given, that he may prove himself the loyal servant, nay even friend, of God. Our Lady was the more sorely tried because she who had the greater love was better able to meet faith's difficulties.

And again, just as she had her greater difficulties to meet against faith in the divinity of her Son, so had she also in the fulfillment of her way of life, her vocation. Here again we have not only a model but a justification in the sight of God. She helps us as always a little better to understand God. At least we are driven to say, as we think of his treatment of her, that we are not in any position to complain if he treats us something like he treated her. In both these matters let us see a method of divine action and recognize it as the way he acts on souls. The New Testament is a revelation of the divine character, not so much directly as by implication. We are shown God at work, the veil is lifted, and we see behind the outward appearance the divine directive power at its work of providence. She then had to face the fact that God does allow himself to be set aside and opposed and triumphed over in his human form. She had to acknowledge that. So have we. She saw herself accused falsely in the very matter of her maiden purity and recognized that this were better left to God to deal with. She made no explanations, no defenses, but accepted the situation, feeling quite sure that God would look after her. No doubt, had St Joseph spoken to her, she would have told him that she was not at fault. It is hardly likely that she would have disclosed to him the secrets of the King. We then must answer accusations which are brought to us by those who have the duty to reprimand or defend. For the others, we may well leave them to their own suspicions, if they have that unhappy nature. Whatever we say is not likely to disabuse them of what they have heard or imagined.

And as for our lives, we can put these without misgiving into the divine care. Put all your care on him, for he hath care of you. There is little to be gained by anger with authority that has used – as perhaps we think – our talents so ill. There is nothing to be gained by supposing that we should make our own lives at the expense of authority. We have rather to remind ourselves that God has charge of the world and that though at times he seems to go all the way round before he brings souls to their real destiny, nevertheless he does bring them there in the end.

The Mother of God is the most outstanding example of this method of God's husbandry. She was led around by circuitous paths to that motherhood, but she left herself in the divine hands and was carried to her destiny. Beneath us are the everlasting arms. Once this has become a living truth to us, the rest of life becomes a merely blind acceptance of the life we find ourselves held to. After that, we have the adventure of waiting to see what sort of life it is going to be. God is the greatest and most unexpected of artists. He will respect his material that he has made, and will fashion of it what it seems good in his eyes to do.

The Immaculate Conception
The law of original sin was relaxed only in one single case, for one soul that needed redemption. Upon the whole human race that was to be born, the curse was pronounced that no descendant of that first pair could escape the need of the Redeemer – however holy or sacred, however allied in kinship or work to the Incarnate God, however destined to precede or follow, to herald or remind the world of its Saviour. Each created human soul stood in need of a Redeemer, required the Blood of Christ to be applied to itself before redemption could come to it. This none could avoid. The privileges of our Blessed Lady were many and great, but they could not include any such gift as that. God could not really allow her to be saved without the intervention of her Son. As much as I, so much did she, require the saving merits of her Son to be applied to her.

Our Lord himself alone out of all created nature needed no such justification. By his own power redemption had come: God as well as man, he stood in need of no redeeming. It was he, indeed, who was offended against, not he who had offended; but apart from him, no other could escape. Even his Mother must fall under the universal law.

She, too, had to be ransomed, and any doctrine that implied her freedom from this requirement would be blasphemy against the word of God. This much must be borne in mind, then, before we can hope to understand the meaning of this privilege: unique as it was, it did not exempt our Lady from the need of redemption.

The difference, then, between her case and mine was not that I had to be redeemed and she had not, but only in the different ways in which that redemption was applied. We were both of us, our Lady and myself, redeemed – both cleansed from original sin. But with her it was, so to say, a preventative cleansing; with me, a cleansing after the stain had already been made on the soul. Original sin, we must remember, is transmitted by means of the body. The soul comes to us straight from the hands of God. It is the only thing that is directly created by God. Everything else comes into the world through the mediation of secondary causes. The soul, since it is from God, could not arrive already laden with sin. There remains, therefore, the body, which is produced by means of the joint action of my parents. All flesh and blood (formed from them and thus descending ultimately from the single pair whence came the human race) brings with it the taint of sin. Not, of course, that the material could be sinful, but that it brings sin in its train. Though soul and body come together in an immediate embrace, it is still correct to say that it is from the body and not from the soul that the stain of sin comes – for this reason, that the soul is of God and the body of man.

By the privilege, then, of the Immaculate Conception we mean no more than that our Lady was redeemed by her Son and that the application of his merits to her soul was made in a way different from the way in which they were applied to others. She had a privilege, a special exception to a general law. Through no merits of her own, long before she was able to merit or demerit, solely through the action of her Son, she was preserved from all contagion of sin. She was already redeemed before she was conceived in the womb. Without in any way interfering with the work of his divine atonement, at the very moment of her conception, the power of God warded from her the least stain of sin. In virtue of his sacred passion, as yet only foreseen, her baptism was wrought without any ceremony and at the instant that her body and soul were united in an eternal embrace.

Thus it is seen that so far from her privilege detracting in any way from the power of God, or her sinlessness being in any sense due to herself, God went out of his way to deal with her. She is, as always, the highest example that we know of the supreme mercy of God.

Sometimes, perhaps, we are led to think of her as though she were in some way less beholden to him than we are. Really she has received much more at his hands and owes him love and gratitude that are far greater than ours. By the very splendor of grace with which he endowed her from the first instant of life, and by the never-failing spring of grace that grew greater from day to day, she has become the greatest miracle of all creation, the one part of creation that more than any other owes to him debts beyond the possibility of humanity to repay. Salute her, then, my soul, because of her excellence, but salute God more for the existence of such perfection shown to our eyes and for the wonderful thing that he has done for that human nature which she bears in common possession with us.

Our Lady

To her clients, our Lady has stood, above all her other glories, as representing and inspiring the virtue of purity. Whatever claims she has to our reverence, the claim of her purity has probably been more obvious to Christians than any other, more compelling, more effective, more popular. Note, for example, what Catholic dogma has to say about her. The first thing that Catholic dogma says is that she was conceived immaculate. What does that mean? It means that what happens to us at baptism happened to her at the moment of her conception through the foreseen merits of the Redeemer who was to be her Son. Not only, however, was she preserved beforehand from that sin from which we afterwards are cleansed, but she was also prevented by God's grace from suffering the evil results of it. She was saved from the least defilement of original sin and from the spiritual effects of it, whereas we have gradually through life to try to get ourselves absolutely under control. A saint is one who, through heroic love of God, reaches a high level of this self-mastery. Where the saints end, our Lady began. God gave her to start with, what he gives to others only as the fruit of a hard war with temptation painfully sustained and loyally persevered in.

The angel saluted her as 'full of grace,' and that before she had received the special graces of her motherhood. Before the offer had been put to her and accepted, an angel had bowed to her in reverence, as already greater than himself; then he set before her on God's behalf the great choice. Her acceptance was made in the perfect language of humility, and 'in her eyes there shone the light of motherhood'. From that moment an increase of grace came to her to fit her for her new office. At once God lay in her womb, was forming for himself from her flesh and blood the material for the body of Christ, and surely took charge of her that she should be as worthy of her high prerogative as it was possible for mortal to be. It does not seem fantastic to suppose that God gives to each the graces and helps needed for his work in life, that those whom he calls to higher vocations have the greater needs, that those who are to be nearer to his person should also be fitted for their nearness by special preparatory graces. If each soul has the grace required for its state of life, what must have been the graces given to her who was to be the Mother of Christ?

We affirm, therefore, as Catholics, that the graces, given to our Lady (given, remember) were the highest graces given to any redeemed human being. Angels bowed to her, prophets foretold her coming, apostles were put in her charge as their Mother. She was full of grace before her Child was conceived, and she steadily grew in grace by corresponding to what had been given her; blessed indeed as his Mother, more blessed because she heard his word and kept it. God spoke to her incessantly and she heard and obeyed. Because, therefore, she was preserved from sin and had been saved from the disastrous dissipation of powers that follows on original sin, she was able to make use of every opportunity of increasing her love of God. Her mental gifts were untainted, unflawed; she could concentrate wholly and without distraction on whatever she did. Nothing led her off from the object that the will set before her mind. She was alert and whole-hearted in all she did, because the fatal consequences of original sin, under which we suffer, troubled her not at all Think, then, of her as of one who was made at her beginning what the saints are in their ending, who from the height at which they finish began her climb; then you will realize how wonderful she is and how the thought of her greatness has filled the mind of the Church.

Tower of Ivory

Our Lady's wonderful holiness was different in degree from the holiness of the saints, but not in kind, for holiness is always the same: it means a great love of God. With the steady increase of grace came also, and naturally, an increase in the love of God. Consequently we have to think of her as ever increasing her love of God with each fresh impulse of grace. Free from sin as she was from the moment of her conception, that the flesh and blood of her Son might spring from an unstained womb, she began her conscious life with a love for God. Then as each event befell her in the marvelous pageant of the Incarnation, it meant a succession of higher grace to fit her for the advancing demands to be made on her, and therefore, more love of God. The annunciation and her stirrings of motherhood, the birth of the Child, his epiphany to the Gentiles, the growing years of boyhood, the loss and the finding of the Boy, his 'first of miracles' at Cana, his parting with her, the passion, Calvary, the taking of his body from the Cross, the burial, resurrection, ascension, Pentecost, the daily Mass and Communion from the hands of St John, were so many increasing moments of grace which deepened her floods of love.

That is precisely why her purity has been so celebrated, for purity means, as we have described already, a love of God; the positive dedication of one's self and one's friendship to him; the making him a third in all our human loves. Think of her love and you see at once how he absorbed all her energies and powers. Mothers, in their extravagant language, speak of 'worshipping' their children; she certainly worshipped her child, for he was also her God. Every inducement, human as well as divine, urged her to love him increasingly: his beauty, his charm, the appealing winsomeness of his childhood, the quiet dignity of his growing manhood, his tender care of her, his strength and vision. Everything human and divine drew her to him. This was the secret of her holiness, of all her virtues, not least of all, her purity. This last especially she had, because it was founded on a special affection for him. Her love of him was so whole-hearted that no room was left for any other appeal to her desires; no evil attracted her, because she was already attracted wholly to him.

Here, then, we shall find in our Lady a great patroness against the temptations to impurity. She shows us the surer way, not of escape, but of prevention, for the firm remedy of these evils is a constant and devoted friendship with Christ. Without this, we shall find ourselves entangled in endless miseries; with this, everything falls into place. We must cling, therefore, to her support, to her intercession, to hold us nearer to her Son. In statues and paintings we find her represented as a Mother holding and delighting in her Child; so did she find her way to that high chastity that has made her an object of devotion to all those in trouble from the passions that stir the human heart. She soothes the perplexities of our nature by inspiring the primary dedication of ourselves to her Son. She lays her calm hand on us and stills our passions, quiets our excitement, by showing us how to center ourselves upon him. Our love for human friends will grow not less, but greater, when it is purged of selfishness, when the mere fleshly pleasure of it is ennobled by looking to a higher purpose, when through our friendship with our Lord, itself deepened through our devotion to his Mother, we recognize the perfect beauty of her character, its inviolate purity, and we see in this no weakness but a towering strength.

Faithful Virgin

Our Lady is a help to us not merely in temptations against purity, but in other ways as well. After all, much as man may be troubled by sex problems or whatever we may care to call them, he has other difficulties to face. Impurity is not the only sin, nor is it the worst sin. We may easily get in the way of being obsessed by this one form of evil, and forget that it is merely one of many enemies with which we are at war. Indeed, the Catholic Church has taught always that though all sin is evil, spiritual sins are, on the whole, worse than carnal sins; that pride, for example, is more deadly and despair is more destructive than sins of the flesh. Consequently we must look upon our Lady not only as an example of chastity, but also of all the other virtues. Let us turn to her now under the invocation of the faithful Virgin.

Consider what is the noblest and most redeeming trait in human character. Probably not everyone would agree as to what he believed this to be. Some might take one and some another, perhaps gentleness, charity, a flaming love of justice, a stern sense of truth. Yet it does not seem unwarranted to say that, to judge from English literature, the most redeeming feature of a man or woman or child is loyalty, consistency in devotion, fidelity to a trust. Success or failure naturally do not very much affect hero-worship. In fact, national heroes are often men who led a forlorn hope, who dared greatly and yet failed; but one thing alone is always said of them, that they were loyal to their cause. A renegade is always distrusted, a traitor is almost the worst name of insult, a turncoat is universally detested, even by the party he joins. We feel that loyalty is the fairest of human virtues, the most stirring, and, in an evil man, the most redeeming.

The reason for this ready praise of fidelity in man is due to the half-conscious realization that it is foreign to his fallen nature. He is a creature of impulse and caprice, essentially subject to change, tempted incessantly to follow the way of fortune and fashion and self-interest. When, then, he sees constant loyalty, he is amazed and touched to reverence. He has come in contact with something that reminds him of the eternal steadfastness of God, who is without shadow of change. Our Lady is evidently a high example of this constancy; in the joy of his presence she loved him, and when he left her to be about his Father's business, she learnt still to accept his will; even to him on the Cross and dying, when the Shepherd was struck and the sheep scattered on the hill, she still remained faithful. Without murmur or complaint, her virginal heart clung to him, faithful unto death. Through the Gospels he seems to deal her strange, unmerited blows that perplexed as well as hurt her; yet she accepted all, 'pondering over them in her heart,' for of her, no less than of us, it was demanded that she should serve by way of faith only, blindly faithful, without knowing reason or purpose. Her sorrows, her loneliness when he had gone, her long wait for release, she patiently accepted, because she was as full of faith as of grace, a 'faithful Virgin'.

Health of the Weak

It was the great prerogative of the Mother of God to live with her Son for thirty years, to learn of him the lessons of her life. She was to face suffering, the greater because of her love for him whose sorrows would thereby become her own. All his action on her life in Bethlehem and Nazareth was to prepare her for this. The scene in the Temple shows us a glimpse of what must have been an unending schooling, labored at day after day. The Mother has indeed left us no record of it, told us none of the intimate parables woven for her out of everyday occurrences, but such slight appearances as she makes in the Gospels are always accompanied by some saying of our Lord in reference to the divine will. He was teaching her more and more to see life through his eyes, to accept it as he saw it, impressed with the inspiration and governance of the Father. Incessantly she was being taught by every kind of lesson to see God's decree in all that befell her, to find him everywhere in her life.

We can see this perhaps more clearly where it is least evident: in that mystic substitution of John for himself: 'Behold thy son.' Too often we are content to accept it merely from our point of view, the divine gift of us all in the person of the Beloved Disciple to her care. It is that, of course, but it was directed actually to her and intended to open up for her the great lesson of her life in another form. Henceforward in every faithful follower she was to see her Son; each was to be to her another Christ. Is it straining a point to see a reference to this scene in St John's own principle that man is to be loved as the visible embodiment of God? 'For he that loveth not his brother whom he seeth, how can he love God whom he seeth not?' (2 John 4:20). He had gone, was no longer visible to her in the flesh, though every day she could yet be made one with him in the sacrament of Communion. She was, however, by faith, to find him in all human creatures. He was handing them all over to her care, but precisely because she would see in them himself. So closely was she made like him that she saw in the world what he saw; she by faith, though, and he by sight. He loved all because he saw in them the mirrored image of himself; she loved all because she saw in all his image mirrored: 'Mother, behold thy son – and henceforth the disciple took her to his own.' And henceforth, too, she saw her Son in every human soul.

That is one reason why she has been so unswervingly the health of the weak. What can strengthen us, lift us above our narrow prejudices, take us out of the pitiful exclusiveness of our views of others, shake us free of the Pharisaism that would let the world that does not happen to be our world go its own way and face its own troubles alone, while we never stir a finger to help it? We want a wide spirit, a kindly appreciation of all the world, a power to trace in human nature, however stunted, deformed, unspiritualised, the ground-plan of that design on which it was originally built: the likeness of God. She is the Mother of us all, because in us all, even in the least of his brethren, she sees himself. We can turn to her and ask her to implore with us of her Divine Son that we may have her great vision of human souls. Not only in St John, nor in the penitent Magdalen, did the Maiden Mother see him reflected, but she found him everywhere. Earlier, when he was told that she and his brethren stood on the edge of the crowd, he waved his hand over the crowd, its motley elements of sick and possessed and unclean, and declared that these were his mother and sister and brother; she learnt a higher lesson from him, she found they were himself.

Seat of Wisdom

There are two things necessary to wisdom: that we should have an opportunity for acquiring knowledge and a mental capacity to make use of the opportunities afforded us. The first resolves itself, more or less, into the need of someone to instruct us. This may, in quite a number of instances, be adequately offered through the means of a book. There are special sciences or branches of learning in which a quantity of reading is necessary, without which it may be altogether impossible to grasp the subject. Thus we might say of the study of history that it is almost entirely built up of materials that demand our closest attention and scrutiny. In other kinds of knowledge the need may be only for a capable master to instruct us in the main lines and principles. This is especially true of those who are concerned with abstract knowledge. In philosophy many of the greatest have dispensed with books, taught by their own minds and the stimulus of conversation and discussion with congenial, though opposingly-minded, friends. In the sacred knowledge of God it is above all obvious that we require instruction rather than books, a master rather than a library. But there is also, again, the necessity for a certain amount of intelligence on our part. Said Dr Johnson on a famous occasion: 'I can supply you with arguments, but not with the wit to understand them.' Hence it is clear that the best master in the world will be altogether unable to effect anything on those who are incompetent to follow him. In fact, the better the master, often on that account the worse the pupil.

Now in the case of our Lady we notice that she was in a marvelous way gifted. She had at once the greatest master of all wisdom, and at the same time the best mental capacities for that wisdom. The Son of God, who is the eternal wisdom of the Father, was in her company for thirty uninterrupted years, during which time she is recorded to have pondered over the words that he let fall. We are always talking about the effect on children of being brought up entirely in the company of their elders. They are exceedingly precocious, acquire the very phraseology of their parents, and have a view of life that is original and fresh. Whether we consider this an advantage or not, we are quick to see the influence that grown-up people receive from their acquaintances: we judge a man by the company he keeps. What, then, must have been the opportunities that lay in the path of the Mother of God! Her acquaintance with the economy of the divine plan must have been profound. The questions and answers of the doctors could not be compared with her manifold intercourse with the substance of the brightness of the Father. Moreover, not merely had she the unique chance in the world of obtaining knowledge of the things of God, but she had also unique opportunities of making the best use of them. She had, out of all the world, the mind most fitted to understand the words of God. We consider always that children have glimpses of God that are lost to us; we judge that their intercourse with God is so intimate and natural, so innocent and pure, that they must have helps to give us in their chance and broken remarks. All that child ever had was hers. The innocence that came from the Immaculate Conception, an unsullied soul that never knew the least stain of sin, where in all the world was anyone so divinely gifted?

It is, then, no mere poetry to speak of her, as does the Church, as the Seat of Wisdom. Over her were outspread the wings of the Spirit of God. United to the Incarnate Word, prepared with angelic purity to understand the divine messages, responsive to the voice of an angel that our grosser ears would not at all have perceived, unclouded by the weakness that sin causes to the intelligence, passionless, without even the dullness of old age, she stands at the head of the long line of the wise who lead onward the children of men. Surely, then, we know where to go in our perplexities of mind. All, in some way or other, must be puzzled by the intricate problem of life. There are so many things in this amazing world that we do not understand, so many stories of the dealings of God that we cannot reconcile with what we have been taught of mercy and justice and truth. There is as well the outstanding perplexity of ourselves when we consider our place and purpose and daily failure. There is, finally, the whole of life and death and after-life, the Incarnation with all that follows from that stupendous mystery, and the meaning of the Church. Where else shall we carry these things that so disturb us save to the Mother who knew and asked and in her heart pondered over all these things? Of surpassing intelligence, she shall be our refuge to her Son. For she is but the seat of that divine wisdom which is in her, but not hers. Her wisdom is not her own, but his to whom we beg her to lead us.

Sorrowful Mother
On the evening of Good Friday we stop to think, not of the passion of the Son, but rather of the passion of his Mother. For him all the suffering is over; for her, suffering remains. For him, death was indeed suffering; for her, death, his death, has made that suffering more intense. We call her the Queen of Martyrs, for she was among all martyrs their queen. She suffered nothing herself in the way that the martyrs suffered. No violence was done her, except the violence done to her heart. She did not suffer for him, as the martyrs suffered. That was her trouble. She could only suffer with him. Thus, she watched him suffer and she could do nothing to help. That is the awfulness of watching people we love in pain. We can do nothing, nothing at all. We can just watch, perfectly helpless, but their suffering, as we watch, becomes our own.

She was the queen, then, of martyrs because she suffered with him. Every blow of the scourge she felt. Every prick of each thorn in the crown pierced her forehead. Whatever hurt him, hurt her. The nails, as they were driven, clenched and unclenched her own fingers. The nails driven through his feet she carried with pain. Her heart hurt when his was opened. The death that eased him gave her no ease. She suffered with him.

In all he suffered, she suffered, and that is where we touch hands with her. We have to watch suffering, be utterly unable to ease suffering, we must think of her suffering. We must ask her to gain for us strength to bear our own. She suffered, even though she knew that death would be swiftly lifted from him, that he would come back. Just to lose him, just to know that death took him, was pain enough, though she knew out of death would come forth life. A mother is hurt when her child perhaps goes away to school from her. She knows she will see the child again. That doesn't lessen the pain. The pain at least is there. It isn't that she doesn't know the child will come back to her, but for the moment all she can think of is that the child is gone. There is a place empty at the table, a bed empty upstairs. Everything is desolate, quiet. She must suffer by that.

Imagine Mary, robbed of him whom most she loved. He was all she had, and he was taken from her, and she stood weeping under the cross. There is no hurt in weeping. She was crying, and no one said her nay. There is nothing wrong in feeling the hurts you suffer. He blessed those that mourn. To mourn was a blessing in his eyes. He didn't say that he did not wish people to feel suffering. He said: 'Blessed are they that mourn. Blessed are they that weep, for they- shall be com-forted.' She wept, and she had at last her comfort. We must think of that, must remember that the depth of her suffering and sorrow shows the height to which her comfort lifted her when at last comfort came.

For all we know, he died without telling her when at last she would go to him. He may have told her, but we don't know that he did, and even so it must have been hard for her to go on living. She might have wondered why she was left. What was she to do? What was her place, now that her Child had left the earth? What was she doing on earth? Why didn't he take her? Well, once before that, when he was quite a little boy, he had gone with them to the Temple at Jerusalem, and then they thought he had gone back with them, but he hadn't. He had stayed behind. They looked for him, searched for him, and couldn't find him, and they came back sorrowful, still looking for the Boy. At last they found him. There he was in the Temple, dealing with the wise old men, asking them questions they couldn't answer, answering all their questions. So wise he was, even as a child. And she came and she said to him. 'Why have you done this? Why have you left me without saying a word? You need only have told me that you were going, and I shouldn't have looked for you these three days. Why did you just go away and leave us, why deliberately hurt your Mother's heart? You need only have said one word, "Trust me".'

Why didn't he say it? She pondered over it; her heart was pierced by a sword. Why did he treat her like that? Why did he deliberately hurt her when he could have saved her all that pain? You wouldn't think any boy was a good son that ran away and never told where he was going when he might have told and so saved them all their pain. Especially you wouldn't think it of one like him, that was so full of sympathy and understanding. It is so strange. But he must be about his Father's business, and her business was to trust him So she learnt to trust him and pondered over these things. That was all when he was a little boy, and now he had grown up and there he was, hanging on the Cross, and then before night fell they had taken him down. Perhaps he had died silent, saying nothing to her, just leaving her to trust. She knew, as all the disciples knew, that he had promised after three days he would come back. She knew that, but she didn't know about herself, how long she was to go on waiting after it was all done. And perhaps he never told her, or perhaps he had just said she was to wait for him Evidently that must have been how he treated her. He said nothing. He asked her to have perfect confidence in him. We may be sure she had. That is how she bore sorrow. This is the way of our Queen.

You and I, whoever we are, whatever our luck in life is, are sure to have all sorts of troubles, and we may sometimes wonder why God leaves us, why all we ever loved or worked for, sometimes at least, may be taken from us, and we left sorrowing and alone. It may well seem strange to us, we being so small, so bewildered. What God does must seem strange, not because it is strange, but because we have such little sight, such little understanding, and God is so infinitely great. What we have got to remember is just how he treated his Mother when he was a little boy, and how when he was a grown man he left her standing, lonely. He went away from her, who had suffered with him, for him, heart in heart. Remember both his silence and her perfect confidence. Thus was she the Queen of Martyrs, but her heart at peace, tranquil, resting in confidence on God.

And so you and I have the thought of her suffering, the dreadfulness of that first night with him dead – not dead only, but buried. How relentless burial seems! As though the dead, while they were unburied, were still in your midst, almost alive. But when they were buried – that seemed the end of things. The earth falling on them; they hid from us. So now he was hidden from her by a great stone rolled. And as she stood, receiving the body in her arms, and then seeing it carried and placed in the tomb, and then the great stone rolled across the front, that must have seemed to make him doubly dead. To that sorrowing mother's heart came only silence, and no words spoken, but she rested on her confidence, on her faith in him, on his love of her.

We are all children of sorrow. For all of us this is the valley of tears. Everyone, somehow, must sorrow – grown-up people, children, everyone. But there is no hurt in sorrowing. It is a blessing. In proportion to your sorrow will consolation come. So it becomes a blessedness. One day he will repay you, but now you must just wait. So we turn to her, this Sorrowful Mother – for all that are sorrowful must come to her – and we ask that she would turn her eyes of mercy towards us. She, so compassionate at heart, so understanding, who had tasted the depth of sorrow herself, had lost the best of all sons, her child and the God who made her, the child that her womb had fashioned, the God that had fashioned her womb. She had lost him, and life was a blank for her, and all her life would now be empty as she turned from the tomb and the closed door. All ye that sorrow declare if there be sorrow like her sorrow, or love or loss like hers. It was God's will. She bore her sorrow and she will help us to bear ours, every one of them, sorrows that others know we carry, and those more hidden sorrows that no one knows but we. She will help us. She has tasted bitterness. She carried her sorrows. She walked tranquil, because she loved. Her tears were not bitter tears. Behind her tears was perfect trust in him. She that is our Mother will put her mantle about us, and when we stand under our cross, we know that she will stand by us. 'Turn then thine eyes of mercy towards us, and after this, our exile' – it is an exile. It was meant to be an exile. Here we are wanderers. Here we have no home. 'After this, our exile, show unto us the fruit of thy womb, oh clement, oh loving, oh sweet Virgin Mary.'

Mother of Mercy

There seems to have been no parable that so much attracted the early Christians as the parable of the Good Shepherd. They have scrawled over the walls of the catacombs the figure of the Divine Master, carrying upon his bowed shoulders the wandering and rescued lamb. Even when they set out to depict the figure of St Peter, the Vicar of Christ, they show him also as continuing the role of his leader, and in their forceful art have carved the apostle in the guise and at the work of a shepherd. The child Jesus himself in their best and most charming statue is the boy David, with a sling, and yet at the same time with the poor and familiar load of a sheep. Then, as though they could not conceive of any more beautiful idea in which to sum up the work of God's Maiden Mother, they have in one case represented her by the side of the Good Shepherd, feeding with her hands a crowd of fluttering birds. She, too, has the high and sacred office that comes to those who the more nearly approach to Christ, of succoring the distressed. We, also, hail her under various titles that so proclaim her kindly privilege: she is Our Lady of Perpetual Help, above all, the Mother of Mercy.

Now mercy, about which the poets have said such beautiful things, implies on the one hand a power of sympathy and on the other a position to show that mercy to others – the fellow-feeling of sorrow and the ability to help.

In the case of our Lady it must be evident that she has an understanding of all distress. We speak of her as the Queen of Martyrs, the Mother of Sorrows, because we regard her as having touched the depths of all human anguish. The whole progress of her life was a progress in suffering from the moment of the birth of her Son, through the early anxieties that the massacre of the innocents entailed, the words of Simeon, the losing of the Child and his seemingly upbraiding words about his Father's business. The shadow of the Cross during all the thirty years of intimacy, the leave-taking, the known plottings of the Pharisees, the detailed pains of those last days, and the terrors of his agony and death and burial, have marked out her burden as above the burdens that have fallen to the lot of the cursed children of Adam.

Is there exaggeration in the way that the Church applies to her the words that the prophets spoke of her Son, that there was no other sorrow to be seen like unto hers? Indeed, apart from his sufferings, which more than any other human being she was able to realize, there have never been sufferings such as hers. Desolation, distress, disappointment, bereavement, were the constant attendants of her life. No one, then, can approach her without feeling that she will understand their own woe. And if she understands as none other can, will she not also desire to help as none other can, since she is the Mother of him who was all love? If his saints are distinguished by love, caught from the fire of his heart, certainly she more than them all must have in her nature the wide sympathy of Christ – the sympathy, and also the will to aid.

Not, then, alone as the spring-head whence broke the waters of wisdom, but as also the nearest and most faithful follower of the divine fount of mercy, we come to her in our distress – confident, indeed, we are, that she will understand by the sad experience of her own troubled life on earth – confident also that, under-standing, she will desire to help – we turn to her. The love of God, which has worked the great deeds of pity since the world began, cannot exist in her without effect; the kindness that she saw for thirty years on earth cannot have left her outlook on life untouched: Mother of Sorrows, she is also the Mother of the Pitiful Heart. Not merely does she sympathize with sorrow, but she is filled with longing to ease and allay it – the consoler, we say, of the afflicted.

Finally, she not only understands and desires to help, but she has far more than any other the power to show that in the fullest way. The chroniclers tell us that when Edward III had made up his mind to destroy the burghers of Calais because of the harm they had wrought upon his subjects, and had refused to spare their lives, even at the request of his best soldier and his favorite knight, the Queen of England hurried from her court across the sea to add her petitions to the same cause. Wrathful at her arrival and at her demand, he could only answer: 'I can deny nothing to the mother of my son.' In applying this to our Lady, is there not in this purely human view of God and his dealings with men, something of comfort? He does not, indeed, repent of his commands, but he may well have willed to spare at the request of the Mother of his Son.

5 THE MYSTICAL BODY

ONE idea to which St Paul frequently returns is the comparison between the faithful who are in Christ Jesus and the members of a human body. He makes use of this metaphor several times to prove several different things – to prove, for example, that each has a separate work to do and that each separate work is dependent on the rest. But while making use of a comparison which has occurred to many writers before his time and since, St Paul gives it an elevation and a nobility that raise it above the dignity of a mere literary device. For him it is a real truth which is to be of help to a soul in its outlook upon life.

We must remember the circumstances in which St Paul found himself. He was a convert from Judaism, where he had been brought up in the very strictest form of the Hebrew faith; he was 'a Pharisee of the Pharisees,' that is, he belonged to the narrowest, most fanatical, and most exclusively nationalistic of the various parties of his nation. Then had come his sudden and miraculous seizure on the road to Damascus, and all the old fierceness was turned now into a burning and impetuous love of Christ. His education, while certainly designed with care under Gamaliel to lead him to a whole-hearted acceptance of the law, evidently brought him in touch with Greek and Roman culture. He quotes passages from the poets, and in his address to the Athenians he shows considerable sympathy with the nobler side of paganism. Moreover, his missionary tours among the Hebrew communities in the Greek cities of Asia Minor made him realize that not these communities alone, but all the world was longing ('groaning') for a new and more perfect revelation. His missionary venture thus became more and more an appeal, not to the Jews (for these had their own valiant apostles) but to the Gentiles.

St Paul took for his own portion the most degraded religion with which he came in contact. Now what is his method of dealing with these poor souls? He at once endeavors to make them realize their own value in the sight of God. He tells them that they are all members of Christ. These people, who have been accustomed to worship idols and who have looked upon gods as heroes of very doubtful morality, who have never been assisted to rise above their own surroundings or to improve their stunted spiritual life, are now confronted by the ideals of Christianity, which certainly must have appeared to them more dazzling and even more impossible than they do to us who are familiar with the character of Christ. And while in this way they suddenly found life become very much more difficult, and were contrasting their old natural or unnatural practices with the new purity and continence demanded of them, St Paul, instead of telling them that they are sinners and upbraiding them with their failures, is at great pains to point out to them how God by becoming man has raised man to God. He reveals the whole story of the Incarnation in its culminating mercy of the Crucifixion. They have been bought at a great price; if man has not valued them, God has. But not merely has Christ died for them, he has made them one with himself. The sacraments knit them to him; the Eucharist is a memorial of that death, transfigured to an abiding presence. Matrimony is but a type of the union between Christ and each single soul; and the ensuing love is so fierce and vehement that it breaks down every barrier, sweeps aside every obstacle, and makes each one with Christ. 'I live now, not I, but Christ liveth in me.'

Here is comfort, not for them only, but for me as well. I am a member of Christ; I have been purchased by the Blood of God. Then I am of value in his sight; he thinks me worth troubling about. Not only has he redeemed me, but he has given me the grace to be a member of his Church, a member of his mystical body. I have, then, a certain definite place in this organization and do a work that others, indeed, might have done, yet which he has confided to me alone. Not only have I my own vocation, but because I am the member of a body, I have a definite function to perform, yet one which needs the co-operation of others. I and they are interdependent. We require each other, and every single Catholic has demands on me, on my good works, prayers, etc. But even more than I am dependent on my fellow-members, I am dependent on Christ and he on me. To me, miserable, poor, foolish, sinful, it is also given to up what is wanting in the sufferings of Christ'; for if 'one member suffers, all the members suffer'. He is my Head.

Surely this ought to inspire me to go on with my struggle in life? This should give me courage to persevere. Just as I find that I can only hope to reform others – children, sinners, the poor – by making them realize the good they can do and the goodness that is really in them, so is it with myself. I shall surely do better when I realize my own dignity as a Christian soul. I, even I, am a member of Christ. Then I shall take care not to sully my reputation or lower myself. I shall have an esprit de corps, a loyalty to my chief, that will keep me conscious that in my hands is the honor, not of myself only, but of all my fellows on earth and in heaven, and of God himself. For 'done member suffers, all the body suffers also'.

Unity of the Church

The Church that Christ came to found was to teach truth. From this central idea it is possible to show that in consequence the Church of Christ must be holy, else the purpose of truth is vain (moreover, the Master prayed his Father to sanctify his children in truth); it must be catholic, for it is the very glory of truth that it knows no boundaries, nor divisions of intelligence or of language or of race; it must be apostolic, for it has not only to show its possession of truth, but that it was commissioned by Christ to teach that truth; and, finally, it can be shown that for the selfsame reason the Church that Christ came to found must be one and the same the world over. Once, indeed, it is granted that to teach truth is the proper purpose of the Church, then the unity of the Church is self-evident. For if it is certain that there can be no boundaries to the limit of the empire of truth, if there can be no language or race or age that can escape its power, then assuredly it must be one and undivided also. If it is to reach over all the world, then over all the world it must be one. If it has to break down the artificial or natural partitions raised up by man's division of the earth, it can do this only at the expense of being the same everywhere.

Truth may be many-sided, as the philosophers of the last generation loved to explain, but it can afford to be many-sided only because it means one thing only from one point of view. But truth as truth must be one and the same always. If it is true that Christ is God, this does not mean that he is not also man, but it does mean that he must be recognized as God always and everywhere. No doubt in his death he died as man simply, for God as God could not die; yet for all that we must say that it was God who died. Because he is God, he is God always. Hence the Church of Christ that is really faithful to his name will always preach the same doctrine.

Here, oddly enough, or rather quite rightly, we come on the ordinary accusation against the Catholic Church, namely, that she never will change. Her opponents, whose name and whose quarrel is legion, at least agree in this, that it is characteristic of Catholicism to be found the same in all the world. In every place where she has set up her altars, she comes with one single faith and she demands its acceptance by all her children. There cannot be one teaching for those who are clever, one for those who are rich, and one for those who are in revolt against the conditions of their life. For all there must be some one message that comes out of eternity, from the lips of God who dwelleth in eternity, and therefore which will be above the restless ebb and flow of changing time. Centuries may vary in their ideas of what is graver and what is lesser evil. Men may have one custom today and another tomorrow; they may declare that a rate of wage which troubled no man's conscience in the generation that is gone would be scandalous to the next; but through it all there must be one only truth. The traditions may alter, but the truth remains.

This is just what the Church has always clung to. When, for example, a new question comes to be discussed, it is her way to find out what has been the teaching of the past upon it, or rather upon some similar aspect of truth, so convinced is she that she must hold fast to that which was, for since it was true yesterday, it is true today as well. In whatever land she is found, she teaches the same doctrine; and in her faith, her sacraments, and her head she is one and the same the whole world over.

It is this that should give me a truer notion of my faith. There is always the temptation – especially when I mix, as indeed I cannot help doing, with people who have no fixed teaching at all – to wish that I could alter some of the things I have learnt as a child. I seem to see that it would make for the spread of the Church if I could only reject one point or another, go back upon this doctrine or that, explain away some decision of some pope in some bygone age. The dead weight of the past seems to lie heavy on the Church. Of course, if the thing in question is merely some disciplinary matter, I may advocate and work for its being set aside; or if a doctrine is merely propounded without the decisive voice of the Shepherd and Teacher of the flock, I may hope that the straitness of the teaching may be modified. But if the question concerns some definite matter that has been decided by the infallible decree of the Vicar of Christ, then I can only bow my intelligence. I am of eternity; I am of truth. Eternity cannot change; nor can truth be other than it always is.

The Church is one because she teaches the eternal truth of Christ; and I must submit myself loyally to that unity, without which I should find myself in the midst of the chaos and confusion that is of man, but cannot be of God. Always, then, I must bring myself back to the spirit of our Blessed Lord when he prayed for the unity of his disciples and of all who should through their word believe in him, that upon us all should descend the very oneness of God. I am one in faith with Catholics over all the world. Let me endeavor by holding fast to truth to bring others too into that one fold, conscious that unity built on any other foundation than truth cannot survive.

Catholicity of the Church

The Church that Christ came to found was to teach truth. By that single sentence alone can be proved all the prerogatives that Catholics claim for their Church, for to teach truth in matters of such moment requires the gift of inerrancy, i.e., the gift of teaching without error the truths that are necessary for salvation, and the gift of indefectibility, i.e., the gift of teaching without ceasing till the end of all the world. To deliver the message of Christ means to preach as one having authority, to tell men how they are to arrive at the same life that he had lived.

But not merely has this Church to appeal with authority and without ceasing till the end of time; she has also to deliver the glad tidings to the whole race. If the Catholic Church is indeed the Church of Christ, she cannot be a national church; she cannot entertain so narrow a view of her mission. If there is one thing more than another that our Lord was most insistent upon in his lifetime, it was that his religion was not intended for one people only, but for all the world. The Pharisees hunted him to death chiefly for the reason that he entirely repudiated the restriction of the kingdom of God to those souls only who could boast of descent from Abraham. He scandalized them over and over again by his appeal to a wider audience than those merely that worshipped upon the Temple-Mount. All their creeds he came to fulfill, to include them in this new faith, this grain of mustard-seed, this leaven, which should affect the whole race of man. He broke through all the divisions of language, or birth, or previous prejudice and would gather into one all the children of man

Now it is just this that the Catholic Church has been able to achieve. She has gone out into the world and has deliberately invited all to the new faith of Christ. At first there was some discussion, as we learn from the Scriptures, and it was necessary that the first Pope (St Peter) should be convinced by a vision before he would agree to allow those converted from paganism the full fellowship of the Christian name; but thence onward all nations found a home within her. She has travelled the whole world over, not as the Church of a nation (for so to label oneself is to repudiate the teaching of our Lord), but as the Catholic Church. She is the Church of all peoples, of all times, of all the ages of man. She has gone to strange countries, not simply to settle there for the benefit of passing merchants, but to take her place in the life of the nations. Then, within the limits of each people, she affects the individuals as well. She is the Church for the children, the Church for the poor, the Church for the old, the Church for the young. The learned find her dogmas wonderful as the flashing brightness of the radiance of God; the simple discover that her doctrine and her practices make life intelligible, though not comprehensible. For each, whatever his state or age or capacity, she has her way of good; she is catholic in every sense of that wide-meaning word; nothing escapes her.

More splendid still, she has gathered together all that is best in all the religions of the world. There is no practice of hers and no belief that cannot be found elsewhere, yet nowhere else are they all put together and formed by the swift revelation of God into a picture, towards a portion of which each people has groped its way since ever the world began.

The Church is catholic. To that Church I myself belong. Catholic, then, must be the whole temper of my mind. There must be in me none of that narrowness that would limit the spirit of God to one single fashion nor would grudge my neighbor his own way of achieving the purpose of his existence. The liberty I claim for myself I should gladly concede to others; for, after all, the Church is large enough to include all. If every nation under heaven can find protection under its shadow, who am I to dictate to my brother how he should serve God? There is the obvious limit of the Catholic faith; beyond that, indeed, there is salvation for the children of men, for the simple reason that God does not bind himself to give grace only in one way.

God, however, wills that all men should come to the knowledge of the truth, and it is the duty of a Christian to bring as many as possible within that fold of Christ. Within the Church there is also the dogmatic teaching which none may with safety deny; she is the teacher from God, and to whom else can we turn? But apart from these fixed truths, there are paths and bypaths which each can follow for himself. Yet the self-centered spirit of man is too easily persuaded that it alone has found the perfect way, not realizing that what is the way of one need not be the way of another; for it is in the power of God to lead me individually to himself by a path singled out from all eternity that I, and I alone, shall take. My past is as the past of none other, and my future must be unique as well. Let me, then, be wide-minded enough not to question or be scandalized in my brother. His conscience is lit up by the glory of God, and that should be enough for me. The silly parochialism that would reduce all to one dead level has no part or lot in the kingdom of God. I must not grudge others their own way, nor seek to drive them into my own; for Catholicism means the freedom of the children of God.

Apostolicity of the Church

The Church that Christ came to found was to teach truth. For that precise object was it established, and by that ultimate end, it is clear, all her institutions are to be justified or repudiated. Her infallibility, her indefectibility, her holiness, her Catholicism, are defended by that simple and primary fact. To it also we can trace that note of apostolicity which, since the fifth century, it has become traditional to demand for the true Church of Christ.

Consider what she has to do to justify her claim to be the true Church of Christ. Not only has she to prove that all that he taught she also teaches, or that she can make good her boast that there is none other that so closely clings to the doctrines that he set out to preach – clings to them in spite of every age-long endeavor to assert their incompatibility with contemporary movements (for she has felt that to be up-to-date is little required by that which is not of time but of eternity) – but over and above this she has also to prove that she bears his commission. That is to say, it is not enough to show that you hold the doctrines taught by our Lord, but it is also necessary to show that you have his permission to represent him There must be some sort of official recognition, otherwise we might be entertaining false Christs and false prophets; consequently we have a right to demand from the Church that she should show her connection with the apostolic band to whom Christ gave the sacred commission to preach his Gospel to every living creature. We have a right to ask her to show how she has descended from that first generation that was of God and taught by God himself. She must, in other words, trace her line back to the apostles.

Now this must not be taken to mean that she has to prove historically that each link in the chain is intact; not, indeed, because this cannot be done, but because we have not the time, the learning, or the opportunity for accurately testing this documentary evidence. Already in the fifth century, St Augustine writes to refute those who would set aside the Catholic Church as not representative of the teaching of Christ, by quoting at length the long list of popes, stretching from his own time to the days of St Peter, who first ruled the Church from Rome; and, of course, from the date of St Augustine in the fifth century to our own it is not difficult to gather from public records the actual names. But this requires more know-ledge and more leisure than can be expected from any of us. It might not, indeed, take much time to compile the list, but it would take a good deal to be certain of each pontiff, whether he did actually follow in the steps of the preceding popes, and whether he did actually connect his own generation to the one that had gone before. But it is necessary all the same that we should be able to see how this direct lineage can be traced back to the apostolic age.

Perhaps the simplest way of all is to take the negative side and explain that there is no evidence that we can see or have ever heard of to prove that at any one time the succession ceased. In other religions that boast the Christian name we can state at what definite date they came into existence; we can tell almost the very day when the world first saw them or knew them as religious establishments. But only of the Catholics we can say this, that popular speech calls them the 'Old Religion'. Now, if our Blessed Lord did come to found a Church, it must have been intended to be continuous; but there is only one Church that can even pretend to make this claim. Therefore we have a right to suppose without further proof that it alone is the Church of Christ.

I belong, then, to this Church, and can thus claim kinship with the apostles. I should not look upon this as mere spiritual snobbery, a craving to find myself well-connected; it has a far deeper significance than that. But there is this lesson to be learnt even from that view of it. The bearer of a noble name must surely take care that nothing base is ever attached to that of which he is but the trustee. He must see to it that no act of his ever reflects evil upon that which was delivered to him not only unsullied, but even glorious. Mindful, therefore, of the apostolic kinship that is mine, I must be careful that so high an honor is not made ridiculous by its association with my own disgrace.

Moreover, there is this also to be said, that not merely should the sense of high lineage keep me from evil, by associating me with those greater than myself, but the sense of greatness is the best incentive to greatness. When I realize what God has done for me, it shows me more the value of my own life, and in con-sequence I shall take more pains over my soul. If I thought that God did not much care whether I followed him or not, that he was too occupied with the vastness of the universe to spare much time for the single units that compose it, I should indeed be little worthy of blame in making no attempts to love or serve him. But when I see by what myriad chains he has bound me to himself – when I realize that even after he had ascended to his Father, our Lord still wished to keep me close to himself in the Church, and that this closeness is symbolized by the bond of apostolic union carefully preserved, then I love him, for he evidently is at pains to gain my love.

The Holiness of the Church

It must seem at first sight to be very like spiritual presumption and very unlike the spirit of Christ for any one Church to claim, as against other religious bodies, the exclusive note of holiness. It would seem perfectly absurd, because contradictory, for the Catholic Church, for example, to boast that it was also more humble than any other Church; yet surely this is really the case with any religion that claims to be holier than others. Is it not the very central idea of holiness that the possessor of it should know himself to be only a sinner? Might it not almost be made a principle of moral life to say that only those who know their own sinfulness are the least sinful? And does it not really prove the overweening pride of the Church that she sets herself, like the Pharisee, in the Temple of God and proclaims to all the world what wonderful things she has done? This certainly is the idea that other people seem to get, and perhaps at times it is what we are ourselves very much troubled about.

On the one hand, then, we find that the Church claims to be holy, and on the other that the very statement of the claim seems to be its own refutation, for the holiest are those least likely to realize, still less likely to speak about, their holiness. Secondly, we notice in ourselves and others of our own faith that creed may have very little influence on the observance of the commandments, and that even the sacraments do not make us in actual life very different from those among whom we live. Thus we see on every side people who have none of our advantages and yet who are better than we are; so that we Catholics appear to differ in nothing from our fellows, except that they hold certain intellectual propositions which we repudiate.

To all this we can say first that our Lord himself boasted of his sinlessness: 'Which of you will convict me of sin?' but, of course, this is no answer at all, for we are human, but he divine. He can declare truthfully what we never can, for even the presence of the saints in her does not make the Church holy in the sense of being without sin. What, then, do we mean when we claim holiness as one of the notes of the Church? We mean that under the redemption by Christ she is the source whence comes our holiness and that she offers to all the helps to holiness that each requires. There is no one whose desires for intimate union with God she cannot satisfy. Other religions contain many examples of those who follow the footsteps of Christ, but their religion as such is not the means of this achievement. But with us it is the whole wonderful economy of the Church which is put at our disposal. For each there is provided the means most efficient for salvation and perfection. For those who feel called to the life of solitude, for those whom God has chosen to fulfill the honorable state of marriage or to continue his work of instructing the young in the ways of the Gospel, for those who desire means of laboring for others or for themselves or for him, there are the many orders and confraternities with their several purposes and pious prayers. We must not try to join them all, but realize simply that all these different means exist in order to enable us individually to reach the state of holiness designed for us by God.

When, then, I say that the Church is pre-eminently holy, I do not mean that I am a saint, but I do mean that, if I want to be a saint, the Catholic Church holds out to me numerous aids to spur me on to the perfect love of God. There are daily Masses, the many sacraments, the daily visit to the Blessed Eucharist which the ever-open church invites, the countless confraternities and guilds which are willing and eager to satisfy every ideal that can ever have come into my mind; or, indeed, if that which I wish to see established does not yet exist, there is no reason why I should not myself begin it. Saints without number, among whom I can surely find those whose lives most appeal to me as the way in which I too could be brought to serve God best, are to be found in the list of her canonized children, who are canonized that they may be an example to me in my labors. Then by this doctrine I profess belief in an ever-increasing number of blessed souls who here or in the other world unite with me in the grand work of following in the footsteps of Christ. Like a huge army with even pace, and with the impetus that comes from a great movement, I feel that with them the way is made more easy; that the long weary journey seems shorter, and the help that each affords the other adds to the general goodness of all. I am surrounded by this influence, which should overcome that feeling of loneliness that causes so much discouragement to human hearts. My own character and temperament require my own special mode for getting to God, but the grace of God is poured out so prodigally in the Church that I have never any need for bewailing my inability to adopt other people's ways. The Church is so great that somewhere I can find that which makes appeal to me, and I shall be led along my own path to him.

Freedom in Religion
It is a common comparison to contrast the Church with the great

empires of the world and to note the vastness of design in each. We cannot but be struck by the hordes of people that these secular empires contain, differing in race, in religion, in traditions, in culture, in their manner of life and its expression in language and art. Yet, compatible with this huge difference, not merely in external but also in internal and essential ways of existence, there is a unity which appears to transcend the natural divisions of human nature. In the famous essay of Lord Macaulay, which has been more quoted probably than any of his other writings, he has pointed out how out of all the ancient European states the Papacy alone survives, with a vigor and a freshness which seem to show no signs of real decay. He is looking at the Church as he would have looked at the nations with their secular governments. Indeed, from a human point of view, there is much likeness between the two – great empires numbering many millions and bridging over many gulfs of thought and habit. But there is this contrast to be insisted on also: that the empires of the world have survived or lived long only by adopting the greatest freedom in their several parts. As soon as a number of divergent races are gathered into a unit, it is essential, if they are to continue to hold together, that allowance be made for these very differences. No despotic empire of any magnitude has ever for long dominated Europe or Christian civilization. The spirit of our Lord makes tyranny impossible, or rather, drives to revolution the oppressed.

Now in the sphere of religion, the opposite principle is to be noted. For if any empire is held together longest by allowing as much freedom as possible to the separate units, a religion which gives up or diminishes its dogmatic position – which allows 'comprehensiveness' to be the mark of its formularies – has no staying power at all. The more vague religion becomes, the less it appeals to the children of men. It will be found, for example, that in every civilized state the Churches that are the widest in their beliefs, that, to all intents and purposes, make no demands upon their adherents, are those which most bewail a decreasing membership. The contrast is therefore very evident. To give life to an empire, encourage mental freedom; to give life to a religion, insist strongly upon authority in the faith. Nor, when it is examined, is there anything strange in this; for the principle of politics is the principle of compromise. Every politician knows perfectly well that he will never be able to get all he wants; nor, indeed, is he perfectly certain that what he wants is really the best thing for the country, but he judges that on the whole his side is in the right. But the believer is seeking for truth, and consequently does not wish to be put off with the nearest or next best: for there is no next best to truth; it is either right or wrong. It is impossible to work a compromise on the divinity of our Lord or on the question of divorce; one or other must be the teaching of Christ, and religion presumes that it is important to find out which is his teaching. The contrast between the State and the Church is therefore a contrast in essential purpose. The State gives us the next best; the Church gives us truth.

I must, therefore, be careful not to allow my mind, brought up in the midst of the modern political forms of thought, to apply them to the region of the soul. It is so easy to say to myself that the insistence of the Church on certain dogmas and her repudiation of this and that is uncalled for and opposed to the spirit of the age. It really has nothing to do with the spirit of the age, for that spirit has no power over the range of fact; it cannot affect the reality of truth. It would be as reasonable to denounce the theorems of Euclid as no longer harmonizing with the ideas of a 'generation that knows not how to obey'. We should answer at once that truth, objective truth, is always one, and is dependent upon the intelligence, not of man, but of God. Freedom, then, should be the principle of politics, but truth the principle of faith. Naturally, of course, there is wisdom in permitting local customs to enter into the discipline and regulations of Christian life, but no local traditions or prejudices can affect by one hair's-breadth the Gospel of God: rather the Gospel must affect and utterly change the customs and prejudices of all of us. In politics I aim at freedom, and probably I end by obtaining truth; in religion I aim at truth and end by obtaining freedom. I try to advocate among my fellow-citizens that form of government which allows the individual the greatest amount of liberty compatible with ordered and stable government, and I find in the end that I have got that form of government that is most ideal. But in religion I choose deliberately that form which most authoritatively claims to teach me truth, and in the end I find that as a result I am most free; for only 'the truth shall make you free'.

External Authority
All men who think about religion would quite easily agree that once they were really convinced that any doctrine had been revealed by God, they would have no difficulty in accepting. It does not matter how impossible a thing might sound or how contradictory it might appear to the other revelations from God: so long as there could be absolute certainty that God had actually revealed it, we should be bound to

believe it.

For God is the sovereign truth; he cannot either deceive or be deceived; consequently whatever he says we may be certain does represent truth. But the trouble is not this. We would accept whatever God said, but the difficulty is to discover what he has said, or, rather, to be convinced that the doctrines put forward as his by the religions of the world do really represent his teaching. Presumably every creed that has been imposed on the human spirit since the world began, even if it was the faith of only one soul, would have been accepted only because that soul was assured that it was the revealed word of God. If I am convinced that God has revealed anything, I must accept it, but how am I to find out what he has revealed?

All religions come to me, and each tells me that theirs is the true Church of God, or that there is no Church at all. Each, that is, gives an entirely different list of the articles to which it demands my assent, yet each claims that it alone represents the real teaching of God, as revealed in Christ. No doubt some in these times would not in theory exclude other religions from a share in divine inspiration, but the incessant war that they wage on each other shows that in practice they hardly recognize the claims of the others.

Now, for purposes of convenience, we can divide all religions of the world into three classes: those which, when asked for the supreme rule for discovering what God has revealed, would present the inquirer with a book; those who would tell him to look within his own conscience; those who would tell him to look to some external authority. The first set (Evangelicals and Mohammedans) are really reducible to the second (Nonconformists and Agnostics), for the interpretation of the book with them lies finally with the conscience. Hence we have two main divisions: those who say 'look within to conscience' and those who say 'look without to authority'.

Now, the first set cannot be right, if it is granted that there is such a thing at all as truth; for if the conscience is the real test of truth, how is it that conscientious men differ? If I am to look into my own heart to find out whether Christ is God or not, whether divorce and remarriage is allowed or not, and if my decision (as these people imply) will really be the true answer, how comes it that there are any differences at all in the world? But if they answer that they do not mean that it is right in itself, but that it is right for me to follow my conscience, then our obvious answer is that in this case, if they do not pretend to be able to find truth at all, what is the use of their calling themselves a religion? Surely they have no business to pretend to teach what they do not know to be right. It is presumptuous in the extreme, as well as very wicked, for a preacher to endeavor to tell people what he is not sure is true. He ought to leave them to their own consciences and not dare to interfere with the direct inspiration of God.

This is not intended to be controversial, but to let me see exactly what I mean when I proclaim my belief in the authority of the Church. It means that I am convinced that she is the divine representative of God on earth and that when she announces to me any doctrine concerning faith or morals, then I am bound to accept it – not because I understand it or approve of it, but because it is the very revelation of God. For if there is such a thing as truth to be got on earth (and our Lord evidently thought so when he commanded the apostles to teach), then I can be certain that nowhere else is it obtainable than within the borders of the Catholic Church. Other religions may retain fragments of truth, but she alone has the whole truth.

I must, of course, convince myself by every means in my power that she does stand for the Church that Christ came to found – that grew up in the days of the apostles and has lasted as a living and deciding voice for so many centuries. I have first to be convinced of that, and then I believe quite simply whatever she tells me is the faith once delivered to the saints. To follow his conscience is all that is demanded of any man, but each is obliged to find out where truth is, that through the truth he may reach God. For me, then, by the divine mercy, the way of truth has been made manifest and I have, therefore, to be thankful for the wonderful favor shown me; and the best way of showing my gratitude is by seeking always to see in the Creed the actual story of God, as told me by himself.

I must look on the Church as just his mouthpiece. There is compulsion in truth, and from it no one may swerve; but if there is compulsion, there is also liberty, for it is only the truth that can make us free.

6 THE SACRAMENTS

THE three great virtues, faith, hope, and charity, teach us the true following of Christ – they point out to us, that is, wherein the pathway that he chose can be traced; they tell us what we have to do in order to be saved. By means of faith we learn what are the mysteries that God has vouchsafed to reveal to our race, and thereby, because truth and knowledge open to us the kingdom of God's love, we are led closer to him. Hope enables us to see on what grounds future attempts at holiness and the firm purpose of amendment are made possible. We grow confident of the divine mercy and, conscious of our own weakness, place in it all the source of our courage. Thus there arises the full flower of charity. Faith is taught through the Creed, hope through the voice of prayer, and charity through the commandments. As our Lord more than once insisted, love of God is no emotional experiment to be narrowed to its expression in words, but it must find in acts the sole sure showing of itself: 'If you love me, keep my commandments.'

But all this is not enough. It is not enough merely to know what the right thing is, though this too is essential; I must know how to please God before I set out to please him. Yet even when I do know what he would have me do, there are still difficulties in the way. To know what is right is one thing; to do what is right is another. Here is the unique power of Christ our Lord. It is sometimes said that the whole of Christianity is contained in the sermon on the Mount. If it may be said reverently, the sermon on the Mount is the least original side of our Lord; almost every religious teacher has said what was said then. But to this he added another thing; he taught us what to do, and further gave us the strength to do it. This strength comes through the sacraments.

Just because he was God as well as man, he had power over all creation and could help man even in the most intimate portion of his being, within the boundaries of his will. Herein lie the force and value of the sacraments: they give us the help of God, by which we are enabled to do that which we know to be right. Divine himself, he can give us divine strength. He can lay down the commandments and then give us also the sacraments to enable us to keep them. It does not take us long to find out the need we have of help, and consequently he has given us these seven means of obtaining his aid. These correspond to the various stages of the soul's development and are the recurring helps, chosen with regard to the sevenfold needs of life. Baptism begins our life with its new birth, then Communion becomes the food of the soul; confession is the medicine whereby our ailments are removed and our health restored; confirmation fills up the gaps in our strength that the early dawn of battle discovers to us when we stand upon the threshold and begin to see the long line of foes drawn up against us; marriage affords us those graces of loyalty and duty required for the exact fulfillment of the marriage contract towards wife and children; holy orders confer on the priest those high powers and that high vocation whereby we too are made partakers through him of the deep life of the mystical body of Christ; and the last anointing prepares the soul for its last long journey or gives (if God sees it to be good) health and strength to the body. Thus, all along life's highway stand these helps from which the power of God is imparted to us and by which we are made partakers of the divine nature.

Now the way in which these things are communicated to us has been itself a stumbling-block to some, for our Lord has chosen to give his grace by means of material things. In every sacrament there is what is called an outward sign, which represents the inward effect on the soul, but also does actually produce that effect. Thus in baptism the water itself, chosen because it shows the purpose of the sacrament in cleansing from sin, through the merits of Christ's passion causes grace to operate on the soul. Again, in confirmation the oil hallowed by the bishop, by its being applied to the forehead, works in this way also upon the soul, conferring upon it the gift of strength which in the East is often typified by the produce of the olive.

Now to many outside the Church it seems to be a difficulty to suppose that matter can so affect the spirit, yet is it not one of the commonest principles of God's dealing? Especially since the Incarnation, he has often made use of the body or the visible appearance of things to show and to cause his works on earth. In the miracles of the New Testament how often he made use of clay or water or the outstretching of a hand, or nails or spear or a cross. These things are surely in the same fashion, as the blessed body that he chose for himself, a thing of matter, yet, as with our own, the living Temple of the Holy Spirit, and in his case united hypostatically to the Word of God. The whole tendency of Christian worship and doctrine is to make use of visible things to produce invisible effects. Here, then, I must realize the material side of the sacraments and see their place in the economy of the divine plan. But, above all, I must use them for the saving of my soul. They are the channels which he has chosen for imparting his grace to me. Without them I shall surely perish, but with them I shall become a partaker of his divine nature.

Baptism

It is through this sacrament that we are made the children of God. The fall of our first parents bequeathed to us an inheritance that put us at enmity with God and so affected us that we were unable of ourselves to follow steadfastly the paths of the divine commandments. The original sin so upset the harmony of our nature that the perfect kingdom was reduced to a state of anarchy, and it is precisely this state of anarchy that is the original sin we inherit. Revolutions, betrayals, treachery, make up the history of my soul; foes within leagued to foes without, plotting to overthrow the rightful government. In the earlier state of Adam, called by theologians the state of original justice, the powers of the soul were organized in perfect order. The passions or non-rational faculties obeyed the commands of the will, the will obeyed the reason, and the reason obeyed the infinite reason which is the law of God. Thus was his whole being in absolute harmony, and everything done by him was orderly and right. Then came the fall, which disturbed this harmony by discord; for henceforth the emotions or passions strove to dominate the will, which in turn dictated to the reason what it should justify or denounce. In a word, the inferior powers assumed the reins of government and lorded it over the man. They obscured his intelligence, so that through passion he was no longer able to judge correctly; they disturbed the will to such an extent that St Paul could accurately describe himself in the paradox: 'To will is present with me, but to accomplish that which is good I find not, so that I do not the things that I would.' Then comes the sacrament of baptism. At once, through the merits of Christ's sacred passion, we become the children of God. All the enmity that we had incurred by our sinful state falls from us and we stand openly as the sons of the Most High.

Original sin, as we have spoken of it, can be seen to be not an act, but rather a state of ill-health to which the soul has succumbed. It is not that we have done anything wrong, but only that we have inherited an evil condition. It is a state, indeed, of positive guilt in which all men share through their inclusion by God's ordinance in the will of Adam. But we can here consider the effect of original sin as a disorder of the soul, wherein the passions dominate will, the will overrules the reason, and the reason defies the law of God. We are told that baptism sets right the effects of original sin; but surely, we ask, does not the sad state that St Paul described still continue even after we have received the sacrament of baptism? How, then, can it be said that baptism restores us to the friendship of God? What really happens is this: through baptism the whole order and properly regulated harmony of the soul is at once re-established so that we become even as Adam was before he fell, yet there remains the terrible possibility of further sin. We are not healed of all our tendency to sin nor of that corrupt desire of our will which turns our thoughts to evil, but we enter into the position of being able to conquer that desire and lead it in the right direction. We are not led back into those golden days of peace, but we have now the power in ourselves, under God's grace, to set up once more on earth the kingdom of the Father.

The value, then, of baptism is that I am no longer a child of wrath, but that I become a child of God. A seal or mark or character is stamped upon me, whereby I am set apart forever as a son. The very sinful nature whence I was rescued by this saving sacrament is now made, as it were, of the nature of God; I partake of the divine nature. I am lifted up from the depth of my degradation to the height of God himself. Hence it is that in the Fathers and early writers there is so much in their commentaries on that wonderful mystery of the Incarnation, so far as it brings him to earth and lifts earth to him. Surely if I could only realize what great things have been done for me, I should never again lose courage or hope. If I could only get myself to understand that God has indeed made me his child, that I am no longer his servant but his son, I should never more put to myself the querulous and foolish question as to what use I am here at all. Sometimes I am tempted, when things spiritual are very dull and seemingly not very successful, to cry out that it is no advantage my going on or attempting to go on, when I am evidently of so little consequence in the sight of God. He has so much that is more worthy of his attention that I cannot conceive his having the time or the desire to look after me also. But then I have to say to myself: 'I am now his son.' I am a son of God by that sacrament that can never be repeated, for it has no need to be repeated, since what was done once has been done for all time. The passions, through prayer and austerity, and the power of the sacraments, are to be brought into subjection. The will resigns its sovereignty to the reason, which in turn more closely observes and obeys the will of God. Baptism does not set us right, but, by the high privilege it affords, it gives us the power to set ourselves right.

Confession

The State has set up courts of justice, the Church courts of mercy. The State in the name of justice punishes, the Church in the name of mercy forgives. The whole apparatus of the civil law is intended to track down the criminal, to follow the traces of his work, and discover his identity. It gives him, indeed, every possible means of escape in the sense that it affords him opportunity for proving his innocence, or establishing such an explanation of his action as should procure his release. He has an impartial judge who probably has not heard his name ever before mentioned. His jury is presupposed to be altogether uninfluenced by personal motives, so that he can actually challenge and reject every member of it whom he may consider to have a personal antagonism to himself; and his counsel may be offered him at the expense of the State. The whole boast of the law is that it is utterly impartial – the unfaltering judge, the deliberating jury, the legal accuser of the advocates. But parallel with this, and intended as the result of the whole organization, is the action of justice, a strict rendering to each one of what is his due – punishment to the guilty, acquittal to the innocent. The confession of the criminal would not ordinarily affect his penalty at all, so that the plea of 'not guilty' is almost always put forward so as to throw the whole burden of proof on the shoulders of the law.

But the Church has no such ideas, does not at all contemplate the action of justice. To trace the criminal, to confront him with witnesses, to twist his evidence from improbability to sober fact, is to violate the seal of secrecy and commit a crime so rare that the annals of Church history have to be ransacked to find even a doubtful occurrence of it. There is never any attempt at any such thing. It is a principle laid down for the guidance of priests that the penitents must be believed when they accuse or excuse themselves. Hence the very personality of the culprit is shrouded in the hushed whisper, the free choice of the confessor, the rigorous suppression of all details of place and name that would be likely to lead to the confessor's knowledge of the people implicated. The penitent may desire to unburden himself to the priest, but the priest himself cannot force him to do so. Even if he does happen to recognize him, he will not remember outside what he has learnt within. This shows the different methods pursued by Church and State, the different purposes of mercy and justice. Perhaps some will declare that confession does really achieve more justice than do the courts of law; but such is not the intention of the Church. She seeks only after mercy, waiting for the penitent to come that she may listen and by God's power forgive.

Confession, then, is the tribunal of mercy. I go to it, perhaps shrinking from the avowal of my misdeeds, not because I have done anything particularly shameful (though this would almost necessarily add to the effort required), but from the very disinclination of telling another of my hidden faults. It offends my humanity; really it offends my pride, for it is difficult for man to beg for mercy, even from God. It is really that which makes confession so hard to me; to ask for mercy seems contrary to all the self-respect that makes man rise to the heights of his nature. Had he to stand and receive a punishment in some sort adequate to his failure, it might be easier because more heroic; but to have to beg for forgiveness is an achievement which only Christianity has been able to produce in the nobler souls of her children. To recount my tiresome and petty delinquencies is harder to flesh and blood in some ways than to make avowal of a deliberate act of passion. Yet it is the mercy of God which alone can bring me to my knees and make me ask for my forgiveness; and this mercy I must regard as a high privilege, something which adds to and in no way lessens the value of human dignity. On him must my eyes be fixed so that even my sins are remembered, not for my own humiliation, but for his tender love. I go to seek his mercy, not simply because I love him, but far more because he loves me; not because to err is human, but because to forgive is divine.

It is to be regretted that the English name for this sacrament is confession, for it seems to make the essence of the sacrament consist in the mere avowal of sin, whereas that is of lesser consequence than the act of sorrow that precedes and follows it. In other languages than our own it is sometimes spoken of as the sacrament of penance – that is, of penitence – and this is really a more accurate description of it. But it would be a less difficult doctrine for very many, if they could only realize that it is in fact the sacrament of sorrow. Indeed, sorrow is the whole essence of it; for there are times when the avowal of sin is quite impossible. It happens at times that a man may find himself in a country where he cannot speak the local language, nor the local priest understand his; he cannot, therefore, make his confession. Or again, a still more common case is that of an illness which does not allow the power of speech. Here it is clearly impossible for a confession to be made: yet in each of these instances the unfortunate man may well desire to have his sins forgiven him. What is he to do? He cannot confess, yet he may approach the sacrament of confession. How? By asking for absolution, not perhaps in words, but by signs; and, as the priest says the words of absolution, by making an act of contrition or sorrow. Here, then, it is evident that the whole essential portion of the sacrament is the sorrow, for the sacrament has been fully performed without the telling of the sins. The confession and the satisfaction are necessary, but they are not essential.

Sorrow for sin is the one thing which is of absolute necessity in this sacrament. It is, therefore, the part of the confession on which I must most dwell. Sometimes am I not apt to worry a great deal about my list of sins, taking surprising pains to discover every single fault and the exact number of times that I have fallen, and then hurrying over my actual sorrow as of less importance? Of course, I know perfectly well that the sorrow was really the more necessary of the two, but it does happen that I devote perhaps less time to it than to the other. Here, then, I must see what can be done to set this right – not the persistent torture of the conscience till confession becomes a thing to be avoided, but rather dwelling far more effectually upon the sorrow and its motive. Certainly this would make my spiritual life happier, and whatever does that is sheer gain. I think, therefore, of my sins and then try to realize what they cost our Lord. So many times have I been forgiven and so many times has that forgiveness been forgotten; all his love wasted! The alabaster box, filled with the most precious ointment, broken across my heart; the fragrance still fills the world with wonder, and I forget. He is my lover and he is waiting for me at the trysting place. To confess is surely a little thing compared with what I have done that required forgiveness; to confess is even a satisfaction, it unburdens my soul of its great weight. But beyond confession is the sorrow.

Surely, then, it is not difficult to be sorry for my sins, not difficult to turn as Peter turned when he had looked upon the face of Christ, and going out wept bitterly. But Judas, had not he, too, tears upon his eyes when he had hurled back the money till it rang upon the marble steps of the temple and went out into the night with the consciousness of how he had transgressed against love? Yes, he too 'wept bitterly,' but where he failed was that sorrow for him did not lead on to love. If he had only gone back to the Master, we should have kept his feast each year as the most blessed of penitents. My sorrow, then, must make me turn to love him more. On the other hand, I must not think that I have to feel sorrow. I must not suppose that I have no real contrition because I feel sure that if the opportunity arose I should fall again into the same sins; nor imagine myself to be a hypocrite because I am afraid that next week or next month will find me once again telling the same list. For I have to realize that by sorrow I mean that, together with regret for the past, I have also a firm purpose of amendment, i.e., a determination that in the future I shall try to do better. I have no right to promise that the next confession will find me free from sin, for I am promising what is above my power to perform; but I can promise that I shall try. Failing or successful, I shall at least have made the attempt, and for the rest God himself must needs supply. My sorrow, then, in the confession is the essential part of it, and to it must be devoted the greater portion of my time. Then the sorrow must be super-natural; it must lead on to God. It need not be emotional, but it must include a real determination to do my best to overcome myself. By the pitiful sight of his five wounds, by the generous kindness of the Creator, by his own absolute lovableness as the supreme and perfect Good, I must fix my will resolutely and forever try to fulfill his service.

The Sacrament of Sweetness

The Blessed Sacrament is often looked upon, as indeed it really is, as the sacrament of strength, but one title cannot exhaust the ways of viewing this sublime mystery of God's mercy. There is need always of courage and hopefulness and the power of persevering, which comes to us from God in this sacrament. The added greatness that the nearness of God inspires must unfailingly affect us whenever we approach the altar rails. But sheer forcefulness in religion will not suffice unless sweetness comes as well to temper the rigidity of our will. There are people, undoubtedly, who have a very welcome influence upon our lives by imparting to us the bracing atmosphere in which they live, the high mountain air, the freshness of soul that comes from those strong characters whose thoughts are always soaring to the high altitudes of faith and principle, but this is not a lasting influence unless it is accompanied by something more. The military genius may be necessary from time to time in the national life, but no military despotism has ever lasted through more than one generation, simply because it is strong and strong only: it is too rigid to accommodate itself to human affairs. The human spirit lives; that is, the human spirit is always changing. Now the main feature, the main helpfulness of strength, is just that it does not change at all; it is fixed. A dictatorship was proclaimed in Rome in times of national crisis; it could restore order, but could not act as a permanent form of government. Even the genius of Cromwell could do nothing against the sentiment of the nation; with all his glories, his undoubted success, he could only for his own lifetime secure in military hands the powers of government.

Religion is much more susceptible even than social life to the evil consequences of mere strength. To be strong of will is only one portion of the moral life. It is necessary, but by itself it is short-lived. The fierce and gloomy fanaticism that begins in a flame of enthusiasm will bear down conqueringly upon any obstacle and sweep it out of the path. But its power is only of today; it cannot last till tomorrow; it has no real hold on human nature; it is too inhuman. One generation, or two generations at most, have been found to accept Puritanism. Just when it is felt by all to be necessary to save the national life from absolute corruption, it has done good; but the final result, unless it is speedily changed, is to drive people to far worse lengths. The interplay of action and reaction is the inevitable consequence. The licentiousness of the Restoration follows upon the white-washing puritan Commonwealth. The total disregard for Sunday has been produced by the Pharisaic observance of it. The militant forms of religion, like Mohammedanism, have held their place only by proclaiming a general permission for what Christianity repudiates: they have forbidden wine, but degraded women. A religion, therefore, which attempts to rule by sheer force and to give to its faithful followers nothing more than strength, is not a religion that can last. Oppressive dullness gives way to riotous amusements. The fear of God, which was the motive power of the Old Testament, could not have the hold of the hearts of men that has been obtained by the new commandment of love. The reign of Christ has outstayed the law and the prophets.

This, since he had made the human heart, our Lord perfectly understood. The system of the Incarnation was precisely to appeal to that which was most yielding in the nature of man. The little Child in the stable has no rival in the minds of children, and for grown men and women his winsome robe of childhood does not hold out its little arms in vain. The Boy of Nazareth, the beautiful young man whose appearance on the seashore drew from the disciples of John the question: 'Where dwellest thou?' has not ceased from then to now to draw to him youth and age. His wooing infancy, his charm of person, the fascination of his appearance, still attract to him the love of the generations as they pass. Nor was he content to come that once and then depart, leaving behind but the fragrance of his visit, for he did all things well. To use his own blessed word, he 'abides' with us. He is with us all days even to the consummation of the world. Now his return to us on altars at Mass, at Communion, is not simply that we might worship, but that the need we have of sweetness in religion might be amply supplied. We must approach his presence, gather about him, for the refreshment of our lives, to break down the hideous monotony of our work, to add the brightness of love to the grey streets and greyer skies. Not holiness alone, but the beauty of holiness, is required to bind our hearts, our whole souls, to God. The child, which with its wistful trust demands protection, asks for something more than strong defense: it needs also the warm welcome of love. And so far are we all children, we need the gentleness and mercy of God to be made manifest, else we shall be too frightened to go on. If religion is to mean much to me, I must approach the altar of the sweetness of God, that giveth joy to my youth.

Holy Communion

The types of the Old Testament not merely foreshadow, they help our understanding of the fulfillment. They foretell and interpret; for God, whose power designed the world, can arrange life and the chances of life so as to portray some future happening. Now one of the most splendid types of the Blessed Sacrament was given in the story of Elias, whom in the desert angels fed. He had passed through a time of adventure and excitement. His challenge to the priests of Baal to prove the authority of their gods by bringing down fire from heaven to consume the sacrifice had ended in his triumph. The altars had been set up on Carmel, a trench dug about them, and a day set apart for the journey. First the priests of Baal clamored to their god, while Elias with terrible mirth mocked their failure. Over the altar they leapt, cutting their flesh with knives as the dervishes would do today. Then, when his turn was come, the prophet poured water over the sacrifice till it ran down and filled up the trench. But at his prayer God sent fire which burnt up altar and sacrifice alike with so fierce a heat that the water in the trench was licked up by the flames. After so wonderful a proof of God's power, the king, Ahab, submitted, the priests were slaughtered, and in further token of the divine pleasure a storm of rain broke on the country that had been three years waterless. Elias was wrought up into a state of overconfidence. Consequently the hostility of the queen, who threatened him with death, drove him to over-depression, till he fled into the desert where he prayed to die. Then came the angel with food: 'Take ye and eat, for ye have yet a long way to go.'

Now this surely is a very true interpretation of the purpose of Holy Communion. It is to give me the courage to persevere. Too often probably to me as to Elias has come the same swift change from presumption to despair. Perhaps I had thought that I had finally quelled some temptation or sin that had long bothered me. A chance sermon, or a passage in a book, or the remark of a friend, and at once the old world had come back to me. Or it may be that it was some trifling but frequent failure which for long distressed me, and then was for a time overcome and driven from power. Always, however, the result was that, however successful for the moment, I found myself ultimately returning whither I had first begun. All the exceptional efforts and fierce resolutions and elaborate addition of prayers, all the feeling of having done great things, ended at the best in a respite, which after all the stress appeared a complete victory. I thought that the battle in that part of the field had been won, that I could rest now without precautions or guards. Then swiftly has come my fall, though months may at times elapse before my undoing is manifest. But all the same the effect in my soul is a quick despair. What is the use of struggle if it is always to end in defeat? I find myself utterly weary, hopeless. The old faults are still there unconquered – or at least not slain.

Now it is just at this moment of discomfiture that I need the voice of God's angel to call me to the Bread and the Wine, for I have always 'yet a long way to go'. By no means has the end come. For Elias the victory of God over Baal, the slaughter of the priests, the downpour of rain, and the fierce run which he made by the side of the king's chariot from Carmel to the royal city of the northern kingdom, had produced a sense of exaltation that was utterly unsound. The nervous excitement was so tense and strained that the least failure at the moment was bound to become as exaggerated as the supposed triumph had been. The opposition of the queen had been forgotten, or its strength underestimated, and as a result nervous prostration brought him to despair. Instead of triumph, defeat; so off he goes to the desert, where his feelings entirely change. Not now is there any talk of having been more successful than his predecessors, as had evidently been his previous idea; but only: 'I am no better than my fathers,' and a cry for death. So with me, the victory, the over-confidence, the despair; whereas the struggle is only just begun, and it were foolish at the first assault or repulse or reverse (or even after many) to lose heart or run away or submit. Rather, because of my weariness and dismay is my need for the Food more urgent, that in that externally provided help I may walk the rest of my appointed path. Courage is my greatest requirement, and it is here I shall find it. Even if my age is failing and my time on earth to be short, I have need of that Viaticum for the long last journey of the grave.

The Sacrament of Sacrifice

The paradox of life was well voiced by Caiphas: it is expedient always that one man should die and that the whole people should not perish. How or why such a law should enter into the world we cannot tell, but the existence of it is unquestionable; over and over again one single victim has set a people free. The Old Testament enshrined it in the ritual of the Temple-worship and in the religious practices of the Tabernacle. The scapegoat was little else than this mysterious law consecrated and sanctioned by God. Irrational, incapable of guilt, it was driven into the desert, and there, in solitude, atoned for the sins of the whole nation. This process of vicarious atonement is frequently evident in history, where over and over again we find the death of one man, himself frequently innocent, being required for the abolition of some injustice or the setting free of some people. The story of the hermit who journeyed to Rome to put an end to the gladiatorial games where human life was sacrificed even in Christian times for the amusement of the populace, and who found no other way to achieve his purpose than by throwing himself into the arena and thus by his death forcing the evil side of such an entertainment on the crowd, is but one instance out of many The same sort of story or legend can be found in the history of every nation, for in the attempts made by a people to throw off the yoke of a tyrant there is always one man who comes forward and at the risk of his own life rescues the lives of his people from their oppression.

In the New Testament the teaching of Christ seems at times to contain little else than this doctrine that, to save life, life must be lost. It is the one consistent principle that explains all the rest – itself remaining a mystery above all comprehension: one Man dies that the world may go free. Somehow upon his head are all our sins placed: 'He hath borne our iniquities.' He took upon himself the sins of all the world. Nor should it be overlooked that our Lord does not suffer the loss of life because he despises life. It is not as though he surrendered something the value of which he underestimated, since to give freely away what is of no consequence to the donor can hardly be considered an act of generosity. He surrendered life just because he put so high a value upon it and realized the responsibilities of it very much more than anyone else has ever done. For him all the world was full of beauty. No one ever spoke as he has done of the charm of nature, of field flowers and falling sparrows, or the graceful fascination of childhood. He lived more intimately with the deep joys of sheer life, for in him was life. He died that others might live, just because he knew their need of life, certain that life alone could be of any avail for them. He himself in one place made the comparison of the mother in labor who put herself in peril that she might set free her child. It was the lesson that better the peril of one than the death of all. It is, therefore, he would seem to show, only with the pangs of death that life can at all begin.

On Calvary, therefore, this teaching received its highest sanction; but its richest expression, as far as we individually are concerned, is evident in the Blessed Sacrament. Daily I can draw upon this unfailing fountain of sacrifice. Let me look upon the daily Mass and Communion as the living gospel of vicarious suffering. Dying daily for me is Christ, here upon the altar. It is the most eloquent missionary venture of all our Lord's life. To have preached it was, indeed, of great avail, nor will the world willingly let his words die. Men who do not believe him divine have yet taken his parables as the most expressive utterances on the duty of brotherly love. But his example was even more splendid than his words, for the example of the dead is never so potent as the example of the living. He died, but death did not exhaust the scope of his action, for he rose again, and again acted the same principle. He is sacrificed always for the world, and in the Eucharist puts himself at the mercy of men. How can I be selfish in my relation to others once I have received within me this Victim of the world's redemption? How can I be unjust in life or even watch in silence the injustice of others, the oppression of the poor, the spiteful persecution of the rich, the revenge of Capital, or the pent passion of Labor? If I go every morning to this sublime sacrifice, it must surely have an influence on my day, the influence of having seen God die. I must take home to my life the saying of Caiphas, and prefer that I should lose all than that all the world be lost, prefer their success to my failure.

The Mass
Think how the Mass is in a real sense the center of Catholicism. All the faith is gathered round it, so that from the mere wording of the Mass the rest of the Creed could be almost wholly deduced. The divinity of Christ is clear in the wonderful power that is given to the priest to perform this amazing act of worship, else could man not even have imagined its possibility. So staggering is the doctrine, that when first announced, even by a Preacher who spoke as none other ever spoke, it broke up the little band; and only the implicit trust that the apostles

had in their Master made them continue as his disciples. They stayed only because they had nowhere else to go. Then if he is God, it can only be because he is the Son of God; nor can he be God only, for the words of consecration tell us of his body and his blood. So, again, besides the Trinity, the Incarnation, we can arrive at the divine motherhood of our Lady and the other mysteries of faith. The sacraments also are arranged round this wonderful sacrifice as the setting round the gem. Baptism pre-pares us for our part in it; confirmation strengthens us in our belief in it; confession makes us worthy of it; holy orders ensures for us the continuation of it; matrimony, says St Paul, is the symbol of it; the last anointing imparts to us its fruits. For it all our churches are built. It is the center of their construction, it unifies all their archi-tectural lines. Without it, the most splendid places of worship seem empty and cold, and with it, however poorly or badly they may appear, they are made alive. Our faith, our ceremonies, our lives are grouped round this supreme act of worship.

The reason why it stands as the most central of all our mysteries is because it is itself nothing other than Calvary continued. Calvary meant for us the undoing of all our woe and the upbuilding of our lives for the service of God; in consequence, the Mass being but a prolongation of that 'far-off event,' it, too, becomes the living reality of that which is most real in all the world. It is not, indeed, a repetition, for the death of God is so unique an event that repetition becomes impossible: moreover, St Paul proclaimed that 'Christ being risen from the dead dieth now no more; death shall no more have dominion over him'. The Mass, then, is not the repetition but the continuation of Calvary; one with it in essence, though not in appearance, as the Body of Christ on our altars is the same as the Body that walked the earth, though it has not the same outward seeming. The priest, by the double act of consecration, slays as by a mystic sword of sacrifice the Divine Victim, for though body and blood cannot be severed while life remains, they are represented as distinct in the difference of accidents, and thus is the death of the Lord shown forth until he come. This, then, is the reason of the acknowledged supremacy of the Mass, witnessed to by persecutor and persecuted, that it is for us Calvary still continued; and since all our happiness and all our chance of happiness come from that saving redemption, obviously that which is only a continuation of it must necessarily be held in deep reverence. It is the eternal testimony of God's love for man; the eternal stimulus to man's love of God.

In order to encourage my own devotion to this tremendous mystery, let me consider what the morning Mass must have meant to the Mother of God. When her Child had been taken from the Cross and laid in the tomb, she was to see him on earth again after he had risen from the dead; but after the Ascension she was to see him no more till that day when she passed to the Day. But at her Mass, when she watched the Beloved Disciple hold up what seemed bread, and when she heard the whispered words of power, she knew him once again in the breaking of the Bread. Dare we trespass nearer on that sacred intimacy? She saw, as on Calvary, her Son's death. For St Peter, St John, and the rest, how fervent must have been at Mass their reparation for that sad night when they left him, or denied him, or stood far off from him! What comfort, consolation, encouragement, in their missionary ventures, that were ventures of faith indeed! Let me think of the strength that came to them every morning that they held in their hands the Bread, and knew it, indeed, to become that Body they had seen and handled – for the men and women and troops of little children imprisoned in the catacombs, who found in the Mass said in the wind-swept passages amid the tombs of the martyred Christians, the grace to meet with patience the trouble that each day brought, who saw in the sacrifice the open door beyond their narrowed lives. However dreary or intolerable in itself, the hour was made glad and cheerful by the savor of this saving rite. Our fathers in the days of persecution risked all for the chance Mass, and the infrequent visit of a priest who might repeat for them the ceremonies of the Upper Room in Jerusalem, and make the loss of lands and life easy compared with the gaining of that 'seldom presence'. If I wish to value aright my privilege of the Mass, I must follow intelligently the whole ceremony, from the Confiteor to the Last Gospel.

Confirmation

I will probably acknowledge that, to a very large extent, I have neglected to make use of this sacrament. Of course, I have received it, and I know well that it cannot be repeated. How, then, can I be held to blame for neglecting that which I have received just the one time that I can possibly receive it? To realize this, let me ask myself why it is that it can be received once only. The answer is naturally that thereby I receive a character or mark on my soul which can never be effaced. But what does all this mean? It means that I cannot receive confirmation more than once, for the simple reason that I have no need to repeat it. Once given, it is given for always, because the effects last as long as life lasts. The grace of Communion may refresh me all my days, but the Presence fades. Absolution removes all my sins from me. They are forgiven forever. But if, unhappily, I fall again into sin, again must I approach this saving sacrament. With confirmation, on the other hand, the sacramental grace perseveres till the end. Once I have been marked with the grace of confirmation, I have had set up in my soul a power, a force, that never runs dry or can be drained or even wholly affected by sin. When I do wrong the grace ceases to work, but it does not cease to exist; so that as soon as I have reconciled myself to God, back again comes the flood that confirmation established within me for good and all. Hence the value of it does not consist simply in the day of my reception of it, but is to be made use of all the days of my life. The indwelling of the Spirit of God, begun in baptism, is now made perfect, and the wonderful sevenfold gifts of God are put into my charge, so that with me it lies whether I have the benefit they can confer or not.

But every sacrament has both an outward sign and an inward grace. What are these in confirmation? First, the external thing, material instrument of God's grace to my soul, is the anointing of my forehead by the bishop with the consecrated oil. That is the essential outward sign. And the inward grace? Strength. In the East, oil, which is at once a food and a preservative of the skin, is in frequent use among athletes. It is, indeed, the source of the strength of the toilers and is mentioned in the Sacred Scriptures as the symbol of that which it helps to produce. Hence it is the external representation of that inner strength that the soul stands in need of. Usually confirmation is administered to children just when they stand upon the threshold of life and are beginning to feel that there are many difficulties that they will have to overcome and endure; just when they are becoming conscious that life grows not easier, but harder. Can I remember that at that age I discovered that not everyone quite held with me about the duties owed to God and all that they entailed? I found that the things I held sacred, and the people that I had been taught to reverence, were now held up to my ridicule; and the things I had been afraid to do, afraid even to think about, were spoken of and done openly before me without shame Even my own inclinations began suddenly to become more forcible, and unsuspected instincts and hidden forces I did not yet understand began to be felt and to give pleasure. Thus the full practice of faith, hope, and love also in turn, grew increasingly difficult to observe. Then I was confirmed, i.e., these tendencies were henceforth to be counteracted by the indwelling within me, not merely of grace, but of the very Spirit of God. He himself was to take charge of my soul.

I have been taught, surely, that the object and effect of this sacrament was to make me strong, that this strengthening of me was to be achieved by the abiding presence of the Holy Spirit, and that this abiding presence was to continue for the whole of my lifetime. As the need endures, so must the remedy endure. This sacrament, therefore, is tremendously alive, nor is it right that I should regard it, as perhaps I have often done in the past, as though it were some childish thing that had to be

got over while I am quite young. Do I not find sometimes that people look on it much as they look on the measles as a normal heritage of children? But surely in my fuller age the need of divine strength increases rather than diminishes. As a child I probably thought that I was only naughty because I was a child, but that when I grew up I supposed that I should find life the easier. Instead, I discovered that I looked back upon my childhood as the innocent time of my life, and looked upon my older years as necessarily years of wrongdoing, though perhaps I clung to the salve of conscience that in youth a man might be a little wild, but in his old age had time to become a saint. Thus it is always yesterday or tomorrow, never today; but confirmation suddenly reminds me that it is now that God calls, and now that the Holy Ghost makes appeal to me to remember his presence and to make use of it. Do I, indeed, think of that presence in my times of stress? In the struggles of temptation do I sufficiently have recourse to that Divine Helper given me? Do the sevenfold gifts really signify anything practical to me? Let me turn in devotion to the Holy Spirit, recite the hymns to him, and be conscious always of the resident force pent up in my soul.

Matrimony

Here our Lord makes sacred the most intimate act of life, wherein two become one flesh. The purpose of the married state he has himself commanded, and it cannot, therefore, be in itself evil. Without it the race would cease to exist and all the designs of God come to naught; it is consequently essential to the economy of the divine plan. From this, then, we may quite rightly argue that not merely is it not evil in itself, but a great good. Indeed, God himself ordained it as a command upon all his creatures that they should increase and multiply and, as though to remove forever from his children any fear of its being evil, he has in the New Law made a sacrament to safeguard its interests and to ensure its proper fulfillment. Marriage itself is an act whereby two are made one in mutual love. All the other ideas that have gathered round the family life have sprung from this as the primal idea. The concept of a family and of even wider relationships, the hoarding of possessions and the encampment or settlement in a house, the setting up of a sacred hearth round which the family might assemble to ask the protection of its own particular deity, have all evolved out of the rudimentary notion that by marriage two have become one. Whatever may be the theories by which we explain the origin of the family – and these theories are as numerous as the professors in universities – we are forced to suppose that the two came together who were before looked upon, as we say, as 'single,' and that from this they became one – two notes in complete harmony, a union that transcends all difference.

Now it is perfectly clear from any study of human nature that the whole tendency of individuals, especially when thrown into each other's company, is to separation; the ideas of two tend on the whole to spring apart; the very fact that the other person holds a view is reason sufficient for holding its opposite. Especially is this likely to happen where two are forever facing each other at all times of day, in moments of irritability, in all moods and tempers. The very likeness in taste or temperament or habit is bound to appear at times when it should not, and to produce friction that will lead to serious trouble unless it is treated with a tact which is rare to find and still rarer to find continuously. The effect of a family, which should prove a bond by linking the parents together in a mutual love of at least a third person, in fact turns sometimes to the other result and produces such divergence of views on education, etc., as to produce, rather than peace, ultimate estrangement. Of course, the answer to all this is that it supposes the absence of love, whereas the idea of marriage is based on love, and apart from love has no significance. Once let love come in, and then the things that might prove a source of difference result on the whole in a deeper affection. Difference itself becomes a bond of union; the two souls become complementary to one another; each supplies what is lacking to the other. This is true. It is obvious that love does bridge over the chasm and holds souls together. But is not this, too, part of the danger? For though love unites as can nothing else, so long as love is there, what is to happen at those times when love is least powerful, when human charms cease to appeal or by their satisfaction have extinguished all desire? Love is strong while it lasts; but who shall guarantee love lasting?

It is just here that the sacrament of marriage enters into its place in the stream of Catholic tradition. It brings to love the safeguard of a divine protection. It wards off the approach of dullness and boredom by illuminating the whole of family life with the outpouring of love divine. The Spirit of God in virtue of the Passion of Christ sets in the soul the power to hold on in spite of every difficulty. It adds to love the wisdom and discernment to allow to each that freshness and spontaneity that is required for the full tale of love. When pleasure in such a life might make men forget the responsibilities of their high calling, it is the infusion of grace that brings back the vision of earlier days. It is the sacrament that makes the father and mother realize that they have duties to perform to their race and holds them to the labor and travail whence is born the joy of the world. Abolish this and in how many cases would not the result be the end of the family, often the end of the national existence? So highly has the married life been exalted by this sacrament that St Paul, to whom in many ways the single life evidently made personal appeal, sets it up as the very image of the intimate union that exists between Christ and his Church. So high is it in his eyes that it stands as a great mystery, that is, a shrine of the dwelling of God. For a Catholic, therefore, the married state is itself a high calling from God. The duties therein incurred are of divine origin, blessed by God, and safeguarded by the grace that this attracts; they have become the living symbols of God's union with man. Mutual acceptance means one single law of faithfulness for both, which no amount of custom or tradition can be allowed to impair. Thus does the blood of Christ make holy a calling that is the exact reproduction of the central fact of the Christian revelation, for it takes God to make a family.

Holy Orders

In an analogy that might be drawn up between the life of the soul and social life, holy orders would correspond to the various grades of government that are necessary for the well-being of the nation. This sacrament is simply to constitute the hierarchy of priests and bishops, by which Christ our Lord desired his Church to be ruled. Since, then, these were to receive certain powers that were proper to them alone, it was obvious that some sort of ceremonious consecration had to be adopted that this special and exclusive gift might be recognized as accurately bestowed. Below the priests are a whole series of lesser ecclesiastical persons – deacons, subdeacons, the four minor orders, and the tonsured clerk; but it is the traditional teaching of the Church that those only receive the grace of the sacrament who have been ordained to the diaconate, the priesthood, or the episcopate. Here again we have, as in baptism and confirmation, the conferring on the soul of a special character, which cannot be repeated for the simple reason that it has no need to be repeated, for the power once conferred remains efficacious for life. Once ordained, there is no need for the service to be repeated, but, morning by morning, Mass can be offered, sins forgiven, the living strengthened for the long last journey. Once a priest, then a priest forever, according to the order of Melchisedech. However unworthy or un-ideal, a consecrated minister of God must remain sacred in his office to my eyes. Nothing can ever remove him from his position which he holds in the sight of all heaven: a priest forever.

My attitude to the priest must therefore always exhibit a consciousness that he stands for something more than merely the official representative of the Church. He has received in a special way the anointing that, in the words of St Paul, makes him the mediator (because the continuator of the work of Christ through the power of Christ) between God and man. He offers to God the things of the people, and to the people the things of God. I have, therefore, to put out of my mind his particular personality or want of it, to forget his social position and my own, and to consider him as the representative of God in the things that appertain to the altar. Obviously there will be many things that I shall dislike in his methods and ideals, but where the altar is concerned he is to be treated with the respect that is due to his sacred office. It does not matter who he is, it should be enough for me that he is a priest. In this way it is obvious that the Catholic places the priest on a higher post of advantage than do other religious worship-pers; yet, on the other hand, Catholics value less than any other the particular gifts of the individual. For them it hardly matters who is saying Mass, for it is the Mass itself that they go to hear. At the Benediction service it is again our Lord, not his minister, that concerns those present. Hence, for us less than in any religion, the priest does not stand between the soul and God, but is an instrument; as water is the instrument of baptism, whereby the union of God and man is made effective. Respect, then, for the office of the priesthood is the first lesson that we learn from the sacrament of holy orders.

But not respect only should be shown to him, but a willingness to help him in any way that seems to offer. Of course, there are members of the laity who are already too inclined to interfere in the priestly work, just as there are priests who seem determined to stifle every effort of the laity and who look upon lay work in a parish as though it was something heterodox. Apart, however, from these extreme cases, it will obviously be of the utmost importance for a priest to have members of his congregation on whom he can rely for the more effective administration of it. There are sure to be clubs for boys, or clubs for working girls, which need the constant attendance of their secretaries and helpers; there are the altar societies, etc.; above all, there is the Society of St Vincent de Paul, which may have an untold effect in any congregation. It supplements the work of the priest by being more regular in its visits than he can well afford time to be; it can continue cases which he has once begun or even begin the visiting of families or individuals where the priest might at first have a difficulty in finding an entrance. Zeal, then, is the other requirement that the priest has a right to look for from us. Says Lacordaire: 'The priest is a man anointed by tradition to shed blood, not as the soldier through carnage, not as the magistrate through justice, but as Jesus Christ through love. The priest is a man of sacrifice, by it each day announcing to every soul the primordial truths of life, of death, and resurrection, and by it each day reconciling heaven and earth.' It is the Mass that makes the priest possible, the confessional that makes him necessary; but without a laity who have at heart the welfare of their fellow-Catholics, who are filled with reverence for his office and zeal for his better accomplishing of it, his time may be reduced to utter distraction. I must realize my duties, examine my past, and make a resolution to offer my services.

Extreme Unction
This sacrament of healing has been in constant use in the Church. From the story of the life of our Lord, as told us in the Gospels, we find that the record of miracles achieved was looked upon by him as a sign that his mission was approved by God. In his answer to the disciples of John the Baptist he called attention to the wonders that he daily worked among the people: 'The blind see, the dumb speak, the deaf hear, the lepers are cleansed, the dead rise again.' In another place it is written of him that on account of the unbelief of some of his hearers, he could do no miracle, 'except that he healed the bodies of some that were sick'. This last was evidently looked upon as so ordinary an event that even their want of faith could not prevent it. Nor, apparently, does our Lord regard this part of his ministry as something particular to himself, for he was at pains, when sending out the apostles in his lifetime, to give them power to heal them that were sick, and he foretold that when he had gone the same powers were to continue in

the Church, so that things even greater than he had himself done would be done in his name. Nor is it simply in the light of an extraordinary sign, but rather as an ordinary event, that the power of healing is spoken of by him and by his apostles; they all seem to take it for granted. In the Acts of the Apostles this power is exercised with perfect freedom by Peter and John immediately after Pentecost. It is found in every record of the early Church and no surprise is shown at its continued existence; but rather the impression is forced upon us that the ceasing of such a power would, indeed, have caused no little wonder.

So common was this gift that it could not even be regarded as an adjunct of sanctity, though it was that also. Not merely was this gift of healing to be committed to those whose nearness to God made them as potent to work good as the hem of the garment of Christ, but to every priest the same power was confided. Thus the gift of healing became part of the ordinary heritage of the Church. It became a sacrament; and, because it thus came into the ritual and ceremonious usage of the Church, it was certain and wise that regulations would be made to safeguard its proper administration. The conditions which are now exacted are simply, therefore, to be interpreted as growing up round something that else from the very frequency of its repetition would be in constant danger of being abused. It is not to be supposed that the Church has forgotten the marvels committed to her for the use of her children. She has never allowed this miraculous power to lapse or imagined that it was something that failed with the apostolic body. It was to be a persistent sacrament. In the prayers which compose its ritual performance, the idea of healing is repeated over and over again: 'By this holy anointing and of his own tender mercy, may the Lord forgive thee whatever sins thou hast committed by thy sight, hearing, sense of smell, taste and speech, hands, feet' is the actual phrasing whenever the members of the body are anointed, but the idea running through the whole ceremony is rather the bodily ease that the sacrament is to give. Health to the body, forgiveness to the soul, is the burden of the ritual, and such also is in a true sense the burden of the life of Christ.

The care of my life is partly the preparing for my last end. No doubt I best prepare by living as I would be found when death comes to me, but it does not follow that every sickness is unto death, nor should I suppose that it is my business when I am ill to make no effort towards recovery. However great the pain, I should be content to remain here and do my best to use the wonderful body God has given me – resigned to death, but resigned also to life. Nor should I be like those who imagine that the last sacraments are to be received when there is no more hope; rather they are to be given as soon as there is any danger at all, and it is to be remembered that they are given precisely that hope may come, precisely that I may have the courage to go on struggling for my life. The outward sign is, as in confirmation, the consecrated oil, and this surely shows that what I most need is strength – courage to face the alternatives of life and death, the long-drawn agony which must precede them both, the tremendous struggle, with my soul already exhausted from illness, to battle my way out to life. The kindness of those about me should nerve me against the weariness of giving in. For all this the sacrament is sufficient. It aids my body, it aids my soul. It gives me the grace to accept whatever God has in store for me, but it also is at pains to emphasize the importance of the body and the hope we have that it will be 'restored to its former health'. Let me, therefore, make use of this sacrament as a preparation for my last end and as an acknowledgment that even my body and its health is of value in God's sight, so that for it he was willing to institute a special sacrament.

The Liturgy
It is the work of Christ to complete, through the direct teaching of the Holy Spirit, his preached Gospel. Scripture thus in the main tells us what to do, but not how to do it. Scripture gives us the sacraments, but the Church adds their formularies, prayers, setting. The Scripture most often shows us the spirit; the Church describes the body in which that spirit is lodged. Therefore it is that she is denounced by her enemies as some-thing formal, whereas she is but the outward and visible sign of an inward, invisible grace. Because her children are not souls merely, but men, she has to give them not God only or some gifts divine, but all that is sacred tabernacled in its incarnation. So, too, prayer must be a natural, spontaneous act; it must be the free talk between friends, between God and myself. Nor, indeed, is there anything on earth so free as prayer; even the air is only 'a chartered libertine'. To taste the joy of life, to feel its rush of pleasure in the spring-time, to know all that is meant in the sheer ecstasy of existence, to take delight in some flower or fruit, to be alive in the sunshine, to experience the relief when duty has been done, or the pleasurable sensation when we have been generous, or to have found once again a friend – all this is perfect prayer, prayer unspoken, but fully expressed. But prayer must be of endless variety to suit our endless need. Sometimes it must be

formless, for our whole sensations cannot be formally represented; but sometimes also it must take on forms – the stiff, brocaded dignity of life; for these, too, are human, none the less worthy of God because they are wholly the work of man. Those who wish to pray always without form, often end by praying not at all.

There are, then, certain formal prayers which are also required by the nature of man; the Psalms, the Canticles, and the Our Father represent the Scriptural use of this kind of prayer; and the lives of good and holy men have very frequently closed with verses of these upon their lips. Savonarola and St Francis sang the Psalms; and as he chanted the twenty-first Psalm, the Master on the Cross bowed his head and died. There can be, therefore, no objection to the mere face of formal prayers. Acting, then, on the inspiration of the same Spirit through whom the Scriptures themselves became the Word of God, the Church composed her liturgy. In this, as in the Biblical prayers, it is worthy of note that the main method is the prayer of praise. It is this precisely that suffers least from being formalized, since we praise God, not for what is in us and therefore changing, but for what is in him and therefore unchanged. Hence these can have, without any danger, the impersonal touch which formal prayer must always exhibit: in the *Gloria in excelsis* we have a very good example of what is meant. This language can be common to the wide world; and since the liturgy of the Church is intended exactly for the devotion of a congregation, it must be composed to suit rather the mass than the individual. It is always, therefore, general rather than particular, and consequently has practically no danger of be-coming stilted. For this reason, accordingly, the liturgy of the Church is the one exception to the rule that prayer in order to be really meant should be spontaneous. This, while on the whole true for the individual, is false for mankind generally.

We should, therefore, though there is no compulsion in the matter, be eager to follow the liturgy, by understanding its own words. We become in this way united to the Church Catholic of all tongues, ages, and climes. We find our faith becoming stronger and less timid when it feels itself one with such countless numbers. The sense of isolation, of dwelling as strangers in a foreign land, is lost when we grow conscious at Mass or Benediction or at the reception of any of the sacraments, that we are bridging over all times and places. All the world over, what we see and hear and are saying is being witnessed by others besides ourselves. We are not lonely travelers toiling after some lost trail, but a huge army, whose uniform and whose battle-songs are the traditions of our race. We enter into the inheritance of all the saints. All that is best in literature, art, religion, is swept up and gathered into one – the wonder of the Mass, the depth of the Psalms, the night-prayer of Compline, the radiance of the office of Prime, the consoling tenderness of the Office for the Dead. Here Hebrew, Greek, Latin are like three solemn kings who bring their gifts to Christ. Out of all nations have come the creators and preservers of the liturgy; and these bring with them the spirit and the genius of their own peoples. All find there some lot or part in the magnificent yet simple services, the curious, often now unmeaning rubrics that speak as relics of bygone cultures and civilizations, the cumbersome classicalism of Byzantium, the decadent paradox of Carthage, the fantastic interpretations of Alexandria. Yet not the past only is mirrored there, but the present: 'French lucidity and German depth, the ordered liberty of England, the flaming heart of Spain.'

Part Two: God's Handiwork

7 THE CREATIVE WORD

WE LEARN as children that God created all things by his word, and St John, in the tremendous preface that he puts to his Gospel, tells us who this Word of God is: 'In the beginning was the Word . . .all things were made through him, and without him was made nothing. . . .The Word was made flesh.' It is obvious, then, that God the Father created everything through the Son, who was the image according to which everything was formed. Thus is the whole world stamped with a divine personality, whose traces are conspicuous in the details and laws of created nature. The old idea of a blind force working its way through all creation, trampling under foot in its mad fashion the ineffective and inefficient wastrels, slaughtering the welter of all unselfish being, cannot readily obtain any evidence to support it. Even evil as well as good shows clear signs of an intelligence directing, controlling, planning Here too the whole value of evolutionary research, such as has been gathered by the science of our own and past times, can be appreciated by no one more than by ourselves.

I as a Catholic welcome the many detailed laws that are now found to govern even the formation of a crystal. Some take shape in one figure, some in another, all in definite mathematical precision. As in the child's story of Robinson Crusoe, there are evident traces of intelligent being on the shores of nature. And the deeper our knowledge becomes, the more clearly do we see the gradual break-up of that old-fashioned materialism that supposed nothing rational in the organization of the universe.

Indeed, so full is the world of personality that it is the lover alone who discovers the full meaning of life. Unless you are in love, you will never find a purpose in the ebb and flow of existence. Thus, to love is to understand. The lover, as he sets about his daily toil, finds in all the earth things that remind him of his beloved. Every corner of the street comes to him and tells him of some excellence or the memory of some past happiness. The whole world spells to him just one name. Hence the object of his love, because it is a personality, does give him the meaning of life. The personality may actually, because of the very vehemence of his passion, obscure for him the divine idea, human forms may block out the radiance of the divine, but the fact remains that they alone who are in love find an answer to life's riddle.

The old pagan idea that found the gods lurking in field and wood and stream was evidence of the instinct of man's nature. Faulty were their legends, gross and carnal their interpretation, but human nature did find out the high secret of earth – that it sprang from the hands of a personal God. A mother discovers the meaning of sorrow in the heart of her child: she sees that God deals with her as she with her little ones. The lover finds the name of his beloved written across the stars; the sighing of the wind, the fragrance of the flowers and delicate hue of the rose, and the music of the birds, do but repeat to the friend his friend's loveliness. For the love of a person alone can unlock the secrets of creation, and make pain almost divine, and even parting such sweet sorrow, since it was through a Person that the world was made. It is just, then, this personal touch that can alone explain it.

Further, it will be noticed that the nearer the person we love approaches to the divine ideal through whom all things were created, the more true is our understanding of life. The more clearly their souls mirror the perfections of Christ, the better is the vision that they unfold to us of the inner depths of life. One meaning of the devotion to the saints is precisely for that purpose. They are the imitators of Christ, and because they so closely followed in his footsteps they do the better explain to us, once we have found a love for them in our hearts, the troubled perplexities of our existence. Our love for them, just because they are human and because they do reproduce in some way the life of our Master, helps our own lives along. But it is only in him that we shall find the complete answer; the saints are at best faulty copies of a faultless original.

By taking, then, into our hands his Gospel and setting the Crucifix before our eyes, and feeding upon his broken Body and his outpoured Blood, we shall be getting into our minds the real vision that alone will make the universe explainable. Through him all things were made; it will be therefore in our increasing knowledge of him and in a corresponding love of him that we shall find our way about in the little furrows of our lives. In the perfect realization of him alone can the meaning of all things be made clear; not indeed as though the world explains him, though this too is true, but rather that he explains the world. Frequent communication with him, frequent communion in the Blessed Sacrament, will therefore be of great help to me. It will help me to know him better, experience his love, and find the answer to all the troubles of life in him.

God Made Me

God made me. How many men have desired to hear the things that we hear and have not heard them! To think that for thousands of years before the coming of Christ and for all the hundreds of years since he came, there have been unnumbered souls who were anxiously longing to hear that answer with assurance. The problem has always troubled the children of men. As the human race began its uphill climb to the full story of revelation, which it has felt for unceasingly in its heart, it has gradually grown more interested in the problem of its origin, whence it took its rise, and for what purpose, if even for any purpose, it is here. Reason has always faced life with the question on its lips as to what is the business of its existence. The traditions that the race had gathered from its primitive revelation were soon obscured by many myths, so that we are expressly told that when God chose Abraham he called him out from his family that worshipped many gods; but at any rate they worshipped. Somehow, though the truth had become overgrown with the strange growths of time, the light still glimmered beneath all this obstruction. Falsely, inhumanly, distorted into fantastic shapes, the remembrance of the Divine Master lingered as a memory. Man, despite his primitive knowledge, gradually lapsed from the sure doctrine of a Creator; then, also gradually, he began again to piece together the scraps of truth that yet remained, and out of them of formed for himself a faulty and variable gospel.

Then God broke through the silence. Gradually, in shafts he illumination, in growing glory from prophet to prophet, the light began to break upon the horizon and to herald the perfect day. In the Old Testament may be followed the unfolding of successive revelation; then when the fullness of time arrived, Christ our Lord appeared; no longer in broken gleams, but in the full splendor of the sun came his revelation. He made known to us the divine life and the mysterious working of the Three-in-One, and brought to the human race knowledge of many things that helped it to understand some of the problems that had for so long perplexed it. What had seemed to the wise and devout beyond all human power to know – what still appears so to many of our own generation that are seeking after God in perfect faith and hope and love – can now be understood by a Catholic child.

From my earliest years I have been familiar with the thought of God, my Creator, Redeemer, Sanctifier. No doubt the very simplicity of my belief, the very fact of its familiarity, the clear way in which it does at once help to the understanding of life, the complete answer it affords to so much that perplexes others, may blind me to the fact of the greatness of the revelation. I cannot conceive myself as without the truth of God's personal creation of me, and consequently do not value as I should the preciousness of that knowledge. Yet the remembrance that it was the death of Christ that purchased it for me should convince me of the divine compassion whereby I was made conscious in my infancy that God had made me.

That acknowledgment of my dependence upon God for the first beginnings of life, as well as for my continuance in this present existence, is the keystone of my faith. The infinite mind that can, because of its very infinity, attend as industriously to each single member as to the whole race, called me into being, purposed my end for his own greater glory, and arranged my life to achieve its decreed destiny. I find myself handicapped by this and that: my passions, my circumstances, the tendency of the environment in which I find myself – the evil effect, perhaps, of my hereditary weakness – all seem to prejudice my freedom. Ah well, he made me! I did not choose, but he, the surroundings of my life; therefore he knows more clearly even than do I the difficulties of that life. He is to be my judge, yes, but he made me and will understand. The very fact that I am his creature is itself of great consolation. Just as I ease my anxieties about others by my consciousness that they are in his keeping, and that if I with all my inherent selfishness can feel disquieted about them, his care and solicitude can be no less, his love being greater; so also is the same thought to steady me, too, in life's perplexities. At my Communions the nearness of that Presence should force the ejaculation from my heart: 'Cast all your care on him, for he hath care of you.' Surely St Peter, when he wrote that phrase, had his mind full of the mystery of the death that he had watched from afar off, with eyes that wept bitterly. But no less does the text tell me of his tender care for me, since I am his own handiwork. I shall walk, then, in perfect trust, for God made me.

The Dignity of the Christian

The whole force of events in every civilized country has surely been to make us recognize the dignity of the human soul. In matters of social organization, in the economic labor market, we can see that one chief means of the present terrible oppression of the poor has been the wanton and deliberate neglect of the individual personal worth of the worker. In the ordinary manuals that are issued on the social question, the arguments for both sides are seldom taken from any view of the individual, but from social reasons for the betterment of the community, or from the exchange between work done and wage paid. 'By himself,' says a modern economist, 'a man has no right to anything whatever. He is part of the social whole; and he has a right only to that which it is for the good of the whole that he should have.' This is obviously a very splendid basis for any act of social tyranny.

This case of political economy is symptomatic of a great deal that is present in modern life – a desire to exalt the community at the expense of the individual, springing from a disregard of Christian teaching. For the Catholic there can be no such method of argument. Society may fall in ruins, but the individual must be saved. Of course, as a matter of fact, society will become much more prosperous when the individual dignity of human personality has been recognized. Yet, certainly, regard for the individual must precede regard for the whole community. For if the individuals were of no worth, then neither could the sum of them be worthy of a man's labor. To belittle the individual is evidently to belittle the society, but to exalt the individual is to make of a society something, says St. Antoninus, 'almost divine'. Christ came to save the whole world, because under his teaching the individual soul alone would have been as worth the ransom of his death as was the race.

In all these things, then, in the whole of my outlook on life, in my attitude towards others, and in the care I should have of my own soul, I must be continually realizing the supreme value of the individual man. Some saint has said that the thing that is deathless, that is exalted by grace till it becomes a partaker of the divine nature, that required the death of God for its own ransom, must be indeed worthy of the highest possible attention and reverence. There cannot, indeed, be any conflict between the good of the individual and the good of the society, for the advance of the members must advantage the whole. But I must begin with the human unit, with myself. I can never value others, nor act charitably towards them, till I am fully conscious of the worth of my own soul. Without that appreciation I can never be of real service to any of them. Once I have perceived my own dignity, I can perceive the dignity of others; and realizing the importance of saving my own soul, I shall be led also to help others to save theirs. The proverb is indeed justified: 'Charity begins at home'. The very basis, therefore, of all Christian virtue, of any attempt to be made by man to achieve something greater than himself, must rest upon this stable foundation – the value of my own being, its high call and destiny, the very divinity that inhabits me, the spark of God that remains inextinguishable to kindle again into flame the dying embers of my life.

8 WHY HAVE WE NO HOME?

WHY are we not perfectly at home here on earth? All about us is the wonderful world of God's creation, and everything on the earth fulfils some purpose of its own. Man alone, on the earth's surface, seems so restless. Something, as we believe, has happened to him. Indeed, something has been given to man. That something we call grace. We mean by this that through a gift of God the actual soul of man has been altered. The soul of its own nature, naturally, though immortal, is of the natural order. We believe that God has now given to the soul something kindred to his own divine nature, that by grace the soul is no longer left in the order of natural existence, but is lifted up to a higher order – a supernatural order. Man is now not only man, but has something of the very nature of God. So truly is this so that it is the ultimate destiny of man living here, as he should, on God's very level, to gaze at last on the supernatural beauty of God. Not merely shall man who has been faithful live this life hereafter and see God as wise men might, in some dim way, even on earth discern him, but he shall reach out to and behold something that eye hath not seen, nor ear heard, beyond our imagination, beyond the most rich and most splendid of our dreams.

Grace holds the roots of glory. The supernatural is at the level of God. We believe that the soul of man is fashioned through grace into something higher and more splendid than itself. This, of course, is why we are pilgrims, why also we are restless. Of course we can never settle down for long here on earth. If you think of the story of our Lord on earth, and of his complete acceptance of his Father's will, you will remember nevertheless that in his heart there was something all his life long that was crying for that other life, for heaven. More than once his words show us what lay in the depths of his soul. Thus, when he told his disciples that he must go from them, he made as though he were almost astonished that none of them gave him the congratulation that should so obviously have been his. Here he was indeed, but he was not meant to be here always. His human nature was destined for the peace of heaven. Even he, accepting the divine will, felt in his heart a cry for something beyond this earth, a cry for heaven.

And he is not the only one who feels it, but all souls, too. Every soul that cometh into the world, every soul, in some degree or measure, has been enlightened and is not at home here on earth. You wonder why people are restless. You wonder why people can so seldom settle down. There is something missing to them in life, and, foolishly, they imagine that it is some material circumstance lacking. They have only to alter this or that, and all shall be well. It would be dreadful if man were ever at peace here on earth. We must look elsewhere than in persistent change or desire for the true remedy for our trouble. We are strangers because we were made for something much greater than the life we know; and because we share that divine nature, there is in us something that understands and longs for God.

Man understands man, not because of some stored-up experience, but because he is a man himself. He knows what men are thinking, he is conscious of other people's minds, conscious because he is a man himself. He knows his own human nature, and knowing it, knows the human nature of the world. People will say, sometimes with astonishment: 'But how could Shakespeare know all that huge assembly of mankind? What chance had he to store so much in his life, to understand all those various types of human nature?' It was not obtained from outside, it was obtained from within. 'He has no education in knowledge of this or that. How does he under-stand life?' It is not really by searching the heavens or wandering over countries and strange peoples that you understand human nature. It is not from education that this comes, though true culture should help it. It is merely by taking cognizance of yourself. St Paul can touch every note of the instrument of the human heart, not because he knows mankind in any wide, general way, but only because he knows himself. Being a man, you understand human nature if you have any quickness of intelligence or sympathy at all. No man knoweth a man but the spirit of man.

Sharing the divine life, you know something of God already by a God-given instinct. There is something in you that gives you, of itself, an understanding of God. Grace has lifted you up to that level so that you share a common nature, and therefore so that you understand. Hence supernatural man shall always be restless like people in better circumstances who, as our saying is, come down in the world. They are always chafing against the circumstances in which they find themselves. They are restless because of their memory of better and happier days. 'A sorrow, crowned with a sorrow, is to remember happier days.' Something like that is in man always. There is a memory that he shares with God. Just as dimly, sometimes, in the winter, if you sit solitary by the fireplace, you can almost let your memory run back to prehistoric man. You can almost feel in yourself, as you watch the embers falling, you can feel in yourself all that man has ever felt. You can think of his dreams varying from age to age, in the mere material expression of them. In such a mood all that man has ever felt you feel. You are human nature in yourself.

Now, you have been given a share in the divine nature. You, too, in some mysterious way, echo to God. You are sensitive to God because of this thing that has happened to your soul, as people, by instinct, know when those they love go by. Some-thing much more mysterious, but no less vivid, comes to the soul that chooses to dwell in God. What is asked of you is that you should dwell in God. There is already something established between you and God. It is there. It is fundamental, not by nature, but by supernature. Just as truly as you share something with all mankind, so too you share something with God. You have the very condition and foundation of intimate knowledge – understanding – sensitiveness to him. By his deliberate choice you are one with him All that is asked of you is to keep that oneness. Remember that you can lose your sensitiveness to human nature. Men can grow selfish and forget the instincts of man. You can lose all contact with beauty. Remember, always, there is in us something which puts us on a divine level, which makes God friendly with us from the start, which establishes a unity between us: 'That they all may be one, as thou Father in me and I in thee. That they also may be one in us.' All that we are asked to do is to remember that there it is within us. It is not our doing. It is due to no merit of ours. It is his sheer establishment in us. Live your life remembering it, and you will find yourself set down in a wonderful world. It is the particular glory of the saint that he has found this. This is the wonder of his life. He lives sharing life with God consciously. We all share it, but the saints knew what life they shared We are told the world is restless because of the speed of its traffic, because of the noise of the streets. Do not believe so superficial a cause to be the real one. It is restless for some much deeper reason. It is restless because it was made for God and because it has forgotten God. That is why it is restless. That is why the married folk are changing partners because the one Partner their soul cries for has been put outside the door. They blame each other for this unhappiness. Listen! 'I stand at the door and knock,' said he. To your last day you shall hear him knocking. He will not open the door. It is opened from inside. That is your fatal power – to let God in, or show God out – consciously.

In another way, God is always there. We share life with him and nothing can alter that. But this is why we are pilgrims: we have been made citizens of another fatherland and, wherever we may wander, here we shall never find a home.

Following Christ
The very phrase 'following Christ' shows how voluntary must be our service of him. He recognizes the freedom of choice that he has himself given us. There must be no compulsion, no being dragged after the chariot wheels of his triumphal car, no long line of captives grimly led behind him. His own ministry among men – though it might be at the behest of his Father ('I am come to do the will of him that sent me') – though even his death, according to his own phrase, might be 'necessary,' was yet the free and willing service of his subjection. 'I lay down my life,' said he; no one took it from him. The imagery of our English poets such as Milton and Dryden, who have attempted to depict in language the offering made by the Son of himself as a propitiation to the Father in atonement of the sins of the world, shows him as stepping forward in the divine presence and offering to take the proffered burden from which the angels shrank in fear. This is, of course, purely metaphorical, for to none other than him could the office of Redemption have been suggested. But it is so far true in that it expresses the doctrine that the whole tragedy of the Incarnation was freely undertaken by the Second Person of the Trinity. He became man of his own choice, without any necessity from his own nature, acting in this way not from any inherent compulsion (such as that from which the Trinity proceeded), but by the simple decision of his will.

As, therefore, his own ministry was freely undertaken and pursued to its own sublime end, so of the same nature was his own appeal to be made to those who wished to come after him. The purity and strength of his life, the fathomless tenderness of his love, the keen agony of his sufferings, the winsome appeal of childhood and boyhood, the charm and fascination of his manly grace and bearing, the wonder of his language, the sympathy of his heart, the boldness of his denunciations of hypocrisy and cant, his love of freedom, his passion for justice, his devotion to truth – all these, we say, compel our love and our affectionate disciple-ship, but it is the compulsion of free service. This marvelous appeal to human nature is the sole secret of his power. What alone he asks of us or would be willing to accept, is the devotion of a son, not the forced labor of a slave. His parables and sermons and prayers are full of this idea of sonship; and through his apostles, whom he had instructed in his own principles and teachings, he is forever insistent upon 'the glorious liberty of the sons of God'. We are free, therefore, in our choice, can take or reject his yoke. At the most and best, our highest title must be that of follower; that is, of one who comes behind, perhaps a very long way behind, but who deliberately and of set choice, without any penalty of force, walks in the footsteps of love.

Yet if there be any penalty, it is the penalty not of force but of love, since though the choice be free, the cost must always be paid. And the cost here is the yoke of Christ. The yoke is sweet indeed, and the burden is light; but for all that there is a yoke and a burden. There is something to be borne by us, some difficulties to be overcome, some disappointments, some agonies in the garden, some cross-carrying in the busy streets, some loneliness, some betrayals, some jeers. We are free, yet have called ourselves followers, and he will take care that we do follow him. Perfectly conscious of what will meet our eyes on each day's awakening, and of what will form the retrospect of our working hours when we turn to our sleep in the evening, we yet freely follow in the footsteps of love. Not spasmodically, like Peter – at one time zealous and promising to die for Christ, at another denying all acquaintanceship with him – but deliberately and with full knowledge of what the consequences are likely to be; calmly striving to keep up to his stride and pace, we hurry after him. Certainly we shall never catch up to him. He will go forever swinging down the great highway, his figure heading the great crusade. His form showing against the grey and dusty pathway, he can be seen leading his followers. But at least I am going in the same direction: stumbling, failing, footsore, hot, tired, weary, it is a blessed thing for me to be still following with a glad heart.

God's Will

God has a purpose for me and he wants me to carry out that purpose. There can be nothing far-fetched in either of these two notions. God is wise, then he acts for a purpose; God created my soul, then he has something for me to do. So far so good. Now since he has a purpose for me, it is clearly a purpose he wishes me to fulfill. But if he wishes me to do it, he will make it clear to me. Moreover, since he knows my foolishness and blindness, he will – so to say – go out of his way to make it clear. He knows me through and through, knows how very easily I can mistake his meaning, and because he wants the thing done he will be telling me endlessly what he wants of me! Do I find it difficult to know what his will is? Then I can be sure that the fault does not lie with him. He wants his will carried out – else it would not be his will; hence I can be sure that he is making it clear; and if it is not clear, the fault must be mine

Have I, then, any way of finding out God's will? I am sure he must be illuminating me all day long, speaking to me in a thousand voices, yet I miss these hints and expressed desires. How can I learn where to look for them? He makes signs to me; how can I discover these signs? Perhaps it is not very easy to lay down laws about them, because God has a disconcerting way of treating each of us differently, so that drawing up a guide book is not very helpful when you are dealing with One who refuses to be reduced to little, human, tabulated, statistical columns Still we can get a certain distance in the right direction by saying that these signs are of two sorts, within and without.

First of all, take the signs within. God started us off in life with a certain bias of temperament. We have certain likes and dislikes, sympathies, antipathies, con-natural, born with us, beyond choice. *De gustibus non disputandum.* Why cannot you dispute about tastes? Chiefly because they are not a matter of reasoned argument, they are instinctive; you can correct them, modify them, sublimate them, but they remain. Now why have I this particular temperament? Evidently it was given me by God for some purpose. It will fit in perfectly with some design of his. Without it, I shall not be able to do the work he has designed for me. When faced by alternatives as to which is his will, I must first analyze my intuitions and examine my natural preferences. Presumably they are there for a purpose.

Secondly, there are signs without, which we call circum-stances. We are not perfectly free to follow our impulses and preferences. We are hampered by the world in which God has set us, the age, the stage of life. This also is of God, and may not be ignored. So life, then, is made up of two forces that fit in with each other, that check each other, modify, play into each other's hands and yet against each other. Impulse drives us, but is checked by circumstance; then when we are blocked, comes a fresh impulse, which again is blocked or deflected by circumstance; thus shepherded we are urged along the path which God would have us choose. He drives us by their interplay. He drives well. What is asked of us in this battle of impulse and circumstance? Three things chiefly: (a) a sensitiveness to God's call; (b) a cheerful humility that is not rooted in its own will; (c) a quiet and patient surrender not to self, but to the work and to God.

Circumstances

Circumstances are the scapegoat of the failure. He always throws all the blame on them. He is no end of a fellow, but he has never had a chance. He bids you look at that and that other, what a success they are; but then, what wonderful chances they had. His whole philosophy lies there. Life is a medley of chances; if the opening happens to come, you can do something fine; if it does not, you never can. That is about as far as he can see into the brick wall of life. Then biographers and autobiographers play into his hand. You read a man's life, saint or sinner, and you begin to believe in circumstances. You find the hero's birthplace and surroundings make him what he is one day to become; his town, country, hills, or wild moors, gave him from the start the gifts he was one day to need; his ancestry explains so much of his success, explains it away even, so convincing is it all. His schooling has its place, of course, and then you are led right up to the breathless moment when his chance comes. He takes it – immense relief, you know he is a made man. Biographers do that sort of thing. It is their way. To their understanding, the hero, for all his heroism, is a mere puppet in the grip of forces beyond his control.

Now it is the easiest thing in the world, once you have got this idea into your head, to become a complete cynic. You have all the necessary ingredients to hand. You know perfectly well that whatever befell the lucky hero, it would help to pave his way to success, or turn up later and account for some curious accident that just saves him from ruin. In the end you rather wonder why he is a hero at all. He was merely a top that spun into fame because it bumped against the projecting side of wood, and got jockeyed into the hole which was marked with the big number. After all, you feel the biographer has made it altogether too easy. He has destroyed his hero's personality, left it out of account. Just so the failures we meet equally leave out the real cause of their troubles, namely, not their circumstances, but themselves. We are so apt to blame every culprit but the right one, to blame circumstances instead of self.

Now the Christian lays down as his first principle that, since each has his own vocation, God-planned, the circumstances must always be favorable to that vocation. First, however, remember that the vocation is unending, goes on all life long, is bound not to the single choice of a profession, but all day and every day. God has a work for us at every moment, and consequently at every moment the circumstances are favorable to the carrying out of his will. God is just; he could not, therefore, fairly demand anything of us which the circumstances did not permit. But secondly, of course, we have to be patient if we are to carry out these purposes of our life. The man born blind had to wait all through boyhood to manhood before that moment came for which he was created and by which he will be to the end remembered. We must steadily push forward in life, every fresh advance will meet with a fresh difficulty, the line will never run quite straight ahead; but we must be on the look-out for God's opportunity, take it when it comes, never grumble that we have not had our chance, for we always have the chance to do at any given moment what God wants of us; finally, steeping ourselves in patience, waiting for him without fret.

9 OUR EYES ARE HOLDEN

IT is this life of God in us that makes us pilgrims and strangers on the earth. Earth is too strait a home for us whom God has lifted up into the circle of his own life. It is only because we share that divine life that earth and all it has to give, must of its own nature be insufficient for us. What he has done for us entails the giving to us, if we be faithful, the reward ultimately of himself. To make men for finer things is really to give them a very desperate hunger; and all the world was made for God, God in his infinite variety. God's absolute truth, goodness, and beauty – man must inevitably and essentially pursue these things, though he may think them hidden under many disguises. The grace of God that is in us, as our Blessed Lord said of it, works in us 'while the man sleeps'.

So often, in the parables, our Lord compares it to the seed that is cast into the ground; and through these parables, followed one after another, we realize that this living thing, the seed, is not us, but something divine, and therefore of its own nature it is inevitably fruitful. What we are in the parables is the soil, so that what fructifies and opens in us is none of our own doing. The life in us is not our action, but something beyond the reach of our human, created action, something spiritually above us, something divine. As our Lord phrases it, this divine life falls into us. All we can do is minister to its growth. All that is alive in us is his life, not our own. He compares it, as we have said, to the seed that is scattered; now the seed everywhere is vital, the seed everywhere is the same. What makes it reach here a rich harvesting, what makes it fail there and drop, what makes it here dwindle and die, and there grow luxuriant, is not the seed's fault or favor; everywhere it is fruitful, alive. It is the soil that is helpful or harmful to it, enables it to produce its own natural fruit or hinders it from becoming what it might. Again, our Lord speaks of it as cast into the field and growing through daylight and darkness while the farmer sleeps. True, he prepares the soil for the seed, he cleanses the soil, he breaks the soil, he scatters the seed, he scares away the birds from injuring it, but the seed will grow while he sleeps as well as while he works. So with us. Our Lord's teaching is that the same law of spiritual growth continues while we go about our business as well as while we pray. Life grows or dwindles. The life is within us; it is a divine life, a seed cast into the soil, nothing of our own production. It is not the result of evolution from within; it is something thrown into the soil by the divine hand; not of our making or gathering, but divine in itself and given by divine choice. We are just sharers in its efficacy, ministering to this divine life such virtue as our soil can give. It grows of itself. And, as is true of all growth, it grows not only when you are actually attending to the growth, but so long as you are doing nothing to hinder it. A child grows fastest at night. You have seen a child ill, and then when he got up from his bed of sickness again, you suddenly found he had grown very swiftly. Indeed, lying in bed will set him growing, walking will not let him grow so fast. In our Lord's phrase, while we sleep the seed grows.

So in your life, when the divine seed is thrown into you, when this divine grace, this share of the divine life, is cast into you, do not imagine that its growth will be visible to you while you watch it. You do not imagine that you can hear it grow. Up, up, through the tree, comes the sap mounting. You do not see it pushing its way along the branches to the softening tips. It is hidden. You never hear the ebb and flow of that tide. Life is silent. Always, growth as we know it is silent, only to be noted afterwards. Silence and the darkness alone can measure the mounting height of growth. You do not watch things growing to see them grow – not in nature, not in life. God's seed is sown in our hearts; shall we know that it is growing? Shall you know whether you are growing holier in life? Certainly not. You will never know. The seed is growing by itself. You minister to it; you cannot measure its growth. Silence and darkness are its needed conditions and the thing grows of its very nature. You can help it and you can hinder, but you do not really make it grow. Our prayers, are they improving? You will never know whether your prayers are getting worse or better. Prayer is not a measurable thing. It is something invisible, something that no eye can ever reach, that even no intelligence can ever watch flourish or decay. Do not imagine that if your prayers were better you would know they were better. You will never know. Do you think a saint stops and says to himself: 'Now my prayers are better'? Sinners may do that, but not saints. Do not suppose that the saint, as he grows in sanctity, suddenly awakes to the fact and says: 'I am a saint.' Sinners – oh, yes. Sinners may be self-complacent, perfectly self-satisfied, but that is dreadful. The saint, as he grows in sanctity, grows in self-disesteem. When you think your prayers worse, they are likely to be better. Likely, that is all that can be said. They may be worse, as you think them worse, they may be more distracted, there may be less comfort and inspiration in them, but whether they be better or worse, you will never know this side of death. Darkness and silence alone can measure a thing's growth.

The most beautiful prayer, so the Church teaches us, and the highest and the noblest, is the prayer of absolute silence. Not in this silence can a man stop and think of any such desperate self-measurement. Any examination in the midst of its prayer to see if the soul is progressing, would be either mischievous or fatal. You can never know. It is hid from you and always will be hid from you. Not when you are striving can you stop to remember. Not when the child is running about is it growing. Not when you think, not while you are working at your soul, will your self-examen help you here. Probably you are only thereby torturing your soul. What God asks is simplicity and confidence in him. Leave your moral worth to him to be judged. We are so small-minded that of ourselves we are encouraged only by what our eye can measure in the spiritual world. If we live at all in the spirit, we must live by faith. We live by not troubling over whether we know or not. We live, really, by ignorance. We live by making no effort to discover exactly where we stand in the divine judgment. We live by absolute trust. To that we are always reduced as the final principle of our perfect serenity. You would be no happier if you saw you were better; at least, you would not rightly be any happier. All that can make us happy is the consciousness of the compassion and care of God. Never can happiness be based on self, never on our knowledge of our own growth, but on God only and always. It is foolish to be looking at ourselves. Only to be looking at him is wise. Let us go back almost to the first thing we ever learnt in our Catechism: 'God made me to know him ' Never fully shall I learn that lesson until, at last, I see him. Till then I must go on learning. But no command is laid on us that we should know ourselves.

So the essential business of the soul is prayer, prayer always, not action. Not what I do matters, nor so much how far my virtues are cultivated, nor my sins gradually laid aside. All that must be attempted, truly, but that is a lesser work. Watch and listen to the saints! They will tell you, one by one, that all the great work of their souls was achieved in prayer, while they were not thinking of self at all. Is it not a phrase of one of the saints: 'You are only truly praying when you do not know that you are praying?' Prayer should be something unconscious in itself. Perhaps on a spring morning, when you feel life coursing in you, you may be aware of it, but ordinarily you do not stop to think that you are alive. Life is natural. With us the supernatural should be like the natural. Thus will the soul be growing best in its prayer when it is thinking not of self, but of God. Its gaze should be riveted on God's wonderful goodness, God's haunting mercy, God's untiring forgiveness,

God in himself, the marvelous truth of God.

'How interesting!' we say when someone gives us the explanation of something we have seen repeatedly but never found an answer for; noticed but never understood. Every little bit of truth is interesting, but truth absolute, complete, must be fascinating above all else. Endlessly, too, goodness attracts us always. How marvelous to grow in the knowledge of God's goodness! The better we know him the more evidences should we find of his goodness. They only see God cruel who see him not at all. The more they know of God, the more will they know of his infinite goodness. The answer to: 'Is there a God?' is to know him. He is his own answer. That riddle you will only answer on your knees. And beauty! God is that infinite beauty. You grow more cultured as you gaze on beauty, more holy as you gaze on infinite beauty. We reach goodness by knowing goodness, by loving goodness, that is, by prayer. By prayer we are brought nearer to God. Prayer is getting somehow into touch with God, but not necessarily being conscious of knowing him. You are not conscious of being alive, not in the daylight, nor conscious at all when you are asleep. Yet we are as much alive sleeping as waking, as much alive, as truly growing. So is it with our souls and God. It is foolish to attempt to measure our spiritual self. It is foolish to worry about securing a true judgment on ourselves. So is it foolish to say to ourselves: 'I am no good at prayer. Therefore I had better lay prayer aside.' Prayer is trying to know God better. Then persevere in prayer. There is no other rule than that to learn how to pray. There is no measure for prayer in prayer. There is no measure for prayer except constancy. There is no reward in prayer except to those who hold on.

There are times when you feel more alive, but at those times you are not necessarily more alive. Even when they are dying, folk will sometimes tell you they never felt so well, and that they know they are improving. Yet you know that the doctor has given up hope for them. Still they say: 'I feel ever so well today.' Feeling is a poor judge in this court of human life. It is a poor judge equally in that other court of supernatural life. Just as of the body, it is true to say while we sleep the growth goes on, so remember that all the growing of the soul is achieved by divine action. All we can do is to help or hinder that action. We cannot do anything else at all. 'I can do nothing of myself' is the everlasting Christian Gospel. I must be humble and remember that I can do nothing. Whatever is done, is done by God. 'Paul may sow, and Apollo water; but it is God who giveth increase.'

To vary the metaphor, we are pilgrims; and we are pilgrims because

God has made us pilgrims by the greatness of his precious gift, because he has given us a share in his own reality, because he has lifted us up out of creation and set us by his side. 'I have come that they might have life, and have it more abundantly.' Whose life are they to have? His. We are pilgrims because he broke our relationship with earth, because he dusted away the soil that clung about our feet, because he fitted us with wings. You remember, in the Scripture, how with touching beauty he compares the way he deals with souls to the mother eagle teaching her young to fly. If you read the story of the eaglets, you will read how-the mother eagle teaches her young to fly by making them dare the great depths and heights. Nearly always, out of every brood, there is one that grows timid, that has not the courage to flutter off from the rock where the nest lies. Then the mother bird takes the nest away from the ledge, twig by twig. She will make its ledge most bereft, desolate, lonely. Meanwhile, the others go sailing by on their new-found wings of flight. There is always one that is timid, that stands and twitters and cries, and will not dare. Do you remember how the prophet describes that, at last, but not impatiently, only with exquisite and disciplined affection, the mother eagle will beat the little one off the ledge with her wings? Then, as it falls, crying with terror, she dives under it and catches it between her wings. Then she shakes it off and again dives under and holds it between the spread of her wings until at last what of itself it would not dare do, it is made to do. It finds that flying is not so difficult as it dreamt.

In our life, whatever is done is done by divine action. Does this explain better your life to you? There are souls God treats like that. He gets rid of their home about them, stick by stick – the nest that might give them some comfort – and makes them cling to the rock from which he wishes to free them. Stick by stick is their nest broken up. But still they will not dare to attempt what he asks of them. So cowardly is human nature! 'How should I learn to fly? However should I?' It is the cowardice of the man with only one talent. It is the coward that falters: 'But, I have so little. I was never intended to do this wonderful thing. I – to go praying? You do not know me, if you think that. What do I know of prayer? I cannot pray at all.' But, you have never tried to pray properly. You have never ventured out into the depths. Some cannot walk much, who yet could fly well. Birds can walk but little, yet they can fly – wonderful is it? Nay, not so wonderful as souls! There are souls that are as small and yet as great as that. If there be such, God will beat them with his wings. Only because he loves them will he un-nest them. If they will only dare where God wants them they will find they can do it; find that the free open spaces are nothing to be afraid of. If we thought merely in terms of human power, these would be something to be terribly afraid of! If you think of the depths below you, you will never dare the immeasurable flight. Think, instead, of God's wings under you, of the divine action. Beneath us are the everlasting wings. It is not what we do that matters. It is only and always what God does. That is why in this world we can be so great, though they try to discourage us by telling us that we are descended from animals and by insisting to us the immeasurable distance of the stars. They say: 'Look how little man is.' But man can look at these wonders; and these wonders cannot look at man.

We can measure the stars though they be right beyond us. No star has measured us. Little? Oh, yes, we are but 'earthen vessels,' still the treasure we carry is immeasurably great. We only carry it. It is not ours. With us it cannot mingle. It grows in us. We, in a sense, never grow.

We are pilgrims, we are travelers. We are meant for finer cities. We are finer than this life we know. This will perish and we shall abide. We need always to remember that what is done in us is done by divine power through prayer. Thus can we help or hinder. But what is living in us is not ours but his. It is the thought of this that makes us great on earth with a greatness no eye can measure. Rest in his power perfectly content, without attempting self-measurement. Do not look down, look up. Do not look within, look outside of you. Do not question your soul, but pray.

10 GOD'S PRESENCE IN US

SCRIPTURE is very full of the idea of the nearness of God to his creation. The Old Testament is alive with that inspiration, for there is hardly a chapter or verse that does not insist upon that truth; the New Testament, teaching so tenderly the Fatherhood of God, is even more explicit and more beautiful in its references to this intimate relationship. Now this notion of God's nearness to his world depends for its full appreciation on the central doctrine of creation. He has made the world, in consequence it is impressed with his personality. The more vigorous the artist in character, will, and personality, the more is his work stamped with his individuality; hence, the tremendous personality of God must be everywhere traceable in the things he has made.

When we say that God is everywhere, we mean that he is in all things because he made all things. Not only does the whole world lie outstretched before his eye and is governed by his power, but he himself lurks at the heart of everything. By him things have come into existence, and so wholly is that existence of theirs his gift, that were he to withdraw his support they would sink back into nothingness.

God, then, is within all creation, because he is its cause. He is within every stone and leaf and child. Nothing, with life or without, evil or good, can fail to contain him as the source of its energy, its power, its existence. Not only, therefore, must I train myself to see with reverence that everything contains him, but I must especially realize his intimacy and relationship to myself. Religion, indeed, in practice is little else than my personal expression of that relationship. I have in my prayers, in my troubles, in my temptations, to turn to God, not without but within, not to someone above me or beneath supporting me, but right at the core of my being. I can trace up to its source every power of my soul, and I shall find him there. Wholly is God everywhere, not as some immense being that with its hugeness fills the world, but as something that is within every creature he has made.

Degrees of God's Presence

God is intimate with all creation because he made it, for creation implies that God remains within, supporting, upholding. God is within everything, and therefore he is everywhere. But while we thus believe that God is wholly everywhere, we also believe something which seems the exact opposite, for we believe that God is more in some places than in others, more in some people than in others. How is it if God is wholly everywhere that he can be more here than there? To understand this, we must also understand that every created thing shares somehow in God's being. He communicates himself to it in some fashion, for apart from him it could have no perfections. We have a way of saying that we reflect God's greatness and that we are 'broken lights' of him, but that is far short of the truth. We do more than reflect, we actually have some participation

in God, so that St Thomas boldly takes over a saying of Plato: 'The individual nature of a thing consists in the way it participates in the perfections of God' (Summa theol., I, 14, 6).

Now since everything participates in God and since some things are more excellent than others, it stands to reason that some things express God better than others. The higher a thing is in the scale of being, the more of God it expresses, for it participates more in God's being. The more life a thing has and the more freedom it acquires, then the nearer does it approach to God and the more divinity it holds. Man, by his intelligence, his deeper and richer life, his finer freedom, stands at the head of visible creation; consequently, he is more fully a shrine of God than the lower forms of life. He bears a closer resemblance to the divine intelligence and will and has a greater share in them. It is in that sense that we arrange in ascending order inanimate creation, the vegetable kingdom, the animal kingdom, and man.

Consequently, we can now see in what sense God is said to be more in one thing than in another. He is more in it because he exercises himself more in one thing than in another; one thing expresses more than another the perfections of God because it shares more deeply than another that inner being of God. The more nearly anything or anyone is united to God, the more does his power exercise itself in them, so that, since God's gifts are variously distributed and are of various degrees, we are justified in saying that though he is wholly everywhere, he may be more fully here than there, just as, though my soul is in every part of my being, it is more perfectly in the brain than elsewhere, because there it exercises itself more fully and with more evidence of expression. Thus we say God is more in a man's soul than anywhere else in creation, since in a man's soul God is more perfectly expressed. It is therefore with great reverence that I should regard all creation, but with especial reverence that I should look to the dignity of every human soul.

God's Special Presence in the Just

While God is in everything in creation, he dwells in the just by grace. Scripture quite noticeably uses the word dwelling when it wishes to express the particular way in which God is present in the souls of the just. He is in all things, but in the just he dwells. The same word is applied to the presence of God in the souls of those in grace as is used when speaking of God's presence in the Temple. But here again it is necessary to say that God's dwelling in the Temple never implied he was not elsewhere, but did imply that somehow his presence in the Temple was quite different from the way in which he was present elsewhere. The same kind of difference between the presence of God in all created nature and his presence in the souls of the just is intended by the careful use in Scripture of the word dwelling, namely, that God has, over and above his ordinary presence in every single created thing, a further and special presence in the hearts of those in friendship with him by grace, and this new presence is a fuller and richer presence whereby God's excellences and perfections are more openly displayed.

Another way in which the same idea is pressed home in the New Testament is by the word sent or given. Frequently, in the last discourse of our Lord on the night before he suffered, he spoke to the apostles of the Holy Spirit, the Paraclete, the Comforter, who was to be sent or given. Ordinarily, by using the expression 'sending someone,' we imply that the person sent is where he was not before, that he has passed from here to there. Obviously our Lord cannot really mean that only after his crucifixion and ascension would the Holy Ghost be found in the hearts of the apostles, for we have already insisted that the Holy Spirit must be in every creature, by virtue of its creation. Hence, the only possible meaning is that the Holy Spirit will descend upon the apostles and become present within them after some new fashion in which he was not before. 'Because you are his children, God has sent into your hearts the Spirit of his Son whereby you cry Abba Father' (Gal. 4:6). From the beginning, the Holy Ghost had been within them; now his presence there is new and productive of new effects.

By God's indwelling, effected by grace, the Holy Spirit is present in the soul differently from the way in which he is present by creation. By creation he is wholly everywhere, yet more in the higher forms than in the lower, for he is able to express more of himself in them. Among these highest forms of visible creation, there are again degrees of his presence, so that even among men he is more in one than in another. This gradation is in proportion to their grace. The more holy and sanctified they become, the more does the Holy Spirit dwell in them, the more fully is he sent, the more completely given, while the Book of Wisdom says expressly that God does not dwell in sinners. As soon as I am in a state of grace the Holy Ghost dwells in me in this new and wonderful way, takes up his presence in me in this new fashion.

Nature of this Presence
We have taken it for granted that God is present somehow in the soul by grace. We have now to consider what sort of a presence this really is. Do we mean absolutely that God the Holy Ghost is truly in the soul or do we, by some metaphor or vague expression, mean that he is merely exerting himself there in some new way? We absolutely mean what we say when we declare that by grace the Holy Spirit of God is present within the soul. Scripture is exceedingly full of the truth of this and is always insisting on this presence of the Holy Ghost. St Paul, especially, notes it over and over again, and in his Epistle to the Romans he repeats it in very forcible language: 'But you are not in the flesh but in the Spirit, if so be that the Spirit of God dwell in you' (Rom. 8:9), and he goes on in that same chapter to imply that this presence is a part of grace.

To some it will seem curious to find that the Fathers of the Church in earliest ages were not only convinced of the fact of this presence, but appealed triumphantly to it as accepted even by heretics. In the acts of the martyrs, too, there are frequent references to this, as when St Lucy declared to the judge that the Spirit of God dwelt in her and that her body was in very truth the temple and shrine of God. Again, Eusebius relates in his history that Leonidas, the father of Origen, used to kneel by the bedside of the sleeping boy and devoutly and reverently kiss his breast as the tabernacle wherein God dwelt. The child in his innocence and grace is indeed the fittest home on earth for God.

This presence of God in the soul is a real, true presence, as real and as true as the presence of our Lord in the Blessed Sacrament. We look on all that mystery as very wonderful, and indeed it is, that day by day we can be made one with God the Son by receiving his Body and Blood. We know the value to be got out of visits to his hidden presence, the quiet and calm peace such visits produce in our souls, yet, so long as we are in a state of grace, the same holds true of the Holy Spirit within us. We are not indeed made one with the Holy Ghost in a substantial union such as united God and man in the sacred Incarnation, nor is there any overpowering of our personality so that it is replaced by a divine Person, for we retain it absolutely. The simplest comparison is our union with our Lord in the Holy Eucharist, wherein we receive him really and truly and are made partakers of his divinity. By grace, then, we receive really and truly God the Holy Ghost and are made partakers of his divinity.

Object of Knowledge

The fact of this presence has been established and its nature explained It is a real presence, a real union between the soul and God the Holy Ghost. We have, however, a further point to elucidate: the mode whereby this presence is effected. Now this is twofold, so far as this presence of the Spirit affects the mind and heart of man. First we consider the knowledge of God that is generated in the soul by this presence. By natural knowledge we can argue not only to the existence of God, but in some way also to his nature. Not only do we know from the world which he has made that he certainly must have a true existence, but we can even, gradually and carefully, though certainly with some vagueness, argue to God's divine attributes. His intelligence is evident, his power, his wisdom, his beauty, his providence, his care for created nature. Merely from the world about them, the pagans, painfully and after many years and with much admixture of error, could in the end have their beautiful thoughts about God, and by some amazing instinct have stumbled upon truths which Christianity came fully to establish. The writings of Plato and Aristotle, of some Eastern teachers, of some of the kings and priests of Egypt, are evidences of the possibility of the natural knowledge about God.

Faith, then, came as something over and above the possibilities of nature, not merely as regards the contents, but also as regards the kind of knowledge. Reason argues to God, and therefore attains God indirectly. Then faith comes and puts us straight into connection with God himself. Theological virtues are the names given to faith, hope, and charity, because they all have God for their direct and proper object. Faith, then, attains to the very substance of God. It is indeed inadequate so far as all human forms of thought can only falteringly represent God as compared with the fullness that shall be revealed hereafter; nevertheless, it gives us direct knowledge of him. I do not argue by faith to what God is like from seeing his handiwork; I know what he is like from his descriptions of himself.

Now the indwelling of the Spirit of God gives us a knowledge of God even more wonderful than faith gives, for even faith has to be content with God's descriptions of himself. In faith I am indeed listening to a Person who is telling me all about himself. He is the very truth, and all he says is commended to me by the most solemn and certain of motives; but I am still very far from coming into direct and absolute experience of God. That, indeed, can be achieved fully only in heaven. It is only in the beatific vision that the veils will be wholly torn aside and there will be a face-to-face sight of God, no longer by means of created and therefore limited ideas, but an absolute possession of God himself. Yet though absolutely I must wait for heaven before I can achieve this, it is nonetheless true that I can begin it on earth by means of this indwelling of the Spirit of God. This real presence of God in my soul can secure for me what is called an experimental knowledge of God. It is not only that I believe, but I know. Not only have I been told about God, but, at least in passing glimpses, I have seen him. We may almost say to the Church what the men of Sichar said to the woman of Samaria: 'We now believe, not for thy saying, for we ourselves have heard and know' (John 4: 42). 'For the Spirit himself giveth testimony to our spirit that we are the sons of God' (Rom. 8:16).

Object of Love
There is something that unites us more closely to our friends than knowledge does, and this is love. Knowledge may teach us about them, may unlock for us gradually throughout life ever more wonderful secrets of their goodness and strength and loyalty, but knowledge of itself pushes us irresistibly on to something more. The more we know of that which is worth knowing, the more we must love it. Now love is greater than knowledge whenever knowledge itself does not really unite us to the object of our knowledge, so that St Paul can deliberately put charity above faith, since faith is the knowledge of God by means of ideas which are themselves created and limited and inadequate, while charity sweeps us up and carries us right along to God himself. Hence, it was an axiom among the mediaeval theologians that love is more unifying than knowledge, so that in the indwelling of the Holy Spirit in our hearts we must expect to find not only that he is the object of our intelligence, but also that he has a place in our hearts. Indeed, it is impossible to conceive any experimental knowledge which does not also include in it the notion of love.

This love or friendship between ourselves and the Holy Spirit, if by friendship we mean anything like that of which we have experience in our human relations, implies three things. First of all, friendship implies that we do not love people for what we can get out of them, for that would be an insult to a friend; it would mean selfishness or even animal passion. Friendship implies that we come for what we can give

far more than that we come for what we can get. We love because we
have helped is more often the true order of the origins of friendship
than we help because we have loved. Secondly, friendship, to be complete, must be mutual. There may indeed be love when some poor,
forlorn soul is never requited in its affection, but that is not what we
mean by a friend or by friendship. Friendship implies action, a desire
for each other, a sympathy. Thirdly, friendship implies a common bond
of likeness, or similarity of condition or life, some equality. Of course, it
is evident from classic instances that friendship may exist between a
shepherd lad and the son of a king (though perhaps Jonathan's
princedom was very little removed from shepherd life), yet the very
friendship itself must produce equality between them. Said the Latin
proverb: 'Friendship either finds or makes men equal.'

Now, to be perfectly literal in our use of the word, we must expect to
find these things reproduced in our friendship with the Spirit of God;
and, wonderful as it is, these things are reproduced. For God certainly
loves us for no benefit that he can obtain from his love. He certainly
had no need of us, nor do we in any sense fill up anything that is
wanting to his life. Before we were, or the world was created, the ever-
Blessed Three-in-One enjoyed to the full the complete peace and joy
and energy of existence. We are no late development of his being, but
only came because of his inherent goodness that was always prodigal
of itself. He is our friend, not for his need, but for ours. He is our friend,
not for what he could get, but for what he could give – his life. Again,
his friendship is certainly mutual, for as St John says: 'Let us therefore
love God because God first hath loved us' (John 4:19). There is no
yearning on our part which is not more than paralleled on his. I can
say not only that I love God, but that he is my friend. Thirdly, I may
even dare to assert that there is a common bond of likeness and
equality between myself and him. He has stooped to my level only that
he might lift me to his own. He became man that he might make man
God, and so, equally, the Holy Spirit dwells in me that I may dwell in
him. 'Friendship either finds or makes men equal.' It found us apart, it
makes us one. By grace I am raised to a supernatural level. I know him
in some sort as he is; I am immediately united to him by the bond of
love.

This Presence the same as that in Heaven
This union, then, between God and my soul, effected by grace, is real
and true. It is something more than faith can secure, a nearer
relationship, a deeper, more personal knowledge, a more ardent and

personal love. Indeed, so wonderful is this union, that the teaching of the Church has been forcibly expressed in Pope Leo encyclical, by saying that the only difference between it and the vision of heaven is a difference of condition or state; a difference purely accidental, not essential. Heaven, with all its meaning, its wonders of which eye and ear and heart are ignorant, can be begun here. Moreover, it must be insisted that this is not merely given to chosen souls whose sanctity is so heroic as to qualify them for canonization; it is the heritage of every soul in a state of grace. When I step outside the confessional box after due repentance and the absolution of the priest, I am in a state of grace. At once, then, this blessed union takes effect. Within me is the Holy Spirit, dwelling there, sent, given. As the object of knowledge he can be experienced by me in a personal and familiar way. I can know him even as I am known. As the object of love he becomes my friend, stooping to my level, lifting me to his. At once, then, though still in a merely rudimentary way, can dawn upon me the glories of my ultimate reward. Even now, upon earth, I have crossed the threshold of heaven.

In order to enjoy that ultimate vision of God, two things will be necessary. First, I shall need to be strengthened so as to survive the splendor and joy of it. No man can see God and live, for, like St Paul on the road to Damascus, the splendor of the vision would wholly obscure the sight. Just as a tremendous noise will strain the hearing of the ear, or an over-bright light will dazzle the eyes to blindness, or an overwhelming joy will break the heart with happiness, so would the vision of God strike with annihilation the poor weak soul. Hence the light of glory, as it is called by the theologians, has to be brought into use. By this is meant that strengthening of the human faculties which enables them without harm to confront the truth, goodness, power, beauty of God. Secondly, this vision implies contact with God. It is no question simply of faith or hope, but of sight and possession, so that there should be no more reproductions or reflections of God, but God himself. Those two things sum up what we mean by the beatific vision. Now, then, if there is a similarity of kind between that union in heaven and the union that can be reflected on earth, then grace in this life must play the part of the light of glory in the next, and I must be able in consequence to enter into personal relations and immediate contact with God.

Such, then, is the likeness between the indwelling of the Spirit and the beatific vision. Wherein comes the difference? The difference, one may say, is largely a difference of consciousness. Here on earth I have so much to distract me that I cannot possibly devote myself in the same way as then I shall be able to do. There are things here that have got to be done, and there is the body itself which can only stand a certain amount of concentration and intensity. If strained too much, it just breaks down and fails. All this complicates and hampers me. But in heaven I shall take on something (of course a great deal intensified) of the consciousness and alertness of youth. A child can thoroughly enjoy itself, for it has the happy faculty of forgetting the rest of life, all its troubles, anxieties, fears. Heaven, then, means the lopping off of all those menaces, and the consequent full appreciation of God in knowledge and love. Hence I must not be disturbed if here on earth all these wonderful things which I learn about concerning the indwelling of the Holy Spirit do not seem to take place. It is very unfortunate that I do not appreciate them, but it is something at least to know that they are there.

11 INDWELLING OF THE TRINITY

So FAR it has been taken for granted that the indwelling is proper to the Holy Spirit, but it must now be added that it is really an indwelling of the Blessed Trinity. It is true that Scripture seldom speaks of the three Persons as dwelling in the soul, stillness of their being given or sent. But every reason for which we attribute this to the Holy Ghost would hold equally well of the other two Persons. By grace we are made partakers of God's divine nature; he comes to us as the object of our knowledge and love. Why should we suppose that this divine presence applies directly only to the Spirit of God? The only reason, of course, is the impressive wording of the New Testament. But even here, there are equally strong indications that more than the Holy Ghost is implied: 'If any man will love me he will keep my word, and my Father will love him, and we will come to him, and will make our abode with him....But the Paraclete, the Holy Ghost, whom the Father will send in my name, he will teach you all things and bring all things to your mind whatsoever I shall have said to you.' Here it is clearly stated that, after our Lord has died, his teaching will be upheld by the Spirit, but that this indwelling will include also the abiding presence of Father and Son.

Why, then, is it repeated so often that the Holy Ghost is to be sent into our hearts, is to be given to us, is to dwell in our midst? It is for the same reason that we attribute certain definite acts to the Blessed Persons of the Trinity, the more easily to discern and appreciate the distinction between them. In the Creed itself we attribute creation to God, the Father Almighty, though we know that Son and Spirit, also with the Father, called the world out of nothingness. So again to the Son we attribute wisdom and beauty, turning in our imagination to him as the Word of God, the figure of his substance, the brightness of his glory, and to the Holy Spirit we more often attribute God's love and joy.

Consequently, it must be noted that this indwelling of the Spirit of God is not so absolutely and distinctly proper to God the Holy Ghost, as the Incarnation is proper to God the Son. There the Son, and he alone, became man. It was his personality alone to which human nature was joined in a substantial union. But in the present case there is no such unique connection between the soul and the Spirit of God; it is rather the Blessed Trinity itself that enters into occupation and dwells in the heart.

Of course, that makes the wonder not less, but greater. To think that within the borders of my being is conducted the whole life of the Blessed Three-in-One; that the Father is forever knowing himself in the Son, and that Father and Son are forever loving themselves in the Spirit; that the power and eternity of the Father, whereby creation was called into being, and by whose fiat the visible world will one day break up and fall to pieces; that the wisdom and beauty of the Son, which catch the soul of man as in the meshes of a net, and drive generations of men to a wandering pilgrimage, at the peril of life, to rescue an empty tomb in the wild fury of a crusade; that the love of the Holy Spirit, which completes the life of God and was typified in the tongues of fire and the rush of a great wind at Pentecost; that the power and eternity of the Father, the wisdom and beauty of the Son, the love and joy of the Spirit, are for all time in my heart. What reverence for my human home of God, reverence alike for soul and body!

Effects of this Presence

It is clear that so tremendous a presence as this indwelling must have tremendous results. If, as I believe, Father and Son and Spirit are always within me by grace, the effect upon my soul should be considerable. To begin with, the very nearness to God which this indwelling secures must make a great difference to my outlook on life. To have within me the ever-Blessed Trinity is more than an honor, it is a responsibility; it is more than responsibility, for it is the greatest grace of all.

By grace, then, I receive this indwelling of the Spirit of God and thereby come into a new and wonderful union with the Blessed Trinity. Now such a union must have its purpose. Our Lord told us that he was going to send to our hearts the Holy Spirit. I must, consequently, expect that the results of this indwelling are judged by God to be considerable, and that it is of much moment to me that I should discover them. The Incarnation brought its train of attendant effects which I have to study: the redemption, the sacraments, the sanctifying of all immaterial creation by its union through man with the divinity. This indwelling also must therefore have its effects, the knowledge of which must necessarily make a difference in my life.

By baptism the beginning comes of this great grace. As a child, with my senses hardly at all awake to external life, I had God in my midst. Do I wonder now at the charm of early innocence, when a soul sits silently holding God as its center? It is not that there are dim memories of a pre-existence before birth, but there are always haunting dreams of a true friendship on earth. Baptism begins that early work. At the moment of conversion, when suddenly I was drawn into a tender realization of God's demands and my own heart's hunger, the indwelling of the Spirit became more consciously operative with its flood of light and love. Since then, the sacraments have poured out on me fuller measures of God's grace and that divine presence should therefore assume larger proportions in my life. I am now the dwelling place of God.

Forgiveness of Sin

To understand this first and great effect of grace, I must know what sin is, and to grasp sin in its fullness I must comprehend God. To see the heinousness of what is done against him I must first realize what he is himself. I have to go through all my ideas of God, my ideas of his majesty, his power, his tenderness, his justice, his mercy. I have got to realize all that he has done for man before I can take in the meaning of man's actions against God. Now, it is against one so perfect, so tender, so divine, that sin is committed; a wanton, brutal outrage against an almost over fond love. Ingratitude, treachery, disloyalty, united in the basest form.

God is just, as well as merciful, so that there had to be an immediate result of sin. Man may see no difference between himself before and after he has sinned, but for all that a great difference was set up. His soul had been on terms of friendship with God, for it had turned irresistibly to him, as a flower growing in a dark place turns irresistibly to where the hardy daylight makes its way into the gloom. That friendship is at once broken, for sin means that the soul has deliberately turned its back upon God and is facing the other way, and thus it has been able by some fatal power to prevent God's everlasting love from having any effect upon it. God cannot hate; but we can stop his love from touching us. At once, then, by grievous sin the soul becomes despoiled of its supernatural goods: sanctifying grace, which is the pledge and expression of God's friendship, is banished; charity, which is nothing else than the love of God, the infused virtues, the gifts, are all taken away. Only faith and hope survive, but emptied of their richness of life. Even God himself goes out from the midst of the soul, as the Romans heard the voice crying from the Temple just before its destruction: Let us go hence. Let us go hence.

Grace, then, operates to restore all these lost wonders. Sin itself is forgiven, all the ingratitude and disloyalty put aside, not simply in the sense that God forgets them or chooses not to consider them, but in the sense that they are completely wiped away. That is what the forgiveness of sin implies. God is once more back in the soul. He had always been there as the Creator, without whose supporting hand the soul would be back in its nothingness, but he is now there again as Father and Master and Friend. We are far too apt to look upon forgiveness as a merely negative thing, a removal, a cleansing, and not enough as a return to something great and good and beautiful, the triumphant entrance into our souls of the Father, the Son, and the Spirit.

Justification

There is something in the forgiveness of sin which implies an element of positive good, and this is called justification. It means that the attitude of God towards forgiven sin is believed by the Catholic Church to be no mere neglect or forgetfulness of its evil, but an actual and complete forgiveness.

Briefly, then, it may be stated that it is not simply that God does not impute evil, but that he forgives it. It is as though a rebellion had taken place and its leader had been captured and brought before his offended sovereign. Now the king might do either of two things, if he wished not to punish the culprit. He might simply bid him go off and never appear again, or he might go even further by actually forgiving the rebellion and receiving the rebel back into favor. It is one thing to say that no punishment will be imposed, it is another to say that the crime is forgiven and that everything is to go on as though nothing had happened. In the first case, we might say that the king chose not to impute the sin; in the other, that he forgave and justified the sinner. It is just this, then, that the Catholic Church means when she teaches justification as implied in the idea of forgiveness. It is just this, too, that our Lord meant when he detailed his beautiful parable about the prodigal son. The boy's return home does not mean merely that the father refrains from punishment, but that there is a welcome so hearty and so complete that the serious-minded elder brother, coming in from his long labor in the fields, is rather scandalized by its suddenness and its intensity. Such, indeed, is God's treatment of the soul. He is so generous, so determined not to be outdone by any sorrow on the part of the sinner, that he overwhelms the converted soul with the most splendid favors.

But in this connection we must see in justification a process by which the presence of God is again achieved by man By sin grace was lost, and with grace went out the Divine Three-in-One, the temple was desecrated, the veil of the Holy of Holies was utterly rent. Then sin is forgiven and once more the sacred home is occupied by God. Moreover, when God comes to the soul he comes with his full strength of love and thereby gives a new energy and life to man. We love because of some beauty, goodness, excellence, that we see in others. We love because of what is in them. It is their gifts that cause or ignite our love. But God, who is the only cause himself, created excellences by love. We are not loved because we are good; we are good because we are loved, so that this indwelling fashions us after God's own heart. 'It is the love of God,' says St Thomas (Summa theol., I, 20, 2), 'that produces and creates goodness in things ' The divine presence of God in the soul, effected by sanctifying grace, makes the soul more worthy a temple, more fit a home. God does not come to us because we are fit, but we are fit because God comes to us.

Deification
This strong expression is used by St Augustine and many of the Fathers to describe one of the effects of grace. By grace we are deified, i.e., made into gods. Right at the beginning of all the woes of humanity when, in the Garden of Eden, Adam and Eve first were tempted, the lying spirit promised that the reward of disobedience would be that they should become 'as gods'. The result of sin could hardly be that, so man, made only a little lower than the angels, can at times find himself rebuked by the very beasts. Yet the promise was fulfilled in the end, since the Incarnation really effected that transformation, and God, by becoming human, made man divine. St Peter, in his Second Epistle (4:1), insinuates the same truth when he describes the great promises of Christ making us 'partakers of the divine nature'. The work of grace is something superhuman and divine. Creation pours into us the divine gift of existence and therefore makes us partakers in the divine being, for existence implies a participation in the being of God. The indwelling of the Blessed Trinity does even more, for by it we participate not only in the divine being, but in the divine nature, and fulfill the prophecy of our Lord: 'Ye are gods.' Justification, therefore, is a higher gift than creation, since it does more for us.

This divine participation is what is implied in many texts which allude to the sacrament of baptism, for the purpose of baptism is just that: to make us children of God. The phrases concerning 'new birth' and 'being born again' all are intended to convey the same idea: that the soul, by means of this sacrament, is lifted above its normal existence and lives a new life. This life is lived 'with Christ in God,' i.e., it is a sort of entrance within the charmed circle of the Trinity, or more accurately, it is that the Blessed Trinity inhabits our soul and enters into our own small life, which at once takes on a new and higher importance. In it, henceforth, can be nothing small or mean.

For the same reason, our Lord speaks of it to the Samaritan woman as 'the gift of God,' beside which all his other benefactions fade into nothingness. Again, it is a 'fountain of living water,' it is a 'refreshment,' it is 'life' itself. Not the stagnant water that remains in a pool in some dark wood, but a stream gushing out from its source, irrigating the ground on every side, soaking through to all the thirsting roots about it, giving freshness and vitality to the whole district through which it wanders. Life indeed it bears as its great gift, and so does sanctifying grace carry within it the vitalizing power needed by the soul.

The participation in the divine nature is therefore no mere metaphor, but is a real fact. The indwelling of God makes the soul like to God. I find myself influenced by the people with whom I live, picking up their expressions, copying their tricks and habits, following out their thoughts, absorbing their principles, growing daily like them. With God at the center of my life, the same effect is produced, and slowly, patiently, almost unconsciously, I find myself infected by his spirit. What he loves becomes my ideal; what he hates, my detestation. But it is even closer than this; no mere concord of wills or harmony of ideas, but a real and true elevation to the life of God. Grace is formally in God, at the back, so to say, of his divine nature, the inner essence of himself. By receiving it, therefore, I receive something of God, and begin to be able to perform divine actions. I can begin to know God even as I am known, to taste his sweetness, and by his favor to have personal, experimental knowledge of him. To act divinely is only possible to those who are made divine. This becomes the formal union with God, its terms, its end, its purpose. Therefore, we become deified in our essence by grace, in our intelligence by its light, in our will by charity..

Adopted Sonship

Here again we have to realize that the sonship of God is no mere metaphor, no mere name, but a deep and true fact of huge significance. 'Behold what manner of charity the Father hath bestowed upon us, that we should be called and should be the sons of God!' (1 John 3). We become the sons of God. St Paul very gladly quotes the saying of a

Greek poet that men are the offspring of God, making use of a particular word which necessarily implies that both the begetter and the begotten are of the same nature. A sonship, indeed, is what our Lord incessantly teaches the apostles to regard as their high privilege, for God is not only his Father, but theirs: 'Thus shalt thou pray, Our Father.' With the Gospels it is in constant use as the view of God that Christianity came especially to teach. The Epistles are equally insistent on the same view, for St Paul is perpetually calling to mind the wonderful prerogatives whereby we cry: 'Abba: Father.' We are spoken of as co-heirs of Christ, as children of God. St John, St Peter, and St James repeat the same message as the evident result of the Incarnation, for by it we learn that God became the Son of Man, and man the son of God.

Yet it must also be admitted that this sonship of God, which is the common property of all just souls and is the result of the indwelling of God in the soul, does not mean that we are so by nature, but only by adoption. Now adoption, as it is practiced by law, implies that the child to be adopted is not already the son, that the new relationship is entered upon entirely at the free choice of the person adopting, that the child becomes the legal heir to the inheritance of the adopting father. It is perfectly evident that all these conditions are fulfilled in the case of God's adoption, for we were certainly no children of his before his adoption of us as sons. Strangers we were, estranged indeed by the absence of grace and the high gifts of God. Naturally we were made by him, but had put ourselves far from him. 'You were as sheep going astray.' Then this adoption of us by God was indeed and could only have been at his free choice, through no merits of ours, but solely according to the deliberate action of his own will, for 'you have not chosen me but I have chosen you'. 'So that it is not of him that willeth nor of him that runneth, but of God that showeth mercy.' Finally, the inheritance is indeed ours by right and title of legal inheritance. We are co-heirs with Christ and our human nature is lifted up to the level of God; not, of course, that we supplant him who is by nature the true Son of God, but that we are taken into partnership with him and share in him the wonderful riches of God.

Here, then, I may learn the worth and dignity of the Christian name. I am a true son of God, and what else matters upon earth? I have indeed to go about my life with its vocation and all that is entailed in it. I have to work for my living, it may be, or take my place in the family, or lead my own solitary existence. I have to strive to be efficient and effective in the material things of life that fall to my share to be done. But it is this sonship of God that alone makes any matter in the world. What nobler ideal, or fancy, or desire, can a man have than to be called and to be the son of God; to know that he has been drawn into the close union of God; to feel within his very essence the presence of God; to have personal experience of the Father, Son, and Spirit as the objects of his knowledge and love?

Heirs of God

One of the conditions of adoption is that the newly-chosen son should become the legal heir of the new father. Without this legal consequence adoption has no meaning. Merely to get a boy to enter a family circle does not imply adoption, for this last has a distinct meaning with a distinct purpose. If, then, we are the sons of God, we are really possessed of a right to his divine inheritance. Heaven has been made indeed our home. We speak of it in our hymns as patria, which we can translate as the 'land of our fathers'. We claim it in virtue of our parentage, and our parentage is of God. If, then, he is our Father, not by nature, but by adoption, i.e., by grace, we are nonetheless his heirs and have some sort of right over his possessions and riches.

I can, therefore, truthfully speak of myself as an heir of God. Of course, I cannot mean that there is any possible question of 'the death of the testator,' i.e., of God. That is quite clearly of no significance here. But adoption does give me some sort of claim to the heritage of God. Now the law defines a heritage as that by which a man is made rich. It includes not the riches only, but the source of the riches, so that if I have a claim to God's riches, I have a claim also upon the source of those riches. For the heir is entitled not merely to a legacy, but to the whole of the fortune. I have a right to the whole fortune of God, to the whole universe. At once, as soon as I realize it, the whole of the world is mine. It is the doctrine of the mystics, which was misunderstood and led astray the communists of the Middle Ages. These claimed a common ownership of the wealth of all the world, whereas what was intended was that we should look upon the whole world as ours. To me, then, in life, nothing can be strange or distant or apart. No places can there be where my mind cannot enter and roam at will and feel itself at home; no things can be profane, no people who are not tabernacles of God, no part of life that is not steeped in that living presence. The only possible boundary is the love and the grace of God. There will, indeed, come evil frontiers beyond which my soul could never dwell. But all else is of God and is therefore my right. All creation is mine; the wonder and beauty of it, life and death, pleasure alike and pain, yield up to me their secrets and disclose the hidden name of God.

Here, then, I can find that divine wealth, to inherit which has been the purpose of the adoption by God. Wherever I turn I shall find him. Whether life has smooth ways or rough, whether she hangs my path with lights or hides me in gloom, I am the heir to all that earth or sea or sky can boast of as their possession. Indeed, these are only the rich things of God, whereas I have a claim upon even more. I have a claim upon the very source of this wealth, that is, upon God himself, for he is the sole source of all his greatness. I have a right to God him-self. He is mine He who holds in the hollow of his hands the fabric of the world, who with his divine power supports, and with his providence directs, the intricate pattern of the world, has himself by creation entered deeply into the world; at the heart of everything he lies hid. But even more by grace he comes in a fuller, richer way into the depths of the soul. Here in me are Father, Son, and Spirit. Dear God, teach me to understand the wonder of this indwelling, to appreciate its worth, to be thankful for its condescension, to reverence its place of choice, to be conscious of its perpetual upholding. By it I am an heir to the fullness of the divine riches. By it I, a creature, possess in his fullness my Creator, Redeemer, Lord.

12   FRUITS OF GOD'S LOVE

I HAVE God the Holy Spirit within me. He comes to me in order that I may surrender myself to him. Of course, I cannot merge my personality into his to the extent of having no power of my own, but God has such infinite dominion over the heart of man that he is able to move the will without in any sense violating its freedom. In the liturgy of the Church there are several prayers which speak about God 'compelling our rebellious wills'. Now, for anyone else to 'compel my will' would be to destroy it as a will, since 'the will suffereth no compulsion'. I cannot be made to will against my will; that would be a contradiction, though I can be made to act against my will, for my actions do not necessarily imply that my will is in them. Hence, no one else but God can move my will without utterly destroying my moral freedom, for God is intimate to the will and moves it, not really as an external but as an internal power. St Thomas Aquinas repeatedly refers to this and says over and over again that God is so intimately united to man and so powerful that not only can he move man to will, but move him to will freely, by affecting not only the action of man but the very mode of the action.

Man is such that, whether in a state of grace or not, his will is in the hands of God, to be moved by man freely, but not so as to exclude God's movement. Naturally enough, it is far easier to say this than to explain it. Indeed, the mere statement is all that is actually binding upon faith, and the particular explanation favored by St Thomas, in his general acceptance of St Augustine's teaching, comes to us largely as of deep and abiding moment on account of the clear reasons given and the great authority of his name; but in any case there is something far more special in the guidance of the Holy Spirit sought for by the soul in its endeavor to 'live godly in Christ Jesus'. It has to yield itself to the promptings of God, be eager to catch his every whisper, and quick in its obedience to his every call. For this to be achieved, the first work is an emptying-out of the soul. Every obstacle has to be got rid of; any attachment to creatures that obscures God's light has to be broken through (though not every attachment to creatures, since unless I love man whom I see, I cannot possibly know what love means when applied to God, nor can I suppose myself to be able to understand or love God, whom I do not see). First, then, to cleanse my soul by leveling and smoothing and clearing its surface and depths.

Then I must yield myself into his arms. I shall not know very often the way he wishes me to go. It may be only one step at a time, and then darkness again; or I may be taken swiftly and surely and openly along a clear road. That is his business, not mine, only I must be prepared not to be able to follow always the meaning of what he wants of me. It is not necessary at all that I should know. If I am faithful and loyal and full of trust, things will gradually settle themselves, and I shall at least be able to look back and understand the significance and purpose of many things that at first appeared accidental and even in opposition to the end I considered God had in view for me. Thus, by looking back, I can sometimes get a shrewd idea of what is to follow; but often it is only a guess, nothing more than that. Still, generally, it would seem that people who surrender themselves to God do get a sense or a feeling which leads them right and makes them sure. It is the divine tenderness stooping to poor muddled humanity and making it transfigured with God's own glory. The advance, then, whether consciously grasped or not, is in due proportion to the purity and fidelity of the soul: purity in its act of cleansing, fidelity in its subjection to the promptings of the Holy Spirit.

Gifts of the Holy Spirit
To live the spiritual life to its fullness, we need the instinctive governances of the Holy Ghost. All day long the Holy Spirit is speaking to us in many ways. He is offering us his heavenly counsel, enlightening our minds to an ever more complete understanding of the deep truths of faith, and generally imparting to us that deep knowledge without which we cannot make progress. Reason and common sense have their own contribution to make in opening our minds and hearts to a proper interpretation of all that is about us and within us, but reason and common sense have themselves also to be supernaturalizes, to be illumined by the light of a far higher plane of truth. Hence the need of this divine instinct is patent to anyone who considers the purpose and destiny of the soul. But it is difficult at times to understand and to grasp surely the words of divine wisdom, since by sin's coarseness the refinement of the soul is dulled and rendered but little responsive; or rather, it is not so much a matter of being responsive to a message as primarily of hearing and understanding it. It seems obvious that God must be speaking to me almost without ceasing; it is equally obvious that very little of this is noticed.

Here, then, am I in the world and needing the governance of God's instinct. Here, too, is this whispered counsel and enlightenment of God perpetually being made to me. Yet, though given by God, and needed by me, this counsel and enlightenment must frequently be entirely lost to me. Hence it is clear that neither my need nor God's inspiration suffices. Something else is required by means of which I can make use of that inspiration, hear its message, discover its meaning, apply its advice to myself; else am I no better than a general who possesses the full plan of his allies, but written in a code that he cannot read.

To produce this reaction or perception is the work of the sevenfold gifts. They are habits infused into the soul, which strengthen its natural powers and make them responsive to every breath of God and capable of heroic acts of virtue. The gifts enable my eyes to see what had else been hidden, my ears quick to catch what had else not been heard; the gifts do not, so to say, supply eye or ear, but make more delicate and sensitive the eye and ear already there. Their business is to intensify rather than to create powers established in me by grace. Less excellent necessarily than the theological virtues, which unite me to God, they are yet more excellent than the other virtues, though, being rooted in charity and thereby connected among themselves, they are also part of the dowry that charity brings in her train. On this account it is clear that from the moment of baptism the sevenfold gifts are the possession of the soul, and whosoever holds one, holds all; yet by the sacrament of confirmation it would appear certain that something further is added, some more delicate perception, some livelier sensitivity; or it may be, as other theologians point out, that by confirmation they are more steadily fixed in the soul, more fully established, more firmly held. But in any case, it is clear what they are to me: habits whereby I am perfected to obey the Holy Spirit of God.

Beatitudes
The possession of the sevenfold gifts results in the performance of certain virtuous acts, for it is obvious that if I am so blessed by the gifts that I find myself made increasingly perceptive of divine currents previously lost to me, I can hardly help acting in a new way. Not only shall I find that what seemed to me before to be evil now appears to me to be a blessing, but on that very account what before I tried to avoid, or, having got, tried to be rid of, I shall now accept, perhaps even seek. Similarly, whereas then I was weak, now I am strong; and increase of strength means new activities, new energy put into the old work, and finding its way out into works altogether new. My emotions, finally, which dominated my life, slip now into a subordinate position, and while as actively employed as before, are held under discipline. It

is clear, therefore, that the gifts will not leave me where I was before, but will influence my actions and alter my vision.

I find, then, that these new habits will develop into new activities. But this means also that I have a new idea as to the means of achieving the full happiness of life. Once I thought happiness meant comfort, now I see that it means something quite different. My view of happiness has changed. I am therefore obliged to change also my idea as to the means and conditions whereby and in which happiness can be found. That is what our Lord meant by promulgating the eight beatitudes. These are the new blessedness, so to say, which results from finding that happiness now means the knowledge and love of God Things that previously I fled from I now seek; things once my bugbear, are now the objects of my delight. Poverty, meekness, mourning, the hunger and thirst after justice, cleanness of heart, the making of peace, mercy, the suffering of persecution for justice's sake, are now found to be the steps to be trod, the conditions to be secured before happiness can be finally secured.

These things, then, are beatitudes to me. They are acts which I finally achieve by means of the new enlightenment gained through the gifts of God. Actively I am merciful and meek and clean of heart. I perform these actions, and they are the result of visions seen and counsels heard, through the new sensitivity to the divine instinctive guidance that formerly passed me by without finding any response in my heart. To be forever pursuing now peace and sorrow, and, at whatever cost, justice, is an energizing state of life which is due entirely to the new perception of the value of these things, so that we are right in asserting that the beatitudes are nothing other than certain actions, praised by our Lord and practiced by us, as a result of the establishment in our souls of seven definite habits. But not only are they actions, they produce joy in the heart; for which reason we call them beatitudes. They show what is truly blessed and thereby give me, even here on earth, a foretaste of the bliss of final happiness.

The Fruits of the Spirit

Besides the beatitudes, there are other acts that follow from the gifts when properly exercised. The beatitudes are means which, under the light infused by God, are valued at their true worth as leading finally to happiness in its more complete sense. But when these are thus put into practice, for the soul understands the new meaning life gathers, they do not terminate the wonders of the action of grace. As a boy, one finds life full of interest and dawning with the glories of success. The world of nature has such manifest beauties that these quickly entrance and thrill the soul. The sun and grass and flowers and woods and waters make no secret of their kinship with their Creator; Francis Thompson found them 'garrulous of God,' so garrulous that in our youth we see that life is full of very good things. Then comes the reaction (to many even before full manhood), when life is found to be full of illusion. Life is now judged a melancholy business, apt to fail you just when the need of it is most discovered, hard to be certain of; it is the age of romantic melancholy, when most people put into verse their sorrow at the disappointment to be found in all things of beauty. Every tree and flower and 'dear gazelle' is no sooner loved than it is lost through death or misunderstanding.

Then, finally, the balance is set right. The two phases pass. They are both true only as half truths. There is no denying that life is good and beautiful and thrilling. The boy's vision is correct. Yet it is equally true to say that there is sorrow and suffering and death and disappointment in all human things. But a new phase, blessedly a last phase, dawns upon the soul. Sorrow and pain are real, but the old happiness of boyhood is made to fit in and triumph over them by the sudden realization that strength is the lesson to be learned. Sorrow comes that discipline may be born in the soul, self-restraint, humility Life is hard, but its very hardness is no evil, but our means of achieving good. That is the atmosphere of the beatitudes, the message they bring, the teaching they imparted from the Sermon on the Mount. Poverty, cleanness of heart, mercy, meekness, are all things difficult to acquire, but they give a real true blessedness to the soul that will see their value. Life is no longer a disappointment, but the training ground of all good.

Finally, there follow other acts, too many to number, though there are twelve usually given, which result from the gifts and the beatitudes. These are called the fruits of the Holy Ghost, for they represent, in that metaphorical sense, the ultimate result of the gifts. They are the last and sweetest consequences of the sevenfold habits infused by the Spirit. Indeed, just as trees are grown in an orchard because of their fruits, and just as it can be said that the fruit is, from the gardener's point of view, the purpose for which the tree is cultivated (for of the fruitless fig tree our Lord asked why it cumbered the ground), so these fruits of the Holy Ghost (charity, joy, peace, patience, benignity, goodness, longanimity, mildness, faith, modesty, continency, chastity – Gal. 5: 22) can be looked upon as the purpose for which the gifts were given. Endlessly could the list of these fruits be extended, for St Paul has chosen only a few; but these that he names are what a man delights in when he has received the gifts and has understood and valued the beatitudes. Sweetness is what they add to virtue, ease, comfort. I not only hunger and thirst after justice, but enjoy the very pain of the pursuit.

Knowledge This gift of God illumines and perfects the intelligence. The purpose of the gifts, it has been explained, is to make the soul more alive to and more appreciative of the whispered instinct of God; not to create new faculties, but to increase the power of those already existing. My mind, then, has to be supernaturalized and refined to that pitch of perception which will enable it to grasp and to understand God's message. Now the mind works upon a great variety of subjects. It has whole worlds to conquer, planes of thought which are very clearly distinguishable; yet in its every activity it needs this divine refinement so that four gifts are allotted to perform this complete enlightenment of the mind. Knowledge overcomes ignorance and is concerned with the facts, visible and sense-perceived, in creation; for by the Council of the Vatican it is laid down as part of the deposit of faith that human reason can prove the existence of God altogether apart from the supernatural motives which grace supplies. The visible world is held to contain ample proofs which in themselves are adequate logically to convince human understanding of the existence of God. Individual reason may fail to satisfy itself; people may declare truthfully that they are not convinced; the Church insists only that it can be done.

Knowledge, however, in this sense is a gift of God whereby we discover him in his own creation and in the works of man It is no mere task set to reason for detecting the Creator in his handiwork, but an actual vision by which the soul is super-naturalized and sees him patently everywhere. The beauteous face of nature is seen as a veil which hides a beauty more sublime. Things of dread as well as things of loveliness come into the scheme, things trivial and things tremendous, things majestic and things homely, all that God has made. Even man's work, who is himself only one of the greater masterpieces of the great Artificer, is affected by this new light with which the world is flooded. The delicate pieces of machinery constructed by human ingenuity, that gain in wonder and in power, are still God's work at one remove; they are the fruits of a mind that he has constructed, and they do not exhaust the capacity of that mind. They reveal hidden potentialities and express actual achievements. Weapons of destruction, with all the horror they inspire, are witnesses again to that parent-intelligence whence was begotten man himself. All this, of course, as soon as considered, is admitted by every believer in God, but the gift of knowledge makes it realized and seen steadfastly.

Life, then, of itself is full of illusion. That is the cry, desolating and pitiful, which arises from the higher followers of every religious faith. Man is bound to the wheel, his mind is compassed with infirmity, he is born into ignorance. Desire tumultuously hustles all his days. He needs, therefore, some light whereby he may find the true inner meaning of all with which he comes in contact. In the gift of knowledge is such a true vision, understanding, vouchsafed him of the visible things of creation. He will realize as much, perhaps even more, than before the attraction of beauty, only it will be no snare, but a beckoning light. He will find in it now no illusion, but the perfect image of a greater beauty. The charm of the world about him will become greater, the wonders of nature, the intricate pattern of mechanical appliances, the fury of storms, the tumult of the wind, the terrific force of pestilence, the psychological facts of man's mind, the construction of his frame, the grouping of his social instincts, all now will be alive with God, shot through with the divine splendor , elevated to his order of life, eloquent of his name – a deepening knowledge of God achieved through a knowledge of his creatures.

Understanding
There is another gift required to perfect the intelligence when it is engaged upon the principles of truth. The mind was created by God to exercise itself upon truth; primarily, the Supreme Truth, and secondarily, all truths which by their essence must be radiations from the Supreme Truth. These truths are of endless variety, both in their relationship to each other and in the particular line in which they operate. They are the truths of arts and science, the intricate yet unchanging laws that govern the growth and development of matter, the complicated processes whereby organic beings build up their tissues and multiply themselves by means of the cell principle. There are also the 'curious' laws, as they are called, that effect gravitation, that have to be counted upon in the science of architecture, and in all the various kindred crafts of man. There are principles, too, that underlie the whole series of the arts, principles of truth and life and beauty. Upon these the mind must feed, and in them all the mind must be able to trace the character and being of God. But there are also far higher truths which are taught only by revelation, safeguarded by authority, grouped under the title of faith. These truths are higher than the others, since they directly concern a higher being, i.e., God. All truths are truths about God, but the truths of faith concern themselves immediately with the being, life, and actions of God. Understanding,

therefore, is the gift perfecting the mind for these.

It may seem, perhaps, that the light of faith is itself sufficient, and that no further gift were needed, since it is the very purpose of faith to make us accept this revelation of God, enlightening and strengthening the intelligence till under the dominion of the will it says: 'I believe.' It is true that faith suffices for this, but we require something more than faith, or at least if we do not absolutely require more, we shall progress more rapidly and further when we are not only able to believe but to understand. In every article of faith there is always something which is mysterious or hidden, some obscurity due not to the entanglement of facts, but to the weakness of the human mind. Of course, this must to some extent always exist, for man can never hope to comprehend God till by the beatific vision he sees him face to face; but a good deal of the obscurity can be lifted by the mere operation of the mind under the light of God, not arising purely from study, but from the depth of love enkindled by God. It is a commonplace in the lives of the saints that without instruction they do yet manage to learn the deep mysteries of God; the same is true of many simple souls whom we meet from time to time in the world. They not only believe, but penetrate the truths of faith.

Here, then, I have ready to hand a most useful gift of God. I desire not only to believe, but to absorb and to penetrate the mysteries of God. I want to taste to the full the meaning of life as a whole, to develop every power that lies in me, to make the truths of revelation blossom out ever more fully, till their hidden and mystical significance becomes gradually more clear. The pages of Holy Scripture are full of instruction, but they will not yield up their secrets save to a soul attuned by God. That can be effected by the gift of understanding I shall find by its means that these treasures are inexhaustible, that from mere abstract teaching the sayings of the Master and his apostles become full of practical meaning, that all life about me takes on a new and richer significance. History and social life open their doors to whoever has this blessed gift, and it becomes clearly seen that their maker and builder is God. The dullness of souls who will not believe, or only believe and then stop short, becomes painful to note and bothersome to put up with, but this is the price one has to pay for so fine a vision. By this, then, we peer into the depths of faith, and find them gradually and steadily growing more and more clear and penetrable.

Wisdom

All writers on the gifts of the Holy Ghost place wisdom as the highest gift of all. It takes this high position partly because its work is done in the intelligence, which is man's highest power, and partly because it is that highest power occupied to its highest capacity. Like knowledge and understanding, its business is to make us see God everywhere, in the material and spiritual creation of God, in the concrete facts of existence, and in the revealed truths of faith. It produces in a soul a sense of complete certainty and hope. Hence it is sometimes described as neighbor to hope; indeed, its finest side is often just that determined and resolute conviction with which the soul rises superior to every possible disaster and is prepared to brave every contingency in its sureness of God's final power and the efficacy of his will. It comes closer, therefore, to God himself than do either understanding or knowledge. These do, indeed, enable the soul to be continuously conscious of the divine presence, of God immanent as well as transcendent, God in the heart of the world as well as wholly above the world, and they affect this consciousness by enabling the soul to see him everywhere. They lift the veil. They show his footprints. They trace everywhere the marks of his power, wisdom, love. But it is noticeable that they lead to God from the world. I see a flower, and by the gift of knowledge I am immediately aware of the Author of its loveliness; by understanding I perceive with clearness the wonder of God's working in the world. By them I lift my eyes from earth to heaven, but by wisdom I look from heaven to see the earth.

Wisdom, therefore, implies an understanding of the world through God, whereas knowledge and understanding suppose a perception of God through the world. Wisdom takes its stand upon causes, the other two on effects. They work from creatures to Creator; wisdom looks upon all the world through the eyes of God. Consequently, the effect of wisdom is that the soul sees life as a whole. Matter and truth are to it no longer separate places of thought, but one. There is at once no distinction between them in the eyes of God, for both are manifesttations of himself and creatures of his making Hence the soul that is dowered with wisdom climbs up to God's own height, and looking down upon the world sees it 'very good,' noticing how part fits in with part, and how truths of faith and truths of science are linked one with another to form the pattern of God's design. Each has its place in the divine economy of God's plan, each is equally of God, equally sharing in his purposes, though some more than others able to express God better. The effect, then, is largely that the whole of life is co-ordinated, and equality, fraternity, liberty, become not the motto of a revolution, but of the ordered government of God.

The opposite to this gift is folly, for a man who fails in wisdom loses all true judgment of the values of human life. He is perpetually exchanging the more for the less valuable, bestowing huge gifts in just barter, as he imagines, for what is merely showy and trivial. Not by causes, but by effect does he consider life and its activities. The wise man, then, estimates everything by its highest cause. He compares and discovers, gleans the reason of God's providence, its purpose, its fitness. First principles are his guide, not the ready and practical proverbs that display the wit and worldly wisdom of the lesser man. Eternity becomes of larger moment than time, since time is merely for eternity. God's law is more convincing than man's, for man's enactments are not laws at all when they come in conflict with divine commands. Faith is so deeply in him that he judges between propositions and discovers truth against heresy. He has climbed to the heights of God and sees all the world at his feet, and knows it as God knows it, the world and its Lord and the glory of it.

Counsel

The fourth gift that perfects the intelligence acts rather as a moderating than as a stimulating influence. The soul is often impetuous in its decisions, moved by human feelings and passions, urged by desire, love, hatred, prejudice. Quickly stirred to action, it dashes into its course without any real attention or understanding of it. Frequently in life my lament has to be that I acted on the impulse of the moment. There is so much that I am sorry for, not merely because now I see what has actually resulted, but because even then I had quite sufficient reason to let me be certain what would result. I was blind, not because my eyes could not have seen, but because I gave them no leave to see. I would not carefully gaze at the difficulties, not puzzle out in patience what would most likely be the result. Even my highest powers are often my most perilous guides, since, moved by generosity, I engage myself to do what I have no right to perform, and find that I have in the end been generous not only of what is my own, but sometimes of what belongs to another; not as though I deliberately gave away what belonged to another, but just because I had no deliberation at all. I need, then, the Holy Spirit of God to endow me with the gift of counsel which corresponds to prudence.

Now prudence, which counsel helps and protects, is eminently a practical gift of God, not so high as wisdom, not so wonderful in the beauty of its vision as knowledge or understanding, yet for all a most important and homely need. The other intellectual gifts of the Spirit are more abstract. They give us just the whisper of God that enables us to see the large ways of God in the world. They give, in consequence, the great principles that are to govern us in life. Hence their importance is very great. We do so seriously need to know by what principles we are to measure life's activities, on what basis to build up the fabric of our souls, to be sure that God's laws are very clearly and definitely made manifest to us. But, after all, that is only one-half of the difficulty, for even after I know the principles of action, I have still the trouble – in some ways more full of possibilities of mistake – of applying them to concrete experience. I know that sacrifice is the law of life, I know that meekness over-indulged may be cowardice, I know that I may sin by not having anger; that is all evident, a series of platitudes. But here and now, have I come to the limit of meekness? Must I manifest my angry protests? Am I obliged to attend to my own needs and renounce the idea of sacrifice? These daily are questions that puzzle, torture, bruise me with scruples.

Just here, then, I have intense need for this practical gift of God in order to apply principles to concrete cases with nicety and precision. I am in a hurry or cannot make up my mind – shall I answer those who attack me, or shall I be silent? Our Lord was silent and made answer by turns. Counsel, then, is my need from God, the spiritual instinct whereby a practical judgment is quickly and safely made. All the more have I a tremendous need for this if my life is full of activity, if pressure of work or social life or the demands of good and useful projects or the general tendency of my family surroundings make my day crowded and absorbed, for the very combined and concentrated essence of life will need some exceedingly moderate influence to produce any sense of balance or proportion in my judgment. The people about me, I notice, become more and more irritable, mere creatures of impulse. I feel some such malign influence invading the peaceful sanctuary of my soul, disturbing its even outlook on things, driving out my serene calm. I must anchor on to this gift of God, become prudent, detached, filling the mind with the counsel of the Holy Spirit.

Fortitude

After the intelligence comes the will, which also, because of the very large part it plays in all human action, needs to be perfected by a gift of the Spirit. It is necessary to repeat that the Holy Spirit does not by his gifts bestow on the soul new powers and new faculties, but develops, refines, perfects faculties already there. It is not the creation of new eyes to see new visions, but the strengthening of the eyes of the soul so as to see more clearly and with a longer sight. The will, then, has also to be strengthened, for it is the will that lies at the very heart of all heroism. Merely to have a glimpse of greatness is but part of a hero's need. No doubt it is a larger part, for many of us never at all touch on the borders of greatness. We do not see or understand how in our little lives we can be great, we have not the imagination lit up by God, no vision. But even when that sudden showing does by God's mercy come to us, we still fall far short of it. It is too high, too ideal, too far removed from weak human nature to seem possible to us. That is to say, our will fails us. We are faced by some huge obstacle, or even by a persistent refusal to budge on behalf of someone (ourselves or another), to go forward and to do; we struggle, fail, lose heart, surrender, cease our efforts. What do we want? Fortitude, that 'persistive constancy' which to Shakespeare was the greatest quality of human wills.

How is this achieved? By appreciating the nearness of God to us. The gifts make us responsive to God with an ease and instantaneousness that operate smoothly and without friction. That is God's doing, not ours. He gives us this wonderful power of being able to register at once every passing inspiration. The gifts that refine the intelligence allow it to perceive sights which else were hidden. The gift that refines the will must do this by some kindred action. Now the difficulties that beset the will must necessarily be difficulties for whose overcoming strength is needed. Therefore the will must be refined by being made strong. How can it be made strong by the Holy Spirit? What exactly happens to its mechanism to secure for it the power of endurance? The easiest way of understanding how this effect is brought about is to suppose that the soul by its refinement, by that delicacy whereby it responds instantly to a divine impression, is quickly aware of God's nearness to it. It perceives how close it is to the Spirit of God, and the sense of this nearness makes it better able to hold on to its duty. In the old style of warfare we often read of wives and mothers coming to the field of battle that their presence might awake their men to the topmost pitch of courage. Even in the modern methods of fighting, the moral effect of the presence of the emperor or king is considered to have an effect upon the troops. Of course here it is more homely, since the familiar presence of the Holy Spirit strengthens and inspires by love, trust, sympathy.

For this reason the name Comforter was given to the Holy Spirit, in its original sense of strengthening, becoming the fort of the soul; and the result is that the recipient is able to hold on, or, in our modern slang, to 'carry on'. By nature so many of us are prone to seek our own comforts at the expense of what we know to be the higher side of us. Human respect also makes us cowardly, or the sheer monotony of perseverance dulls and wearies the soul. We get so depressed with the strain of making efforts that we are very much inclined to let the spiritual side of life go under, or at least be rendered as little heroic as possible, for it is real heroism even just to 'go on'. The 'silent pressure' of temptations, when their passion and fury have died down, is a constant worry, an unconscious weight on the mind, like the thought of war that lies heavily at the back of the consciousness of those whose external lives seem empty of war-reminders. We want to be courageous and fearless, to undergo. Then we must hold fast to God's nearness to us, and feel the virtue going out from him to us, though he does but touch the hem of our garments by his indwelling.

Piety

Besides our intelligence and will we have other faculties that go by a diversity of names; sometimes they are called the emotions, sometimes the passions, sometimes they are alluded to as the sentimental side of our nature; but by whatever name we may happen to call them, it is clear that they represent those movements of our being which are not really rational in themselves, though they can be controlled by the reason. It is simplest to divide them into two classes and to realize that they lie just on the borderline between spirit and matter, partly of soul, partly of body. These two classes are arranged according as the emotion attracts or repels man. The repelling emotions are fear, anger, hatred, etc.; the attracting ones are love, desire, joy, etc. The gift of piety enables even the emotions to be made responsive to God. It is always the notion of some perfect instrument made harmonious that most clearly shows us the work of the Holy Spirit in the gifts of God, some perfect instrument, which needs to be so nicely attuned that its every string shall give out a distinct note and shall require the least movement from the fingers of God's right hand to make its immediate response. Here, then, we have first to record the fact that the purpose of this gift is to make the emotions or passions so refined, so perfectly strung, that at once the slightest pressure of the divine instinct moves them to turn their love, desire, joy, towards God, finding in him the satisfaction of their inmost heart.

Piety, in its Latin significance (and in theology, of course, we get almost all our terms through the Latin tongue), means the filial spirit of reverence towards parents. Virgil gives to the hero of his Roman epic the repeated title of *pius*, because he wishes always to emphasize

Aeneas' devotion to his aged father. Hence it is clear that what is primarily intended here is that we should be quickly conscious of the Fatherhood of God. The mediaeval mystics, especially our homely English ones like Richard Rolle of Hampole and Mother Juliana of Norwich, were fond of talking about the Motherhood of God in order to bring out the protective and devoted side of God's care for us. Of course, God surpasses both a mother's and father's love in his ineffable love for us. But it is just that sweetness of soul in its attitude towards God that this gift produces in me: a readiness to perceive his love in every turn of fortune and to discover his gracious pity in his treatment of my life. It requires a divine indwelling of the Spirit of God to effect this in my soul, for though I may be by nature easily moved to affection, prompt to see and profit by every opening for friendship, yet I must, no less, have a difficulty in turning this toward my spiritual life without God's movement in my soul.

Perhaps the most unmistakable result of this is in the general difference between Catholic and non-Catholic nations in their ideas of religion. Even if one takes a non-Catholic nation at its best and a Catholic nation at its worst, the gulf between them is enormous, for at its lowest the religion of the Catholic nation will be attractive at least with its joy, and the non-Catholic repellent with its gloom. There is a certain hardness about all other denominations of Christianity, a certain restrained attitude of awe towards God, which, though admirable in itself, is perfectly hateful when it is made the dominant note in religion. Better joyous superstition than gloomy correctness of worship; better, far better, to find happy children who have little respect, and much comradeship, towards their parents, than neat and quiet children who are in silent awe of their parents. It is, then, to develop this side of religion that the gift of piety is given. The result is a sweetness, a gracefulness, a natural lovingness towards God and all holy persons and things, as opposed to a gloomy, respectable, awkward, self-conscious hardness towards our Father in Heaven. Clever, trained people have most to be on their guard, for the intellectual activities of the soul are apt to crowd out the gentler, simpler side of character.

Fear of the Lord
Catholics as a whole claim to be not in awe of God, but holding themselves to him rather by love than by fear; yet for all that there must come into our religion a notion of fear, else God will be made of little account, dwarfed by his hero-followers, the saints. It is possible

that familiarity with God may breed something which seems very like contempt. The majesty of God has got to be considered just as much as his love, for either without the other would really give a false idea of him. Just as there are people who would give up all belief in hell, because they prefer to concentrate upon his mercy, and, as a result, have no real love of God as he is himself, so there are people also who do not sufficiently remember the respect due to his awfulness, people who think of him as a Redeemer, which indeed he is, but not as a Judge, which is equally his prerogative. Hence, this side of our character is also to be made perfect by the indwelling of the Spirit of God. Our fear, anger, hate, have got to be sanctified by finding a true object for their due exercise. No single talent must be wrapped away in uselessness; I must fear God, be angry with, and hate, sin. Fear, then, as well as piety is a gift of the Spirit.

The chief way in which the absence of this gift of fear manifests itself is in the careless and slipshod way we perform our duties. We are sure to believe in God's justice and majesty; but we are not so sure to act up to our belief. Accuracy in devotion, in prayer, in life, is the result of a filial fear of God, and if I have to confess a very chaotic and uncertain procedure in my spiritual duties, then I can tell quite easily which gift I most need. What are my times for prayer like? Are they as regularly kept to as my circumstances permit? How about my subject for meditation, how about my following of the Mass, my watchfulness in prayer, my days for confession and Communion? Again, my duties at home, in my profession, in the work I have undertaken? Are they on the whole punctually performed, accurately, with regard to details? That is where my fear for God should come in, for fear here is part of love and love is enormously devoted to little things; indeed, it finds that where it is concerned there are no little things, but time and place and manner and thoroughness have all faithfully to be noted and carried out. Here, then, is where I shall ford I need a reverential fear of God.

Yes, of course, pride and laziness will protest all the while, by urging that all this is a great deal of fuss about nothing, that God is our Father, that he understands perfectly, that we should not worry ourselves too much over trifles. Now pride and laziness often speak true things, or rather half-truths. It is true that God is my Father and understands; but it is equally true that I am his child and that love demands my thoroughness. Horror of sin, devotion to the sacrament of confession, the Scripture-saying about a severe judgment for every idle word, all these things have got to be taken into account as well as the first set of principles. Piety needs fear for its perfect performance. The boy at first may have to be scolded into obedience to his mother. He does not at first realize, and is punished; but watch him when he is a grown man, no longer in subjection or under obedience; see how charmingly he cares for her by anticipating her wishes, how much he is at her beck and call, proudly foreseeing for her, protecting, caring. That is love, no doubt, but a love of reverence. They are comrades in a sense, but she is always his mother to him, someone to be idolized, reverenced, yes, and, really, feared, in the fullest sense of love.

Grace
The indwelling, then, of the Holy Spirit is a true and magnificent phrase. It means that we become living temples of God. Elsewhere indeed he is in tree, flower, sky, earth, water; up in the heavens, down to the depths of the lower places, in the cleft wood and lifted stone, in the heart of all creation by the very fact of its creation. Yet the higher a thing is in the scale of being, the more nearly is it after God's image and likeness, so that man by his sheer intelligence is more representative of God as the highest masterpiece is more representative of the author of it. Yet over and above this intelligent life of man is another life, which secures God's presence within him in some nobler fashion, for it is noticeable that Scripture repeatedly speaks of God's dwelling in his saints and not dwelling in sinners. He is even in sinners by the title of their Creator, so that dwelling must be a deliberate phrase chosen by the inspired author of Scripture to represent some presence above the mere general presence of God everywhere. Consequently, we are driven to the conclusion that the saints, in virtue of their sainthood, become dwelling places of God, temples, special places set apart, where in a more perfect way, with richer expression and more true representation, God is. Sanctity, therefore, constitutes something wholly supernatural, attracting God's indwelling, or rather resulting from this indwelling of God.

Now sanctity itself cannot mean that one man is able to make himself so alluring to God that he draws God to himself, for in that case God's action of indwelling would be motived by a creature, and God would have found some finite reason for his act. This cannot be, since the only sufficient motive for God can be God himself. 'He hath done all things on account of himself,' says the Scripture. We can be sure, therefore, that the indwelling of the Spirit is the cause and not the effect of the goodness that is in man, for the saints are not born, but made by God. Hence, we understand what is meant by saying that the justice of the saints, their justification, is effected by grace, i.e., by God's free gift. It is not from them, but from him• 'Not to us, O Lord, not to us, but to thy name give glory.' Grace, therefore, is the name given to that divine habit whereby the soul is made one with him. It is clear, then, also why in the Catechism grace is called the supernatural life of the soul and why mortal sin is called the death of the soul, since it kills the soul by depriving it of sanctifying grace.

This leads us to the last notion of grace: that it is in the super-natural order what the soul is in the natural order. My soul is everywhere in my body and gives evidence of its presence by the life there manifest. Cut off a portion of the body, amputate a limb; it dies. The soul is no longer in it. So does grace work. It is in the very essence of the soul, at the heart of it, and works through into all the faculties and powers by means of the virtues. It is the life of the whole assemblage of these habits of goodness. As soon as it is withdrawn, at once charity goes, for we are out of friendship with God, and charity is nothing other than the love of God. Hope and faith still remain in some form, but without any inner life or energy to quicken them. All else is a crumbled ruin, without shape or life, a sight to fill those that can see it with horror and disgust. With grace the soul is once more thronged with vital activities, for grace is life. Grace it is that gives the same charm to the soul as life gives to the body; it imparts a freshness, an alertness, an elasticity, a spontaneous movement, a fragrance, a youth. By grace we are children in God's eyes, with the delicate coloring and sweetness of a child; without it we are old, worn, dead, not only useless to ourselves, but a pollution to others. Need one wonder if all life is different to the soul in sin? Religion, God, heaven, Mass, prayers, have lost all attraction and are full of drudgery. Outwardly we feel the same, but our attraction to these higher gifts has gone; a prodigal as yet content with the husks of life's fruitage, relishing only the food of swine – without grace – spiritually dead.

Part Three: Growth in Holiness

13 THE CULTIVATION OF PERFECTION

IN OUR Lord's view of holiness, the central part of it lies hidden within. There is little means of judging a man's holiness, since it is concerned not with acts but with motives, and motives are out of sight. We need reminding that it is never what we do, but why we do it, that most matters. If we can get our motives right, the rest can be left to follow its own way. Moreover, motives themselves are commanded us in the saying that we must love. Love is less an action than a motive for action. We are bidden, not to do, but to love.

So we have set out what constitutes the essence of that perfection which our Lord laid on us as a command. Then we have spoken, too, of the way in which that perfection manifests itself, namely, in the acceptance of the divine will, for it is clear that we shall be perfect if we leave ourselves to be trained by God. Hence, we must trust him absolutely and suffer in serene love whatever he shall do to us. Then will he gather us to himself. But we must needs have a consciousness of our native sinfulness, and because of our insufficiency be led to put all our confidence in him. We must not only remember that we are worth nothing, but also that he is worth all. Since he is all, he also does all. In the language of the old mystics: 'There is no doer but he.' Even sin has a place in his economy of grace, so that we must not let ourselves become impatient of our faults but use their memory to love God better. This the Passion of Christ can achieve in us, through the compassion of God's Mother, in our prayer and contemplation. Thus shall we be made perfect in hope.

'Be ye perfect as your heavenly Father is perfect.' That saying of our Blessed Lord is one that continuously puzzles us. Thus, we listen to what he says and we know ourselves and we know too that he knew us better even than we do. We know ourselves and know that the idea of the infinite perfection of God is something not only above us, but utterly impossible to us, beyond our very dreams; and yet our Lord, who knows human nature, for he made it, gave us not as an invitation but as a command that we should be 'perfect as our heavenly Father is perfect'. How can we be perfect? How can we be perfect as God?

But when we use the word 'perfection' or say of a thing that it is perfect, we may mean all sorts of things, we may mean 'perfection' in all sorts of ways. Thus, we even use the word of a ruin. People say that Tintern Abbey is a 'perfect' ruin. We do not mean that it is complete, for it is a ruin; but we mean that it is perfect as a ruin, perfect in its own order, perfect in its place. We may say of speech that it is 'perfect,' and by that mean that it contained no word too much, no word too few. It could not be improved on. It was perfect. We say of a witty answer that it was a 'perfect' reply, meaning that it fitted the situation exquisitely, that nothing better could have been said. Or again we can say that the silence was 'perfect'. We mean, of course, that it was absolutely complete or in place.

Can we not then describe perfection as implying completeness in a particular order, so that the perfect thing does completely what it is wanted to do? Thus, a mechanical instrument is perfect or complete if it does its work thoroughly, exactly fulfils the purpose for which it was designed. Thus also we can say reverently that God is perfect because he fulfils all that he is: 'I am who am.' God is perfect; in him everything is in order. Again, his world is a perfect world in its own order, for everything in it is in its proper place. God is perfect. But man was made after the image and likeness of God. Man therefore – you, I, all men – was created to be perfect, but perfect only as man,

perfect only as a man should be: all his powers, his passions, his emotions, his intelligence, his will, all are to be perfect, each in its own place, doing its own work, fulfilling its own purpose as – if it is properly in order – it will do. That is what man was intended to be; he was made after God's image and likeness. That is why it is, and how it is, that man can be perfect. He is formed on the model of God.

If you remember, even as a child when you learnt your Catechism, you were taught that man is like God, that is, like the Blessed Trinity. Since then, you have better understood that he is so by nature. God made him so in his first creation. And you have learnt too that, besides his nature, he received a supernature – treasures of grace by which his soul is again made like God a second time by participating in the divine life. God is perfect; man, fashioned after God's likeness, was also intended to be perfect in two orders, both by nature and by grace. And also he was to be perfect by a determination of his will. He cannot be perfected against his will.

Our Lord said: 'Be perfect.' That is evidently a command. Are we perfect, that is, are we fulfilling our purpose? Are we perfect, having everything in order, our intelligence, our will, our love, our anger, our hopes, our desires, everything about us doing what it should be doing, every power and faculty exquisitely obedient and alive? That is what he meant us to be, that is how he fashioned us.

But this perfection was to be aimed at deliberately, by our own will. You will never be perfect unless you want to be perfect. Honestly, do you want to be? Do you want to have your anger completely under control, never to be angry except when it is reasonable to be angry, never to love unless you should, never to enjoy what you ought not to enjoy? Do you want to be perfect? They that have tasted it – saints, we call them – say that it is a thing blessed beyond dreams. They were men and women who set themselves perfectly in order, aimed at perfection, wanted it, heard of it, and acknowledged it as a divine command.

Can we be perfect? What have we to do to become perfect? It can be maintained that quite truly we have very little to do. We believe this to be God's world; we believe God to be in charge of it and us. We believe that God fashioned our world, and that God made each one of us. But God made us, intending that we should know our own way, goal, and purpose, and achieve it for ourselves, and thus reach the perfection he meant us to have – a perfection, that is, within our scope. How can we achieve this goal? Leave it to him, leave it to him entirely; he will get us there, if we will but let him. That is all that we have to do, to let him make us perfect. It is his job. God governs us, God governs our life absolutely. Every moment of our life, then, we are under the infinite power of God. Because you believe this, you must try not to chafe against God. Do not fight against him. Let him deal with you; he will treat you in the way he sees you need. Nothing is asked of you but this absolute acceptance of the divine will affecting every detail of your life.

Have you grown old? Or are you middle-aged or young still? Whoever you are, God is watching you, who slumbers not nor sleeps. God is watching you, not to do you hurt, but to make you perfect. All that is asked is that you should surrender yourself absolutely to him. He will give you what he sees you need for the perfection of yourself. Have faith in him and you will remain tranquil, putting yourself into his hands.

'But what will he do with me?' He will make you more truly and more fully after the image and likeness of himself, as he made his Son. 'Shall I be happy under what he does to me?' Do you remember how God treated his Son? It is a foolish question to ask, if you do remember. You certainly can be happy. But whether you will be or not, depends entirely on yourself. 'Will he treat me hardly?' God chastises those whom he loves. That is the price you must pay for your divine fashioning after the image of his Son. You will be bought and sold, denied, betrayed; you will have false accusations brought against you. Yes, but the point is: what are you going to do about it? Are you going to leave yourself absolutely in his hands? Or are you going to fight for your good name? Do not so act! Dare to leave yourself to his fashioning After the example of his Son, if you wish to be perfect, be submissive. Surrender yourself body and soul to his will. 'Be ye perfect' – dare we even aim at that? What were his blessed words? He knew human nature as we cannot know it. He knew its baseness, as even we do not know it; he knew its frailty, its inconsistency. Yet, knowing it, he dares to say to us: 'Follow me.' How well he thought of us, how nobly he judged us who said to us: 'Follow me. Come where I go, follow me to the heights of self-sacrifice that I have climbed.' He would not have said it unless he meant it, unless he knew that we could.

Was he a dreamer? He was no dreamer. He knew mankind, for his fingers had fashioned it. He knew the shallowness of those who then followed him and of those who would follow him, but he knew also their depth, their greatness. And knowing this, he calls all of us to follow him.

What he asks is that we should come willingly. So we must answer him personally, one by one. Are we willing to follow him, really willing? I do not think we really are; I think we are desperately afraid of what he may ask us to give up. St Augustine, as a youth with his dreams and idealism and yet with that frailty of his flesh, prayed his broken prayer: 'Give me chastity, but not yet!' Not yet! Not yet! Is that not like our own heart's prayer? Perfection? Yes, but not yet!

He says to us: 'Be ye perfect as your heavenly Father is perfect.' We were made after his image and likeness, made so by nature, made so by grace. He tells us that, even after we have sinned, he will again re-make us to that blessed likeness, if we will let him deal with every detail of our lives. All that is asked of us is to accept his divine overmastering will and this may well include the crown of thorns, the scepter set in our hand by way of mockery, the garment of a fool flung round us. Do not be troubled by these. Take them as part of life. If you will but let him, he will make a saint of you.

14 SANCTITY

A SAINT in the meaning of the Church is not a mere ordinary Christian who at last has managed to enter the gates of heaven, but is essentially a heroic soul. When the process of canonization, is set in motion, the judges are not content with everyday goodness, with piety or charity, or a quiet life of peace, such as could be discovered in almost any good Catholic home in all Christendom. They are on the look-out for something a great deal more vigorous than this. They are searching for such a love of God as shall be expressed in energetic and forcible ways, such a love as will do heroic things, raised above normal standards; often a scandal to some, who suppose it to be too tolerant or too intolerant according as their own measures are under- or over-sized. The phrase, indeed, in which this is expressed is 'heroic sanctity'. A saint, then, in this sense is a hero – a man, woman, or child, with a genius for morality. Of course, everyone has some love of God, some goodness, just as everyone has some power of expressing himself in language; but as there are people whom we recognize at once as possessed of a special fluency and distinction of style, and whom we therefore regard as masters of literature, standing head and shoulders above the crowd, so also there are those whose very goodness has a distinction and a fluency which puts them in a category apart. They are God's heroes, the saints. They are possessed of 'heroic sanctity'; that is to say, they have expressed their love of God in a heroic degree.

When, then, I say to myself that God sent me here to love him, that he has called me to him and from time to time I do feel that he wishes me to be a great deal closer to him than I actually am, I am surely criticizing very severely my present way of life. Is there, of a truth, much heroism in my method of carrying out the Gospel? My hours of rising are regulated by my work; are they ever regulated by my piety? Week-day Mass persistently followed may be a difficulty, but it is certainly at least an occasional possibility. How many times do I assist on a week-day at that which I profess by faith is the very sacrifice of Calvary! It would be hard to go regularly: precisely, it could be heroic; an outward and visible sign of an inward invisible love that passed the love of ordinary souls. Nor it is merely in relation to God's worship that this heroism is to be shown – there is the monotonous grind of daily life. My charity, my patience, my tolerance, my truthfulness, my love of justice, are they not rather carelessly interpreted and put into practice? Is there much heroism in the way I manifest them? Perhaps I am very often repeating to myself that it is easy to be heroic; easy to die for one's faith, but hard to live for it; easy to bear in patience the great sorrows of life, but difficult to put up with daily and hourly annoyances. But the heroic is precisely that which is most difficult – the word means no more than that. If, consequently, to live for one's faith is harder than to die for it, then of the two to live for one's faith is the more heroic. Perhaps for certain souls to bear quietly the break-up of a friendship (than which it is difficult to imagine anything more terrible in life) is not so trying as to refrain from impatience when in a moment of hurry a bootlace is broken. This last for them would be the true test of sanctity.

Now, have I not to confess that these true tests of holiness would find me, indeed, very far from success? Have I not avoided too often any way that seems to be rather out of the ordinary? I do not mind doing good, whereas it is of far greater importance to be good. For me kindness, generosity even, may be cloaks of malice and excuses for not loving God. It is no use my being kind, or philanthropic, or prayerful, unless God's love burns within me. If I have not charity, the rest profits me nothing Just as it is possible that I may make fasting an excuse for omitting the weightier things of the law, so it may well be that I sweat my employees and build a hospital; am impatient at home and go out to console the sick. I am avoiding the heroic things and not in reality showing holiness. Heroism consists in being heroic, and just as it is easier to do gentlemanly things than to be in one's soul a gentleman, so it is much easier to feed a starving foe or tend him when wounded or succor him when drowning, than to forgive, love, and pray for him when he is boastful and full of success. Yet this last is just what a saint and only a saint would do: it is heroism, or the love of God expressed in a heroic degree. I have, then, to realize my dignity as a Christian and see that in my vocation to follow Christ it is just the difficult things that I must try to do, simply because I have first made my soul instinctively apprehend the spirit of Christ.

Saints

God, we say, is wonderful in his saints, and in so saying, though we may mistranslate Scripture, we yet state a truth, for God is made full of wonder to us when we see his saints. A saint is a sinner who is conscious of sins, who is sorry for sins, and who seeks God. Is there anything very wonderful about that? Indeed there is. To be conscious of one's sins is a grace of God. It is he alone who can show up to us the dark places of the soul, and by this means the contrast between ourselves and him dwarfs our goodness to insignificance and deepens the shadows of our sin. That is God's way of dealing with those whom he loves and whom he intends should love him. In the lives of the saints, whether of those who have once strayed from God or of those who have never left him, you will find how, with growing clearness, they saw their failures and the evils in their lives. But the saints in so doing were not led to despair. They were not only conscious of their sins, but sorry for them.

Now this is the positive side of sanctity. It faces facts without weakening under the self-revelation they produce. To be conscious of one's sin is indeed a grace of God, but others besides saints have received it. Modern literature is full of that consciousness. Blanco Posnet is aware of his sin, and the author of *De Profundis* and even *Barbellion* found it stabbing them with a sudden pain. But sorrow for sin is nonetheless a gift of God, because it implies unselfish sorrow, the sorrow begotten of love and burgeoning into love. To regret the past with shame need not be sorrow, unless with it runs a wistfulness of soul that turns away from self and is urged forward to further love. Hence, beyond consciousness of sin and sorrow for it, saint-ship implies a seeking for God. But does the mere seeking for God make a saint, even though it follows on sorrow for sin? Yes, it does, for the saints are the lovers of God. All who are his lovers are his saints. A mere seeking after God will do this? A seeking, if it be real and persistent, is a finding, for no one goes to look for God who has not already found him. Whoever looks for God must first have missed him, and to have missed God is already to have had some knowledge of what he means to the soul, and to have had some knowledge of what he is, is already to have dimly found him.

God is wonderful in his saints? Of course he is wonderful, be-cause his greatness is made manifest to us through them. They are but broken lights of him, and he is more than they. Their goodness is a mere fragment of his goodness, a participation in it, a reflection of it. Since, then, God himself in his immensity is infinite, our only chance of finding any contact with him is to see him in what he does. The sun is too dazzling to be looked at in its full splendor, but the divided colors of the spectrum give us an idea, inadequate indeed, but suggestive of the glory of the whole. In some such fashion, the saints, distinct and individual, representing in diverse and varied forms his perfect being, inadequately indeed, yet suggestively reveal him to us.

Of course, the bigger the city to which men journey, the more roads must there be that lead to it. The little village, that straggles along a single high road, has but the ends of its one street to guide men to it. But the great cities of the world have numberless approaches. So it is with God. Immense beyond human categories, he must be a center of roads as infinite in number as himself; a city set high on a hill, the beacon of the wise, sought by souls whom no man can number, must necessarily be approached by each in his or her own way. We come to him by the way he chooses for us, and whosoever cometh by whatsoever road was chosen for him, God will not cast out.

God is really made wonderful to us in his saints; their variety of goodness enables us to grasp better what God is like. Hope, too, is to be found in them, hope for others and for ourselves. We can hope when we see how each of them has climbed to God along a separate path. Of all ages, trades, and nations, of all kinds of culture, learned and unlearned, of all degrees of moral excellence, we find only one common likeness in them: that they all (save one only have been sinners and conscious of their sin and sorry for it, and have been seekers after God.

15 FORMATION OF CHARACTER

UNDOUBTEDLY, our first step to achieve holiness or goodness is to discover our predominant fault. This requires some looking for, since it may possibly be hidden underneath a good many other sins which have concealed it. Thus, it may well be that the fault I have most frequently to confess is not really my predominant fault, but only the result of it, while the real sin skulks away and refuses to come to the surface. Impurity may be caused by other things, such as love of ease, selfishness, even pride. Often it happens that we are wrestling with the wrong enemy, not getting hold of the source of his strength, but fighting frontal attacks against an ugly mask; all the time the cause of our failures will be quite undisturbed and in possession of the field. First, then, I have very carefully to examine my conscience. I must go very thoroughly to work, and sift the whole of my actions with some trouble. Just as I find that week after week my list for confession is practically always the same, so in all probability I shall find that, whenever I examine my conscience, the results are pretty much alike; hence there will be no need for me to make this examination very often – once

it is done thoroughly, that will be sufficient for some months. Nor should I fancy that it is helpful to look every now and then to see how things are going on, or, indeed, to busy myself overmuch with whether it is going on at all: for it is a foolish gardener who persistently digs up his bulbs to see if they are sprouting, and I shall find it extremely difficult, even when I have dug up my soul, to know whether I am progressing or not, for it must surely happen that, when I am at my best, I shall see only more clearly than ever in how much I have failed. So that the worse I see myself to be, the better, perhaps, I shall really be.

Hence, I must beware of making purely negative resolutions, for then I shall simply look back at the past as measured by failure. If I make up my mind to avoid this or that, the result will be that I shall have no other standard of judgment in moments of spiritual stock-taking than the occasions on which I have broken my resolutions; the final result of this will be that I shall exclaim in disgust that I had better never have made any resolutions at all – a perfectly logical conclusion. The more cheerful and helpful way is to reverse this procedure. Already I have found out what my predominant fault is, for I have made a thorough and careful examination of conscience. Then, when I am certain, or at least as certain as I can be, I must concentrate not on the sin, but on the corresponding virtue. My resolutions now will not be to avoid this or that, but to increase or develop this or that. I shall not measure my past by a series of faults, but by the number of times, few perhaps but nonetheless real, when I have actually managed to achieve success. The gardener who spent all his time digging up the weeds and never thought very much of strengthening his plants would produce a very tidy but depressing garden. He would have hurt his back by stooping, and never stood upright to enjoy the beauty of his garden. But a good gardener knows well that if he will only do his best for the flowers, they will derive goodness from the soil and so leave less from which the weeds can get the nourishment they need. Weeding must be done; but the first thing is the flowers. So in my soul, all my energies should first be spent upon encouraging my poor feeble virtues to grow strong, and then by their very strength they will cause the sins to diminish. I have, therefore, not to make my resolutions to avoid this or that, but to improve in this or that.

Let me suppose that I have discovered that my chief failing is uncharitableness. Then my resolution will be to take up as strongly as I can a charitable judging of my fellows. I should not simply try to avoid the temptation when it comes, but make positive efforts to increase what little store of charity I have. I must start with my thoughts and gradually get into the way of trying to find a good motive for everything I see. St Catherine of Siena, in a humorous moment, told our Lord that if he had only given her an opportunity for it, she would have discovered an excuse for the devil himself. We cannot, indeed, say that right is wrong or wrong right, but we can, while denouncing a fault, suppose that the motive was good, for the motive forever eludes us. Often, when I went out of my way to help someone, they saw not the motive that I had, but only its result, and were annoyed; and as others have misjudged me, so it is possible that I misjudge others. In this way I shall find that it is not difficult after a while to think kindly of everyone, and to think kindly will end in speaking and acting kindly. I must, therefore, develop the virtue corresponding to my predominant sin rather than look to the sin itself; develop my charity so that I have no longer any temptation to judge unkindly, so that gossip will not please me; encourage in my heart so great a love for purity that foul thoughts will not remain with me, and foul conversation will bore me; seek after truth and justice, so that lying and the defrauding of my neighbor revolt me.

Habits

Once we have discovered our predominant fault, we have to endeavor to cultivate the virtue most opposed to it. But it is just here that the difficulty begins; for surely I have tried over and over again to compass this and have failed. What is a virtue? There is this difference between a good action and a virtue, that a good action may be quite isolated, whereas a

virtue is a definite habit established in the will. In the same fashion, a vice is an established habit of wrongdoing. It is possible for me thus to do good, to tell the truth, be charitable, patient, without really having the virtues of truth or charity or patience. What, then, do we mean by an established habit? What is a habit? Of course, we have a vague idea that it means we have got into a way of doing certain things and have got the knack of them; and certainly it is difficult to describe in other words this apparently simple thing. However, we may start by saying that a habit does not incline us to do anything, does not give us a push in its direction; but once we have made up our minds to do it, we find that the fact of the habit enables us to do the thing much more easily, promptly, without friction. Thus, supposing I have obtained somehow the habit of being tidy; then it is much more easy for me to seize hold of a confused mess and put it into order; I have such a horror of untidiness and such a custom of putting everything in its place that it becomes much more easy for me to do it than it would be for others who had no habit of the kind. But I must realize that having the habit does not make me tidy, but only makes it considerably easier to be tidy. In other words, to make use of the expression of psychologists, a habit does not force the will to act, but enables it to act with greater smoothness.

This will be more apparent, perhaps, if I try to see how a habit is formed. Let me take a habit of the body, so that by visible things I may the more clearly understand things in-visible. I am learning to shoot. First I shall be trained probably at a stationary target. Slowly and deliberately I take my aim for firing, until in process of time I have got my eye into the way of it and find I can score a good number of 'bulls'. Then, perhaps, I am taken out to the moving target, or the clay pigeon, and finally to the actual flying bird. But in the meanwhile an extraordinary change has taken place. At first I was very slow and deliberate in taking aim; now I shoot at once, lifting the gun, aiming, firing, all within a few fractions of a second. Or, again, a favorite example is the simple dressing in the morning. As a child it was an intensely laborious process, requiring at first the constant assistance of the nurse to pilot me through the vast array of garments. If every morning the same efforts had to be made as I had then, my day's work would never get done. The toddling of a child is strenuous to it, not simply because its limbs are weak, but because the effort at balancing is a tremendous strain upon its energy, which, if it continued all through life, would make all walking intolerable. It is to be noticed that what has happened in each case is this: from effort I have passed to effortless action – at first slow and deliberate, with attention required so as to be certain of every step in the process; then a stage when effort slips from the action, and by a sort of instinct, swiftly and without thought, as it appears, we do promptly, easily, and without difficulty what we have learnt by habit. Habit, therefore, is simply a faculty of our nature whereby, by repeated action, we acquire an ease in movement.

Now it is just this that we require so incessantly in our spiritual life. For us the great trouble is the determined efforts that have to be made: we find the struggle so fierce that in despair we relinquish the effort altogether. We should remember that at the beginning there is bound to be extreme difficulty, extreme deliberation, extreme slowness; it is only gradually that we shall find it possible to lay aside effort and fall into the pleasant lines of habit. But what a gain to be able to hand over to mere instinct (it is not really that) what had first been so tiring a task. It will be useful for me to think over the three rules that are given, so that in the formation of the habit of goodness that is most opposed to my besetting sin, I may gradually, positively, set up something really efficient. These rules are: (1) As far as possible to accumulate circumstances such as will make the forming of the habit least of all interfered with – to avoid, for example, those places and people whose proximity I find to be on the whole tending to make me break it; in simpler words, let me avoid the occasions of sin. (2) Never to allow exceptions till the habit has been firmly established; to beware, above all, of that very deceitful excuse: 'Just this once,' for that phrase is never accurate; Just this once' leads easily to many other times. (3) To find every opportunity for exercising these habits; do not let me wait for the opportunities to arise, but let me go out to seek them, for it is clear that in order to establish these habits by means of repeated acts, I require to exercise the acts frequently, and the only way to achieve this is to go out of my way to find these opportunities.

Character
Many people seem to worry themselves a great deal more over the

things that they cannot help than over the things that they can. They are greatly agitated over the color of their hair (for which they are not responsible), and but little over their tempers (for which they are). This want of proportion is doubtless observable in myself. Do I think more of the accidents of birth, fortune, personal appearance, than of the self that I have created? For I myself am responsible for myself. 'To be born a gentleman is an accident, to die one is an achievement.' Other things, then, I may not be able to help, but myself I can. As I am at this very moment, as my character is – truthful or untruthful, pure or impure, patient or impatient, slow to wrath or quick-tempered, eager, enthusiastic, energetic, or lazy and dull and wasteful of time – I have no one to thank but my own self. Of course, I may blame my temperament and say I was born so; I may accuse the hereditary tendencies of my family, or excuse myself because I have been spoilt or cowed or left to my own devices, or have been deluged with too much religion or starved with too little. But, despite all this, the fact remains that I myself alone am responsible for my own character; for character is an artificial thing that is not born, but made; it is the result of human effort and human guidance, of human wisdom and human folly. I am as I am now to the eye of God because I have so made or marred myself, either deliberately and of set purpose or by allowing myself to drift along, never moving hand or foot to save myself from peril.

But surely there is such a thing as temperament? Surely people really are different from birth? Surely even the physical formation of the body, the whole stream of tendencies inherited or instilled in early childhood, the evils produced by a neglected education or an upbringing that is not Catholic, do most certainly affect my nature and make some difference to me? Have I not, on their account, some justification in excusing myself from being wholly responsible for the evils in my character? Here I must begin by realizing that I must make a very real distinction between temperament and character. Temperament is natural, I am born with it; character is artificial, the result of my way of life. I am born with a certain definite temperament, and for this I am not responsible; and on this account, too, I may well suppose that God will make allowances for me. At any rate this temperament gives me a set-off, a push, in one definite direction; for some are by nature gentle, generous, and obliging, while others as naturally are cross-tempered and easily ruffled. But this need not settle my character. Of course, if I make no effort to tame any evil tendencies of my nature, then temperament and character will coincide and my actual life will only mark more deeply and emphasize more pronouncedly the original defect with which I started. But that is my own affair, for it is possible for me to act in opposition to my temperament and to produce a character that is the reverse of my nature.

St Thomas, indeed, in a very brief passage, seems to suggest that the worse our natural temperament is, the better for us; nor is it at all difficult to understand his argument. If I have a bad temper by nature, let me first of all go down on my knees and thank God for it; for it is surely highly probable that if I had a good temper I should be obliging and kind, not from any supernatural motive but from sheer nature. Supposing I was of that comfortable disposition which says 'Yes' just because it finds it impossible to say 'No% surely my acts would hardly ever be supernaturalizes. But, on the other hand, supposing I am so cantankerous that I can be generous and helpful only at the cost of a mighty effort, then I can be certain that every obliging thing I do is done only from a high motive; it is the very contrary force which stiffens me into goodness. Just as an enemy is the necessary material out of which to fashion victory, so is an evil temperament the foundation on which a strong character is to be built up. This character is, of course, nothing else than the group of habits formed round the axis of the will; and these are achieved only by repeated acts, so that it is by deliberate and energetic actions alone that I can react against my own temperament. Above all, I must beware of allowing myself to be careless in life, without ambition or ideal or plan; for to drift through existence is at least as dangerous as deliberate evil consciously performed: I am quick, then, by nature, or mean or thronged with impure imaginings. It does not much matter what my own trouble may be, but instead of bemoaning it, I should set to work by deliberate and conscious reason to reform myself under the grace of God, and not follow the blind impulses of nature.

16 EMOTIONS AND SENTIMENT

CONSIDER the immense power that feelings have over us. Our attitude to life, our efforts at improvement, or the ceasing of all effort, are unfortunately very largely affected by our feelings. Prayers are often taken up and then dropped, simply because we do not feel in the mood. We seem to think that God is pleased, not by our prayers, but by how we feel during our prayers, and suppose ourselves to be saints when we feel saints, and sinners when we feel sinners; while probably the very opposite is true, for on the whole we may be certain that we are never nearer to God than when we feel furthest away from him. I find myself distressed when my thanksgivings after Communion are dull and cold, when I do not experience any of those waves of emotion with which, as I fondly imagine, everyone else is thrilled. Perhaps if I looked into every other soul in the church I would find them very much as mine, and if I looked into the heart of God I should find that he was content. But first I have to impress upon myself the fact that I have very little command over my feelings – indeed, I suppose that is really my very complaint, whereas it should be my excuse. I should like to feel the sweetness of his presence and I do not feel it. Is that my fault? Not at all, for evidently I do want to feel it; therefore, as far as I am concerned, I should be experiencing the very raptures of the blessed. The reason, then, that prevents me is evidently beyond my control. Instead, there-fore, of losing heart, let me take heart, for the cause of the trouble is not mine to remedy. It is probably some external thing weather, health, digestion – that adds or takes away my feelings in my prayers.

If, then, I cannot produce at will the several emotions proper to the occasion, the fault evidently does not lie with me, and is in fact no fault at all. I cannot be held responsible for lacking what is not, indeed cannot be, under my control. Inability to feel devout, to enjoy one's prayers, to find pleasure in visits to the Blessed Sacrament, to taste the sweetness of Holy Communion, to discover sensible sorrow for my weekly or monthly tale of sins, to thirst after the rewards of heaven or even to understand that they are rewards at all, to appreciate with proper devotion the pageant of the Mass, etc., is not sinful, since it is not willful, deliberate. Try as I may, I cannot command these feelings. The speaker whose kindling words rouse my enthusiasm and work me up to a pitch of emotional frenzy has more command over my feelings than I have myself; in fact, I might almost make it out as a principle of psychology that others have always more control or more effective influence over my emotions than I have myself. They are more likely to compel me to weep, to love, to laugh, than I can force myself to do. But then I must deliberately realize that religion cannot be built of such frail and uncertain material. The City of God rests upon foundations surer than these that ebb and flow; it is upon the reason and the will that the whole fabric must be reared. As long as my will is turned to God and endeavors to keep hold of him, to follow his teaching, to obey

his law, I am doing the best I can, and he can expect no more of me than that.

Can I not really go one step further? Not only can I not control my feelings, and not only therefore does their absence prove no sin to me, but is it not very much better for me that these should rather be against me than with me? Are not my prayers more valuable because they have no such accompanying thrills of pleasure? For consider that the object of the Christian life is union with God, and that this union is achieved by self-surrender, which is itself stimulated by the example of Christ and by his merits, communicated through the sacraments. Now, to obtain self-surrender I must above all else be unselfish, and therefore probably shall have to battle against all the instincts of my nature. My talks with God, my prayers, the sacraments, etc., must be supernaturalized, deliberate; but if these pious exercises brought with them such torrents of delights, would there not be a danger of my taking them up, not because they were a duty, but because they were a pleasure; not because I wished to be unselfish, but because I thought only of myself? Actually, I have no such temptations. If I persevere in my prayers, then my efforts are certainly supernatural, for there are no natural motives for continuing them. I get no delight, no repayment; of my good works it cannot be said as once it was to the Pharisee, that I 'have already had my reward,' for so far I have found no reward. To go through all my exercises of piety is, moreover, my only way of love; not that sensible love which keeps me alive and active in my human friendships, but a deeper love that follows upon duty done, a love that hastens after its Lover, not for the consolations that he gives, but for himself.

Sentiment
I cannot always control my emotions, cannot command my sentiments or feelings. Well, then, let me beware lest I undervalue them, for their influence upon life is enormous Think how much of the day is

arranged for by mere sentiment. My hours of rising, of business, are regulated by little else; or at least by custom, which is largely sentiment crystallized. For I can soon notice that different nations have their different hours when the streets are busy or silent, and the variety is based not merely on climate, but on that vague and uncertain principle: 'We have always done so.' Again, the arrangement of my room, the knickknacks upon the mantelpiece, the pictures on the walls, the photographs, indeed the very idea of having photographs at all, are not all these things due entirely to sentiment? My day, my work, my pleasure, the things with which I surround myself, my calling in life, my prayers, my home, are they not one and all steeped in emotions, dominated by emotions, ruled and regulated by emotions? I say that I cannot control my emotions; can I say as truly that they do not control me? Before answering that question, let me at any rate be clear upon this point, that emotions are not necessarily unreasonable. Occasionally the argument is heard by which something is dismissed as being 'mere sentiment'. Now the fact of anything being merely sentimental does not degrade it at all, for in some ways and at some moments our emotions are the finest things we have. Men are, in given instances, at their best when they obey instinctively the call of emotion; and what puts reasoning beings at their best cannot fairly be called unreasonable.

I have, therefore, to start with the idea that very much of my life, and of the life of the race, is governed by reasons of sentiment; there is no contradiction in this phrase, since sentiment in man can be reasonable. When I have faced that fact deliberately and begun to realize its meaning, I can then go on to consider sentiments, etc., in relation to religion. I find that in dealing with my fellows and in dealing with myself, sentiment plays a considerable part, and that it does so (when under proper safeguards) without any harm either to them or to myself; in fact, that the world would be harder and poorer if sentiment was barred out. Hence, I expect to find the same in my relationship to God, namely, that sentiment should have its place in the united and harmonious worship that my whole being renders to its Maker. A religion, therefore, that neglects, ignores, or denounces whatever is sentimental simply because it is sentimental, stands itself condemned, for it is the religion not of man, but of only a part of him. It is inhuman; it can have effect only upon a starved and stunted portion of mankind, and then only for a time. My worship of God, my religion, must appeal to the whole man; it must induce me to put into his hands the whole offering of myself. Puritanism may work wonders of good when it follows upon a period of laxity and disorder, but it cannot last. It holds the seeds of its own decay, since it scorns a part of nature and makes Christianity not a fulfilling but a distinction of the law. My dealings with my fellows, my dealings with myself, my dealings with God, will all be considerably affected by sentiment: and if religion is to rule me all the day, it must rule all of me.

I should, therefore, be very careful that my attitude to sacred things does not become harsh, gloomy, unnatural, inhuman. It is one thing to say that I cannot control my feelings: quite another to say that I should ignore them. It is one thing to say that my prayers are likely to become more deliberately super-natural if they are untouched by feelings of pleasure, quite another to say that therefore we must abolish feelings. I cannot repose on feelings, but that is no reason for expelling them. St Gregory wrote to St Augustine in England, not to destroy, but to hallow to divine service the heathen temples of our Saxon forefathers. Let me, too, consecrate to God that buoyancy and gladness of soul which is all too frequently supposed to be a sign of the pagan joy of life. It is not pagan, but human; and, like the rest of man's nature, needs to be baptized unto Christ. If my devotions tend to cast out love, to sneer at the poetic side of religion, to crush out enthusiasm or gracefulness or youthfulness, then I must be on my guard at once, for such devotions cannot last. My faith should not be uncouth, rigid, stilted, repulsive, but glad, easy, natural. Devotion to the comeliest of the sons of men, the thought of his beautiful boyhood, of the firm majesty of his splendid manhood, will keep supple the sinews of love. The ideal of God's Maiden Mother, pure, yet womanly, the mother of fair love, will prevent my emotions becoming divorced from religion and growing befouled.

17   FREEDOM OF SOUL

BEFORE setting out to mould our characters, our souls must be in perfect freedom. I cannot address myself to such an undertaking until I am unhampered in my movements. It is essential for me, in order to achieve anything that requires much effort, to avoid everything that prevents action, even though in other ways it might be useful, and might, indeed, later be ultimately repossessed. Thus, in a sort of parallel, a battleship going into action clears its decks of every obstacle. Things that have their use at other times, that will again become useful, are for the moment sacrificed in the immediate and compelling interests that dominate the situation. Danger of fire from shell, and danger also to the free movement across the deck that might, at any moment, become essential to the safety of all concerned, are sufficiently pressing to force the destruction of everything, however useful, that might possibly impede this freedom. The same thing is observable whenever there is any occasion for swift and determined action. Thus, in military operations liberty and mobility of attack are themselves of such life-or-death necessity, that houses, industrial centers, cultivated plains, may have to be ruthlessly harried and great national loss inflicted on his own dominions by the general, in the interests of final victory. Or, in a more homely illustration, a man going to work, or going in for sport, rolls up his sleeves.

Something of the same is necessary in the work of forming our characters. I must have perfect and unhampered liberty of soul if I am to work at all easily. In a certain sense, this is also the final result of the whole spiritual life – that it produces a detachment in the soul and effects a real freedom that marks off the saint from the sinner. The great-souled lovers of God need nothing else upon earth than God's constant presence. They have attained that liberty that was promised to the sons of God, so that neither life nor death nor any other creature can separate them from their Friend. The attainment of this in part is essential for the beginning of the spiritual life.

Before the Fall, the soul of Adam must have been especially beautiful from this very freedom. The whole harmony of passions, will, and reason united in acting with solemn and pleasing smoothness: nothing disturbed, no discord broke in upon the matchless symphony. It was as though a perfect piece of machinery were working without friction, and with such absolute adjustment and nice balance as hardly to suggest the possibility of any untoward accident dislocating the mechanism. Then befell the terrible sin of disobedience whereby 'came death into the world and all our woe'. Thenceforward the only possible remedy was, under the grace of God, to be achieved by man's own energy. Freedom must be grasped; it is never given. It is something to be fought for, something that is bought only at a great price; indeed, for some it is death alone that frees the soul from all the entanglements of existence. There must be nothing to hamper or clog the free movement of the will or the reason, nothing to obscure or ruffle the one nor to blunt the energy of the other. As with the boxer whose every limb is by training and practice brought into immediate subjection to the mind, so that the rippling muscle moves under the silken texture of the skin at the slightest instinctive prompting of the intelligence, so must every emotion and passion obey the will in the light of reason.

Although it is true that this perfect adjustment and nice balance can never be completely recovered, yet it is both the basis and the goal of the spiritual life. I cannot go forward till I have effected the subjection of myself; and when finally I overcome and enter into my kingdom, then only shall I have achieved perfect freedom. I must begin with this, and thus I see the necessity of acquiring a spirit of detachment from all things in the sense of subordinating my own will to the will of God, realizing by faith that I cannot escape from it, that whatever happens comes to pass only because God has allowed it in his wisdom and love. I must frequently meditate upon this divine will. Then again, I must try to be perfectly truthful in life, i.e., my life should correspond absolutely to my thoughts. Once I start posing or pretending, I am become the slave of a pretence. Never shall I be able to free myself till I revert to myself, and am not content to act as others expect of me. Compromise, just because it is a lie, cannot be allowed within these limits which circumscribe truth. To be prudent, to be on my guard, yet to keep myself undisturbed, to possess my soul in patience, that is the great secret of life. Especially in these days, when speed enters so enormously into life, when everything is at a rush and hurry, I must take care to be in perfect serenity of mind, lest I add to the disturbance of existence and break in upon my peace of soul and perfect freedom, without which spiritual life is rendered impossible.

Faithful in Little

'Receive not the grace of God in vain.' That is a warning of the Apostle, showing us that it is quite possible to receive grace in vain, that is, to let it be without result in our life. In some measure, perhaps, we have had experience of that. Perhaps we can go back to a day when things, good things, came more easily to us, so easily that we hardly valued (as we should have valued) this gift of God. Then, because in little ways we laid aside our former habits of self-discipline and a delicate fulfillment of the divine will, gradually, by laying it aside and neglecting it, we lost our sensitiveness to it. We grew not to be quite so responsive as once we had been.

You must keep your faculties active if you are to keep them sensitive. You must be always perfecting your gifts if you are really to keep them alive, alert. Whatever gifts you have, if you lay them aside for a while, they will lose something of their activity; they must lose something of their power. This is true of everything we know in life. It is true of man's natural gifts. It is true of things material as well as immaterial. To let a power die down is to let it die out. So, too, in the spiritual world. What we need through all our lives long is a daily addition of grace. This means not so much doing more, but doing better. It does not mean more prayers, but prayers said better. It means that when I attend Mass, I try to get from Mass what it has to give me. There is a danger of just settling down to life, taking ordinary, everyday views, losing our perception of the supernatural in life. It is a danger of which we are all aware. What alone can keep us free of it is this daily, almost hourly, infusion of the grace of God.

This grace of God that has been lavished on us so freely, we gain in proportion to the way in which we use the small opportunities of life. If you ask someone who has come to the Church from outside why he has become a Catholic, nearly always he will tell you that it was something small and trivial that finally brought him to the faith. The sight of someone's obvious belief in Catholicism, some chance faithfulness, some surrender, that had this extraordinary reward and brought him, at last, to his home. Always, it is true that in proportion to my use of what has been given me shall fuller use and fuller gifts be made. He that is faithful over little shall be given greater things to rule.

A man may say: 'I am not going to trouble over little things.' That will not do. It will be followed shortly by this confession: 'I am losing my power of observation. I am losing my familiarity with divine things.' Half a gardener's work is done upon his knees. The work of the cultivation of our soul is done humbly, in prayer and service, in quiet moments, and through the use of what we have. You and I are not fit to have the greater graces; we must be content with a very little. All the more, therefore, so that we may use the little things that come our way, must we value them, must we try to secure from them all that they have to give. Prayers – ordinary, everyday prayers – must be used faithfully. We shall not be treated even to little things, if we lay these aside. We shall be even less responsive to graces than now we are. What is asked of us, then, is a steady faithfulness to divine grace, realizing the greatness of our need and realizing that this need is daily, hourly, urgent and realizing that grace comes to us through apparently insignificant ways. Thus, God's revelation, apart from his revelation through our Lord, is a daily revelation to us as to what is his will

This will, we have said, comes not in a thundering fashion We shall not be struck off horses on our road to Damascus. That is right for a great character like St Paul, not for us whose dramatic value is so much less. We must go much more quietly and use the things we have not dreamt of, only because they are the things that are actually at our door. We have no cause to imagine that our call is to serve others in some wide way, but be perfectly content with home; not dreaming of a vast work which we shall one day be called upon to administer, not taking things merely in quantity, but in quality. Every little thing can be made great, great because of the power we put into it, because of our faithfulness and carefulness in the use of what we have.

Our Lord dealt so patently with the little things of life that to many he seemed no great saint. The chroniclers of the world in his day are silent of him. An apparently small life his! Yet it was charged with an affluence of divine greatness. His human body seemed so ordinary in spite of its radiance. That tiny child! To kneel in front of that! You know what a child is like? – so pitiful, so small. Must I kneel in front of that and say: 'This is the God who made me. This wee Child is the Creator of the world!' Is it possible to believe that this Child is God? Faith gives that vision to us. In the little things of life we shall then learn how to find the infinite greatness of God. To despise nothing, to use everything, to realize how near, all our life, we are to the infinite power of God. We have only to take our life as it is, the people we meet, our work, our prayers, and use these to the full. If only we used all these precious things that he has set in our way! To pay no regard to them is to lose our due sense of perception. To shut our eyes to them is to lose the nearest we shall get to the beauty of God. Carefully, deliberately, with a sense of responsibility, not torturing but inspiring us, shall we try to live a life closer to this infinite friendship of God.

Yet, we must realize the solemn warnings of the Apostle. To watch our Lord dealing with people is to realize that there must come an ultimate moment, a last divine grace, though the mercy of God is in itself without end. He is infinite, endless. It is we, we who have an end. God's mercy shall go on forever, but we, at last, close down. There must be a last grace. What shall we do with it when it comes? As we have lived, so shall we deal with it. In the life of grace you never stand still. You go forward or backward. You move the whole time. You are a pilgrim, you are being hunted, driven by God across the face of the earth, but you can halt and go back. He that looketh back is not fit for the kingdom. He cannot reach it if he is turning his back on it, going the wrong way. As long as we realize what is asked of us, as long as we try, out of our store of small things, to gather the good things given, we must trust to the infinite mercy of God that all shall go well with us. Our need is then to use daily the grace of God. Grace is given often; all we need is to awaken to the fact. Use his grace, trusting to his mercy, that we shall be led where he would have us go.

18 SIN

IN THAT part of the Gospel in which the Last Supper is de-scribed, our Lord is shown us breaking off in the middle of it to say to those at table with him that one of them is about to be-tray him When St. Matthew recounts it from his own vivid memory of what happened, he tells us that everyone was much troubled at what the Master had said to them, and each questioned him anxiously: 'Is it I, Lord?' Our Lord had told them that someone sitting there at table with him and with them had done a most contemptible thing – had sold and betrayed him. To this, each answers with the question: 'Is it I, Lord? Is it I?' They had lived with him for the three years of his public ministry, had listened to his exhortations, and knew the type of character that he wished them to become, knew the virtues that he most extolled. Surely they had learnt their lesson well! We can see that here. Not for one moment do they think of accusing one another of this terrible sin. Not for a moment do they suspect the others of it. Not even Judas crosses their minds as the likely offender. At the back of their minds is no thought as to who it could be. No one says even to himself: 'I can guess who that is.' They say at once, each one of them, John, Peter, James, Thomas, Andrew, and the rest: 'Is it I?' Only self-accusations, and by all.

We feel at once that these twelve gathered round their Master, these twelve priests at their very ordination service, have realized that they are, each of them, very near to evil, not as an outside enemy, but as part of their very make-up. There could be no evil so loathsome as treachery; yet each is at once as willing to suspect himself of it as suspect another. As we read this, we cannot but admire these men who so little suspect each other that they are ready to suspect themselves of being guilty of a crime that they have not done. Each knew how near he stood to falling into evil. Have we not to see in this a point of view which it would beseem us to have? Our Lord wants his followers to recognize what a little gap there is between themselves and the most revolting sinfulness, and also to be utterly unsuspicious of others' sinfulness; to know our own frailty and to be blind to the evil of those amongst whom we live.

When you open your paper and see that some ghastly crime has been committed, perhaps your first impulse is to ask yourself how it can be that human nature can fall so low as that. Let your second at least be the frank recognition: 'I share that nature. To those depths I myself can fall.' We know that, whoever the criminal was, he was as much human as we are, that he had a home, was a child, played with children, grew up with his family, was at school, went to work, had his friends, his hobbies, his pleasures, his quiet moments, his favorite books. There is no doubt a type of criminal of a mentally low grade, a sub-normal being; there are also those whose surroundings from childhood have seemingly condemned them to a life of crime. We can have pity in our hearts for these. But even those who started in good surroundings have slipped and fallen. We share their nature.

No crime, however dastardly, is ever beyond us. Perhaps once upon a time we can remember (is it a long while ago or only a short time?) thinking of some wrongdoing as having no power to tempt us, as the sort of thing to which we should not fall a victim, and yet we have fallen to it, at least in thought. Once upon a time there were things that seemed to us dreadful. Are they quite so dreadful now? Once there were things at the very thought of which we imagined the human heart would shudder. Yet now we may have to confess that they no longer appall us as they did. We have at least become accustomed to them. Once we were shocked at things people said; now perhaps we say them ourselves. Once upon a time – well, once all sorts of things distressed us, and now we are doing what then we scorned others for doing or, it may be, so far we do not do them, but only think them and are restrained from doing them, not from any motive of religion, but out of human respect. How we denounce human respect, yet from what have we not been saved by this same human respect! We were saved because we dared not let others know what was in our hearts and eyes. Someone was looking, someone might tell. Of course, in the world there is evil. Our Lord teaches that there is evil in every human heart, except in those two that are our great inspiration.

Let us hold by this, that we live close to evil. Suddenly it may be laid bare – like lightning at night when the sky is torn with a sudden flash, and the dark world and some near horror is made manifest Suddenly, too, we may see a menacing beast revealed to us within. At another time this is manifest to us when false accusations have been made against us or we are suspected of something petty or wrong. Our impulse is to be furious, indignant that anyone should think us capable of anything so base. We never even dreamed of doing it, we say by way of expostulation. Never even dreamed? When other people are bois-terous in their denials, we are led to suspect that there must have been something in what was alleged against them. Over-strong protests have the contrary effect to what they are meant to create in our minds.

And our denials? Do we think people were taken in? But the accusations really were false. False in fact? Probably. False in desire or consent? Perhaps; perhaps not. Perhaps at least we very nearly fell.

Almost worse is it, not when they suspect us, but when they praise us, when they say to us: 'Oh, you are different from other people. You are not that sort of man.' We dared not say anything by way of protest lest we should seem to be seeking for more praise. Yet, though we said nothing, our hearts knew how false were the fine things they said of us. Then we realized how far short we had fallen of the praise they showered on us. Nor do we realize it any less when we have resisted evil but known how close to falling we had been. It is true that by the grace of God we escaped it, but escape was the right word; it very nearly had us in its mesh.

Evil in the human heart! Evil in every one of us! There is no crime so contemptible but we are capable of committing it; we share the same nature as the person who has done this thing Between us and him, between our dreams and desires and his desires and dreams, there is something common. This our Lord taught the apostles; and this they learned. His training was to self-insecurity, never being sure of self. Now, our Lord brought them there, not to leave them there, but to lead them on to something higher. Our Lord did nothing merely to darken their world. He never tried merely to destroy their self-confidence. Not even for this did he speak so sharply to the Pharisees. He broke the self-confidence of his followers, their good opinion of themselves, only that he might build something better on the broken, contrite heart. On the ruins of self-respect he will fashion confidence in himself.

So he wants each of us to realize that he is a sinner, that there is something contemptible in him, that in him is that which would make his dearest friend loathe him if he knew. Because of that native menace in all men he came; because every man needed redemption from the beast within This was to be accomplished by giving us confidence in himself, by our resting entirely upon him. By so doing, the grace of God – the power of God, reaching us through the sacraments – transforms us into him. But the work begins by making us aware of our sinfulness. We must first be taught to recognize that we are sinners. Once we have reached to this self-knowledge, we have begun the work of our saving. Our salvation in effect will start in this way. The Light of the world will turn his light on the dark places of our soul. He will show us, as no one else can, the secret shrine of evil within us. He does this that we may realize how weak we are.

'Is it I, Lord? Is it I? Am I really like that? Am I really so mean as to be no better than that after all that you have done for me?' Yes, the whole point is that we, all of us, are and shall always remain capable of the greatest villainy. This is no exaggeration of the pious preacher or the dreamy nonsense of some dithyrambic moralist. This is good, solid, Christian teaching. Moreover, its purport is not to discourage us but to lift us up. He wants us to realize our weakness only in order that he may substitute for it his strength. He never does anything to put us off his service, but everything to bring us into his service. He urges us this way to ask for pardon and help and confidence in himself.

Even children have their hidden source of evil. What dreadful nonsense is talked about the innocence of childhood! Children know less evil than we do, but they enter on the evil they do know quite as deliberately as we enter upon ours. Compared to us, they are innocent; but within them, as they know so sadly, there is a capacity for wrong. There is evil everywhere. All our nature is most frail. Where one has fallen, all may fall. Our Lord came to repair mischief, not to say there was none.

So he gave man faith that he might have his eyes open to the wonderful things he has put to our hand, and hope to enable us to continue our efforts against temptations, and love that we grow not lonely in our fight but remember that he is by us. You will have found that in difficult mountain-climbing it is wiser not to look down. Even though the height above you is a great way off, it is safer to look up than down. Looking down shows you the awful depths below. The sight of these may paralyze you and make you lose your balance. If you would climb, put fear aside. Hope is what you need. Hope is what he gave us. Hope? Yes, even in the cry: 'Is it I, Lord?'

In the parable in which he described the judgment at the world's end, our Lord says to the wicked: 'I was hungry, I was thirsty, poor, naked, in prison, dead. Yet you did nothing for me.' They answer him-'When did we see you hungry, thirsty, naked, dead? There were many indeed in prison and rightly so, but we never saw you there.' To whom he answers: 'You had your scorn for others. They were my brethren, so that in them it was me their brother that you also scorned.' And then, when the good were praised because they had cared for him, they had likewise to admit that they were not aware that they had done him service. Even the good were blind: 'We did that sort of thing, but we were not convinced that all the cases we helped were genuine; yes, we did do what we could for them, but we did not realize that they were you.' To whom his reply is instant: 'Come, ye blessed of my Father.' 'What? Is it I, Lord? Is it I?' In that last scene the good look timidly

behind them as though they could not really be the people addressed
by him as blessed of his Father. Who were they to be summoned to the
Father, who had helped just some few folk in human distress?

God will show us always the evil of our character, how close to the
surface of us is the untamed beast. But, if because of this we put our
confidence in him absolutely, one day in his infinite mercy he will
show us our good. Only if we lift our eyes from our good and look at
our evil, and also look beyond it at that blessed compassion of his
loving heart; only if we can keep our eyes both on our weakness and
his strength, will he say to us too: 'Come, ye blessed.' We shall be
abashed and say the words that have so often been on our lips here in
self-abasement: 'Is it I, Lord? Is it I?' 'Surely,' will his blessed answer
be, 'surely, thee am I calling. Enter thou into the joy of thy Lord.

The Loneliness of Sin

The gravity of sin comes from its being an offence against God; but its
effect on the soul is to be measured neither by the guilt nor by the
temporal punishment inexorably affixed, but by that deep sense of
loneliness it brings with it. Scripture is full of the comparison between
the soul and a waterless desert; in one place comes the phrase, 'the
desolation of the wicked'. Now this represents a quite apparent effect
that sin has upon the soul. It makes a man realize as nothing else does
the terrible loneliness of life. It is possible that after a while this
perception wears off, and the soul becomes in this way, as in others,
hardened to the sense of sin; but at first, when the conscience is still
delicate and refined, after an offence against God, human nature feels
itself to shrivel up and become cut off from the rest of the world.
Notice children when they have done wrong; how difficult it is for
them to face their fellows again; they seem to have severed themselves
from the companionship of those with whom they are wont to play. A
scolding drives them entirely upon themselves, and the punishment of
solitude which grownups rather thoughtlessly inflict on little people is
as nothing compared with the terrible desolation that has already
overspread the tiny nature. The sense of sin brings with it a feeling of
loneliness, when the first pleasurable excitement has worn off. This
loneliness our Lord himself submitted to in the hour of his dereliction.

Nor is it to be supposed that the desire that so many saints have
shown for solitude is in any way a contradiction of this. Really, it is a
further proof; for it is, on the whole, just the saints who do desire
solitude: the sinners are far too lonely to find a desert at all suitable or
even tolerable. Notice who those are that spend most of their time in

rushing from one distraction to another: they are those who have felt the torment of loneliness so fiercely that they cannot endure to be by themselves. So lonely are they that they spend all their time feverishly pursuing one pleasure after another or one work after an-other – anything or anybody that will take their minds from the torment of themselves. The oppression that sin effects in them makes them anxious to live their lives to the utmost in the full stream of human existence. Pleasure is heaped up in crowded hours to make them forget the aching void of their hearts. Indeed, it is their greatest punishment that they finally succeed, until they lose at last all perception of their pain, whereas the saints are so full in themselves of love that they must needs draw off alone to be away from all others; so accompanied are they by the dear presence of their Friend that they cannot stay and waste (as to them it seems) the precious hours with any other thought than of him. Thus, Mary sat at the feet of Jesus, while Martha, busied over many things, hurried to and fro, sometimes in his presence and sometimes out of it. This does not mean that we can show our love only by retiring out of the world to the cloister; but it does imply that only those can stand the loneliness of life who have their hearts aflame with the love of another; while the effect of sin is to produce a feeling of loneliness which irks humanity.

Sin's loneliness is evident, and the cause of it no less clear; for by sin the presence of God by sanctifying grace is removed. After all, God is the most intimate neighbor of the soul; no other power can creep so close to the heart and tangle itself so cunningly with the roots of our desire. The will is at his mercy alone, so as to be moved by him without in any sense destroying its freedom. Every movement of goodness is effected by the special impulse of his virtue, and every thought that turns to the things that are more excellent must have been inspired by his illumination. For him, then, was my soul wholly formed, and without him it is baulked of its purpose and reduced to a hungry longing for what it cannot achieve. Thence is it restless till it finds its peace in him; thus is it lonely, deprived of all that is most required by its several faculties. Man, in other words, was made for love, the diviner part of him for divine love.

By sin is all this love dried up; the parched and thirsty soul feels, therefore, the need of the dew of God and rushes madly as the beasts wander in the jungle looking for the water that they cannot find. The soul by sin is thus made solitary. I have therefore to take care that the grace of God is not removed and the life of my soul destroyed. When I am feeling particularly the loneliness of life, perhaps the cause is that I lean too little upon God; perhaps it is that my sins will not let me feel that inward presence that is the sole real source of peace here below. I was created by Love for love, and when by sin I act contrary to Love, my heart must necessarily feel his absence.

Sin in the Divine Economy

If we were truly humble, we should never be astonished to find ourselves giving way to sin. We should indeed be horrified, but not surprised. This is one of those things that are so hard to understand. Once we have really begun to try to see what we are like, we recognize ourselves to be the most evil of all creatures. This is no mock humility. At least, we can put it another way round by saying that we know more evil against ourselves than against anyone else. I know others in history or amongst my acquaintances who have done worse things than I, but I cannot say truthfully that they are worse, because I do not know. I do not know either their temptations or their conditions of interior life, nor do I know their motives; and until one knows motives, one cannot tell whether what was done was sinful or not. The Catholic Church never claims to judge intentions, to judge why people do what they do. She may condemn acts, but never persons in their own consciences: 'All judgment must be left to the Son.' It follows, then, that I know worse against myself than against anyone else. I know that I am a sinner.

I have also every reason for supposing that I shall always be a sinner. There is nothing in myself to warrant any supposition to the contrary; consequently, I have to keep in view, as far as my own power is concerned, the prospect of sinnership to the very end. To hold this in memory is at least to avoid any disturbing discouragement when I find myself giving way to my old sins. I shall not be surprised at their return, even if I find that for some reason or other I remain free from them for some time. To be surprised because I had kept clear of evil is more reasonable than to be surprised because I had fallen back into habits of sin.

The value of recognizing this seemingly depressing truth is, first, that it prevents me from falling into the habit of confusing hurt vanity with an act of contrition. To be distressed because of sins – especially of returning sins that I thought I had rid myself of – is not contrition, as like as not, but mere hurt vanity. Such an act of sorrow cannot well be supernatural, since God does not come into it, but myself only. It has not a supernatural motive but a natural one; it is not in the least a motive of conversion, but the beginning of despair. Let me, on the other hand, hold to the conviction that I am a sinner, and at least I shall not be discouraged at my falls; and this is no mean accomplishment.

We shall always be sinners; consequently, we must not allow ourselves to lose heart over our sins. But why is sin allowed in the world at all? We do not know, and perhaps never will know till the very end of all. But we do know this, that God allows it. Unless he allowed it, it would not be found here. We know also that God does not will it, because he could not be the perfect holiness he is if he willed it. Yet, though it be contrary to his direct will, it is not contrary to his permissive will. God allows it, and therefore God has a good motive in allowing it, for God cannot have motives other than good.

God allows sin; God allows me to sin. Why? I do not know, but it is something to know that God does allow it and that he has a good motive for so doing. Now, the fact that God allows it does not in any way excuse me from the guilt and responsibility of my wrongdoing. These sins are sins, and I know quite well that I deliberately chose evil rather than good. It was a deliberate choice of my will. God's permission does not, therefore, absolve me, but it does give me reason to think differently of my sin after the event than if it bore no relation to God at all. For it is clear that, since he allows sin and since his motive in so doing is a good motive, and since his only motive can be love, I am allowed to fall into sin because God loves me. However disconcerting this thought is, undoubtedly it is a valuable one because it makes me realize that something can be done with sin to make it useful to me.

What else can that mean but that God wishes me out of my past sin to come nearer to him, to find somewhere in that un happy past a motive too for love? Nor is this difficult to find, for the past seen in this light is not merely full of my failures, it is also full of God's for-giveness – the remembrance of which shall surely be as important to me as the remembrance of my sins.

Let me not suppose on this account that I have reason to presume on God's forgiveness. I must not take as my conclusion that it does not matter that I sin, for God will forgive me. God will not forgive me if I am not sorry for my sins, and sorrow I cannot have if I take no trouble to avoid sin and merely think of the infinity of God's mercy. But the way it should affect me is this: I should try to make capital out of this past sin by letting it bring me nearer to God. The starting point of this concept must be that there is a divine purpose being achieved by this permissive act of God. We know that he is so powerful that he could have prevented sin. We know that he did not prevent sin. We know, therefore, that sin must in some way fit into his plan. Let us say, as St

Augustine did, that God is so powerful that he can bring good out of evil.

There is a passage in the writings of Juliana of Norwich in which this idea is stated in the terms in which a mystic would see it. She was privileged, as it seemed to her, to ask God why he should have let sin come; and his answer, as she understood it, was not a direct answer and yet an answer after all. God set in front of her the fact that by Adam's sin more harm was done than by any other sin, more harm to man and more dishonor to God. Yet, the remedy for this was the Incarnation, which was more pleasing to God than the sin of Adam was displeasing; else we should never have been saved. But also the Incarnation brought to man finer and fairer things than sin had brought him hurt and pain: 'Since I have made well the most harm, then is my will that thou know thereby that I shall make well all that is less.' This was to show her, as she thought, that even the sins of men have a place in the economy of God, and that man can, if he so chooses, use them for finding an additional reason for loving and serving God better. Indeed, what else is the act of sorrow but some such act as this? It is the act of a soul that deliberately turns to its own sin, but not merely to its own sin. Sorrow is not merely self-regarding, else it would be no act of religion at all. Religion is looking at God and paying to God what is owed him. What do we owe God when we have sinned against him? What is sin? It is an act or thought or word or omission against the law of God. Truly so. But it is also against his love. It is an act, not only of disobedience, but of malice God therefore asks of us in return by way of recompense not merely that we shall be obedient, but that we should love. It is love exactly that we must have in our act of sorrow, or else it is not sorrow at all. Love is turning to God. Turning to God means that he is in our thoughts as an aspiration to help us to a deeper and stronger resolution to do better than we have done in the past. Past sin can thus be made to re-assert to us the claims of God on us. This does not justify sin, but it can be made the way in which sin also plays into the hands of God.

Indeed, so strong is this idea in the New Testament that our Lord almost seems in a well-known scene to put a premium on sin: 'Which of the two loved him most, Simon? The one who had been forgiven a little or the one whose forgiven debt had been the greater of the two?' Surely the answer of Simon is reasonable: 'He to whom most was forgiven has more reason to love most.' It sounds as if our Lord wanted to teach that the converted sinner had more reason for loving God than those have who have never done wrong. But this he cannot mean. What is evident is the positive teaching that those who have been forgiven much have much reason for love.

Sorrow, then, is an act of love. In it the soul looks beyond its own fault to see God at the end of the vista. Sorrow, to be supernatural, must bring in God, and that means that in my act of sorrow I have to think more of God than of myself, give more time to the consideration of him than of myself. That is why our Lord, when he meets St Peter after the Passion, does not say to him: 'Art thou sorry?' but he asks: lovest thou me?' There is a whole world of difference between these two. Peter was sorry, of course. So also was Judas; else he would never have hanged himself. But the sorrow of Judas is a purely human sorrow, the sorrow that is the offspring of hurt vanity. He suddenly woke to the meanness of what he had done and was terribly ashamed. But shame is not sorrow. Shame is a much less inspiring emotion. It leads indeed of its nature to depression, as the sequel showed. Love, on the contrary, is inspiring for the simple reason that it takes the soul away from the contemplation of itself – always a depressing sight to those who are honest – and focuses its attention on another. That is what we mean by love. So the remembrance of past sin can become either of two things: an emotion which is self-regarding and depressing, or an emotion that is other-regarding (to wit, God-regarding) and inspiring to further effort. The difference between these two is the whole teaching of Christ. He came to lead men to God, and that in every part of their lives. He came to lead them there through everything they did. There must be no exceptions, no bare patches which are exempt from this. Even sin, once over, must be brought under the dedication of the Gospel teaching. Not even evil can be allowed to escape.

Sin, then, can be used afterwards to make the memory of it an inspiration towards a greater love of God. This is also the real act of sorrow, the perfect contrition that thinks of sin and is sorry for it because it has offended God. Here is true sorrow in which self is forgotten and God only remembered. It is not sorrow only, but sweet sorrow: it is love.

19 CONSCIENCE

THE reason why we fail so often in our attempts to overcome our faults is that we start quite the wrong way round. Usually our efforts are directed to the task of overcoming evil, a dull and spiritless endeavor. As a result, our eyes are trained to look on the less pleasant side of our character, to the discouraging occupation of counting up the number of times we have done wrong. What can come from this but an unhopeful vision of life? We look back on the past day or year, and it is measured for us simply by the sins we have committed. No doubt it is very important to be conscious of our shortcomings, for otherwise we shall grow into the fashion of the Pharisee and be self-complacent sinners, but, on the other hand, a too exclusive view of our falls from grace will absolutely paralyze all our efforts and we shall be so numbed by despair as to be unable to proceed. But worst of all is it that we call this unedifying process an 'examination of conscience'. Surely this is to confuse all sorts of ideas. If I examine my conscience do I really expect to find only evil in it? Have I not a right to peer about and see whether or not there is some good there as well? Is it fair to myself to suppose that I have never done anything well? Surely this will necessarily be the result of concentrating on what I have done wrong without keeping equally before my eyes what little, of course under God's grace, of real good there has been in my life. In any case, I have no business to call it an examination of conscience, for conscience is not simply composed of evil. To examine my conscience I must actually review my whole being, good and ill alike; it must be thoroughly undertaken and not lightly rushed through. Do not many of the terrible scruples that grow so easily out of modern spiritual training arise from this practice of scrutinizing too closely the evil and avoiding the good in ourselves?

Conscience is simply my whole nature articulate. It is the voice that results from my faith, my actual way of living, my ideals, etc.; hence the better and finer my state of soul, the more refined and delicate my conscience. As I advance up the scale of creation towards the perfect figure of our Master, I necessarily look more and more askance at wrongdoing, and feel a terrible hatred for all injustice. But as I get more and more hardened in sin, naturally my conscience becomes less and less susceptible to the prompting of any higher ideal; indeed, no prompting at all comes from within, for it has no longer any meaning to me. If, then, I am to examine my conscience, I must go behind all the merely apparent actions of good and evil and see the causes of my deeds. It is not examining my conscience to know that I am uncharitable, untruthful, impatient, impure. I want to know why I fall, or what makes me fall. The sin is a sin, but when I have learnt that much, I cannot hope to make progress unless I can also find out the reason of it. A general would be a foolish fellow who was content to count up merely the number of times he had been defeated, and considered that he had done all he ought to do when he had published the statistics of his losses. In every case it is necessary to find the failures, but still more important to discover their causes; and for this it is essential to go over the whole ground, to discuss both good and evil, and not to be content with a bare enumeration, but to probe more deeply into the ultimate reasons for things. Yet does it not happen that I speak of an examination of conscience when I have hurriedly gone through in my night prayers my sins during the day?

What, then, have I to do? I must examine my conscience: that is, I must look at myself as nearly as I can as God sees me. I must not be as that foolish man of whom St James tells us that he saw himself in the glass and then went off and forgot what manner of man he was. Perhaps I am even more foolish and never even look at the glass to see what I am like. To change the metaphor, I stand on the brink of my own soul, shivering and never daring to sound its depths, for fear that I should find much that I should have to change. But I must face myself and count up the evil and the good, not be content with the enumeration. I must look for the causes of things. Thus, surely, many a child has been confessing its sins of untruthfulness and never realized that its real trouble was cowardice. Night by night it had examined its 'conscience' in the sense of finding out what it had done wrong; but it had not been taught to discover the causes of its troubles, with the result that it never improved. Had it been properly instructed it would have found that it was not really untruthful, had no desire to tell a lie, but was simply terrified into lying because it feared the consequences. Thus, it should have set to work, not to meditate on the virtue of truth, but on the virtue of courage. It has never improved, because it never knew what caused its untruthfulness.

Because of all their efforts to secure Catholic education and a Catholic atmosphere for their children, Catholics must admit that conscience can be changed, trained, developed. We protest that it is possible for the consciences of children brought up under non-Catholic principles and with non-Catholic ways of regarding life and its obligations, to become distorted and even destroyed. All the promptings that are right and normal and that should be almost instinctive, may become hopelessly obscured, and their fine delicacy so blunted as no longer to produce that feeling of shame and moral reprehension that should at least follow an evil deed. No doubt there are certain principles that are so fundamental and elementary that it is very difficult to imagine them wholly inoperative – such, for ex-ample, would be the rudimentary idea that a man should do to others only what he would wish them to do to him. In varying forms, this idea seems to be of universal acceptance; but other subsidiary notions can certainly become obliterated by custom or ignorance. St Paul uses a most expressive word to describe the effect made by sin upon the conscience, for he speaks of sinners as having their consciences 'seared'; that is, the delicacy and responsiveness to evil suggestion have been lost through a hardening of the perceptive faculty of the soul, comparable only to the loss of all feeling produced by a burn, which hardens the skin and deadens its perceptive power. Thus, by everything that we proclaim, we show that we Catholics regard the conscience as something easily affected and capable of education and refinement.

Conscience, therefore, is subject to influence; hence it cannot be a mere collection of principles. Sometimes in our conversation we speak of a man of conscience as 'a man of principle,' as though the two things were necessarily the same, whereas they are quite distinct. Principles are unchanging, whereas conscience is alive. Conscience is more accurately what the poets have always described it to be – a voice, not in the sense that it is a voice external to us, but that it is the inarticulate expression of our whole being. Perhaps we have had the notion that con-science was the voice of God whispering in our ears, a voice that tells us of things of which we are ignorant, an instructive suggestion, much as revelation is. But conscience is nothing of the kind. It is the voice simply of ourselves, though based upon certain rudimentary principles such as we have already described. It is, if you like, a faculty, like the musical faculty, which must first of all be inherent before it can be cultivated, but which assuredly requires cultivation. Left to itself, it might go off into all sorts of wrong paths. It needs to be taken in hand by someone who has both judgment and taste, by whom it may be fashioned to its best purpose. Conscience is always changing, always fluid, so that we do things today that our conscience is silent about, whereas tomorrow it may furiously upbraid us for even thinking of them. I have, then, obviously to train my conscience, for of itself, except in the very simplest things, it will not necessarily act aright. There are souls, indeed, that are naturally Christian, but how few, and even these not on every point!

To train my conscience I have need of some definite principles by means of which I can be certain that I am on the right path. What are these? Perhaps I may notice that there are three such sources: (1) The principles of the natural law, such as justice, truthfulness, etc.; (2) the principles of the supernatural law, laid down in faith and morals by the Church as representing the teaching power that Christ left to continue his work; (3) the actual life of our Lord, which takes in concrete form the abstract principles that the others profess. In the first two we see simply how life should be lived; in the last we can see it actually lived. These separate sources, if properly studied, will give us the main ways of achieving a properly regulated conscience; for the real trouble of conscience is that we are responsible for conscience itself. It is not enough for me to say that my con-science lets me do this or that, since the further point can quite properly be put: Has my conscience any right to do it? Certainly it is possible to have a false conscience, and it is possible also that this falseness of conscience may be my own fault entirely. The question, then, is not so simple as it sounds, for conscience is not the external voice of God whispering to me, but is really just the voice of my whole being. To see, therefore, whether or not my conscience is correct, I must make frequent meditation on the faith and on the Gospels, and on that code of moral life which I find accepted even by those who make no pretence to be following the teaching of Christ. Only when I have done this shall I really know whether my conscience is healthy or scrupulous, whether lax or too personal, or whether it follows the lines laid down by our Blessed Lord and continued after his design by the Church. Conscience is above all, but that is only because it has been formed after the fashion of Christ.

Conscience is, therefore, a voice springing from the whole being. It is partly a judgment on principles, as when my con-science tells me that such and such a principle is wrong, and partly an application of principles, as when in the ordinary round of events I reject a temptation to do something because my conscience informs me that this would not be right, would not accord with certain principles that my faith has taught me to accept. On the whole, and chiefly, it concerns the application of principles rather than the mere selection of principles, for these are selected by the reason or the light of revealed truth. In the voice of conscience, then, we notice the idea of moral obligation of moral insistence; the root idea of it is: 'I must.' This voice of conscience, then, we certainly have to obey, for it is the sole personal command that reaches us. Even authority could not be accepted nor its ordinances respected unless it had been backed by the full majesty of conscience. Conscience must sit in judgment on the claims of authority before investing it with the sanction of the moral law. A Catholic has first to convince himself of the divine mission of the Church and be sure that she represents the teaching body that our Lord came on earth to found, before he can allow her to make any demands upon his allegiance. Either deliberately or by implication he has to be made sure of his ground by conscience. So, again, in every action in which the moral obligation which we summarize under the name of duty is felt and attended to, I have to convince myself of the authority of conscience, and have to put conscience in judgment over the claims that are made upon me.

But while in this way I am completely under the dominion of my conscience, I have to remember that, in consequence, I cannot move until my conscience is sure. I may not act until my conscience is really determined; I cannot act, that is, when my conscience is in doubt. The reason of this principle is that, were I to do so, I should in effect be saying to myself: I don't know whether this is right or wrong, but I am going to do it anyway. Obviously, this would be altogether a dis-respectful attitude to God, a complete disregard for the law of God. Yet, on the other hand, it is surely difficult to make up one's mind on all the points that have to be settled by conscience. Often I have to admit that I am not quite sure, but that I think a certain thing is allowed. And here am I doing wrong, for I am acting on a doubtful conscience? No. Why? Because really and practically my conscience has been made certain. What has happened is that I have put myself into some such position as this: I have said I must act from a sure conscience, but in this particular matter I am not quite certain what is right. However, it seems to me that under the circumstances I have enough to justify my doing it, for I do really think it to be allowable; hence, I have done the best I could under the circumstances, for if I were certain that the thing I was going to do were wrong, I should, of course, not have done it. But as I must act somehow, and as this does not appear to me to be actually wrong, I am justified in going through with it. In this way, by getting as it were behind my conscience, I have in reality made my conscience sure, and can proceed to act on it.

I have, then, just to do my best, for my conscience is in-fallible; that is to say, if I make up my mind seriously that a certain thing is right, it becomes right for me. My conscience is not infallible, of course, in the sense that whatever I think right is right in itself, but only that it is right for me. Even when other people tell me what they think I ought to do, even when the priest gives me advice in the confessional (unless I have been rendered abnormal and incapable by scruples), I have to remember that with me and my conscience lies the ultimate responsibility of it. I may not plead their words in my excuse, for my soul is my own. Guided by conscience, which itself has been trained by faith and the moral law and by the example of Christ's life as I find it in the Gospels, I have to steer my own way.

It is the teaching of the Church that I must always follow my conscience. I can never shelter myself behind authority and say that though my conscience objects, I have a right to put it aside and follow authority blindly. Put in this way, I am certainly wrong, for in that case I should be using authority to break up conscience; I should be using that of which the whole basis is an appeal to conscience in order to violate conscience. Yet, on the other hand, is it not true that authority once proved divine must be obeyed, that authority can even instruct conscience, teach it principles of right and wrong, such as left to itself it might never find out at all? This contradiction is sometimes, perhaps, a puzzle to me as a Catholic. How am I to deal with the situation when my conscience and the authority of the Church, whose divine mission I accept, come into conflict? This puzzle, which is simple for Catholics once they examine the matter, is altogether a scandal for non-Catholics. Forgetful of the fact that, during the whole of her rule, the Church has been the champion of conscience against tyranny of the state, or tyranny of superstition, non-Catholics are in haste to suppose that conscience and authority are in opposition, whereas they are necessary for each other – it is impossible to find the one safe-guarded without the other. Wherever authority has broken down, I shall find that in effect conscience has also been overridden, and where authority has been upheld, it has but confirmed the rights of conscience.

But I must begin by recognizing the distinction that, on the whole, conscience is rather concerned with the application of principles than with the settling of principles. Our Lord came to teach truth, and consequently I am sure that in his creed I shall find what I want to guide me through life; but where I shall fail is that I shall from time to time be uncertain as to where or how these wide principles are to be adopted in my ordinary life. Faith says to me that I must not kill, and conscience has to settle which sort of killing is really murder: the two spheres are thus, on the whole, divided. Yet it is certainly possible for them actually to come into conflict. Thus, I can suppose that my faith tells me of an everlasting place of torture called hell, while my conscience tells me that I cannot believe that God would be so cruel. What is to happen? First, am I certain that this is of faith? Yes, I am certain. Then why does my conscience object? Because it cannot square such a place or condition with God's mercy. Then I look back at my conscience and say: well, our Lord uses the phrase 'ever-lasting fire,' and if we follow his words we cannot go wrong. Then the Church has never said that she quite knows what the punishment really consists of, nor can we really have any very accurate concept of eternity. Lastly, at the most, all I can say is that my conscience does not quite see how divine mercy and eternal punishment fit in, but I cannot honestly say that they do not fit in. Thus, the only point that conscience blocks is merely a personal difficulty in seeing how things which faith tells me are compatible can really be so.

Thus it is in every case. Conscience may stick at the explanation, but it has to leave the principles alone. My conscience it-self is a growing thing, quite capable of training and cultivation. For years I may consider certain things allowable, and only come to find them forbidden later in life. Whatever the voice of conscience dictates I must fearlessly follow. But I have also to be sure that conscience itself is properly taught the correct view of life, comparing its acts from time to time with the authoritative decisions of the faith and with the familiar example of the life of Christ. I must in this way take care that I do not yield to authority in those matters where authority has no right to interfere, nor, on the other hand, erect into a principle of conscience what is really nothing else than some foolish fancy of my own intelligence.

20 LAW

THERE is something majestic about the sound of the word law, and something exceedingly irritating. It is majestic because it calls up pictures of stately judges with scarlet robes and venerable wigs, looking so gravely out of family portraits or in the National Gallery, and with these pictures go, too, the remembrance of their sober and dignified judgments, their wise and austere diction, their careful arguments, their power to pronounce the death sentence with its awful ending: 'And may God have mercy on your soul.' Majesty, too, seems linked with it in English history, for, despite occasional exceptions, the law has stood on the whole for the liberty of the subject and constitutional justice. Yet law conjures up not only majesty to our imagination, but sometimes galling restraint. It has done such irritating things, we think it cumbersome, gripped by the dead hand of the past, with its quotations from statutes and cases settled in far-off days under rule of long-dead kings. Its stateliness looks majestic, but proves irritating. It is too majestic altogether and not human enough. It sentences the wrong people and dismisses the wrong people; some wretched woman is harried for murdering a child with which a dishonorable man has left her as a pledge of her constancy and his fickleness, while well-known and public swindlers elude for so long, sometimes finally, the unwieldy operations of the courts. A judge may be most impressive, but a policeman can sometimes be exasperating.

We demand law and order, yet there is nothing under which we chafe more than law and order. The simple truth is that human nature is too moody a thing to fit in for long with regulations and injunctions. The law is fixed and dead; man is unstable and alive. Yet undoubtedly law is from God. By law we mean primarily the principles of justice revealed by God to us, either through faith or the native operations of the mind. A law implies a lawgiver. It cannot be of itself. We notice that motion has its laws, that vertebrates have certain inseparable characteristics, that light is conditioned, and thought, and numbers, and finance. These things we notice, but the explanation of them is guesswork, an hypothesis which states but does not explain. Over all, then, we place God. God made the world and gave to each thing in creation its number, weight, and place.

It is a principle of creation, then, that things are true when they correspond to what God meant them to be, as a portrait is true if it faithfully represents its subject. Now the same principle is to be applied not only to the laws of nature, but to the laws of men. Man was created by God for a certain purpose, to be guessed at by envisaging the nature given him by God. Further, besides the laws of his nature, he needs other laws, that he may live in peaceful society with his fellows. Laws are imposed because man is a sinner. Were he perfect, he would fulfill righteousness of himself. Because of wickedness or ignorance or thoughtlessness or perplexity, he does the thing he should not; laws are to help the man to do the thing he should. For that very reason no law can hold him unless it be according to the law and nature of God. Anything against God is no law; it would be unjust, a violation of justice, a contradiction of man's purpose. Human positive laws, then, must be measured against the eternal principles of truth and justice; they must not oppose these, they need not refer to God or the faith, but they must not oppose the natural principles instilled into our hearts. Majestic or irritating as law may seem to us, according to our moods and our desires, the only view of it that really matters is that if it be law at all, it is divine.

The Commandments

The coming of Christ was not to destroy, but to fulfill. Hence our Lord never in any way abrogated the moral teaching of the Old Law. Whatever Moses had declared to the people as the moral code of Israel was never to be slackened, but rather, under the New Dispensation of love (for which men had been laboriously trained and educated under centuries of fear), to be filled out in fuller detail. The commandments were not, therefore, to be lessened, but to be increased. Whatever had been ordained was still ordained; what had been at one time permitted might not, however, be permitted now. All this is the inevitable result of a higher grade of holiness.

As the soul draws nearer and nearer to the holiness of God, it absorbs more and more of the meaning of sanctity. Things that at one time seemed hardly to suggest a scruple now become considered in a new light, from a higher plane. The soul has become more sensitive, and can detect flaws and defects where before it would have noticed nothing amiss. As we get holier, we think ourselves always worse, for always more pronounced is the great gulf fixed between what we are and what we should be. And what I can see taking place in my own soul has taken place in a larger way in the upward movement of the race towards God. Before, Moses forbade adultery; but now: 'I say that whosoever lusteth after a woman in his heart hath already committed adultery.' The New Law thus fills in the details of the Old.

It is interesting to see, as a result of this, that without Christianity man would have no real proof of the idea of racial progress. Destroy or deny the truth of Christian teaching, and nothing can be found to show any advance on our part towards the 'perfect day'. The whole doctrine of progress rests upon a supposition that man has grown towards a larger and freer hope. Christianity alone, especially Catholic Christianity, can ratify and confirm this. Abolish our idea of a Redemption accomplished and our channels of grace through the sacraments, and the whole fabric supporting progress falls to the ground. Apart from the advance made by Christianity upon both Judaism and paganism, there is very little evidence of an upward movement; for neither in art, nor even in crafts, have we – considering the length of time the human race has occupied the earth – made progress. It is difficult for us to improve on the masterpieces of ancient art or literature; and, even in technical skill, some of the builders of antiquity were ahead of us. We are simply unable nowadays, with all our resources, to do what some of them have done. Doubtless we have discovered things they did not know, but also how many things have we not forgotten? The note, therefore, of optimism that pervades modern scientific circles rests upon the moral teaching of Christianity.

This, too, is enforced by the commandments. The new interpretation which Christ has given to the Old Law, the spiritualizing influence which he has shed on what was to a certain extent a material view of moral life, are all advances which will be made noticeable to anyone who will take the trouble to study them severally. He cannot but be struck by the huge advance in ethical values which has been made in this New Dispensation. Under the previous code, the whole relationship of God to man in the matters of moral life was a relationship of rewards and punishments. Was man obedient, then he would be rewarded; was he suffering, then had he done evil and was but fittingly punished. But the new code meant, in some ways, a reversing of the old. Suffering and success were now proofs neither of rewards nor of punishments, but of love only. Whatever happens, I am now to find love as the sole solution of life and its problems. I am not to be searching my heart to see wherein I have failed, but rejoicing myself that in all God is showing me his love. The commandments come, indeed, as restraints to human nature, but as restraints that impose the burden of love. 'Decline from evil' is the least and lowest act of religion; the highest and best is 'Do good'. Man was created, not to avoid sin, but to love God; and we show that love – so he has taught us

– not by calling upon his Name, but by keeping his commandments.

Rights

What constitutes a right? The word has a significance sacred in civilization. It is a word invoked by all who are oppressed, and it finds a response in every heart. It is a phrase that crosses my lips very often, but what exactly does it signify? Though it has been the battle cry of freedom, it has also been used to justify the most terrible tyranny. Every rebel against authority takes to himself the name of right, and every act of authority bases itself on the same sacred claim. How am I to know in my own case, and in the cases of others, what is meant by the word? How can I tell whether really I have a right to this or that? What do I mean by my right to live, to serve God according to my conscience, to hold property, to demand from the State that my children be educated according to my religious beliefs? Of course, I am using these expressions every day of my life, but let me calmly in the presence of God try to make out what they really signify. I am led to this thought first of all, that the word right is not primary, but secondary; that is to say, it is based upon something else which is even more sacred.

Every right is dependent on some duty which must precede it. I can have no rights except so far as I have duties; and apart from what I owe to God, myself, and my neighbor, I have no real justification for any of my rights. That is the first and most important idea that I have to impress upon my mind• the intimate relation between the two things, so that I should never in my mind think of one without thinking also of the other.

Rights must, therefore, be described as the means to achieve duties. Once I find that I have a duty to perform, I shall find all sorts of conclusions following at once, and these conclusions establish definite rights. Thus, my conscience informs me that I have certain duties to God, therefore I can fitly argue I have a right to all those things that enable me to fulfill those duties. I find, again, that I have duties to myself, to the cultivation and development of my own soul, to the application of the various talents which God has confided to me. Then, obviously, I have a right to all those things which enable me to carry out these duties. Parents have rights over, because they have duties to, their young children; and the children, just because they have duties to their parents, must have rights also from their parents. Similarly, if I have certain duties to the State, I must also have claims of my own that are valid against the State. To repeat, the two ideas are interrelated, interdependent. I may, therefore, quite shortly define a right as the necessary means to achieve an essential end. Once I am convinced that I have something to do, incumbent upon me in my position as a creature or a member of a state or family or Church, then I must claim and endeavor to make good my claim to those things which are necessary for my so doing.

This enlarges at once my idea of my rights and imposes a responsibility on me on every occasion that I use that sacred word. I cannot claim anything as a moral right until I can prove that it is necessary for the fulfillment of some essential duty. Hence it is that, if I can keep this idea well before my mind, I am in little danger of getting selfish in my life. If, whenever I find myself speaking of my rights (even in ordinary conversation), I set to work at once to see whether they are rights at all and what corresponding duties they oblige me to perform, I shall find that I shall not be so quick or so insistent in asserting them. It is a pity that the word 'right' has become so popular a word, and the word 'duty' so dull and respectable; for many people cannot stop talking of the one who imagine it to be old-fashioned even to mention the other.

Duties themselves do, indeed, demand in their performance some tax upon my pleasure or my will. I must deny myself something; to do what I ought to do, there must always be some self-sacrifice. My rights, therefore, become nothing more than the requisite opportunities for denying my own will. Let me clamor, therefore, through life, never for rights, but for the better understanding of my own destiny, and only assert that I must be allowed to fulfill my duty. Let me never use the word 'right' without the swift consciousness of the duty involved; for rights from the very nature of the thing have nothing at all to do with private privileges (which are exceptions on the whole to be reprobated, and seldom if ever to be demanded), but sacred obligations.

21 OBEDIENCE

OBEDIENCE is an essential virtue of the religious life, but it is no less essentially the virtue of the Christian life; it is an essential for all those who would follow Christ. The Gospel story, indeed, reads in that sense like a Greek tragedy, for there is a persistent insistence upon the idea of necessity working its way throughout. When watching the tragic plays of the great poets, we feel that the characters are like puppets in the hands of some higher power; struggle as they may against the fatal end, they are driven relentlessly to the divine purpose: the human will is forced to accept the divine. Of course, as Christians, we know this to be untrue, because the will is free; yet, for all that, we are assured that the plan of God is never disarranged. 'I come to do the will of him that sent me' is a refrain which comes repeatedly in the Fourth Gospel; and as a counterpoint, we have his relief when all is ended: 'I have finished the work thou gayest me to do.' It was this, too, that his last conscious breath confessed: 'It is consummated.' Even in the Synoptic Gospels (as the first three Gospels are called), where the dramatic side of his life is obscured, or at least not brought out in full detail, we read his saying to the protesting apostles: 'It is necessary that the Son of Man should die.' His life, then, was planned on simple lines; it meant that he came into the world to do a certain definite work and that he was straitened until it should be accomplished. His idea of goodness consisted almost wholly in this immediate subjection to his Father. His model prayer contained it; his own prayer in the Garden meant little else; his chosen ones were not those who said: lord, Lord!' but 'who did the will of the Father'.

What, then, became a dominant principle in our Lord's life must become equally the dominant principle of mine – obedience. It helps to make life so much simpler, and the good life a thing of practical clearness. First of all, I have to get clearly into my head what it is that God requires of me; and this itself means a good deal. I find myself a child in a family, a citizen in a state, a worker under some employer, a Catholic member of a Church. Here, then, straightway I am subject to four separate authorities, and have to discover the rules and requirements of each; I have to find out for myself what orders these four authorities lay upon me, and the limits of the obedience they may claim. There will be a great easing of my troubles when I have become convinced of these things. It shows me at least some of my pathway and prevents to a certain extent my stumbling. I have, therefore, to discover these four leading sources of governance, their actual and binding commands, and then to fulfill them to the best of my ability. Secondly, it will be of importance for me to find out further to what vocation God calls me: for I am convinced that there is a certain work in the world that God has created me to perform for him – each has his vocation, and each has his capacities for that vocation. God wants me for some purpose. What is that purpose? Unless I can find it out, I cannot ever say: 'I have finished the work thou gayest me to do.' This vocation will be disclosed to me in different ways, and it will be added to indifferently throughout life by countless opportunities for doing good that will be continually opening to me. I must obey in lawful command those lawfully set above me, and must follow the calling marked out for me by God.

Obedience is, indeed, a law in all finite things, for the Infinite can obey nothing but itself. But in the graces of finite creation 'we may observe that exactly in proportion to the majesty of things in the scale of being is the completeness of their obedience to the laws that are set over them. Gravitation is less quietly, less instantly, obeyed by a grain of dust than it is by sun and moon: and the ocean falls and flows under influences which the lake and river do not recognize.' Ruskin's physics may, in this example, be not entirely accurate, but they form an allegory, for it is certainly true that the higher in the scale of being, the more exacting the commands. Obedience, therefore, does not debase, but rather exalts mankind. It is the sign of the nearness of our approach to Christ, and in Christ it is the sign of the complete union between his will and intelligence and the will and intelligence of God the Father.

The superman, whom our generation has been taught to honor by prophets of Prussia and the philosophers of our own press, is placed above all law, unrestrained by morality or any other hampering influence. Yet when I analyze what it all means, I find that even the superman rests upon obedience, i.e., the obedience of others; and if this obedience is good for their characters, then it is justified as being beneficial; but if it spoils them, then the superman stands self-condemned. And if he himself, above all law, is to govern by his whim or fancy, then reason itself is overthrown and all the arguments in favor of his supremacy have lost their value. The gospel of anarchy is a contradiction, for it teaches the law that there is no law; but I, though the child 'of an age that knows not how to obey,' must endeavor to copy in my life the obedience of Christ.

Who Would Resist his Will?

In this pilgrimage of ours, in our life, we are taking our journey under the direction of God himself. Therefore, in our life we are receiving from God messages as to how we should walk. Often, both in the Old Testament and in the New Testament,

phrases and sayings suggest to us that here on earth we are directed by God himself. Somewhere in the Old Scripture it is written: 'Thou shalt hear a voice saying to thee turn to the right, turn to the left. This is the path – walk therein.' I am sure that none of us but must often be aware of this divine voice directing us in life, not merely in the choice of a religious vocation, a profession or a way of life to which we are called, but, once there, once started on our road, still conscious of God's daily speech with us, directing us, sometimes to go back and speak to someone, to go where we had refused to go, or to take this rather than the other. Moreover, we do, almost surely, know that it is the voice of God speaking to us. Not in the whirlwind, not with any overpowering of us as he overpowered St Paul on the road to Damascus, but with that still, small voice, that whisper of his, God has directed us nonetheless surely in our life.

Of course, what is asked of us is that we should be prompt in our obedience to this voice of God. Sometimes, perhaps, people may be puzzled or bewildered as to which of two possible choices is really the divine will for them. This is sure, that if when it is at all clear, you have always promptly obeyed God's voice, you will gradually get to know by spiritual instinct which is the voice of God. If you have a friend, the better you know him the more quickly you know what would be his choice in any particular matter, even where he has not yet told you his mind. You know the sort of play he would like. You know, instinctively, the book that would not interest him You know him so well that you know where his will would lie. So to be able to know God's will, we must have been faithful to God. If we are faithful when we know God's will is manifest, if we are prompt in our obedience, I do not think we normally need trouble ourselves but that we shall know the will of God where it is not at first very clear. To live with God, to obey God, is to learn what God is like, and knowing him we shall, instinctively, know which of two possible paths is his path for us. We are here to do God's will. That, after all, is the purpose of our life; and in our faltering and inconstant fashion, that really is our will, too. We really want to do the divine will.

Promptitude is the first quality of our relationship to this voice of God that is directing us all the time on our road. We should be prompt in our obedience to whatever is asked of us because the voice that speaks is God's voice directing us, because we are on a journey, and because he is the ultimate goal of our journeying.

Prompt in obedience!

Again, it means not only that we must be prompt, but that we must be humble in our obedience. We must take God's view of life and not our own. It is often possible for us to confuse ourselves by laying down as axiomatic our own preconceived ideas: 'This is what I ought to be doing. This is how I should be employed.' Thus we persist in our own will, choosing beforehand what we should be about. We must be humble. We must empty ourselves of our own ideas. We must wait for the voice of God to settle things and not be determined on our own choice.

What is so evident in Scripture is the way in which people who merely listened for the voice of God, get where you think they never could get. Look at our Lady. She was marked by God to be the Mother of his Son, yet she had had the divine will, somehow, manifested to her that she must vow her virginity to God. You as a spectator would say that she had thereby spoiled her chance of becoming the Mother of the Messias; that she could never be the Mother of God. All the maidens of Israel had always hoped to be the Mother of the Messias. It is a great dream that still haunts the hopes of Jewish women, that they may be called to be the Mother of the Messias. But here was this voice of God speaking, so she took her vow, knowing it should surely prevent, one might think, every chance of the ultimate fulfillment of this dream. Yet she is the Mother of God despite her vow. 'How can this thing be done?' was immediately her question to the angel. 'I who know not man, how can I become the Mother of God?' 'The power of God shall overshadow thee. . . .The Spirit of God shall descend on thee, and he that shall be born of thee shall be called the Holy One, the Son of God.' What seemed therefore to frustrate her motherhood, actually helped towards it.

Put yourself in God's hands and you will get where God wants you to get. It seems to you that if you obey God's voice you may be spoiling your ultimate chance of success. How can God's will be hurtful? Rather be humble. Not your wisdom, but divine wisdom, will best guide you. Go his way and you will get what he wants you to get. Be prompt and humble.

Another quality required is to be brave in doing the divine will. We require courage in the service of God. You would think, really, if you listened to the people about you who are always disapproving of religion, you would think that what was wanted in religion was fear, not courage. Submission of our will, fear and reverence for the majesty of God, are certainly asked of us. That is true, but courage, undying courage, that is no less asked; and if anybody really sets out in life to look for the divine will and do it, he will need all and more than his mere natural stock of courage. He will need courage reinforced by divine grace, divine power, and divine help. Courage? Surely courage to go the way God wants him to go. It must seem at times to us that though God must be wonderful in his knowledge, and complete and sure in his wisdom, his ways of guiding us and others are not the best ways. You say to a child: 'Don't touch that!' 'Why? Why?' asks the child. A grown-up person often seems foolish to a child. 'Why must I do this?' it asks again. And you try patiently to explain why it must. Yet what child really understands? If the ways of grown-up people, especially wise grown-up people, puzzle a child, will not God's ways be likely to puzzle us? If the gap between mature wisdom and the opening of the child's mind produces bewilderment, what shall not the immeasurable gap between divine wisdom and human wisdom, at the best, occasion to us of bewilderment and dismay? Trust him absolutely and go on, to the very end. Often enough we are not afraid to look for God, but we are afraid, sometimes, to search out the divine ways, but it does terrify us that God shall be searching out ours, that God should be watching and directing us, and that we should have to commend ourselves absolutely to God. We are the children of compromise and what we dread is the full courage that accepts everything unafraid. A child needs courage. It is made to do all kinds of things that it shrinks from. It requires, above all, courage to obey. Well, courage, too, is asked of us – courage to go the way God wants us to go. But if we are obedient, that is, prompt, humble, and courageous in our obedience, God will make us into what we are really capable of being made into, that which he discerns in us.

There is, I suppose, in everyone's heart a desire to be independent, to be let go his own way, indeed, to be himself. We all, at some moment in our life, feel ourselves capable of some-thing, and our lament often is that we have never really had our chance. We grumble that all sorts of things have interfered with us, first this, then that, so that we were deprived of showing the excellences we have. Away back in childhood we were chafed by authority which hindered our desires, hindered our dreams; and we said to ourselves: 'When I am grown up, I shall live my own life. I shall be able to settle things for myself. I shall have freedom.'

Yet, somehow, we never got freedom. Our desires we have never had fulfilled. We never secured our thorough independence. Thus, in the end, we never really dare to become ourselves – except the saints, except the saints! They were fearless. That is what makes them stand out against the background of their time; that is why they are so fine and striking and why round them eddies perpetual discussion. How clearly St Francis stands out! Not because he chose his own life, no! That was the very last thing St Francis ever dreamt of doing. He sought and followed the life God had planned for him That is what made him great. Others did not achieve greatness because they were afraid to go all the way God led. If you and I listened to God's voice directing us and obeyed it, we should be great characters, unafraid of opposition, unbroken by the world's despite. We should be able to scorn mere popular ideas or theories, or the gossip chit-chat that mists human doings in uncharity. We would seem, perhaps, at times to go against our best interests and deny ourselves the use of our own talents and our own gifts; and yet we would never more fail to make use of our possession of them. We should live the life God meant us to live and be ourselves. God alone knows what we are capable of. God alone knows why he made us. We do not know, really, which way we should go, nor what we should do, nor what gifts we have hidden deep within. But God knows; and if we are only obedient to God, he will make of us that which he had in mind when he first designed us. We shall fulfill all his purposes. We shall have room made here on earth for the due employment of all our gifts. To go our own way is to go the wrong way.

If you want to be independent, obey God, and you will be truly independent of anyone else. God is afraid of none. By his side, of none will you be afraid. The hour of darkness will come, it will find you fearless and unafraid. We shall need to be fearless in these our days. The hard ways of life look as though they would grow sterner; the road seems not to be lightening but darkening; for all we know, the worst is not yet. To listen to God's voice is always to go on unafraid into the future. Indeed, it is our only chance to do that. Panic, suspicion, dreadful rumors will else threaten us all our life! We shall be questioning ourselves. Is this God's world? Am I created by God? Is life but a journey that must pass? Is there a city towards which I journey? Is there someone directing my path? Do I believe that? If I do, then I must listen to his directions; I must promptly, humbly, courageously obey and be truly free. If I am obedient to the divine word, I shall achieve the divine ideal. Once you dreamt of your own future, you had your own idea as to what you would do and be in the world, you had your daydreams Now it may be they seem impossible. Whatever your dream of your future was, it cannot equal his dream of you. All your hopes of youth, so wild, romantic, extravagant, are nothing as romantic or splendid as God's designs for you. Lay your own aside. His vision is more richly peopled, his knowledge truer of you, his knowledge, that is, of the place you still could take in life. Leave yourself in the divine hands. Listen for his voice with humility and promptness and courage, and you shall reach at last to the very stature of Christ.

22 SUFFERING

OUR faith, our life, our ideals, our actions should be proof against human respect. We should prefer to obey God rather than man. It is the perfect quality of our Blessed Lord that he was staunch to all the principles that he came to teach. He would rather die than surrender them. He would rather the crowd drifted from him than change one jot or tittle of the message he came to bring. After that dramatic sermon on his Body and Blood that he was to give to be man's food and drink, he preferred to let men leave him rather than alter his teaching to suit their prejudices or their ideas. He was the living truth. Truth is unfaltering; and though it may be many-sided, it is changeless. It is of eternity, it is God. God is truth as well as love. We pilgrims, strangers on earth, in order that we may the better hearten ourselves for our pilgrimage, have to remember that towards which we are journeying, to remember that life here is a passing life, that, though now many things press on us, one day we shall be out of their reach, that life's troubles, perplexities and bewilderments, all that hurly-burly, will at last be done and finished with.

If you go walking, often it is only by a distinct effort that you can keep steadily in front of you that towards which you journey. But if you do, even though you may be tired, the very sense that you are getting nearer, that there is an ending to your journey, will of itself give you courage to go on. In our life on earth, too, it would seem that we need to remind ourselves of that towards which we journey, which is now the hope of all our lives. We should be the most miserable of men unless those things we set our faith on were true. So holding them as truths and journeying towards them, there will always be comfort and inspiration. As man grows older, he cannot help the intensifying of his desires. Perhaps, in a sense, this may also be the purifying of them. Something of the material dreams of childhood and youth are still there. These dreams are not false. Almost, we might say, it is the purpose of faith not only to explain God to us, but to explain to ourselves the secret of ourselves, our old hopes and ambitions, their newer modes.

Our Lord comes and tells us that we were made for God, that he is our purpose. Since he is the object of our creation, though, perhaps, we did not realize it, in all our youthful dreamings and hungers it was really for God that we yearned, really God that we desired. Faith does not come and teach us things altogether outside the range of our ordinary human faculties. We could not believe unless our nature was designed by God to be able to accept the living truths. Faith tells us, indeed, of much that is beyond their range, but not beyond their purpose. It tells us of what can comfort us, perfect us; of what, without knowing it, always men hungered for from the start. We were made for God. Well, you know, if we are made for anything, we cannot help hungering for it. Each child is made for its particular, personal vocation and hungers for it from the first. Pick up any biography and read it. You see the man already in a child, beginning to do the things he wants to do and is to do afterwards. We are all children, and God is the vocation or profession for which we all were made.

People forget what the Christian faith is. They often quarrel with the prominence given to heaven in Catholicism. They will sometimes say: 'Is it not rather selfish to work for a reward? Is this not something degrading to mankind?' They forget the essence of religion: 'Thou shalt love the Lord thy God.' It is not degrading to wish, at last, to possess someone or something that is the love of your heart. No man has been degraded by that; man has been lifted by it. Man is always at his noblest when he is in love with someone or something – with a person, a cause, an ideal. He is most unselfish when he is working for that. Heaven is not a reward in the sense that it is something for which we are laboring. God is our reward. That is what we mean by heaven. In our foolish way what we strive for is to love God. He is the reward for which we were made. For him every faculty is crying out all our time. We were made for everlasting things – for God, the knowledge, love, and service of him. We are interested in many of our own particular interests, whatever they happen to be, but it is not hard to show how these really are but fragments that mirror God.

If you look in the history of mankind, all the arts of man began in worship. All the dramas we first hear of are sacred dramas; the first dance was a sacred dance; the first music was the praising of God in unknown and clumsy manners. The first representation that we know was a representation that lifted man above himself to God. It is out of divine worship that has come everything that has helped man to rise above him-self. But eventually each civilization and culture becomes secularized because men so easily forget the object for which they work. The world is so beautiful that it distracts us. Even we are tempted to say to God: 'Why have you put such obstacles in my way? Why have you given me such a wonderful world to live in? Why have you given me such attractive people to live with?'

He has commanded that he alone shall be worshipped. It is the breaking of this commandment that ruins most human lives. For God they have substituted something less perfect. They see what is visible; they miss the invisible. Yet one should lead to the other. From the visible things the invisible are known. That is what our Lord came to teach us. He took the world and showed it as a parable that could lead man to God. He sees a child – 'Of such is the kingdom of God.' He sees the sower – that, too, is a symbol of the kingdom. Whatever he sees is not something which blocks his vision of God, but something which opens and shows God manifestly. This is the definition of life that he came to teach. 'Because you did it to the least of my brethren you did it to me.' That is the true view, the whole view of life for us. That is what should hearten us and should give meaning to our lives. 'My life is small,' you say. Naturally, but only because you are short-sighted. 'I spend my life looking after this one or that one. I am at someone

else's service always. I never am allowed to live my own life.' Yes, but see – cannot you see? 'Because you did it to the least of my brethren . . .' See whom it is that you are serving? St Francis got off his horse to kiss a leper. He did not see the leper. He saw deeper than that ruin of humanity. The leper would pass. His leprosy would fall from him, but that which was eternal in him would abide. That is what you must remind yourself of if you live in darkness, in dullness, this ultimate fulfillment of your desires. 'My life is empty of purpose,' you may say to me. Oh, blind! blind! Your purpose is above, not here. Not here! To complain that your life is purposeless is to deny Christianity. God is what you are made for, not this busy little world below.

God is kind. He has no need of us, and yet he lets us serve him in a thousand ways. Even here we can come on him; he is not far from any of us. For all this business must pass away and he whom we have served will still hold us. This passes. Do not set your heart on it. Look beyond! You are journeying to a city – your city. The saints are there already and the saints are your saints. As you grow older, the city will seem more familiar to you. You will know so many more each year of those who have gone to walk its streets. The tragedy of living is that in this misty world you can lose the living. The dead you cannot lose. Remember that towards which you journey. It will give reality to your life. All those other things, the troubles and the joys, they pass, but that for which we were made remains forever. Whatever passes, that shall not pass away, Our Lord came with a message of infinite peace to humanity. He gave us a hold by which to steady ourselves in the turmoil of life. Your heart is restless? It must be restless until it finds infinite rest. All of us he has called to that ultimate purpose – for that all we were made. Our soul is so shaped that it will fit into God as a key is shaped to fit into the lock for which it is made. To him we belong: to us he belongs. We were meant to be one. We should remember our ultimate purpose. In our moments of misery it shall be warmth to us. Poor are we? Feeble? Tired? Yet we were made for God.

Go We Must

We live our lives as pilgrims and travelers, but directed in our journey by the voice of God. God, when he created us, had a definite purpose in his mind, and created us in order that we might do this work of his in the world as we journeyed through it; and all our lives, since it is his will for us, God is always speaking to us as to where and how he would have us go. All our lives he but asks of us that we should steadily listen to his voice. Every time we ignore his directions or deliberately act contrary to them, it means that we have missed the turning of the road he desired us to take. It means that only very painfully shall we get back to where he meant us to go.

Looking back, sometimes, we can see where we took the wrong turning. Perhaps out of negligence or perhaps sheer in-difference or perhaps deliberately we refused to enter on it. It was rather too hard at the time. It may take us a long time to get back to where we should have been when we faltered and refused. Since life is a pilgrimage and we are always on the move, since we are travelers and have here no lasting city, it means that every mistake we make can only be remedied after a time.

Sometimes the call of faith comes – and people deliberately refuse to listen to it; all the rest of their lives this still affects them. At last, in much more difficult circumstances, they have to go back and again face the cost of buying truth with pain. In all sorts of ways God speaks to the soul and we refuse to listen, or are merely so foolish that we do not hear him, or hearing, we refuse to obey. Thus are we endlessly hindered and our life made far more painful spiritually than it need have been. To obey instantly is to recover the ground quickly – to find, at once, really where we should be, where we belong. Our Blessed Lord came for the purpose of helping us to realize the greatness of the journey, and the importance of paying attention to the directions given. It is one of the Christian heritages to realize that the road, for us, is something in itself holy; that life here need not be something mean and sordid. Indeed, life cannot be sordid if it is lived in obedience to the divine command. Life itself, here on earth, though it be a pilgrimage, though it be just a wandering, life itself can still be extraordinarily great, but it is great only on the terms that we dare listen to the voice of God and set ourselves to go by it deliberately. After all, God is so strong, so overwhelming, that we never really can escape him. We must, at last, come into the very hands of God. There is that ultimate meeting between us and him whose voice has so often spoken to us. At last, we must stand facing our Judge. If we have listened to that voice on earth whenever we have heard it, and tried to go the way God wanted us to go, then all that while we shall have been getting nearer and nearer to him, and, when we meet him at last, we shall meet him as a Friend. But to meet him so then, means listening to him now.

A great artist is not only someone who gives you a beautiful picture, but someone who teaches you, through what he gives you, to see beauty that you had hitherto missed in life. He gives you, perhaps, a picture of the light falling through a window on a common scene of work, as in those Dutch pictures where the light streams through the window on the red tiles, a woman cooking, or a jug of milk. You begin to realize from the picture the beauty of that in life and recognize it when next you see it. By isolating it, he has made it more apparent to you. Whatever else artists do for us, they do that much for us; they help us to appreciate the things that are actually before our eyes. All the world is in front of us; we look at it and miss its beauty as it goes by.

Our Lord comes to show us the beauty of the life we live in. All his parables are just so many paintings to us. Now, never again can you look at them without remembering what he said. He came to teach us the beauty of the world – to show us how, through our life, God is calling us. We are never far from God at any time. God is speaking and calling to us, and what we realize from his teaching is that it is God calling, so we go gladly, not reluctantly, however hard the thing is or painful which we are called to do or bear. He will never leave us alone. He is pursuing us always, because he has clearly in his mind where he wants us to be. He is urgent with us. If we attempt to take a short cut when he calls us, we shall have to take a long way round to reach the place to which he has called us. If we be patient, even so, we shall get there in the end. Though we sometimes act against his will, he is too much for us. We shall gradually find ourselves shepherded wheresoever he wants us to be.

Over and over again in Scripture we have put before us two, of whom one listens and the other is deaf to the call. The good thief and the bad thief were equally thieves, villains, folk who had broken the law. They are both in equal circumstances and he hangs evenly between them. One sees him, and one misses him. We do not know why it should have so happened, but all we do know is that one saw and had his ears open to listen and the other missed the beauty and the call. Or you have Paul called on the road to Damascus and leaving all to follow Christ, while Judas, who lived side by side with that wonderful life for three years, betrays him with a kiss and then despairs. The life of our Blessed Lord seems to be of incredible beauty. Judas lived side by side with that for three years and missed the exquisite teaching of it. Whatever it was that led him astray, we can hardly guess; yet somehow he went wrong, somewhere missed the turning. He missed it. Did he ever come back? Right to the very end, right up to his very betrayal and beyond and after, he could still have come back on the road to the turning. Peter did. What do they tell us? 'The trembling of a leaf between men's choices – just that by which you may see or miss. The child Samuel recognized the voice at last and begged: 'Speak, Lord, for thy servant heareth.' The rich young man knew the voice but would not heed it. Perhaps he came back when he was no longer rich or young. Perhaps he had to be beggared of both youth and riches before he would hearken and follow. God in our lives and God calling; if we miss his voice he will call again, we may still have a chance to follow, still get where he wants us to be, only much more painfully shall we now find him. A nation, too, can live like that, can ignore the signs against it on the road, and be brought back again only after infinite pain. So is it true of souls. Some would not obey God's voice until, at last, they had to.

God then has his will for us, his high designs. Of these we are capable. Finding them, we shall find the real solution of our-selves, our hungers, failures, hurts. If you listen to God, he will make of you what you are capable of becoming. If you will not listen, then you must be compelled against your will to do what he requires. Blessed are they that have served him from their youth. It seems hard at times to be called so early to his service, yet, in the end, these are seen to have gained. They are saved so much. The service of God is surely harder when the soul has grown still with its habits of evil. Easier is it to go when we have all the energy of our nature to help us. A sad pity when we have to limp in tired fashion, worn out and weary, a long way behind. Yet God's grace is marvelous. With his own wonderful power he can rebuild broken lives. He can compress labor that should have been spread over a whole lifetime into a short passage of years.

It is one of life's marvels to find souls who have lived in extraordinary softness, who have faltered along the road and wasted youth's fragrance, suddenly seeing themselves to be face to face with God and overcome with it, living ever so brief a life afterwards, yet having it so crowded with divine understanding and divine suffering that they have been made perfect in a short time. So it is never too late to find the road again, though it is only rediscovered with much costing search. Moreover, it is a pity to give God merely the fag-end of life, when you have already had all the pleasure out of it. Better is it to give God your life while it is the fresh and eager thing. But give God whatever you have. It is all you have.

God calls us; if we do not hear, or miss it, we shall spoil our life. He will get us back at last, but we shall have got hardened in the process. We shall need to have our limbs broken and set again. Perhaps, only so can he mend us and make us walk again so as to go his way. Though it looks hard to you, whatever it is that you know to be God's will, remember that it is easier to accept it now than to let it slide. Easier? To say that is to use a poor argument. We shall not merely say that it is easier. Our call is to love him; that is why he made us – that we might love him because he first loved us. That is the only way in which we should look at life. Not that to do his will is easier in the end, but more loving. He who calls me is my Lover. He is my Friend. He knows me as I never know myself. If I do what he tells me, when I know it is his voice that is telling me, then I should give him all that I have – not much, but all.

When you are in love you realize then how humbling love is. You realize when you are in love what a very little you have to bring to the one you love. Friendship, while it exalts you, makes you realize the poverty of your own heart, the emptiness of your own soul. You wish you had much more to bring, more of yourself, a finer character, a worthier gift. This humility will be found in divine love, too. Once you awake to the knowledge of what God is, you realize how very little you have to offer him. You want to give him at least all of the little that is yours, not because it is easier, but because it is more generous to go God's way when he calls you. He is your Friend. So we ask him (because it needs his own gift to do this) that we may know his voice. We ask him to help us to listen for it, so that we may know it as his voice when it sounds to us; and then that we may have courage to follow the voice wherever it call us, not with reluctance because the road whither it calls us is hard or painful, but gladly because he that calls us is our Father, our Lover, our Friend: 'You have not chosen me, but I have chosen you.' What is love but choice, the choice of a friend? He calls us, because he loves us and he is always calling us. May he give us the silence of heart that will listen, and the discerning wisdom that will recognize, and the courage of love that will obey.

Love and Suffering

God sends us suffering because he loves us: we accept suffering because we love him. Love is the only answer that can be made to suffering; it is the only explanation of suffering save that of the Christian Scientist, who denies that suffering really exists.

Either it has no real meaning or its meaning is love. One set of pagan philosophers, with very noble ideals and with the desire of lifting human nature above itself, tried to make man impervious to suffering. It taught that suffering was stoically to be borne with, for everything that was disagreeable to man was virtuous. The Epicureans, on the other hand, taught man to escape from suffering, saying that it was degrading and debasing to him, since everything pleasurable was alone worthy of the name of virtue. The Christian alone teaches that suffering is to be embraced. This idea is based upon the fatherhood of God and the story of the Incarnation; for it supposes that the Father only allows such suffering to come to each child as shall be for its own good. Naturally, God could have prevented it altogether, but in his wise providence he has not done so; consequently, we are driven to assert as the ground claim of faith that it can only exist because Wisdom and Love and Power are one. We are really as children whom the world's toys have led astray, and who, when scratched or hurt in our play, run back for comfort to his arms. It is not, therefore, simply as a punishment that we should look on suffering, for such a view of it will add more troubles than it can answer. Suffering is also the very expression of love; almost the only language that adequately describes its feelings.

Love, then, which can alone explain suffering when it comes, can also alone give us the strength to accept it joyfully, for life is only tolerable when it is permeated with love. There are hardships for everyone; do what we will, we cannot escape them. Yet it is not the troubles of life, but the way we bear them, that makes life tolerable or not. To complain or cry out does but dig the point-head deeper into the flesh. It is the fretting against imprisonment which makes imprisonment the terrible torture that it is; the trouble is not that the walls are small, but that the mind is too big, and in its desires streams out beyond the narrow borders of its cell. The anchorite was contented in his tower, but the prisoner essayed night by night to escape: their conditions were the same, but their hopes and desires were different. The whole secret, then, is to adapt our desires to our conditions. Love puts into bondage as many victims as hate; but those whom love's chains bind are glad of their lot. It is just so that our whole relation to God leads us to be tranquil in trouble, to be glad even in sufferings. We are told, indeed, that God punishes with suffering all workers of iniquity; but those also whom God loveth he chasteneth; and for ourselves who try, fitfully indeed yet honestly, to love, we can feel sure that it is only the strength of his embrace that we feel. Love, then, alone will help us to understand life and its sorrows. As children in perfect trust and hope, we must rely on him that even our pain is from him and will lead us to him.

Of course, the full realization of this is the attitude of the saints, for they have achieved that same state of soul to which St Paul confessed that he had reached: 'For which cause I take pleasure in my infirmities.' Of one saint we are told that he considered himself neglected by God on any day in which no suffering came to him; it was as though for the moment God had withdrawn his caressing hand; of another, that she began to be afraid that she had fallen from grace whenever her sufferings ceased. Now these 'hard sayings' of the heroes of Christ seem too high for us even to attempt to practice: to love suffering and rejoice in it seems more than we dare even ask for. Yet there is this to be considered, that our Blessed Lord himself found it perfectly compatible to shrink from suffering and yet to be resigned to the will of God. His whole frame sweated blood when faced with the loneliness of sin and of death, yet he could be still in absolute union with his Father; so that the combination of the two is not necessarily impossible. To shrink from suffering and yet to love seems a contradiction, yet it was not only achieved by our Lord but confessed to by the saints. God, then, for us is the Master of Love, and his chosen ones are those who have learnt deepest in his school. Sorrow, then, far from opposing love, is its perfect expression, so that without it love would pine away in silence. It is caused by love and can be made tolerable only by love. It is, above all, in the Sacrament of love which we receive upon our knees and with a *Domine, non sum dignus* in our hearts, that we shall obtain the strength and courage to bear life's troubles with a serene heart. For it is the Crucified who alone explains the crucifixion.

Mortifications

The self-denial of Christ has been made a law for his children. We cannot call ourselves his followers unless we make up our minds to follow, and to follow means quite definitely to take up our cross. Hence, penance becomes a necessity of the Christian life. The whole New Testament rings with this idea. The Gospels show it in action from the Incarnation to the Passion and Death; the epistles of St Paul formulate that example in words that are still striking and arresting. There the Cross is exalted with a vehemence of language that is astonishing in its freshness, and the Crucified is, as indeed he asserts, the central thesis of all his exhortations. In the acts of the early martyrs, and in the liturgy of the Church, it is not at all infrequent to find the term athlete applied to those who fought so strenuously for an incorruptible crown. Perhaps the idea of employing such a word came from the persistent metaphor of the same St Paul; he is always turning to the great public games for his comparisons of the New Dispensation. Time after time he speaks of the training necessary for the fight, of the splendid lure which the prize gives to everyone entering the lists, of the stern necessity for all who so enter not to play with their rivals in half-hearted fashion as though idly beating against the non-resisting air, of the steadfastness and courage required, and of the ultimate reward, itself exceeding great. Through the Middle Ages the same metaphor lingered at least as a literary habit. Nor is the notion at all fantastic; for we can quite readily suppose that the whole of life can be divided between the training and the race, the long days of preparation interspersed with intermittent struggle.

Now, it is just under the idea of training that the true concept of mortification is to be found. It is not the end of life, but the means of achieving the end of life. It is not sought for itself, but because it is necessary in order to attain that faith and hope and love which it is the purpose of our creation to secure. Hence, to those who are at all perplexed over the limits which prudence should set to austerity, it is simpler to make answer that it is essential in itself, but that the particular form it takes must depend entirely on our personal circumstances. Necessary to the Christian in some way, mortification or austerity may exist in varying forms and degrees, which must be gauged to be prudent or not according to the extent they help us or hinder the fulfillment of the Christian ideal. Its whole justification is that it comes as a preparation, leading up to greater things. It is, in fact, merely the training for the athletic arena of the New Law; and just as it is possible, by choosing a foolish system or by exaggerating the limits laid down or by not paying them sufficient attention, to unfit the body and mind for a contest in the games, so also because I mortify myself unwisely, too much or too little, the whole effect of my labors may be to unfit me altogether for an exact following of Christ. Now it may not unfairly be said that the limits of training begin where the needs of life end, and the needs of life end where training begins. Training, therefore, is busied with what is above the margin of decent livelihood. Supervision is to be exercised only over the luxuries, not the essentials.

Hence, I can at once find a ready rule by which to measure my mortification. I can mortify myself in things of the flesh and things of the spirit only just so far as the things I curtail are not necessary. Directly I come upon what is needful to my life not to life in general, but to my life), then I have reached the extreme boundary of penance, and further I need not go. It is, then, very largely a personal matter, dependent on my health and work; consequently it is extremely variable, and I must be prepared to speed up and slack off according as my needs determine me. Consequently, no one is so fit to judge these for me as I am for myself; indeed, others can only judge according to the information and evidence I myself provide. Hence, when I put my case to others, I have probably already prejudged it for myself, and they can hardly do more than ratify my own opinion: thus I do not gain any real confirmation by referring the matter to them. I cannot help describing my state as I judge it to be. But in the whole trouble of it I must remember that beneath it all must be love. The life of Christ – above all, his death – can find no rational solution except in love; for in suffering as such, God can take no pleasure. But love that denies itself for love, is love such as we know it to be, and such as our hearts have found to be a law of their own movements. The self-denial, then, that is commanded us is incomplete without that final call: 'Follow me.' It is that perfect form that beckons and gives heart and life to all creation's toil. The putting away of my own will profiteth me nothing without charity, and charity suffereth all things.

34 COURAGE

COURAGE is one of the most praised of the virtues and the least understood. Cowardice is the least attractive of vices and probably the most rare. More people own to cowardice than have it. What is courage? It is certainly not the same as daring. By daring we mean almost foolhardiness, a boldness that knows nothing of fear, that disdains all risks. Daring faces all these things without fear. Now, courage is compatible with fear, and that marks the whole difference between them. Daring implies its absence, and courage is compatible with its presence. Daring men may be also courageous, but courageous men need not be daring, for daring is the result of temperament, whereas courage is the result of virtue. Daring is rarer than courage and not so meritorious, for one cannot help being daring, whereas one can help being courageous.

Courage seems to be best defined as the act of a resolute will in the pursuance of duty and in the face or threat of known danger. It is an act of the will, and not a physical act, since it is an act of virtue; it is therefore compatible with physical shrinking It must be exercised in the pursuance of duty, for the act of a dare-devil is distinguished against it by being performed out of sheer love of danger. To be too frightened to leap across a chasm is not a lack of courage, unless one is bound by one's duty to do it. Further, there must be known to be danger in the act done, else it might be done not out of courage, but out of mere ignorance, folly, or forgetfulness.

No one, therefore, is a coward except a man who, in the face or threat of known danger, shirks his duty. There are many people who in war, perhaps, will tell you they were cowards at heart. All they really mean is that they were afraid. Now a man may be afraid, and despite his fear may do his duty. That is not cowardice, but the highest courage. To be terrified of a horse or a dog or a madman would never be cowardly, unless we were to allow our feelings to prevail over our sense of duty. Courage, therefore, is compatible with fear and is most in evidence, perhaps, when fear is strongest. Consequently, we may know that at heart we are easily frightened; this is no fault of ours, it is usually the result of some old experience or of mere temperament.

What we have to remember when we find ourselves in difficulties, is that courage is a gift of God that urges us to continue our efforts despite failures and fears. If we have done our best, we have this further assurance, that the result will not be as futile as we may think. We have done our duty in the face of discouragement, and even though what we aimed at has not been accomplished, we have not thereby failed. To have made the attempt is already to have achieved something; to continue to make attempts because we see that our duty lies that way is an act of courage, and therefore, whether the results be disappointing or not, the initial act remains in force. Success is often only an accident due to the concurrence of other forces besides ourselves. We owe success, wherever it comes to us, to causes other than ourselves. Moreover, success without a check would weaken our character, and even our freedom. No people and no individual can remain free without a constant effort. It is this very effort that makes them worthy of freedom, and the freedom thus achieved, unless it requires repeated further defense, gravitates to weakness. Unused muscles grow flabby. Unused powers become atrophied. Opposition is the stem and kindly guardian of the soul. After all, opposition is even a tribute of flattery, for no unsuccessful work provokes opposition. So long as it is unsuccessful, no one bothers to do more than to prophesy its end. In proportion to its success, it offers a target to contradiction, 'gives hostages to fortune,' and therefore, only when it is disturbing or threatening to disturb other forces, human or diabolic, is it likely to meet contradiction. Temptation from the evil spirits is, in consequence, the best testimony to our success, and the more it is redoubled, the more full of hope should we grow; the fury of the fighting merely proclaiming that God's grace has been set around us. Our checks in life are a tribute to our power and God's mercy, and should nerve us to repeated efforts. Even when we have tried our best and failed, we can be sure that if we have not secured what we wanted we have secured what God wanted. Our plans may have gone astray and yet our soul be no less great; and to continue our efforts, despite the past and in fear of the future, is courage indeed.

Perseverance
The virtues of man are the reflections of the goodness of God. Each of his divine attributes, as we call them (the various perfections which we attribute to our idea of what is meant by the name 'God'), is mirrored in humanity, which has been made after the image of God. The fullness of his being cannot, indeed, be found adequately confessed in any single human soul, since that would obviously imply that the finite could express the infinite, an evident contradiction. But the whole creation does reflect, though in an extremely limited and

fragmentary way, the Infinite Beauty. His justice we note in one soul, his mercy in another; in others his power, his wisdom, his compassion, his love, his gentleness, etc. And we declare these who thus reproduce some portion of his excellence to be saints, to be God-like, to be the friends of God.

But of all the attributes of God of which we have know-ledge, it might seem that his constancy and unchangeableness of being defied all reproduction in his creatures: for surely the very note of time (in which here all creations stands) is a note of transition. The very idea of human life, even of the holiest and best, means movement, progress; means, therefore, that the notion of sanctity itself implies incessant change, whereas the whole idea of eternity (where God dwells) supposes neither past nor future, but an unchanging present. How in that which grows, declines, decays, can we find any resemblance to his unchangeableness? We can find it in perseverance, which does feebly indeed, yet truly, mirror that unique perfection of God.

For perseverance is really nothing else than a persistent effort to keep a hold on virtue. That is precisely the very difficulty and labor of it, for it concentrates not simply on the mere performance of good, but on its continual performance. Isolated acts of goodness are not in themselves too high or too great for us; nor would it be discouraging or staggering to flesh and blood to continue the attempts at goodness for a certain period, determined, brief, known. But there is a distinct difficulty in the thought that all these attempts have to be kept up, never allowed for an instant to relax, for a span of years, perhaps of long duration. It is the 'silent pressure' of time that wears down the strongest heart and the most determined resistance. To hold out against a restless foe who takes advantage of every loophole of attack, who worries and never leaves time for rest or recuperation, who has persistence enough to dog and harry our steps – this requires the highest courage of all, the most splendid daring. Just as the unbear-ableness of pain consists in the accumulated consciousness of it, so the unbearableness of virtue consists of the perseverance in it demanded of us by God. To be good is not difficult, but to be always good is a gift that reflects the unending perfections of the Eternal.

What consolation can I hold out to myself? Faced each morning by the idea that this attempt at goodness must be made every day of my life, faced in every temptation by the certainty that the attack repelled now will be repeated tomorrow, driven to disheartenment by the conviction that life is not a warfare but a siege, what comfort can I find, what basis of hope against the long dreary stretch of existence? First, I must boldly acknowledge that I have no right to suppose any such length of life. Tomorrow may well see the end of it all. I have no guarantee of the number of days through which I must struggle in my fight for my own soul. The rich fool built barns for his hoarded grain, and that very night his soul was required of him. Many a man has set out to build and has awoke to another life, has sown seed which he did not live to reap. It is, therefore, altogether without reason that I promise myself a long struggle for goodness. Then, secondly, I must be content to take the life simply of this day. Let the dead past bury its dead, and let to-morrow care for itself. Sufficient for the day is its own evil. Let me resolutely fight the battle that presents itself to me, and leave alone the bogey that my own imagination has created. Even were I assured of length of days, let me be content to take each as it comes. I shall fail tomorrow? Perhaps! Anyway, let me make certain that I do not fail today. Today God is with me. Will he not, who inhabiteth eternity, be able to be with me to-morrow also? Steadfastness in love is the most attractive virtue in God or man.

We Need Courage

If we try to realize that saying of Scripture that we have here no abiding city, that we are here as travelers, it helps us the better to understand what life means. We are always planning and designing for ourselves what one day we shall do. As children we planned what we were to do when we had grown up, in youth we planned for our middle years. As we grow older, it is always in the future that the great event, whatever it is, is to happen. We plan, at last, to settle down in old age. We cannot settle down – we never shall – we are pilgrims. Most of life seems just living from hand to mouth. We seem to be doing things that are not of particular consequence – but one day the thing, whatever it is, will come. Under such conditions the great virtue that is asked of us is courage. If you are to go on a long pilgrimage, you must accommodate yourself to others. So life is an endless accommodating of ourselves to others. You say when you begin: 'This is only for a short time – later on I shall be able to organize my life as I want it.' That will happen truly, but not here. Life is not at our individual choice. No one ever really has here a chance of having exactly what he wants. Only on the other side of death will you really have a home. We belong to a great city, but the city lies over the far side of the river.

When you go on a journey and meet with all sorts of difficulties, you must comfort yourself with the reminder that it will not be for long. You live, more or less, in a muddle. At last you think that you will be able to settle down. Again this is true, only not on earth, but in heaven. Nothing is exactly spread out as you would like it. We say life is in such a rush nowadays. It always has been from the beginning Turn up any letters of ancient days. They always say the same thing of life, that it is so difficult to fit everything in. This must be so in every age. Where people misunderstand life is when they imagine it is home. This spoils all our judgments of life, even all our judgments of the God who governs life.

Why is that child born blind? we ask, half scandalized. Why has someone else grievous trouble laid on him? Why do those who love each other never get a chance of living in one an-other's company? Please remember, this is only a journey. The child will not be blind when it reaches life at the end of its journey. It is sad that it is blind, but nothing really to trouble about. To the pagan, if he thinks this life finishes things, it is dreadful. To us, life's troubles are robbed of half their sting. Courage is our great need. And courage is faith's child, not hope's, nor yet despair's, but faith's. We need to be always pulling ourselves together and saying that our life here is not going on forever. Children play at hide-and-seek--that is like life: it is a search, a finding, a coining home. The dreadful part of death is that we go into God's presence unaccompanied. Yet death is the ending of trouble – compared with what it ends it is no trouble, except the uncertainty of where it will leave us. So lay up treasures in heaven – not here. You will find that whatever troubles you in life, only troubles you because you misunderstand life, either because you cannot have what you want or because what you want is taken away from you.

Say to yourself then: 'I am a pilgrim.' That things should be wrong on a journey is right. The things we complain of are really only the little things that never matter. The only real trouble is how to get home. Courage, then, and the remembrance of what we are going to will support us. You think you cannot go on any longer? Of course you can go on, it is only a journey. Of course you can go on. It will have an end. When on a long walk in winter you see the light of your destination in. the night ahead of you, it helps you to go on.

'Have I always to be keeping back my own ideas and so being a peace-maker in the home? Is that my life? Always doing this or that?' No, that is not your real life. Your real life is to see God face to face. But that you may have to do these things during your pilgrimage may well be, only it will not last forever. Moreover, all you thought yourself capable of here, there, at last, will be reached. You will stand as God meant you to stand, in the place for which you were fitted. You are immortal. You are too great to find complete satisfaction in this life. You were made for bigger things. This life is too small.

God's blessed Mother – what a life she had! What mono-tony! Even Christ our Lord lived such a life as this. Always he lived it quietly. He, too, was on a journey. 'Follow Me,' he said. He goes walking; we come after. That is what we mean by the following of Christ. The great thing is not to let yourself be too tired, but to remind yourself that at the last there is a home. You must gather your strength together. What is courage but the power, not of those who are eager and full of activity, but of those who tire, still to go on. It is not the untiring energy of the child. There is no endurance in that. The child does not find it hard to be moving; the child finds it hard to keep still. But tired and yet going on with our labors, that is endurance. Why should we not? These will come to an end.

It is the part of the traveler to see this thing today and that tomorrow, to enjoy a thing while it lasts, to take life as it comes, not to trouble about the past or the immediate future. The happy traveler becomes as a. little child.. His life has the beauty of a child's life. It is living simply for the day. The past is only to be talked of in the evening when we rest comfortable because of the toil done. And the future? We should not talk overmuch of the immediate future – but take each day as it comes. Courage then! Remind yourself that this journey will have an ending. Do not let yourself be weakened by weariness. Instead, by the grace of God, renew your energies in the thought of his constant assistance and companionship. Look at him, speak to him. Go on!

24 FAITH

IN OUR Lord's solemn prayer for his disciples at the Last Supper, he said: 'Sanctify them, O Father, in truth: thy word is truth.' Since sanctification is the whole purpose of our lives, our Lord is evidently at pains to impress on us the fact that without truth – that is, without the word of God – we cannot hope to fulfill the object for which we were created. The revelation of God is absolutely necessary for the love of God, since sanctification means nothing more than that love. It is clear from the witness of the New Testament that the reason that lies at the back of all the Church's ordinances, sacraments, con-fraternities, etc., all the good works done to our neighbor, all the charity and self-denial in the world, is simply the love of God; for, without this, our sacrifices are vain and our prayers a hypocritical deceit: 'Not he that saith to me, "Lord, Lord," but he that cloth the will of my Father.' WI give my body to the torturers, and have not charity, it profiteth me nothing'; and St Paul goes very carefully through a whole list of good deeds, and points out the faultiness of each, except they be done from the motive of the love of God. Hence, since sanctification means the love of God, and since truth can come to us only through the illumination of faith, the prayer of our Lord must be interpreted in the sense of these words of the Council of Trent: 'Perfect love is based on perfect faith.'

Why should this be? The reason is quite simple. It is impossible to love properly unless we know properly. If we have not a true idea about God, we can never really love him. The pagans and others have such distorted ideas of what God is like that it is impossible for them to know him as he is in himself. Those, for example, who would give up their belief in hell would have no doubt an idea of God as all-merciful, but not of him as all-holy and all-just. Thus, the God whom they would love would only be a caricature of him, not God as he is in. himself. It is for this reason that the Church has been so particular, so fierce even as it seems, against sins of heresy; for false doctrine prevents people from really knowing God and, therefore, from really loving him. Of course, in a certain sense it may be said that love helps us to know, so that unless we love people and have sympathy with them we can never understand them; and this is undoubtedly true, for love and knowledge act and react upon each other. But even so, it is always knowledge that precedes; and the knowledge that comes to us from their own revelation of themselves must itself tend to a better love of them. So of God, the more I listen to his voice, the more I learn of him, the better I know him, so much the more and the better will my love of him be also. For faith must precede love.

Apart from merely making acts of gratitude to God for giving me the faith, I have also to study, according to my ability, the truths of the Catholic religion; for the deeper my knowledge of him, the more I must be drawn to love him. The more clearly I can grasp his revelation of himself, the more surely shall I be attracted by him He is so perfect, so infinite in his perfections, that truer knowledge of him must end in truer love. It is as though I was in some darkened room and could see hardly anything at all; then gradually, as my eyes get accustomed to the darkness, the outlines of things begin to loom out in vague, gigantic shadows; even details, at first obscure, after a while take on definite shape and stand out in clearer relief. So is it with the deep mysteries of God; they strike us as incomprehensible, as indeed they are; as contradictory, as indeed they are not – but by the sheer light of faith and fixity of gaze, the divine beauty becomes apparent, transparent, and eventually transfigures the world with splendor . I have no excuse for my ignorance; I must, therefore, endeavor to increase my know-ledge of my religion, that my love of God may grow to the perfect stature of Christ.

Living Faith
Since our faith is intended to be our life and to enter into every thought and action, it is clear that it cannot be a fixed and stable thing, although it must be conveyed to us by means of definitions that are fixed, in the sense that they represent the best terms in human language that express, as far as it is at all possible to express, the mysteries of the revelation of God. Of course, the Catholic Church has never hesitated to declare that these definitions are always really inadequate, for it is derogatory to almighty God to suppose that the facts of his being and life could be fitted into the limitation of human language and human thought. Hence, while the Church claims that she can define as accurately as possible those mysteries of God, she does not pretend that what she has to say exhausts the subject or even represents the actual truth she is trying to teach. It is the nearest to truth that the human mind is at the moment capable of expressing. Hence, there is such a thing as the development of doctrine, whereby things revealed from the beginning are found to be in the tradition of the Christian people, though they might require the rise of a heresy to make the people conscious of what had always been accepted. In this

sense, therefore, it must be admitted that faith itself is a fixed and final thing, for otherwise it is clear there would be no possibility of acquiring any knowledge of the ways of God. What would be the use of dogma if it were to be constantly changed, disregarded, outgrown? Dogmatic definitions, therefore, are the vehicles by means of which the divine truths are conveyed to our minds.

Yet the real purpose of faith is something more than this. The kingdom of God that our. Lord came to establish upon earth was not merely the elaborate or simple knowledge of the way of God; rather, it was the individual acceptance of truth simply as a means of life. God teaches me about himself so that in the end I may be led to a closer union with him; it is himself for whom I am created; not for faith, but for possession. The kingdom of God, therefore, is something that the individual from the age of reason to the end of life has to be continually realizing for himself. He has to be continually hammering away at the truths of faith, endeavoring to get more meaning out of them, to find in them the help and guidance that daily life continually demands. The whole series of mysteries will certainly be no use to me in my endless advance to God unless I try to make them my own by ceaselessly pondering over them. Of themselves, they are just the bare outlines of truths, yet it is not truths but the facts that are contained in the truths that are ultimately to influence my life. Hence, my first act must be to get interested in my faith. Faith has to be regarded as the revelation to us of the meaning of life, the understanding of life, the effects of life. I shall never become interested in religion until I have come to see that I must make it personal to myself – chew it, digest it, form out of it the sinews of my spiritual being.

Perhaps the reason why we think this a hard thing to do is just because we get into the habit of supposing that faith, and the attitude to life that faith ultimately produces, is something foreign to our nature. I find myself looking at this gift of God as something that is, as it were, dropped on me from outside, something external. External, indeed, those truths are, in the sense that nature left to itself would find no record of them here on earth, or at least a record so misty and incomplete as to distract rather than convince; but it is obvious that they can never influence my actions unless they have become transformed from external into internal possessions. I must so unite them to myself that they affect the whole color of life to me. Religion may be fixed, stable, but my religion cannot be stable or fixed. The truth may be one, final, determined, but my apprehension of it can never be anything of the kind; it is changing continuously. I am always learning more and more, or forgetting the little that I once knew; the meaning grows more definite or more indistinct. I cannot suppose that this alone of all my forms of knowledge remains stationary all through life; and even if such a supposition ever came to me, the facts of life would very quickly disillusion me. My faith must advance or retreat, it cannot remain the same. The real trouble probably is that I look upon faith as something purely official, and only obscurely realize that there is a personal side of it as well. Now it is just here that I shall fund the advantage of it to me. To be called a Catholic because we accept certain isolated truths is hardly worthwhile; once I see that it is as it is called in the Scripture – a 'way' – then I shall find that it opens up large visions to me and reveals me to myself. Notice that the Creed mentions not merely the truth believed, but the person believing: 'I believe in one God.'

Mysteries in Religion

If, as I am taught from my childhood, faith is concerned with mysteries, i.e., truths above reason, how is it possible for me to make them my own? It is obviously impossible for me to acquire such intimate knowledge of a thing that I cannot understand as will enable me to obtain any benefit from it. I may remember the phrase used and be careful not to confuse the way in which it is worded; I may be strictly accurate in my definitions, but what else can I do with it? It is above reason, therefore it is above life. The very element of mysteriousness seems to preclude every effort making these truths really my own or enabling them in any real sense to have any influence over my actions. I can accept them with my intelligence, but they will remain merely truths and have no personal significance for me.

Now, first of all, it is indeed clear that I shall never be able to understand at all adequately the truths of faith. Whenever I come in contact with God, I come in contact with something that is utterly above me. God is infinite and I am finite, so that truths about him can never be packed into my limited intelligence. If I could understand God, I should be at least his equal. We say in English that when we know anything we have mastered it. That is a perfectly accurate expression; we can only know a thing when we are greater than it is, so that if I really knew God, I should be his equal or his master. Hence it is clear that it is impossible for me to understand God's being or his acts. There must be in everything he does a great deal that I can never comprehend nor ever hope to comprehend. Let me begin by realizing that I must expect, when I come in contact with God, to find that he is above my understanding.

It follows that there will always be difficulties in the matter of faith. There will always be much that I shall be able to understand, but God will add also to the difficulties that surround my understanding of him. He cannot help blinding me even while he enlightens me, not because of his limitations, but of mine. When, for example, he told me that he was one and alone as God, I could accept that as shedding light on the world; but when he told me that in that one Godhead there were Three Persons, he told me a great deal more about his own life, but at the same time he at once added to my perplexities. He taught me, yet he perplexed me; nay, the very fact of his revelation was itself the cause of my mystification. When I knew him as the governor of the world and its just judge, I found that no contradiction; but when he told me that he had become man and had died for me, I was grateful for his revelation, but it added also to my difficulties. In other words, just because God is infinite and I am finite, it is to be expected that everything that he tells me of himself, while increasing light, will increase darkness at the same time. In those countries where the sun is brightest, there are the deepest shadows; the very brilliance of the sun adds to the blackness of the shadow that it casts. I have, therefore, to repeat to myself that if all the ways of God were capable of explanation, then I should know for certain that he did not exist, but was the creation of man's mind. It is just be-cause he is so difficult to comprehend that I know he is indeed a revealer of truth.

I arrive, then, at this, that these mysteries are apparent contradictions. He is all-holy, yet allows sin; all-loving, yet allows suffering; full of mercy, yet the builder of hell; all-powerful, yet leaving me perfect freedom; God, yet man; innocent, yet the redeemer of his people; united to the Father by inseparability of nature, yet feeling on the cross the loneliness of his abandonment. What have I to do in the midst of all this contradiction? I am to take the mysteries to pieces. I shall find that it is because the two apparently opposed truths are taken together that their difficulty occurs. I must simply cling to both ends of the chain, and remain ignorant of the link that binds them together. He is one, he is three; he is man, he is God; he is merciful, he is just – all these things I can follow separately, but conjointly they are impossible of understanding. However, there is this much comfort for me that I have to say to myself that I am not surprised that I do not understand him. When people ask me how I can explain the existence of evil or sin, I can answer that I do not know; and that, granted there is a God, it is impossible that I should know. It is to be expected that, if

God created the world, it would be impossible for the world to understand its Creator; but if the world began itself, then it would understand itself. Consequently, I am content to go through life in trust – conscious and, indeed, proclaiming as part of my belief, that the ways of God ought to be mysteries to me, yet not thereby depressed or losing confidence, but rather keeping tighter hold of the little knowledge of God that has come to me through revelation. It is good for me that when I go out at night I do not bump my head against the stars.

Pride in Faith
It is the perpetual platitude of the pious that reason puffs up and faith humbles us; and presumably there is something to be said for this. Reason is quite likely to produce in certain minds a perfectly conceited and foolish attitude, as though we were capable of understanding all things. Just because we find that there are certain things that we can understand, we may possibly take it on us to assert that we are only going to accept what we can prove. It is possible that we may take up this dogmatic position, and on the basis of this pure, unprovable prejudice proceed to refuse acceptance of divine revelation. Fortunately, man is unable to remain for long obsessed by any such foolishness, but such an attitude is really common in the early stages of human development in the natural sciences. The terrible thing is that reason quite soon finds out, not its wonderful power, but its utter hopelessness when up against the problems of life. It discovers, not how much but how little it knows of the ways of God and man It is oppressed by its limitations. It finds that the influence of the body upon it is considerable; this delicate instrument, whereby reason had hoped to discover the whole meaning of life, is at the mercy of all the elements. The slightest ache or pain robs reason of its keenness; weariness makes its movements impossible or fantastic; a serious bodily derangement can reduce it to absolute incapacity. Instead of reason being the plummet by which the depth of the universe is to be sounded, reason is discovered to be so faulty as to render any of its soundings suspiciously incorrect.

On the other hand, the whole effect of faith is the exact opposite. So eager are we made by the wonders about God which revelation brings to us, that we are reduced to disregarding the limits of our creaturehood. There is nothing sacred from our touch; the very sanctuary of God is invaded and we speculate almost irreverently on the doings of God in his heaven. Open any book of theology and you will be amazed at the hardiness of the theologians who seem to dogmatize about all sorts of things of which they are almost quite ignorant. There is nothing that they are not willing to tackle and decide. Every possible point will be settled without any admission or any confession that all the while they are depending upon very slight grounds of argument. All this is not to destroy our confidence in the writings of theologians, but merely to say that the temper of reason and faith is really the very opposite of the popular conception. The effect of reason on anyone who is really intelligent is, by itself, to make one conscious of the little knowledge that the human race has amassed; it is to reduce us to a state of hopelessness; whereas faith is so illuminating that the chief danger is lest we ignore the vast difficulties that there are to be found in life. Place the believer and un-believer side by side and ask which is the more conscious of the limitations of human endeavor. Ordinarily it is the agnostic who sees the real problems of life. It is not that they are not apparent to us, but faith is so inspiriting that we forget all about them. It is the Christian who is the optimist, the agnostic who is the pessimist.

For faith, then, the very infirmities of nature--weakness, sleep, weariness, etc. – that make reason so aghast, make faith, curiously enough, more active. Every obstacle to faith becomes its defense, and every enemy a new recruit. The physical sciences have given to Catholics a much more splendid vision of faith and God than they had before, enabling them to see the wonders of God in greater profusion. Every advance of the enemy only serves to show how intimate and how natural is the supernatural. An older generation startled us by telling us that all other religions contained in fragments what the Catholic Church held in a complete form, but we found on examination that this was one more reason for acknowledging the truth of revelation. If the Christian faith were really divine, then surely man must feel deeply the needs that it comes to supply, and, in consequence, will feebly and brokenly grope his way towards them. Because I can find every single doctrine of the Church taught by some religion or other, and because I can find them gathered together nowhere else than in her, then surely I am convinced that she has obtained, by the swift light of God, what they painfully and falteringly have partly discovered. Surely, then, this should give me a greater realization of the importance of my soul. It is, indeed, depressing to find that my reason is so at the mercy of the world, yet is it reassuring to find the world in turn at the mercy of my. faith. Even the sorrows of existence, the triumph of evil, the apparent impunity that is guaranteed to crime, the early deaths of those that most promise good, find in faith an easy acceptance. We strive for their amelioration, but we are not troubled by their evidence. The despair with which my reason confronts the whole of life is turned into a rapture of entire sympathy with the power, wisdom, and love of God.

Tolerance

I have my own pathway to God. I can find no one on earth with whom on every point I am in complete accord, and therefore I can find no other way to God than the way of my own being. Others may advise and help; but they can never know me really, for they have little else to go on for judgment except what I tell them myself, so that whatever they may say has to be modified and, as it were, re-edited before it can be of any use to me. Their counsel and directions are based upon their own experience, but of mine they know very little. After all, none other has had my life, my hereditary influences, my education at home and in school, my interests and hobbies and tastes and pleasures; in other words, I am myself different from anyone else, and, in the full sense of the word, unique. It is for this reason that my prayers must be my own; no words of others can ever fitly represent the needs I have and the thanks I personally owe to the Creator, Redeemer, Sanctifier. For the same reason also I have continually to be reminding myself that I have something to give God which he can get from none other. There are times when I cannot help wondering what use I am in the world and how he could ever have sent me here at all. Then I have to realize that however much I am a failure, stupid and sinful, yet because I am unique I have a unique offering to make, i.e., myself. God gets from me a peculiar glory which no other work of his hands can show, and therefore in me alone is some fragment of his splendor reflected. My own pathway to him, however much it may resemble the ways of others, must be really my own, in the sense that it is on the whole different from every other.

I have also to realize that as I am unique, so is everyone else. Just as my hereditary tendencies, my upbringing, my temperament, my mixture of faults and virtues, my ambitions, my hopes, my fears, my past, my present, my future, are entirely peculiar to myself, so also are to others their own tendencies and temperaments and tempers. All of them look out into the world from themselves as the central point; they are conscious of their own view of life as I am of mine. We are always repeating our wonder at the endless variety of nature, with every leaf and every flower and every sunset apart and alone and unique. We notice the monotony of life, yet have to confess that no day is really exactly like another; though to us, each sheep in a flock is exactly like the rest, yet to the shepherd each is absolutely distinct, with a character of its own. So God tells us that he has called each of us by a name, that from all eternity he has singled us out for himself, that even the hairs of our head are numbered. As, therefore, on this account I claim for myself the right to go to God in my own way, accepting the truths and practices of the Church, for that reason must I also be willing to allow the same freedom to others. The rights I demand for myself are rights, not privileges; therefore they must be conceded equally to all the world.

Therefore I must be tolerant. Each has his own way to God. I cannot pretend that I alone know the way in which he wishes to be served. I know by faith that he has established his Church to be the sole teacher of truth, and therefore I try to bring all to this wonderful mistress of the ways of God; but, even so, I am certain that he does give the light of truth to all who serve him, and if I find that what I say has no influence on my fellows, I can surely leave it to him to guide them aright. Again, within the Church the varieties of holiness are innumerable, the patterns of the saints endlessly diverse; to each, therefore, his own way, and I must be in no hurry to foist my own upon them. Nay, it is this very variety that produces the beauty of holiness in the world. As in a garden the loveliness of the effect is due to the shades of color, the diversity of form, the contrast of flower with flower, so in the garden of God is it with the glowing differences of soul from soul. Hence, it is noticeable in the lives of the saints that their own growing independence in life has effected an increasing tolerance; as they realized their own special calling (for to each living soul comes a distinct vocation), they came to recognize the sweet harmony that all these notes produced. 'Such a man rejoices in everything. He does not make himself a judge of the servants of God nor of any rational creature; nay, he rejoices in every condition and every type that he sees. . . .And he rejoices more in the different kinds of men that he sees than he would do in seeing them all walk in the same way, for so he sees the greatness of God's goodness more manifest.' (St Catherine of Siena.)

25 HOPE

FAITH is the basis of life and charity is its crown, but hope is its greatest need. Most of the difficulties of life come because man is so prone to lose heart. His distractions in prayer suggest to him that he was not meant for such high acts. His weekly tale of sins at confession seems to imply by its almost identical repetition that it is useless for him to continue his efforts at 'a firm purpose of amendment'. His faltering attempts at perfection disconcert him from any persistent or long-continued service. His cold and listless Communions take away his feelings of devotion and lead him to fancy that it were better not to go at all than to go with so little seeming effect. This joylessness in the sacraments does far more harm than that, for it makes him close the very gates through which alone help can come to him.

The whole of life tends to depress a man who is at all conscious of his capacities, his responsibilities, and his failures. He is, then, a great sinner? Not at all. He has lost his faith and love? Most certainly not. What, then, is wanting to him? Hope. He has given up hope; he is disheartened; he is too discouraged to go on. He is very human, yes, but he is very foolish also; for when hope has gone, all is over. Failure counts for nothing; defeat, disappointment – these matter nothing at all, so long as only hope sits patiently, stirring the embers, watching and tending the fire, coaxing the flame, never despairing and never leaving the wind to work its will. That the clouds should come up over the sky, or that darkness should encircle the earth, brings no real terrors, for we are sure that the dawn will come and the sun will break through with its golden glory.

Now hope frankly starts by acknowledging the certainty of trouble. It implies that life is hard, implies indeed that a perfect life (i.e., life without fault) is impossible for man. That is to say, the first thing for me to do is to realize quite simply and quite definitely that I shall never overcome my faults, at least in the sense that I shall never be able to find myself free from temptations. I may improve, please God I shall! I may lessen the number of my sins by narrowing the occasions of them. I may so far clear myself that the old fault has ceased even to be repeated; for the goodness of God may achieve all these things. But at any rate I must never expect that this will be done for me so completely as to prevent forever any struggle in my life. The certainty which I must face is that always I shall be a wrongdoer. I must reconcile myself quite determinedly to this prospect, not buoy myself up with false hopes of a time when I can rest securely upon my oars. Life is always a pull up-stream. The terrible thing is when people expect to find things ultimately easy and discover them to be continuously very hard; the shock is too much for them; they lose heart and can never recover. This, then, is the first point that I have to get into my mind, and it should need little to make it sure. I am a failure from the beginning, and shall be to the end; at the best, says our Master, an 'unprofitable servant'.

The next point, when that first has been fairly faced, is more reassuring. I can never be perfect; nor does God want me to be perfect. He does not expect perfection from me, for the very simple reason that he knows he would not get it. He knows man, for he made man; he knows exactly the limits of his power. Only the heavenly Father is or can be perfect. It is foolish of me, then, to be discouraged because my prayers are full of distractions, my Communions cold, my confessions always the same. God does not ask from me perfection in any of these ways. Rather, it should fill me with wonder if for any length of time these things went wholly well. What, then, does God ask? That I should try day after day, despite failure, repeated and certain, to overcome these obstacles to my union with him. If, then, I fail, let me not be discouraged, but, realizing my own weakness and confident only in God's strength, let me go on striving to do my best, for my business in life is really little else than to continue to fail, without losing courage or lessening effort. The phrase of St Catherine should ring always in my ear: 'God doth not ask a perfect work, but infinite desire.'

Accepting God's Will
It is a great advantage to us when we realize that our lives lie absolutely under the providence of God. From the point of view of our spiritual lives, this gives us the proper angle from which to judge them, the necessary spirit in which to live them and to receive in them whatever God gives us. Perhaps you have sometimes heard grown-up people, when they wanted to give little children candy, telling them to shut their eyes and open their mouths and see what God will send them. More or less that, I suppose, should be our attitude to God, and that the way in which we should try to take our lives. We should try to realize how the whole of life lies under the divine governance, guidance, providence; and to realize consequently that what God asks of us is to surrender that which alone it is in our power to give.

Look at your life. You know by now your difficulties. Some spring from your own character and remain with you; some spring from circumstances, and these will no doubt change as the circumstances change. Now these are difficulties that you have to meet. You must begin, then, by saying to yourself that all these are supervised and governed by God. You believe this, for this is the first article of your Creed. You believe that there is a God overall. Because he is God, the Father Almighty, he controls the whole of life. What, then, am I asked to do? I am asked to accept his definite ruling of life, to submit my will absolutely to his, and to be prepared for his dealing with me. My will? Yes, we answer, I submit it. I shall try to do faithfully all that I am told to do by God. A child goes through its child life with older people in charge of it. Now the child can say, if it likes: 'I am going to let these older people deal with me. They are wiser than I am. Moreover, they are stronger. I cannot escape them, even if I would. Therefore, I am going to accept patiently whatever they do to me. I shan't understand why they do what they do to me, but I shall know that they are doing it for what they think to be my good.' Or it is possible for the child to rebel and refuse to do anything until it is compelled to do so. It can make up its mind that it is going to take charge of its own life. It can challenge everything that is done to it, and accept only what it is forced to accept. 'What we are asked to do, then, is to take life on the terms of the accepting child, and believe that what is done is done to us by him who knows best what is right for us, who is strongest, most loving, most wise.

But here comes the one trouble of life. We resist. We should submit, because we know him to be wiser and more loving. We should submit before we know what is going to happen to us, on the basic principle that his judgment must be better than ours, that his judgment must be best. I shall not be found fighting against God. But how do I know when it is God who is dealing with me or mere human interference? Our lives are so much at the mercy of one another. There is this one who seems to me unfair, unjust. Why should I submit to him? Can you really expect me to believe that this injustice is an act of the divine will? Is it not due to human folly, jealousy, revenge, dislike? Why should I say that the terrible injustices of this world are the result of a divine will? Why not say that it is a human will that is false, mischievous, spoiling my life or the lives of others? Well, it is not really difficult to know whether it is the will of God or no. If it be of God, you will not prevail against it. Alter all you can, but accept what you cannot alter. Accept whatever is beyond your power to remove. It would, indeed, be foolish to accept everything that happened to you as though no human effort should be made to mend the hurts of life, for there is a remedy for many of our ills. We may try to remove our pain. We can cross out of the shadow into the sun. But if there be no sun? We must then take what we cannot alter. We may better ourselves if we can. But we must also realize that, if human sin and suffering and folly are the immediate causes of our distress, these have their place in this divinely governed world. We know that Calvary was due to human sin and folly. Yet Calvary redeemed the world. That is part of our very faith.

You and I are asked to give up our wills to God. We are asked to accept whatever he does to us; for the most part this will not be done directly, for God does little directly to us. Most of what he does to us, or at least so much of what he does to us, reaches us through other agencies or is due to all sorts of other things. We are asked to take it, accept it, see the will of God ever behind it, keeping our eyes steadily on him.

It means, too, that we do not worry ourselves with the problem of whether we are making a success of our spiritual lives. Why, for instance, do we not pray better or pray as much as we should? Or why are we not constant in prayer? Because we find our prayers so dull, because it seems that we cannot do anything with them. We go into church and kneel down and begin to pray, but nothing comes, nothing seems alive. God does not seem really and truly there. What is God asking of me? My will! My will! He does not ask me to make a success of my prayer. He does not ask me to make a success of anything. Success lies wholly and solely with God. Moreover, so blinded are we, you and I, that we do not know when we have made a success of anything in the spiritual life. God is the only person who knows. He alone knows whether my prayers are a success or not. We may think our prayers are good, and God may judge them to be too self-satisfied. Sometimes we pray and our prayer may seem dull and full of distraction. Yet, for all we know, God may judge it to be well. Success, failure, we know nothing about these. God is the only person who knows. You cannot judge your life or your character or anything that you have done. Leave it to God.

Still less can you judge anyone else. Leave all to God. This is God's world. You and I are under the divine power; we must accept what he does. We should not plague him with our ideas but be content with his judgment, sure that under his guidance our life shall be as it should. God is wiser than we. God knows far better than we what we can do well; so, instead of asking him to take this or that from us, we ought to trust to his choice of what we should have. 'Though he slay me, yet will

I trust in him.'

We must, then, have an absolute trust in him. This trust must never waver, must be held to constantly through life. This will help us to be consistent in taking whatever he sends us – the sunshine and the shadow, the wind and the shelter from the wind. We do not imagine, therefore, that God asks only unpleasant things, nor do we suppose that we ought to have our way simply because it is what we should like. We lay aside our will and make an offering of it. It is the only thing we have to give to God; and we make a gift of it to him by accepting the life that he has planned for us. We meet it on those terms. We cannot escape our life; we cannot get away from it; we are not big enough to fight with God. All we can do is grumble at him. That does not hurt him, but it does hurt us. Nothing is gained that way. God is our companion and he is not to be resisted as a companion. We cannot break away from God. Down God's road we must travel and God only knows the road. So leave yourself to him. You will find that he will take you where he wishes to take you. Fight with him, and you must still go his way. You can accept what he has chosen for you and say: 'I will take his way because it is his choosing.'

We do not know what is the motive of God's action. We only know that God it is that acts. Is not that enough for us? It hardly matters why God does what he does, for it is sufficient to remember that it is he who does it: 'Though he slay me, yet will I trust in him.' Behind his act of slaying lies, as his motive, love. Can you trust yourself to God absolutely? I am afraid that you must. I am afraid that, whether you wish it or not, you must trust yourself entirely to him in life and death and beyond death. But it is our comfort that we have to do this; indeed, that in his love of us we are allowed to do this. To find a comfort in this act of confidence, all we need to know is the sort of person God is. If we knew him we should be glad to trust him. The saints trusted him absolutely, but that was because they knew him. Even when he seemed to treat them hardly, they were quite sure what his intentions were and relied entirely upon what they knew about him; thus, they were not only tranquil under his treatment of them but were happy under it. It gave them pleasure to know from their familiarity with his character that all was well.

After all, we have all had friends on whom we could rely. Here is a Friend greater than any other, wiser, stronger, who has loved us more than anyone else will ever love us. We may get tired of God, but God will never get tired of us. However little there is of lovableness in a man's heart, God still will love him. He will always find something in man to love. His ingenuity in love is immeasurable, is infinite, for in us always he sees the image of himself. Whatever happens, that likeness can never be removed from us. Because he loves us for his own sake, he must love us to the end. We are asked then to surrender our will absolutely to him. To do this thoroughly will take up all our time. It means, in effect, that we accept the life he has planned for us. Whenever our plans go awry, we must see in this his kindly interference to save us from our follies and we must be blessedly content. Go down on your knees to thank him for the obstruction of your plan or your ambition, for it must have been placed there by him to prevent you from going astray. He gave us his own example: learn of me for I am meek and humble of heart.' Do not expect too much in life. Take what he gives you. Though he slay you, still do not lose your confidence in him.

The Lord is my Shepherd
That wonderful gift of God which we call grace brings us immediately into the family circle of God. It is a saying, you will remember, of St Paul, that by it we are made co-heirs with Christ, that we are set in such relationship with God as to be coheirs with his beloved Son, who was of the same nature as his Father, who alone knew his Father, and who was known by his Father with a knowledge which was exclusive on both sides. Into that intimate relationship of nature, of knowledge, and of life, so runs the New Testament teaching, we, by grace, have entered. Because of that, naturally follows the pilgrim state of each on earth. This makes us always restless because, perhaps even unconsciously, we are homesick for a country to which we really belong.

Christ establishes us in the order of God, makes us a fellow with God, and shares God's life with us. We must never forget these articles of faith. As St Peter says, we are 'partakers of the divine nature'. This is what grace has done for the human soul. Yet, though we be partakers of the divine nature, co-heirs with Christ, though we be, to use another phrase of St Paul's, 'living temples of God,' God still asks something from us--the movement of our own. will. When St Paul himself was struck from his horse on the road to Damascus, where, as one might say, faith was not asked of him but given him, since the vision was too overwhelming for him ever to deny or to hold back from faith, when this vision came, this blinding vision, literally blind with the glory and splendor of the majesty of the appearance of Christ, he answered the vision immediately: 'Lord, what wouldst thou have me to do?' Do! The vision is given him. Christ appears triumphant to him. St Paul's immediate question is the practical one: 'What do you want of me? What am I to do?'

Always something is asked of us, some doing, some action of our own soul. This grace lifts us to the divine level, but there at that level we have to live, and live precisely in virtue of this shared life with God. Lowly man lives at that altitude of God. This is indeed what he asks of us. But what have we to do? What can we do? Life! It is not action exactly, is it? Life is surely not: 'What have I to accomplish? What have I got to bring with me when I stand before the judgment seat of God?' Doing is not Christianity, but believing and loving. Action? Is it not that? True. But it is easy to be mistaken and suppose that when we talk about a vocation and a purpose in life this means we have to do something quite definite. It may be, perhaps, that some people have something definite to do. For them life is simple. But many people have not. For them life seems strangely astray. It is very puzzling sometimes for a soul to say: 'Well, what am I doing? Or, indeed, what can I do? Here am I, and the few gifts I have, and the narrow limits set to my experience of life. What do I achieve that is worth achieving? It is all very well to talk about the grace of God and all this splendid life, but what have I to show for it? And what could I show for it? Nothing!'

Now please remember, such souls can do all that God wants. What do you do on a journey? Nothing! That is the whole point of it. You are waiting or you are arriving somewhere. When that is over, you will settle down and do your work. Here we are pilgrims. That is the whole point. Here we do not do any definite work. In an absolute sense we can say that here we do not live.

Apparently most people live just disregarded lives. These have beginnings and endings, but there is no plot in them, no drama. There is nothing sensational. There is nothing in them that a man can say definitely that they have done. We were not meant to do things. There is another life. There will be your real achievements. People pity themselves. They say: have gifts, but I have never had a chance to use them.' They say this so often that others find it tiresome to listen to them. But tiresome or no, it is true of all of us. We have never had our chance, nor can have this side of death. Do not measure the saints by their achievements; or, if you must, not by their achievements of then, but now. All the wonderful things they did. Yes, but eye hath not seen nor ear heard what they are doing now. We only know of it that it is eternal life. Measured against that, this is not life at all. This is but the thin trickle of the stream of life. There torrents pour down.

'So, then, there is no purpose for me? I am just wandering?' Of course you are wandering. So were the saints. So, says our Lord, are all of us. So was he. That is the New Testament teaching. You are a pilgrim. You are a stranger. 'Shall I go on to the end with all the powers in me undeveloped?' Surely your powers are far more magnificent than you ever dreamed; wonderful if you only knew. But this is why the saints were so perfectly content to let the world go by them. They watched 'doing' taken from them, perfectly content. 'What opportunities you are missing,' people would have said, hating their meekness. The saints missed nothing. They were waiting for the greatest opportunity. Death was the call. Here – it is on earth that we are all idle in the market-place – here it will one day seem to have been emptiness and idleness compared with that fullness of life which is to be revealed hereafter. Such is the Christian contention. Not this life shall fill up our measure. it should be unsatisfactory. The dreadful thing would be if we could settle down to it and be content. 'And so I am doing that for which God made me?' If you are, you shall not wholly know it. There is no one who knows surely. The external lives of others seem so perfectly rounded, beginning and ending, and with a perfect scheme between. As we think of them, we say to ourselves in our folly: 'I wonder why these people are not satisfied. Surely they have all they want?' We hope they will want more than they have – always. They were made for God. In this life we have faith in God, not the possession of God in himself really. Darkly to know him as in a mirror, that is really all that comes our way. It is not the invisible made visible that we hold. It is just a veil, it is just the hem of his garment as he goes by, that we are touching. But virtue passes out of him, only him you shall never see this side of death.

We are journeying to a far country. And until we get that New Testament view of life completely into our whole mentality we shall always be misunderstanding and even criticizing God. You may even hear human souls saying: 'God has never given me a chance.' Wait! Cannot you have patience? This is a passing life. There is an eternal life later. It is not fair to judge the artist until he has finished his work. Did you see it in his studio, that great portrait? 'But,' you said, 'that is not a portrait of such a one! His coloring is not like that! You have not caught the expression.' Wait! The artist will say to you: 'Wait till I have done!' And this other Artist? He knows what he is about. Wait, you are God's masterpiece. 'We? Is this all God can do? We so tired! We so feeble! What a poor achievement! We God's masterpiece? Wait, wait – leave the stained glass in the fire and then it will glow. Not at first, not yet, but wait until the whole process is done, wait till the work is over!

Then, if you like, dare to criticize the Artist who made you – wait till then! Do not be unjust! Do not say his handiwork is not beautiful. It does not look beautiful! But then it is only in the process. The completion comes when this life is over and done.

'What would you have me to do?' So live that you remember whence you came, and whither you journey. Keep your eyes steadily fixed on the height towards which you climb. You are content with nothing? Why should you, be? You have not yet what you were meant to have. Forget the things that are behind you – strive earnestly forward. That is the purpose – not 'What do I do?' but 'Whither go I?' Only one bowed his head, saying: 'It is finished.' He that was eternal – the beginning – the end. But not you or I. Our life never 'finishes'. That is the glory of it. That is the promise made to us. On earth lies a doom because nothing here can ever content us. We get past one difficulty only to encounter another. That is right and proper. Indeed, that is the very grandness of life. It is a roadway that leads to something magnificent. Cannot you be grateful for the road? Do not expect, that is all, do not expect to find here your city – the thing perfectly worked out, complete, that you desire, dream of, work for. Do not expect to be able to settle down for long to enjoy your life. You dreamt of a kingdom in childhood. You hoped for it in your working years. In your old age you will never find it. Pilgrims, travelers, strangers, that is all we be! But we seek a city, whose maker and builder is God – a city that is God himself. We shall enter within it by his mercy. God himself shall be our home. Cannot you be grateful for the road though it be rough and uncertain? It does all a road was ever made to do. It takes you home.

26 LOVE

You see the whole of religion can be compressed into the two words, 'life' and 'love,' which are so frequently on our Lord's lips in the Gospel of St John. Try to remember the numberless texts that include one or other of these words, or even both of them, and you will be astonished to find with what frequency they occur in those great passages of the New Testament that have always moved you. And why not indeed? There is nothing else so desirable here or anywhere as those two things: life and love. Life is a condition of all enjoyment and love is a condition, in its turn, for all real life. You cannot separate these two that God has put together. Life drives us to love, and love deepens life. Love demands life; is stronger even than life's rival, death; is stronger even than its own rival, hate; it is a fierce and consuming power, more terrible than an army set in battle-array, more terrible than war which feeds on death, a 'lord of terrible aspect'.

We think of love, then, as something which, for all its attractiveness and unifying power, has nothing to do with dalliance or mere weakness. Sometimes love may find us in a maudlin mood, and then selfishness may creep in; but love itself is a passion, a thing rather of violence than of weakness. What dreadful crimes has it not, in one form or another, driven men to commit, because it is violent and unruly? Life, too, is a violent thing; it courses through one's veins, it stirs, thrills, impels, uplifts a man. It expresses itself in motion. It cannot keep still. Howsoever rhythmic it may be in sleep and unconsciousness, it is never wholly quiet. Death is very still, hushed, silent; life is awake and about and always stirring. Dignity and reserved strength move us just because we can see the sign of strain and guess the pent force that is being held up, and contrast in a swift act of imagination what appears with that which lies behind appearance. The silence of life is tense and awful, because incredibly and actively protected by a barricade of power against the urgent pressure and clatter of noise and cries.

It would be very foolish, then, to think that religion, which is the knowledge and love of God, can be a boring thing if it is really concerned with life and love. My religion may bore me but that can only be because it is not religion at all. It may have the outward forms of religion in perfect order. It may be intellectually an orthodoxy without fear and without reproach; it may have the actual controls of true religion, but it has quite evidently missed the inner heart and meaning of it. What is the test of a man's religion? There are two tests: love and life. Is my religion a stirring thing, not emotionally, indeed, but vitally? Does it move me to live better, more fully, more richly? And does it drive me to love? Puritanism may be called religion, just as revivalism is called religion. Neither of them is religion at all. They are semi-religions.. Revivalism breeds immorality and Puritanism breeds cruelty, whereas our Master came to give us life and love, a noble life expressed in the love of God and man.

Sources of Life

Why do I find religion sometimes – often, perhaps – very dull and heavy? Only because I have not a love of God. Yes, but that is no answer at all; it merely shifts the question further back and leaves us where we were, for we have only to put to ourselves the same question in a new form: Why have I not a love of God? to see that the answer was no answer. We do not want religion to be a bore; we should very much like it to be interesting, particularly if it is possible to combine religion (that is, a love of God) with the happy and pleasant things which are in life and which, after all, were put there by God himself presumably for our enjoyment. Here we get to the heart of our real problem, namely, how am I to make the love of God something more than a mere form? Boredom can only come into religion when that religion is merely formal – a great danger, because religion tends of itself by routine to become formal. Can I keep it fresh and fragrant? Cannot I put lavender in the drawer with it to preserve this freshness and fragrance in it when I lay it aside after each act of prayer?

Does this simile help you to see the remedy? It is not that religion needs lavender. It is that it must never be laid aside. We can vary the metaphor and say that, like a man's muscle, it needs use to keep it fresh and fit. Religion is not like your clothes, which you can put off. It is not even like your skin. It is deeper than these external things, deeper than beauty, It is under the skin. Religion does not become conspicuous by being absent. It becomes conspicuous only by constant presence, by repeated action, by daily, hourly, unceasing repetition. There is no end to it, just because it is alive: 'I am the Way and the Truth and the Life' (John 14:6). Truth, faith, religion, are alive or not at all. Only repeated acts of religion and of faith can keep them alive; and by repeated acts of religion, something more is meant than regularity in prayer or the sacraments. Religion implies this, but no less it implies taking a high and noble view of life. It means aiming at kindness in conversation and act, having ideals of generosity and keeping to them, laying aside suspicion and cynicism, 'believing all things, hoping all things, enduring all things' (1 Cor. 13:7). A difficult task? Good heavens, yes; the most difficult of all. But then he called his service a cross when he first told us of it, a burden and a yoke.

Is it possible to keep my ideals unsullied, and still go on believing in man in spite of experience? Yes, it is possible: first, by a constant reading of the Gospels and by trying to recall the splendid phrases in which are flung at us the tremendous and perilous principles of Christ: 'The kingdom of God and his justice' (Matt. 6:33). Secondly, by endeavoring to live up to our love of our neighbor, whoever he be or whatever he may do. To Christ, who saw truly, the publican and sinners were better folk than the Pharisees; but we cannot judge any man. We must take all into our sympathy. Thirdly, by basing ourselves on the sacramental food of the Eucharist, which means eternal life springing up in us and breaking out into life and love. 'The Blood, that is the life' is given us there. There we can come, if we will, into such close relationship with him, that we are fired by his enthusiasms and find religion a devouring flame.

The Force of Love

Love, then, was given man by God to be of help to him. Without it, he would have found himself alone in a state which God judged to be 'not good'; and we can see how love becomes such a help, for it lifts a man above his own selfishness and fires him with an ideal which endows his work and sufferings with a new purpose, makes them of value and gives a center to them all. Love, therefore, is the great power that God set in the world to move and to establish man. It moves him, bringing him forward, giving a motive for his ambition that will rob his strongest efforts of selfishness.

Love, therefore, must be considered in its practical results if its place in life is to be fully recognized and used. Nevertheless, it is chiefly its romantic side that is thought of and here we meet at once with the humors of literature. The love episode has its comic reliefs in drama and literature. Indeed, the comic element in it, its incongruous ecstasy, its empty and vain repetitions, have overflowed from books and the stage into life. By their elders children are jokingly paired together as sweethearts, and laughed at. The youngster still at school is chaffed over his infatuations: the girl is jestingly accused of her long line of captives. Probably this is quite sane and healthy, but there is a danger also in this belittling, this endless guffaw, that greets on the stage and in life the opening drama of love. Granted that it needs being laughed at from time to time, has it not at present need rather for respect?

The romantic side of love is now at a discount. The lengthening list of divorce cases proves that over and over again. That love should really be stronger than hate, that for richer and poorer, for better and worse, love should hold its worshippers together against every weakness of human nature, seems now to be thought impossible. 'I no longer love you' is the burden of the letter read in the divorce court, written by one or the other to show that the end of their companionship has come; as though love were a thing beyond one's control, and once having begun can die down all by itself, without either party being able to prevent it. This is not true, need not be true. Love can be kept alive. Yet love is romantic, and to save it, its romance must be kept alive. It is not mere emotion, for it must outlast the emotions; it must be supported by every truth and every dogma, it must be nourished upon reverence, it must be realized to be the state wherein men and women are at their finest and best. Cleansed of untruth and selfishness, and yet robbed of none of its beauty, it must be recognized to be the only genuine human force that can give man vitality and virtue, steadiness, courage, enduring hope, and a remedy against passion for the men and women of the world.

Friendship

What difference is there between love and friendship? It is hard to determine, perhaps, with any absolute exactness. To Shelley, the word friendship had a meaning of greater unselfishness than love. Friendship was less passionate than love, and implied that a man gave more of himself and received less in return. Perhaps more usually a man's friends are thought of as of his own sex. If this be so, then, in spite of Shelley's distinction, the friendships of boyhood, school friendships, can be passionate enough and hard to distinguish from what Shelley has called love. It is written that the friendship of David for Jonathan was 'passing the love of women'. We can take it, there-fore, as a fact that the friendships that a man makes with his friends of schooldays, or of later life, may be as passionate as any others. In the artificial surroundings of school and its necessary isolation from home interests, the spontaneous affection of a boy finds no outlet other than the other boys; if he be of affectionate nature, he will turn passionately to his friends. Partly, therefore, by his mere circumstances, a boy is drawn into mysterious and ardent friendships with other boys. This may be perilous: let us admit, however, that it is certainly inevitable.

Now, when school-days are done, this friendship does not always cease, for there are natures that by some turn of temperament are drawn more easily to appreciate, admire, and love their own sex than the other. This may lead to sin in the same way as other loves may do; but it is not necessarily evil. It is a trick of temperament, which may have a psychological origin. Certainly it cannot be safely ignored. Everywhere, in every stage of culture, under every climate and in every condition, the thing has always been; not, indeed, in the majority of cases, but in a large and eager minority. Let us at least recognize that it cannot well be helped, that there is no reason why it should be prevented. It is of absolute necessity, if the matter is to be dealt with at all honestly, that I should recognize these tendencies and facts, and recognize them to be in themselves perfectly innocent: 'Each is drawn by native preference.' This preference for men by a man is, then, of its own nature, innocent, and need contain no evil; but it may become as desolating, debasing, and destructive as any other power or talent worked to an unmeasured extent. A man who falls in love with every girl, who seeks and pursues whatever pleases his eye, is no better and no worse off than he who pursues as selfishly those of his own sex who attract and appeal to him. Uncontrolled emotions are degrading in every direction and for whatever purpose. There are not the same consequences in each excess, but the consequences of each are terrible.

The friendships that we have with others of our own sex may be as valuable to us as those we speak of usually as our loves. They can possess us as wholly, can give us as high a measure of unselfishness, can form as great a joy. But friendship, no less than love, has its rubrics, conditions, and limitations. It must be entered into deliberately and with eyes wide open to the consequence. A friend, like a lover, is for all time: 'That is not love which alters when it alteration finds and bends with the removers to remove.' I must choose warily, for I choose for always. Again, with friendship as with love, with loss of reverence comes friendship's own ruin, for respect is the basis of the enduring equalities of love; so that passion beyond control, a blundering, vulgar thing, which destroys the freshness and fragrance of affection, destroys friendship as completely as it does love. Friendship is a great gift, if we remember that it is carried in an earthen vessel, delicate, 'a seldom pleasure,' and is only to be kept from evil by the thought of our Lord present as a third in it. Thereby it becomes full of unselfishness and sacrifice. It may become evil, it is not necessarily an evil, it may be a great good.

Our lives are made and marred by our friendships. In the world of nature and grace love is more powerful than reason, heart than head, friendship than law. We can easily notice that people have always influenced us more than books. The literature of our time moulds us, it is true, but generally only just so far as we find it embodied in those about us or in one particular person who sums up for us the principles of a philosophy. It is the man that matters. The action of Christ in becoming flesh was motivated undoubtedly by the deep knowledge that he had of the human heart. The whole story of the Incarnation is the splendid attempt of God to appeal to us, no longer in the formless definition given to Moses, I AM WHO AM, but as a definite personality whose actual features and whose life should really stir humanly the human soul.

'He knew what was in man.' He proclaimed not so much a code as a personality, not so much stone tablets as a friend. And what he has done in the supernatural sphere shows us also what is going on in the natural – that our lives are made and marred by our friendships. These are not, therefore, to be considered evils, nor as things merely allowed us. For the pagans, friendship was the very end and purpose of life. For our Lord himself it is a thing right and good. He had his chosen twelve, and out of the twelve an especial three, and out of the three one above others, the Beloved Disciple. Then there were the Magdalen and Lazarus; and what he began, the saints have freely copied: in the biographies of so many we read of special friends. Friendship, then, is allowed and was practiced by the Master whose lessons we try to learn.

Now the reason why friendship is thus powerful in human life can be readily understood when once we have tried to think what friendship means. It is obvious that friendship implies an openness between friends, confidence, the absence of all reserve: between friends there can hardly be any secrets. Friends, therefore, must, in their talk and in their silence, be revealing to each other what are their secret thoughts; consciously, even more unconsciously, they are letting each other in behind the veil that to outward seeming shuts off their lives from others. The deepest feelings and desires become apparent, the little touches that are lost upon others are to each other revealing. The effect of each upon the other is incalculably great. By this friendship the two are made equal.

Though one be but a shepherd boy and the other a king's son, yet if their souls be knit as one soul, all such artificial checks and barriers of class, age, ability, temporal goods, spiritual endowments, are brushed aside quite lightly. Mutual attraction, therefore, means ultimately mutual influence. I cannot go on living with others or feeling drawn to them, and so opening out to them my heart and listening to or watching the language that tells me of their soul, and come away the same as I was before I knew them. I have affected them, and they me; and all the world can tell how much we have in common. The influence, then, of friendship is all-powerful just because it means the absence of reserve and brings friends to the same level of greatness or littleness in character.

Friendship, then, is not wrong; indeed, it is to be found in the scriptures, in the life of our perfect Model, in the stories of the saints, whose deeds here rather than their words are to be attended to – or rather, perhaps, whose words are to be interpreted in the sense of their deeds. It is even, as the pagans declared, the most perfect gift of God to men. There is nothing else which gives greater joy in life, nor the loss of which makes the leaving of life more easily accepted. But, because of the very fascination of it, for its due exercise certain qualities have to be observed. The most sacred things are the more easily profaned; indeed, you cannot profane that which is not holy. The higher and nobler are our helps, the more dangerous does their abuse become. Friendship, therefore, must be loyal: there must be no fair-weather friendship, nor any friendship that allows an attack to be made unparried. A man may sit and say never a word, yet leave the room with the shame of disloyalty on him. Constant, for constancy is of the essence of friendship. Those who are always changing their friends, full of affection for one today, revealing all their reserves, and tomorrow seizing on another and making him also a recipient of their tales, know not what is true friendship. Many acquaintances, yes; many friends, no! Frank; friendship must be based on sincere confidence and trust, but this does not justify constant correction, which is an over-hasty attempt to reach the results of friendship. Ideal; I must see my friend as he is and as he might be.. Respectful, for passion destroys friendship by destroying respect, and cheapens the precious signs of love.

27 PRAYER

PRAYER has been defined as the raising of the mind and heart to God, but it would be more descriptive, and perhaps more accurate, to say that it is the raising up of the heart through the mind to God, for it is a commonplace of conversion that knowledge precedes love. It is true, of course, that the opposite statement would be equally valid, for I cannot know anyone till I am in love (i.e., in sympathy) with him. But though this is so, I must still begin by having some rudimentary knowledge of the existence of that which I love; that is to say, I must at least know of a thing before I can love it. Since, then, prayer means getting into communication with God, it is clear that I have always, consciously or not, to get into my mind some truth about God.

Let us suppose a mother is praying to God to save her son from peril. She really has convinced herself (either deliberately or without realizing what she is doing) of two quite definite things: first, that God is certainly able to help her; and, secondly, that he can be affected by her loneliness and desolation of heart. In other words, she is holding to two dogmatic truths – the omnipotence and mercy of God. And whenever we analyze prayer, our own or another's, we shall find that at the back of it lies some truth about God which we or they have accepted; and it is only because of that particular truth that we turn to that particular prayer. Thus, again, we often praise God because of his greatness, etc.; i.e., we first believe him to be great and then praise him for it: but belief, in any case, comes first. Unless I believed in his mercy or his power or his justice or beauty, or one or other of his many attributes, I should never turn to him at all.

Notice that in all this the word 'belief' is used, for our real knowledge of God as he is in himself comes to us only by faith. Reason can (says the Council of the Vatican) prove the existence of God; but it is at least possible that my reason never has proved it. My reason may never feel convinced by its own reasoning. In any case, the real knowledge of God as a supernatural power, with the full heights and depths of his divine life, cannot obviously be attained to by the reason, except so far as it is illumined by supernatural light; and it is just this supernatural light that we call faith. It is a vision. No doubt it is true, as Cardinal Newman has admirably phrased it, that the act of faith is partly an act of will. There must be the wish to believe at the back of me, a movement of the grace of God. Yet in spite of the fact that this act of will is essential, the gift of faith is still in its purpose and in its effect an enlightenment, an apocalypse, a revelation. This vision is an entrance into the kingdom of truth, for it tells us about God and the soul, this life and the after-life. We become as little children in implicit obedience, and gain also the clear sight of a child. Prayer, then, is based on the knowledge of God, therefore on revelation, therefore on faith.

Consequently, when I look at my prayers I must see what part faith or the Creed plays in them. I must get my faith quite clear, or at least as clear as I can, before I can settle down to pray. Before the Crib or before the Tabernacle, I must begin by making myself conscious of what exactly I believe. I must go over in my mind the significance of the Incarnation. Why did he come? What purpose had he in coming? What was he going to effect? What motive had he in coming? etc. I fix upon one single point and try to see really what I know about it. He came, for example, to redeem me. Yes, but what does redemption mean? It is a common word, frequently on my lips; do I realize what it implies ... And so on. This is the only way to pray.

Perhaps I begin at once in prayer by thanking or asking or praising; then I find I have nothing more to say; I am used up. Really I have begun all wrong; I have begun in the middle. Let me start always by some act of faith, and then go on quite slowly. Notice the liturgical prayers of the Church. They begin generally in some such fashion as this: 'O God, who by the life, death, and resurrection of Jesus Christ, etc.,' i.e., they begin from some dogmatic truth. So, again, our Lord's own prayer: 'Our Father, who art in heaven.' This, too, is a piece of information which faith alone makes known to me. If I leave faith aside, no wonder my prayers are dull, monotonous, a bore to me. But, then, I shall have to learn all about my faith? Certainly; I must go back to my Catechism. I shall find prayer growing easier as my knowledge of God increases. The two run parallel, prayer and faith; the absence of either, or their disuse, paralyses the practice of the other.

The first act of prayer is knowledge, the second is love; for I must always remember that the ultimate purpose of prayer, as of all spiritual life, is to get into union with God. For that end was I created, and to that end I must turn all and every supernatural enlightenment. Love is always the end of acquaintanceship with that which is perfect. I know my friends with a deep and true knowledge, and the knowledge does not remain as though shunted off in some separate compartment, having no influence upon life. I know their kindness, generosity, loyalty; and this makes my love itself, without any deliberate act on my part, increase also very considerably. The more I see the beauty of a thing or a person, the more I am attracted by it. The word 'attracted' is very appropriate, for it shows what has happened: the thing or person, in consequence of the increasing evidence of its beauty, actually draws me to it; it does not come into me, but leads me to it. Thus, theologians who describe the beatific vision tell us that the real act of possession is an act of intellect, but that once we have with our minds seen God, we cannot help loving him. No doubt, the reason is that the division of mind from heart is purely artificial; they are both mere functions of the same indivisible soul, which, when once it knows what is lovable, loves it by the same energy. The very appearance of beauty produces its own effect. In prayer, then, we begin by contemplating some fixed mystery or truth, and our heart then burns within us.

In other words, prayer is not an abstract science or art, but a handicraft of life. It is no use for me to set out, however elaborately, article after article of belief: the medievals said: 'God taketh not delight in logic' – that is, there is no prayer, no union with God, in merely tabulating our knowledge of him and describing it accurately, and remembering it in great detail. All that would be possible without prayer; prayer means that the heart, too, has been touched. The Psalmist sang: 'From my heart broke the good word;' and, again: 'A flame burst forth.' It is not prayer, therefore, when I merely weave theological patterns out of the truths of faith; but it is prayer when, contemplating God as revealed to me, I find him to be so lovable that my heart longs for his company and for the return of his sympathy. Nor should this be difficult. Any scene in the life of my divine Master, as recorded in the Gospels, must, as I study it, make more and more evident to me his mercy, his gentleness with sinners who are conscious of their sin, his meekness and humbleness of heart; and as these become more and more evident, surely my love will follow. So also the mere contemplation of any article of the Creed must certainly light up the depths of the mysteries of God at least sufficiently to let us see how really beautiful they must be. The mind explores all these wonderful things only to draw the heart more deeply after it. The mind lights up the loveliness within, and the heart is aflame with the vision disclosed. No one can gaze for long at something which is genuinely beautiful without being caught up in the rapture which the spell of its loveliness must cast.

While I recognize that faith in prayer is intended to lead me on to love, this does not mean that I must wait for a great flame to burst forth. This is, indeed, a matter about which I must be most careful, for I may discourage myself or be led astray by delaying for too long or rushing too impetuously along. By 'love,' 'rapture,' 'ablaze,' nothing more is meant than an inclination to follow God's commandments and live as faith prescribes. It has nothing to do with feelings, emotions. It does not mean that I do not pray if I do not feel love for God in the same way as I feel love for my friends, or that I must go on working out the particular mystery or article of belief until my whole being is stirred and raised to a white-heat of devotion. I am only a beggar, and cannot be a chooser; I must be content with the crumbs that fall from the table of God. No physical delight or appreciation of God's nearness to me is needed, nor is it in any way a sign that my prayer is fruitful; for this may depend rather upon digestion than upon the love of God; in fact, the very absence of it may make prayer, bravely persisted in, all the more pleasing in the sight of the Most High. Here, then, the up-raising of heart that should follow upon the heels of faith may be unfelt, even unconscious. It is shown rather in the day's work than in the moment's emotions. 'If you love me, keep my commandments.... Not he that saith to me, "Lord, Lord!" but he that doth the will of my Father, shall enter into the kingdom of heaven.' These are the proofs of our genuineness in prayer. Anyway, I must be satisfied with what is given me, nor should I seek to say much. The prayer in the Garden was but the repetition between long silences of one single petition. By faith, then, is his beauty unveiled; and the vision of this beauty sets my heart on fire with love.

The Method of Prayer
The whole doctrine of prayer from its practical standpoint can be summed up by saying that it is talking to God as a friend talks with a friend. That is, indeed, the best test of my prayers. Should I venture to talk to anyone I was fond of in the way I talk to God? We read in Scripture of God walking and talking with Adam in the cool of the evening, and we say to ourselves, that is perfect prayer. What does it matter in what shape God appeared, or whether he appeared at all! At least imagination grasps what the sacred author intended. Or, again, when we find it written of Enoch. that 'he walked with God till God took him,' we say, again, that our ideal of prayer could not be better described. Or lastly, for the quotations could be multiplied to any extent, when we first come across this wonderful sentence, are we not immediately conscious of what is meant: 'God spoke to Moses, face to face, as a man is wont to speak to his friend.' Now here we have in a very brief epitome all that, from a practical point of view, we need to know about prayer. It is simply the converse between my soul and

God, to be carried on in precisely the same fashion of language and the same pregnant silences that characterize my own talks with my friends. These must be the models by which I individually test the value and the sincerity of my prayers. Nothing else will do, nor will anything else for long hold or attract me. Prayers will ultimately bore me unless I carefully follow out these directions. First, then, the matter of prayer is originated by the. mind out of the articles of faith, and the result is that the heart leaps up to love God, and this love itself is expressed in the simple language and silences of friendship.

Now this 'talking as with a friend' involves certain consequences. It involves a view of prayer that should make it much easier for me. For example, prayer must be perfectly natural. I must speak to God in my own language, or else I cannot hope to pray frequently nor well. I may in my life ape the thoughts and style of another, but only for a while, since I soon wear his garments threadbare or show occasionally the real clothing that is beneath. My conversation with friends is perfectly easy. I have no character to keep up with them; they know me too well to be taken in by what I do not mean, and will not be at all impressed by any pose. So with them I lay all that aside, and appear as they know me to be. I say exactly what I think in the language that is most spontaneous and natural to me. Let me see, then, that the same naturalness is to be seen in my prayers. If my temperament is emotional, my prayers should be emotional; but if by temperament I am very matter-of-fact, what good would there be in my attempting to use the rapturous language of ecstasy? The sooner I learn that I cannot fit myself into another's prayers, the better for my own peace of soul. They will either be too large or too small; in any case they will only hamper my movements. Just as ready-made boots do not fit, so neither do ready-made prayers: the former blister the feet, the latter blister the soul. My prayers should therefore be my own, and I should ask only for what I honestly want. It is a mockery to ask God to take me to himself if I cannot really say that I want to go; and it is a lie to speak of myself as the greatest sinner in the world if I know that I certainly am not.

Quite honestly, then, I will speak to God in prayer as a friend speaks with a friend. That at least will be my ideal, and I shall do nothing deliberately that conflicts with it. Am I, therefore, to cast aside all my prayer-books? Not at all. It is true that as far as possible I should endeavor to do without them, for surely my needs, my reasons for thankfulness, and the motives that I have for praising God should supply me with abundance of material for talking to him. But undoubtedly from time to time I do find myself strangely silent; perhaps I am really only very tired. Still, it is helpful always to have a book, provided that we realize it to be merely a model and not the only way. Yet even here, at these times when our hearts can say nothing from sheer weariness, or from whatever other cause, we should still keep to our test and use the privilege of friendship. For surely one chief way in which friends differ from acquaintances is that we can be silent with friends, but allow no pause in the conversation when we are with an acquaintance; should this last happen, we grow uncomfortable and cast about for something to talk about, but to be in the friend's presence is joy enough. Conscious of each other, we are content; walking side by side, we may say never a word, 'make' no conversation; or sit, as on either side of the fireplace sit old cronies, speaking not at all, yet happy. For silence expresses things too large to be packed into language; and out of the fullness of the heart the mouth most often cannot speak. Hence, when I come to Communion, or make a visit to my Friend and find I have nothing to say, let me say nothing, be silent, wait for him to speak; at least be glad that I am near him.

The 'Our Father'

One day the apostles made this request to our Lord: 'Teach us how to pray.' Now so many questions must have been put to him that have not been recorded, that we are very grateful that this has been set down, for it gives us his whole answer.

But before coming to his words, let us just notice this, that the apostles do not ask to be taught prayers, but prayer. They do not say: 'Teach us some prayers,' but: 'Teach us how to pray,' which is obviously of infinitely more importance. It was just this view of things that our Lord himself insisted on, for he does not reply to them by telling them to use a particular form of prayer. His words were: ' Thus shalt thou pray,' not: ' This is what you must pray.' That is, he simply confirms their own attitude, implied in their very particular question: he answers them that the particular words he was using were meant merely as a model. Prayers may be most beautiful and most touching, but they are useless unless they are really intended. To repeat words is not all that is meant by prayer. The apostles had numberless prayers in the Sacred Scriptures, such as David and the prophets had composed under the inspiration of God; but they felt it was not prayers, but the attitude of the soul in prayer, which it was most important they should discover. Not, therefore, was their request: 'Teach us a new prayer,' but: 'Teach us how to pray.' And our Lord's answer endorsed their supposition; not 'this,' but 'thus shalt thou pray'; not 'in these words,' but 'in this fashion'.

This distinction is of great importance. Our Lord never intended that we should merely learn by heart the Our Father and recite it day and night. No doubt it is very beautiful and very simple, and can be meant quite easily by anyone who cares to use it, but that is not the purpose (though it is one purpose) of his gift of it to us. He evidently desires that we should take it to pieces, study its composition, and make it the model of our conversation with him and the Father. Obviously, it is impossible for this to be done in this book, for it would require a great number of meditations to work through the whole and find the meaning of each carefully (because divinely) intended phrase. Moreover, the real benefit would be lost, for the true value would only be appreciated when we had done it for ourselves. I must study it carefully, petition by petition, noting the distinct meaning of the words, the arrangement of the order, and the gradual development of the ideas of fatherhood, etc.

But this much may perhaps be set down, on the understanding that we may use another's remarks on condition that we judge and reject them if they do not touch the personal note which dominates the harmony of our own lives. First, then, it is worthy of comment to observe how easy and conversational the Lord's Prayer is. There are no appeals to God, as though he required forms of address different from anyone else. Indeed, this prayer is little else than a series of remarks made by a child to its father. The very want of connection between each petition, the staccato notes that mark off phrase from phrase, seem to suggest that it should be said very slowly, pausing after each group of notes to let their meaning and harmony echo to the base of the soul. Then, again, it is also worthy of comment that the child does not at once think of itself or its needs, but turns instinctively to the excellence and greatness of its Father: 'Hallowed be thy name.' Without request or word of thanks, it raises its voice in praise, desirous only that this praise should evermore increase till the valleys of earth echo as gloriously with his greatness as do the hills of the heavenly country. Only when this is done does it turn to its own needs and venture to plead for their contentment; and even so, it makes no request for luxuries or high spiritual favors. Bread only does it require, its urgent, instant, daily need; and it does not soar above such an unromantic view of the life of the soul as supposes it only not to be led into temptation, but delivered from evil. Lord, teach me also how to pray!

Distractions in Prayer

It is a constant source of annoyance to find how full of distractions our best prayers become. Hardly have I settled down to my devotions, made the Sign of the Cross, and put myself in the presence of God, than I begin to find myself overwhelmed by endless thoughts which have no connection with my prayers. I suddenly wake to discover that my mind has been wandering along, considering all the businesses of my life, my anxieties, my hopes and ambitions. As soon as I am conscious of this I go back to my prayers and endeavor once again to get into conversation with God. Nor shall I find, unless I am rather unusual, that even now I am really any more safe than when I began; probably the whole time I am on my knees, my mind is practically occupied with the troublesome task of disengaging itself from thoughts that it has no desire to consider. At Mass or Holy Communion it is possible that I have longer intervals of devout contemplation, but even during these sacred moments, souls that are really longing to love God with fervor and generosity are not seldom absolutely overborne by the inrush of distractions. All this is troublesome and distressing to me, but that is all; troublesome and distressing, but not sinful; for sin implies a determination and deliberation that are here obviously absent. The only harmful result can be when I am so wearied by my incessant struggles, so impatient at the apparent emptiness of all my prayers, that I finally in sheer disgust give up the whole attempt, in the thought that I was not meant by God for this kind of exercise.

Though it is exceedingly troublesome to have to wage war thus endlessly throughout all my praying time, it is certainly not at all to be unexpected. From a purely natural point of view, from the physical aspect of it, it seems certain that once I put myself in a state of quiet and have no very definite movement to catch and hold my attention, all the deeper and noisier interests of my life will at once spring into renewed activity. I have silenced the outward clash and clamor of existence, and the persistent inward battle-cries are bound to make themselves heard. I may have paid no attention to them, but they were there all the time; much as I lose the consciousness of the ticking of the clock, and only the ensuing silence reminds me that all the time it was really heard, but not attended to. Much in the same fashion, merely entering into church or kneeling quietly in my room, I am in reality allowing the repeating echo of my anxieties to be heard; all the interests of the day and the deeper mental impressions have been stored by that subconscious memory which never forgets. There is, then, nothing unexpected in all this, for it is the release of perfectly natural energies; and, what is more important, there is nothing sinful, for sin implies willfulness. Now it is clear that whatever direct willfulness there is, whatever will there is, consists in the effort with which I endeavor to get back to my prayers; for the whole trouble of distractions is that they come of them-selves and involve no effort whatever. Distractions, therefore, are not ordinarily sinful, and only become so when, grown conscious of their presence, we deliberately pursue them.

Why, then, do distractions come to us from the evil one, if they are not sinful? To this we may best make answer by saying that they do not all come from the evil one, but arise quite simply from purely natural reasons such as we have already described; and they can be only indirectly traced to the devil in the sense that the weakness of our mind is due to the effects of sin, original and actual sin. But of course every way of assault comes to the hands of the spirits of evil, and these may quite easily make use of distractions which are not in themselves sinful; for the effect of all these troublesome interruptions of prayer on souls timid and impatient is to make them inclined to give up prayer. They are a great source of discouragement, and whatever tends to depress the human spirit is the very best ally that the devil can have. He counts on all this, and hopes that my impatience under them may do me a great deal of harm and spoil my efforts at a close union with God. My meditations, grown dull with distractions, will be omitted; my prayers become more seldom; and the food of the soul being denied it, the soul must starve. I have, therefore, to be patient under the cross and continue my devotions unfailingly; all the more persistently because of my very distractions, for my need of God's strength is greater. One good way of getting rid of distractions is, as soon as I am aware of them, to pray for that person or matter which causes them; if, despite this, the same trouble continues, I must resign myself to the good hands of God, nor lose hope in my efforts after faith and love.

Aridity in Prayer

There is often in our minds as we think of the apostles almost an envy of their wonderful privilege, living so much in the blessed company of their Lord. To have that presence to in-spire them, to watch him as he went about his ways, to see how he treated those who came to him, to hear his words, to see him at his prayers, to know his goodness, to handle the Word made flesh, to have his affection visible and tangible, to be touched by those healing hands, to be called by name by one who thus gathered all men's hearts to his, how easy to fall in love with him, to love God – that is, to pray! It sounds idyllic, too beautiful a way of spiritual life, an experience to be envied. And yet, when the time came, what had they learnt? At the time of crisis they failed. One denied and one betrayed and almost all deserted him. That does not look as though it was a satisfactory way of being trained in the paths of holiness. They had the best trainer of souls that they could have had. His method, too, must indeed have been the best, so that there can be no blame against the Master for what was done by them. It was the condition of their spiritual life that of itself must have militated against their proper understanding of their life-work. They must have supposed that all their lives they would have the dear presence that so inspired them, and made no provision against the time when he would have to leave them.

But actually he had already told them that his going would cause them pain indeed but not hurt. His going would be to their advantage, it would be expedient for them. The reason is not far to seek, for only after he had gone would the Paraclete come to them, and their need now was for the Paraclete rather than for him. This seems to be a truth of the spiritual life stated with clearness by our Lord. There is some incompatibility in the inner life between sensible devotion and the depth of love. It is suggested to us that only when the sensible devotion has died down, gone out, will the real spiritual life come into its proper relationship to the whole man. Man, therefore, needs the fusing into one of his whole being. So long as he retains his devotional fervor in its physical sense, he has little chance of being able to hold to the Spirit. His upper surfaces are too engaging for him to be able to realize his lack. All goes so well with him that he does not see how ill it all is. There is the danger of mere externalism, the child's spirit of prayer that cannot hold out against the pressure of life and its stings.

The beauty of the child's religion lies exactly in its unconsciousness; the beauty of a man's life of prayer lies in its conscious reaction to the life about him. While we are in our childhood years, it would seem that prayer and all that it implies are easy to us. Then, as we grow up out of childhood, we begin to experience difficulties in the exercise of our devotion, partly the mere effect of that period of the development of the mind when romance has become unattractive and feminine and the critical spirit is more respected and desired. Even philosophy has its part in this drying up of the devotional life of the soul. As in the case of the apostles, this should be recognized to be an expedient occurrence, though it must also be reckoned a painful one. It is painful, for man naturally devotes himself more easily and more conveniently to what gives him pleasure, but for that very reason, in this matter of religion, the pain is expedient lest he find in religion something that soothes him and does not inspire him and brace him up to the difficulties of life. We have the parallel case of the doubting apostle who believed as soon as he saw the wounds but who would not believe on the word of his brethren. Our Lord indeed blessed his faith, for it was faith to see the humanity and believe in the divinity, but our Lord also implied that there was a greater faith – that of those who did not see and yet believed. So, it is evident that to our Lord there was a loveliness in the faith of those unnumbered millions who would never have the consolation of seeing or handling or hearing the Master, and yet whose spiritual life would be no less holy and alive.

We accept it, then, as a principle of the life of the soul that it is expedient when the merely emotional side of religion gives way to something deeper, because only with the dying down of the emotional side can the other be liberated – the advent of the Holy Spirit. That this should be so in the world of the spirit is natural enough, for here above all we need to guard against the intrusion of self and self-complacency. Now, it is abundantly clear that if we did enjoy prayer always, we should be with difficulty persuaded from praying always, and yet our motive in so doing might very easily be not supernatural or unselfish but human and selfish. We might easily give ourselves to prayer because we enjoyed it. That would be a poor motive, for we would be seeking not God but self.

Moreover, if we take prayer in its essential concept, it is part of the virtue of religion, which in turn is part of the virtue of justice – the virtue which renders to everyone what is his due. In this particular instance the person to whom we render our due is God. Prayer, therefore, is not so much an indulgence as a duty. Duty is of obligation because it is duty, and for no other reason. If it be also attractive, that is perhaps an advantage; but if it be unattractive, it remains a duty still. Duty is a steadfast and constant thing.

The offering of prayer then (for prayer is an offering to God in testimony of our relation to him as our Creator) survives any alteration of our feelings, any dying down of them. We still have a duty to love God; and we still have a duty to offer him our worship, and worship is expressed by prayer. There is the public and personal prayer of Mass, there is the communal prayer of Office, but there is also the obligation of offering God prayer as an individual. Now, in all these matters it is the obligation that is of the supreme necessity. We are obliged to pray. If we enjoy our prayers, the obligation is easier;

but if we do not, the obligation remains. Supposing, then, that prayer is no longer enjoyable; pray still I should, for God is no less my Creator because I cannot feel any devotion to him.

In these matters it is the will that counts. We can indeed rest content that if we do persevere in prayer, we shall very likely recover something of the earlier fervor that we had, for God does help souls into ways of peace. But if he does, that will not mean necessarily that prayer is now better than it was. He himself, when he came in his human nature, was no less pleasing to his Father when he seemed to be abandoned by his Father than when the good pleasure of the Father in him was publicly announced at the baptism.

Perhaps we shall find, when this life is done, that the most valuable in the sight of God were those times in our existence which gave us less pleasure than those which gave us pleasure. When all seems going well with us, this may be due only to the absence of temptation. When we are tempted and have to fight for our very souls, we feel ourselves hard pressed and we may well judge that things are going badly with us; and yet those may be the very moments when we are meriting our eternal reward. We are so prone to judge things, not as they really are, but only as they seem to us, which means little else than what they cost us. Martyrdom was not exactly attractive to the martyrs, and they may have had no sense of the heroic in their testing; they may even have been assailed at that very time by the wonder as to whether there was any after-life at all. They may have been incredibly weary when the crucial moment came. But that would not matter. What did matter was their acceptance of the contest and their profession of faith by the will.

All this is but to say that the soul is to be measured in its development by the efforts it makes at its duty and not by the pleasure it takes in its duty. So here, then, in prayer we have to consider that the only point about prayer is that it should be done and as well done as we can do it, but that does not mean that it should be done with emotional pleasure. We would all of us like to have that pleasure whenever we prayed, but, since we have it not, we must be content not to have it.

Just as we cannot deserve it, so also we cannot produce it. We can only rightly be blamed for not having those things that we could have, but the very difficulty that here confronts us is that we are dealing with emotions that of their nature lie outside the control of our will. We can keep back our tears, but can we command them to come? We can hold us the feelings of love, but can we summon love in any emotional sense of that word? The answer assuredly is pertinent to this problem, for what so often troubles souls is that they have no sentimental pleasure in the prayers they say. It is something to remember that we cannot bid these emotions come, even if sometimes we have the power to bid them go.

Thus again, when we come at the end of a busy day to deal with God, It may happen that we are in no condition of awakedness to say our prayers as we should, were we in the true condition that wholehearted attention requires. But then we have been busy about the things of God, or at least remotely we have been in his service; or even if we have not, then at least here we are in the state of physical tiredness which makes it impossible for us to attend to what we are saying. It is well to remember that as long as we are doing the best we can under the circumstances in which we are, then God will not ask more of us.

Once, it will be remembered, he stood by the treasury and watched the people come one by one to make their offerings. The stream that passed was of all sorts and kinds, but he noticed that there were many who gave lavishly and perhaps others who gave little at all. One there was who gave but two small coins, indeed the smallest coins of all. Yet in his judgment she had given more generously than the others. For the others gave out of their abundance, but she had given all the living that she had. All she had she gave, and was rewarded by this judgment of his. It is his judgment, too, on prayer. It is not what my prayer is like, for no prayer of ours is worth his while. But because prayer is a duty, I have to ask whether I am giving him all I have to give here and now.

Yet shall I trust in Him

There is something subtle and strange in the way in which nationality or race produces sympathy or antagonism of itself in us. We are often at a loss to discover why, or to set out the reasons or motives that produce it. Something strange, we repeat, about the way in which people of the same nationality understand one another, and, again, strange in those antipathies that race or color produce. A curious knowledge! A curious hostility! In a nation of immigrants from different nations, how strangely the original racial characteristics often continue under utterly different circumstances. How people of the same nation, of the same racial origin, almost naturally gravitate together, how they drift into the same trades. There are certain racial capacities that very quickly establish themselves. People from a common country not only gather together, but adopt the same trade because they have the same capacity for this or the other craft or form of business.

The same is true of that inner life of grace, which constitutes us pilgrims here on earth and fellow-citizens of the saints. There is something about it that produces a strange, unexpected knowledge, a certain sympathy of understanding, a certain strange magic by which the world can be transformed by those who have it and by none else. It carries with it a certain know-ledge, a curious sympathy. Sometimes people are astonished that some book or other, that deals entirely with the super-natural, becomes, as the expression is, 'a best-seller'. And, they say: 'How unexpected that a book like that should have so great a sale.' Books that appeal to or exploit the lower portion of man, works of that sort, that are deliberately written to excite the lower passions, it is easy to understand why they are popular. It is difficult to understand that this, so spiritual in its outlook, can sell and be popular almost everywhere. It is not really strange. There is something in everyone which can be roused into sympathy with God and the supernatural. There is a hidden root upon which this growth can be grafted. He does not destroy our nature when he shares life with us, but fulfils what is already there. There is in every soul something that connects it with the God who made it. Man is no stranger to God, at any time. How can he be? He is a child of God. Essentially and necessarily there is in the soul an incomplete under-standing of divine things, not dominant necessarily, but always there. It can be surprised into quickened life under stress of some great emotion. A man who has forgotten all about God, yet, in a moment of great pain, may be found calling for aid, invoking, almost unconsciously, the God who made him. At times, another, surprised by some marvelous blessing, almost in spite of himself, will say: 'Thank God.' It is not merely a phrase; it is deep understanding; something so deep that the man is hardly aware of its continued existence. For man is fashioned after the divine likeness. There is in man always an intimate relationship to God, the relationship of child and father, and so always a sympathy, always a strange knowledge of God, reasonable but not reasoned.

That this should surprise us is because we neglect these hidden things or push them out of sight; it is because of our utter forgetfulness of these deep things of the spirit that in our time so many freak religions are born. They are the feeling of ill-taught souls towards their full manhood, which holds traces of the faith. They get the truths they stumble on only in part, a fragment; and without complete, rounded knowledge they let their imagination run wild, rim to extremes over it. But they have felt some portion of that which is indeed their spirit. For the truths of faith are not ours only, they were meant to be the inheritance of all mankind. All has been fashioned, all has been redeemed by God. All is loved by God. All has sympathy of blood with God. All the world is God's child. It is because we are hardly aware of our own relationship with God and because we are still less aware of our responsibility to others, that these spiritual truths are but half known in our world. What we need is to deepen our own supernatural life so as to keep ourselves in more or less continuous relationship with God. What we all need is a deeper sense of prayer.

This does not mean that we need to devote ourselves to something that would take up more time than we have leisure to give. Already we say our prayers, but what we need is a greater intensity in our prayer, a deeper sense of God's nearness to us. And this not only when we are kneeling down, but when we are going about our work or duties. What a pity it is that so much of our reading is of material things, that we read so little of the high, spiritual things of God! What a pity it is that men and women, as they go about their business, do not hold themselves quietly in the bus and say their prayers. Why must they needs hold in front of them the record of the world's sins, and be content with it? Murder, violence, court cases, gossip, scandal, shame. Is it not possible to say to ourselves: God is here, and all these people have need of the consciousness of God? Cannot I sit in my place and pray for them one by one? Cannot I realize that God's immensity fills all of it? Cannot we live with God and share our lives consciously with him? Shall we not then be able, all the better, to help the people we meet? To say the right word when we should speak, or keep silent when we should be silent? We do not learn this tact out of books. We learn it from God.

Somehow we must keep close to God if we are to be moved by him, like the planchette on which you put your hand and which then writes your thought. So must we let ourselves be moved under the divine movement. We must let ourselves go. We must put ourselves into the divine power or recognize, rather, that we are there. This involves a life of prayer, not necessarily, though perhaps also, of churchgoing, for instance, a daily visit to the Blessed Sacrament. But it does mean that we live our lives consciously in touch with him. Then will come to us a knowledge of God, an understanding of him. That is why he said: 'Thou shalt love the Lord thy God.' You must have sympathy to understand. Once you say: 'I dislike such a person, race, or type,' your knowledge of them is finished with, it will never be true. If you want to know God you must love him, and that means prayer. Our life should be more consciously full of God; it very easily can be. It is to help us to achieve that that our Lord came. The beauty of his life is not his love for his fellow-men, but his conscious relationship with his Father.

People are always telling us what religious people ought to be like, forgetting the essential thing. All that is asked of us is to love God; the rest follows of itself. Without that, religion becomes mechanical and cannot be realized. Religion is all begotten of God, of our conscious relationship with him. We are God's children; that we must never forget. That fact establishes a certain root of sympathy on which is grafted all our faith, everything that is supernatural in our life. Everyone has it. No one can utterly get rid of it. No one, therefore, is beyond redemption; no one is outside the capacity of faith. If it were something of our own making, yes, it might lapse and die. But it is not. It is something God has planted in us. It can never be done away with. It is essential to us, it is rooted with our nature. It can never be laid aside.

What is true of us is true of the whole world. None is outside his kingdom. All could be nearer than they are to God. We must begin with ourselves, and try to keep ourselves in that divine company and realize what an effect such a consciousness would have on our life, this conscious relationship with God. It means a new life. The ordinary life, but now crowded with God's company. To sit in the bus or while walking to say to ourselves: 'God is infinite power. Nothing can happen to me except God lets it happen.' Now knowing this, let me look at the world! God's wisdom is governing everywhere. I can never have cause to feel a panic. The infinite wisdom of God guides all I know. Let me read about the distresses of the world and see these from the right angle. Who is the Lord of the world? What was he like? He was the most compassionate, was our Master, but absolutely at peace always within. There was nothing frantic or fanatical about him. He was exquisitely gentle, full of the sense of the fatherhood of God. He saw suffering; was touched by it; knew God to be its providence.

People are either passionate and impatient with God or pious and careless. I must say fragments of the Lord's Prayer as I go up and down, and round about. That will do. Anything will do that can be repeated over and over again. Here we shall find the immense value of the Rosary for keeping us in touch with God. If we can only do that our world will be richer, and his magic will transform it. We shall grow larger to the fullness of the stature of Christ.

What a width of vision there was in the saints! It is the width of vision that must most matter, not a width that is a tolerance which does not care, but a tolerance which cares so absolutely, because only out of faith can souls see what is right and true and sane. These are the children of God. What we need is this deeper, supernatural sense, consciously awakened, this steady and daily increasing consciousness of the nearness of God to us in life.

Part Four: The Christian Family

28 VOCATION

WE HAVE each of us our vocation in life. Unfortunately, the word 'vocation' has become restricted to that particular form of life which includes only religious or priestly life; consequently, the idea is not seldom to be found even among pious people that those only have a calling from God whom he has summoned to stand away from the cares and joys of normal existence – all others are 'in the world'. This little phrase again suggests the same unjust belittling of the vocation of the lay-folk, so that these do not realize the high importance of every profession of man or woman After all, the majority must marry and be given in marriage. It cannot be, then, only a minority whom alone God calls. Each of us has been placed here to do a certain work; each has his separate vocation, just as each, according to the Scriptural expression, has been called by a separate name. In the Old Testament this notion of a name whereby God knew us from all eternity is evidently only a way of expressing the particular office to which each of us is summoned in the economy of God. How is it possible for me to know what my vocation is? There are certain obvious clues: my capacity for some particular form of life (whatever it may be that suggests itself), my desire for it, and the possibility for me to attempt it. All these are necessary, but perhaps my desire for the life is what most convinces me and least convinces others. We cannot explain, but are deeply conscious of, the appeal. I have, therefore, to make up my mind as regards my vocation. I must ask advice of my confessor, my parents, or guardians: those that best know me. I have to consult my own inclinations, opportunities, prospects. Then I have to pray for light; and, finally, make up my own mind as to what profession in life it is to which God calls me. But supposing I find out later that I ought to have been something else? That supposition is impossible if I have honestly made up my mind. Is it not possible for me to frustrate my vocation, to remain in the world when I should have entered the cloister? No, certainly not, as long as I did honestly try to make up my own mind. My con-science has judged as best it could, and God can ask no more from me. However, I eventually make my decision, as long as it is my conviction that God bids me do this or that, I must unfailingly, as far as may be, carry it through. To stay and labor and marry requires – as much as does the priesthood – a separate and distinct call. Such a life is a holy and a sacred living. I must realize, therefore, that God has an interest in my life, and that should give a dignity to my whole view of my soul and its work here. What God has made, let no man call common or unclean. Whatever my line of life, I may be sure that to it I have received a divine calling.

Consequently, I must learn to be very patient with life. It is no use now longing for the peace of the cloister and wondering whether or not I was not called to that life. Every Catholic child feels, at one time in life, a desire for the religious state; but that fades with the many and continues in the few. But though all are not, and cannot be, called to such a vocation, to each there is his own vocation. God, indeed, has no need of any of us. Preacher, priest, worker, rich and poor, old and young, may try to do their best, but all that they achieve throughout their whole life, he could have effected by the single act of his decree. He has no need of any of us, yet he has allowed me the high privilege of partaking with him in the continuance of the world's history. He has allowed me to become a partner, a member of his firm, a helper in his voluntary aid society. Perhaps I long to be this or that, feel powers within me that are clamorous for expression, yet find no opportunity to put them to their full advantage. I become miserable, discontented, perhaps bitter. Can I never learn that whither God calls, the road must lie open always? If I cannot do what I would like, then it is because what I like is not what he likes. There may be obstacles which I must endeavor to surmount, but do not let me become impatient of them. Perhaps to struggle only is my vocation, never to achieve. As a model husband, citizen, parishioner, as a model Catholic, I have a vocation sacred and unique. I can imagine a higher vocation than I have, but, for myself, it is certain that there is not a holier one.

29 VOCATION TO MARRIAGE

THE one great result of believing in the unbreakable bond of marriage is, or I suppose should be, that people are more careful how they enter into that irrevocable life. Yet often a priest hears it said to him by one or other who wants to be married that the real reason that is impelling them to marriage is that by it they will escape from the bondage of the home. 'I don't love; at least I can't exactly use that word to describe my feelings,' they will say to the priest, 'but, honestly, I am very tired of home. I have had so much to do. I am so much interfered with that I will take this or any other opening that gives me my release.' Or again, sometimes at least, you will find that they look on marriage as something which will give them a good time.

Now all these reasons show complete misunderstanding not only of marriage but of life. For us, under the faith, we have to look on the married life as a distinct vocation, as solemn, as personal a life as life is in the cloister. The vocation to marriage is as definitely, divinely planned as that. It is not even a mere alternative to the cloister. 'I haven't a religious vocation or a priestly vocation, and therefore I must go and marry.' This is not a true argument. Life is not quite like that. Sometimes in the books one reads, in the novels, people go off to the cloister because they have been crossed in love. That could not be a justifying reason for even attempting a vocation; but though the idea is silly to us, it is also tragic, as it shows us what an insipid view the author must have of every sort of life. It would be impossible for the soul to continue in religion under such a negative impulse.

So, contrariwise, people will say: 'I have no vocation for religion or priesthood, and therefore I must marry That is not a true argument; at least that is not a real argument. There must be something far more solemn than that. Moreover, today, the single life is being lived increasingly outside the cloister. As far as we can tell, more and more people have a vocation from God to a state neither of marriage nor the cloister, but to a very different way of life. Sometimes, perhaps, the single life is sought out of selfishness, because men or women love too much the comforts of their world. To marry would be almost to halve their income, and at least to share it with someone else. They have been accustomed to a definite amount of material comfort so that they have not the necessary unselfishness to enter into the married state. Or as a further reason they defer marriage to a date beyond their endurance of chastity and because of selfishness they open the door to troubles, evils of the soul.

God has his own designs for each one of us. Each of us has his own way of life. The married life is as much a vocation as the life of the cloister, and marriage should dominate the life of the married as the life of the cloister dominates the life of a nun. She has her religious vocation and so she has her religious life to live. Now that fact limits her life. She has probably to fit into her days somehow a great deal of external activity, but a certain amount of religious activity has also to be fitted in. If she be a good religious, she will not allow the activity of life to interfere with her religious obligations. Her first obligation is to her own development, and she may have to diminish her external activity if she finds it to be hurting the religious obligations of her state.

What is true of the religious, is true, or should be, of the married person – wife or husband. Marriage is a sacred vocation of God. Just as the nun, under her solemn obligations of the cloister, must not allow external activity to reach so high a point as to interfere with her spiritual obligations, so also a man or woman must not allow external activity to reach so high a point as to let it interfere with the obligations of the married state. Here, then, is a positive vocation, dominating, limiting the amount of activity to be given to other works, however good. This most, this uttermost, is the solemn obligation of their lives.

We must suppose further that one who is called to a life of marriage will not be safe outside the married life. Those who have been called to it and have not accepted it because of their selfishness, will live lives maimed to the end. Something in them that would have found expression through human love will never find its expression. God's work will be left undone. God is wise, which means that God acts for a definite purpose. A fool drifts; a wise man plans. God is wise. God made every soul for a separate purpose. Each was born for that. Every soul came here marked by God for a definite work in life. Moreover, providence guides the fashioning of the human lives that intermingle. God is over all. So God fashioned our soul deliberately for a work and gave an individual purpose to the individual soul. This purpose is not fulfilled in a single act of life. A nun doesn't fulfill her vocation by the mere act of entering the cloister. That is just one stage of her vocation. A vocation is something always opening, unfolding. It is the pageant of a life, the drama of a life, moving on.

You watch a play, and you see a character unfolding itself in scene after scene. The dramatist who wrote that play shows you the character unfolding to its climax, and then achieving its fulfillment or failing under it; but in the theatre a life unfolds to those that sit and watch. Here it should unfold to the actor himself. Now God has planned each life of ours as a story, scene following upon scene. You can go back to your childhood, and you can see how gradually all sorts of things that at the time you hardly noticed have led on to what you are today. Just a chance acquaintance ripening has molded you. Not a chance acquaintance really, but one divinely planned. It seemed by accident, but this is God's world, and there are no accidents. It is only God's plan gradually fulfilled. God has a purpose for every soul. If you follow it, and as you follow it, your life opens and leads on. You don't notice the plan at the time. Indeed, it seems as though life were almost at the mercy of anything and anyone. It is not really so.

Moreover, if we find our vocation, we find a place where our talents will have their opportunity, for there must be an opportunity always for the talents God gives to man, since we were given our talents for use. God made us for a purpose, and because he meant us to do something or be something, he fitted us for the work that awaits us. Every soul has its work, and because that soul is destined for a work, it is divinely endowed with the gifts necessary to do the work. Further, we know from the parable that we must use our talents, else a severe judgment will await us at the end.

Now there are souls that can only develop their gifts through the married life. Their souls, left solitary, would be maimed, never achieving their real richness. There are others whom God has designed for the way of the cloister – separated, untouched, alone. Each has to find the place to which God calls him and for which he was destined and endowed. His vocation is a positive way of life. The married life, if it is God's choice for you, will contain for you the highest thing you can ever do. One way of life may be higher than another way of life, one way of prayer higher than another, but this can be only in the abstract, for that is highest for me which God has called me to – whatever it may be.

To do God's will is the noblest thing; by this only are both cloister and the way of marriage justified. Now which is God's way for me? That is what I have to find out. That is what I have to discover. To do this is something evidently to be studied solemnly, something that I have to go into with careful thought. I should not drift into my life's work. I may, of course, but that were foolishness. I shall achieve success only if I find that way to which God has called me, for which he has fitted me, and where alone such talents as I have shall find their fitting result.

Therefore, we say that marriage should not be looked at as an escape from the home, not a place where one can have a good time in life. Not that. Not even a cure for some unnatural desire. Sometimes you hear this advice given to people who have a habit of unnatural sin: 'There is something wrong with you. What you need is married life.' But married life is a holy way, not a remedy for unnatural evil nor a legitimate escape from trouble that is not born of natural desire. Lawful desires are achieved in matrimony, not unnatural desires. To remedy such a nature, you must change the nature or discover some way in which these desires can be sublimated and made whole. Matrimony is no cure for something which is contrary to the nature that God gave us; it is a positive vocation to which God has destined the vast majority of mankind.

Again, marriage is not a romantic dream, though there may be romance in it. There is romance in every life for the soul that cares to seek it. But marriage is no romantic dream. It is real and earnest. Marriage is a solemn vocation, something for which a soul must prepare. A doctor has years of study to equip himself for the work he has one day to do. A lawyer has to undergo preparatory studies fitting him for his subsequent career. If he neglects his studies, whether he be doctor, lawyer, priest, or whatever else, and because of his neglect fails in some signal instance in his profession, because he never studied in his schooling years, he is to blame for the mischief that follows his ill-done action. A soul that the priest hurts because he never studied properly in his seminary days is a soul of which God will one day demand from the priest an account. A body mangled through the ill knowledge of a doctor or a case in the courts that goes awry due to neglect in preparatory studies these men are answerable for the damage they have caused. These are ignorant, who should not have been ignorant, ignorant therefore with a culpable ignorance for which they must be blamed Now do you think that marriage is not also a profession needing preparatory study or that people can just drift into marriage and expect, somehow, to find their way through?

You know human nature. You know your own, its curious outlook, personal, unique. You know the strange self of yours, how it hides from you, how difficult it is really for you quite to analyze your own character. Can you with less difficulty understand the characters even of those you love? You that perhaps enter so easily into partnership with another soul, do you realize it has its own life that is worth studying, reading about, that it is a soul as complicated as your own?

The Catholic Church has had a great deal more to say about marriage than merely lay down her laws for it and leave it. She has provided her children with the results of her experience of the conduct and direction of human souls. Surely it is only fair to that other whom you have joined to yourself, and only fair to yourself, that you should try to discover if there be not laws and principles, if there be not some way of conducting the married life as a positive vocation so as to get the best out of both your lives.

The best of you will be called out in married life. That, re-member, is what we mean by a vocation. Your own heart, your own life, your own character need precisely these conditions of marriage if the best of you is to be brought out as it could and should. That is the life God made you for. That is the life you will fit into, but carefully, foreseeing, watching, learning, above all praying, asking God to help you to deal with this other soul so that you may lead it always nearer to his ways. Are you lifting one another Godwards? It says in Scripture: 'He who is alone has no one to lift him ' Eve was given to be a helpmate to Adam, not a burden, that she might help him nearer to God. She failed at first but in the end she triumphed. God has planned his direction of the human soul, has endowed it with definite and personal gifts, and so intended that not drifting, not blundering, but deliberately and care-fully it should build up its own life.

We say, then, that marriage is a positive life to which, per-haps, God calls you. Remembering that, you must give to it the fullness of your capacity. To make it a success you must put all your heart and mind to it. Thus, her married life is above all things the supreme business of the mother. Success in other lines will not compensate for failure here, so nothing must be allowed to interfere with that, with her obligations of motherhood and wifehood. These come first. Let women be eman-cipated by all means. Allow them to enter, if you will, into every business or profession that there is; but if they marry, their family obligations are their first, and no piety, no parochial activity, no hobby or amusement must be allowed or encouraged that hurts the conduct of the home, for this life of marriage carries these obligations for her. This is justice. All other activities are but charity, and, great as charity is, justice comes first. Before you give alms, you must pay your lawful debts to those that are your creditors. The mother's creditor is always the home. That is the reason why the Church has spoken so nobly of motherhood. That is the reason why she sets as our example the Mother of God. To her the ideal of motherhood is most noble because it is most unselfish. A mother has the pains, but she also has the rewards of love. Even the Church has claimed this title; it is the very name that we give her. Our high praise of her is that she is 'Mother Church'. We think of her as though she were a mother. The same title seems to us the finest thing we can say of a human soul.

The mother is the center of the home; and if the home is hurt in our day, by whose fault do you think it is that such a thing should have come to pass? If the family has failed, whose is the cause of failure? Everybody is perhaps in part to blame, but she perhaps most blameworthy who with such little wisdom has dealt with human souls, most difficult and most delicate of instruments, linked to her by duty and love. She has her quiet time for thinking. Though all of her day is busy, she has many a time to think; and in such times she must study each soul committed to her and puzzle out by memory and experience and instinct how to deal with each. She is the mother, even of the man that calls her wife. She is the great protector of the family. So we think of her. Always a mother is carved for us holding her child or with outstretched arms. That is the mother's place in the world, in the home. Indeed, she is the home. It is not a place really, this home of which men sing; it is her heart. She is the priestess of this intimate sanctuary. She is the mother. What more is there to be said?

There have been days when our people have been persecuted. All that while the mother was the inner shrine of the faith. There have been ages when the exercise of everything that is holy has been prohibited us. Then the Catholic family, and in the family the mother, has been the center of the Catholic shrine. There have been ages when the voice of pulpit was hushed, silenced by the persecutor. Then she was the only preacher in the only Temple of God. Altars were leveled. Her knees became the only altars, where age by age the children learned their faith. No catechism class existed, no Sunday School. She was their catechism class and Sunday School, she was the Church of God for them. She taught them their prayers; that they kept the faith was due to her. Oh, that age of valiant motherhood! Not mere love had she, but wisdom, too. Indeed, love must include wisdom, for love is no mere passion or impulse, not even a mere instinct like that with which the hen gathers her chickens about her. Love is not that merely. Love includes wisdom also, for character comes in as part of love. A mother's love, then, is a vocation, a calling; so too is the love of father and child. Into that sanctuary God calls some human souls as he calls others to the cloister. A way for each; and to each of us a call of God to follow the way. And to all of us, whosoever we be, St Paul speaks those solemn words: 'Walk worthy of your vocation.'

What is your vocation? What is your place in the home? Whatever it is, realize that God called you to it and gave you the gifts to manage it. If you have failed, not his has been the fault. One day he will ask of you what you have done with your talents, how you have dealt with these souls. He will question your patience, your wisdom, the care with which you searched for them and used them, whether you have studied to understand them as the teacher studies the children in her class. Love is not enough to help you to deal with them, nor is power enough. You need the blessed trinity of wisdom, power, and love.

God will surely give us the grace to do whatever be our duty in the way to which he has called us. Pray we must that we may do our work, for it is not ours, but God's work, and that we be worthy of the vocation to which we are called, because it is God who has called us to it. It is a highway of life, high and noble, for there can be nothing petty or small in a world planned by God.

30 WHAT IS LOVE?

IN ALL the teaching of the Catholic Church wherein she deals with the subject of marriage or the home, she takes for granted that it is built on the foundation of human love. Hard as she may sometimes seem to those outside her borders, absolute, without the wish or power to relax her laws, this is only because, first, she has no teaching except Christ's teaching and this she has no power to alter; secondly, because she supposes the home, the married life, to be possible as Christ taught it, but on terms of love. It is precisely that love may be preserved and protected, that all her rules and regulations are drawn up. They are to protect love. Thus, she teaches that Christ gave a sacrament to keep love's fire unquenched despite the inconstancy of man.

When we speak of human love, we speak a word which in all our language is the strongest word we know. Scripture tells us that it is stronger than hate, and the power of hate is strong indeed; that it is more powerful than death even; stronger than hell; than an army set in battle-array. Love is a strong word. It is not a strong word only, but one of the strongest powers in human life and human history. What an amount of evil it has done! What an amount of good! To turn over the pages of history is to come on records of the ravages in history wrought through love. Passion – what fabled cities of antiquity were destroyed because of love that went astray! What giant figures in the pageant of mankind in history have been spoilt to us by the stories of their loves. What characters, emerging triumphant, have yet at the last been rotted, spoiled by love. Or – to move away from the great figures of history and come to the world we know – what hearts have been broken by it, what homes ruined.

Love has been hurting, degrading, leading men falsely. And yet, what a deal of good love has done! Man, at his noblest, most unselfish moment, is so, precisely because of love – love of something or someone. The greatness of man is uplifted by its power; the littleness of man is broken and hurt by it. Strange effect it has had on the lives of men! Again, how differently it affects people. Some are made eloquent by it, who else were but dumb, halting in speech; others, who are voluble by nature, find that love halts their tongues. They cannot say what they would care to say, for love has silenced them; whereas the others have been made to speak. The pleasures, the joys it brings, and yet what terrible agony too.

Joy and sorrow, gladness, agony, good, evil, what strange power love has to evoke all these! Yet when we think of it and try to analyze it, disentangle it for ourselves, see exactly, or as nearly as we can, what love is in itself, I fancy that our first idea would be to class it as something emotional, an instinct in man. It is often so strangely sudden that we cannot look on it as rational or deliberate. Sometimes without warning, without preparation, without knowledge, it begins to move. 'I loved at first sight,' men say. Suddenly (they will tell you) it swept over them; it woke an echo between soul and soul. The external appearance of beauty will so seldom account for it. It is something invisible, disturbing, a wave-length that carries its message, irresistible, sure. So men tell us. It is an emotion, an instinct, something that moves them strangely. It stirs and thrills them beyond their power to forbid.

Now that is true, but it is not the whole truth. For man's instincts and man's emotions are not the same as the instincts of the brute beast. Man is rational, we say; man has reason, and his very instincts must therefore be rational, that is, capable of being controlled. The instincts of an animal are almost automatic. You show it something and it follows at once. It matters not who it is or what it is, whether it attracts or repels, the automatic reaction comes at once. Of course, man can train an animal not to respond to its instinct or emotion – can show it food and tell it not to approach it. An animal can be tamed from outside by another; man only can be tamed from within. A beast can be taught all sorts of things, can be taught control by another; man can be taught self-control by himself.

Love is an emotion; it is something that sweeps over man, something unaccountable, but not something beyond his control. Man can fight it down if he thinks it is hurtful. He can bring in arguments to make himself renounce it; he can reject his emotions. Man can at the start control all of his emotions, before they have grown too strong. Love is an emotion, but you have not finished with it when you have said that of it. You must remember also that it is something that can be controlled at the start. It can be controlled even later, when some of the fierceness and violence of it has been lifted from it. No man or woman really can ever honestly make the excuse and say: 'But I was caught; I just fell in love."Fell,' as though it were something beneath them, as though it were something they slipped into, into which they fell. It is always controllable at the start. It is an emotion, and, like every other emotion, needing to be guided by art. It can be dealt with, it can be managed, it can be supported, it can be killed.

People talk of love sometimes as though it were something immortal, but the dreadfulness of our passage through life is to see love so often die. Even when those whom it holds do not break it, yet of itself it may fall apart. It can be managed; it can be dealt with. I suppose those that are acquainted with it could formulate for themselves or others rules for the management of love. They would tell you, I fancy, that it can be easily over-sentimentalized until it reaches boredom. Like food, it can be sweet at first, but then later, because too sugared, tiring; it can lose its force because of the amount of emotion with which it is too heavily stored. Love can't live upon sentiment. It can't possibly survive like that. Men and women, after all, have a sense of humor, and humor at last may kill sentiment. Love should be careful, tactful, managed wisely, if it is to last. Especially, perhaps, in an age like our age, which is extraordinarily sentimental, lovers need, if they would keep each other, to use sentiment delicately, to be ready (as the phrase runs in boxing) 'to break'. Partly this is a sentimental age because our newspapers are full of sensation. They have by now created a generation which lives on its sensations, which must be stirred before it can be interested. This means that we have to be worked on, pandered to. So we have become extraordinarily sentimental. We are swept by sentiment, not by reason, by an appeal to our hearts.

On the other hand, love can get broken if it has not some sentiment to allay the irritating little things of life. It is quite possible to find that those who once loved each other, now are almost tired of each other, bored, weighed down by the dreariness of life, of its material cares. Riches, they say, make men worldly, but so does poverty make folk worldly. It does more than merely distress them, it breaks in on them and hurts them. For, just as wealth can make people too devoted to their comforts and too full of care lest they should lose what they have, so poverty, too, can load people with cares and anxieties and make life full of solicitude. There is no romance in poverty. The poor have little enough cause to see their lot in life colored with glory. It is just a round of daily, dreary housekeeping, menaced with material cares. Those that are affected by it so as to allow their souls to be made grey by it, can never keep the flame of love alive. You must shelter love, protect it from being hurt by these outside worries. Nothing breaks love so easily as the constant irritation of the soul.

I suppose, too, that love always should be mutual, that it should always be active; that if it is to be kept alive both parties must practice love. One-sided love has little chance to survive. Both must go on loving, if love is to go on. Life is more or less what we make it, what we bring to it. If you find life dull, it is because you are dull. It is your dullness that swamps you. If you are always waiting to be enlivened by others, you will be oppressed by your own dead weight. And if life is adventurous for you, it is because you are adventurous, because you are always looking for some adventure beyond the dreary curtains of life. If life is full of laughter for you, it is the echo of your own laughter. If all men smile on you, it is because first you have smiled. Love is but the echo of your own voice. Do not wait to be amused. Don't wait for that other love to uphold you. You must reawaken your love if you would find it again in the other.

Love is mutual. It is not something that one only can carry through, of which one alone can provide enough for a home; it needs the work of all. It is fire catching fire; it is active. Each must bring love and not wait for it. Let no one say: 'I am the one that is tired. I go out to work all day. Love should be waiting for me at the doorway when I return.' Everyone in the home who does his business is working all day. There is no rest for anyone that is really interested in the home-life, really taking his proper share in the work. Both are always tired when the day is ending, both should be tired if they have done their work. Don't let each wait for the other to be the first to show welcome. Bring love if you would find it. It is but the echo of the cry of your own heart. Although it must come differently to each and the other, love runs mainly on the same lines. The mother is always a mother, even to the man she has wed. That is her fashion, she must, she can't help being active like that. The father will play with his children, going on all fours on the floor. Though he is the father, he has no sense of his dignity in dealing with the child. But the mother always has. She is the mother. The child is begotten of her. The ways of love in father and mother run on different lines; love acts differently on them and employs on them different forces. But they must be active always if love is to be kept alive.

You can test love in every age by one simple test – the attitude of man to women. If in any particular age men generally despise women, there is no love in their hearts. Men who follow after sex have no love in them. 'The fallen woman acts the love she cannot have.' He can never respect her and she knows that she is despised. This is not love. This is passion, or you can call it by a sadder name. It is not love. Reverence has gone from it, respect has gone. Where women are not honored, men certainly are not in love. When our quack scientists talk to us about companionate marriages, we know that they have reached the bankruptcy of love. There is plenty of sex possessing them, but no love. Companions – that is all they want to be. What they want is friendliness colored with sexual pleasure. No one can call that love.

Love is unselfish; love lifts people. This other just places them side by side. Love is not humiliating but it is humbling. It makes the man or woman go down on their knees. They don't see each other as companions but as raised above them. It is not so much that they build a pedestal and put on it the one whom they love. It is really that they kneel down low because they recognize their own unworthiness. The very sacrament of love puts this natural cry of man on our lips when we approach divine love. You would not come to the altar until you had first cried: 'Domine non sum dignus – Lord, I am not worthy' in your heart. So is it in the sacrament of human love. Marriage, says St Paul, is the divine counterpart of that which happens in the love betwixt a woman and a man. It is some-thing humbling, something that puts the lover on his knees before her that he loves. Companionate marriage is cheap and costless: it is the glorification of sex and the dooming of love. Love cannot be a companion, love can only be a god. Love has flown out of the window for love has wings.

So, when our Blessed Lord came to bless this great power of mankind for good or evil, he fenced it round about with law. He made love something that should last a lifetime, something that only death could break, if aught at all. Christ exalted human nature, knowing it, and knowing it to be inconstant, restless; knowing how hard it is ever to be permanently loyal to any ideal or to any soul. But he worked miracles to make the inconstant constant. He walked dry-shod upon the raging sea. He hushed the winds and the waves and made them silent and grow quiet. He bade Peter come walking to him on the waters, unafraid. He knows human nature, knows how faulty it is, knows how restless; and so with his grace he blessed the home.

When men, in the early stages of society, drifted aimlessly over the wide plains, when men were nomads, following their food, stalking the other tribes with whom they were at war, when they were thus homeless, their only home was the mother and the child. That was home. Home was not a place set in a single landscape; in it there was nothing permanent but love. Love held them, though they were wanderers. Under God's blessing, though they were restless, they had rest. Man is restless except for home. There he stays. Love holds him there because it is unselfish. Love holds him because it costs him all he has to give. If either of the two must be blamed in love, then both must be blamed. If one be selfish, the other can't be wise. Neither need be at fault. God has taught us love's true ways. But remember that you cannot let it drift, go alone of itself. You can't expect a fire to go on burning; you must feed it, keep it alive. Man is fitful, changes like the wind, but God can make him constant. God can keep the fires alight in his heart. God will. 'This is his will; your sanctification, to keep each his vessel in honor,' says St Paul. God is there to help us stay the restlessness of human hearts and to find constancy where alone it must abide, in the heart of the eternal, for God is love. Through the grace of the sacrament, we can see even human love abide. Through grace, human love can become constant – immortal even. Through the miracle of grace, the restless heart can find in another heart its home.

31 LOVE'S CHOICE

WE HAVE been trying to see, in the unfolding of human life, nothing less than the gradual fulfillment of the individual vocation in life; that every soul whom God has created has its own purpose and destiny here; that its vocation is the fulfillment of that destiny; that not merely those souls that are called to the cloister – not those only – have a vocation, but every soul that God has made; and that this vocation is not determined or not fulfilled by any single action, but by every action of a man's or woman's life. The entrance into a cloister does not finish for the religious the business of their vocation; it is but one important step in its unfolding.

So, too, we have tried to see (as the Catholic Church teaches us, following the way taught by Christ himself) that in the taking of this step of marriage, those who are called to it have fulfilled but a part of the unfolding of their life. A vocation is not completed by marriage. Marriage is merely an important step in the unfolding of the vocation. Again in the old phrase, 'Marriages are made in heaven,' we see a public profession of the belief that a divine providence watches over all; that God chooses; indeed, that God creates souls for souls; that all life is lived under the divine power. That is the teaching of the New Testament, the teaching of the Sermon on the Mount. Every hair of your head is numbered; every moment of your life known to the infinite God. Thus we account for that strange, sudden recognition of soul by soul. 'Love,' they sometimes call it, 'at first sight.' We, in the faith of God's power and love and wisdom, see in this but the recognition by man of a divine providing will who has destined each for each.

So love, as we see it, is no mere instinct. It is not even instinct governed by human reason; not even something which can be managed, directed, fought down. It is not something that just moves and sweeps over a heart by its governance, but something which, if a man cares and wishes wisely, he can manage and control. Rather, we hold that love, this instinct and more than instinct, is a high following and fulfillment of a divine law. Love, because it is divinely planned, enables him that loves to find in the beloved the things that are hidden from other eyes.

In the old ways of art they showed you love as blind. And men, in their cynical outlook, explain unexpected marriages, shrugging their shoulders, saying: 'Love is blind.' Love is not blind. All the world else is blindfolded. Love alone can see! Hate closes the eyes, closes the vision. Hate baulks knowledge. You cannot know anyone you hate. Once you have the firing up of any hatred – racial, national, or individual – for that time men and women and children are blind. Hate blinds people. That is the folly of it. When the hate dies down, they see what fools – blind fools – they have been. Love opens the eyes. 'What did he see in her?' He saw what God first had seen! Love means confidence, means that someone has believed in you. Blessed you, in whom someone has believed! They have believed in you because God first believed in you. God made you. He made you only because there was something he wished from you and gave you power to achieve. And love sees that, sees capacity and greatness as divinely intentioned; love loves the soul because of the treasure hidden in the soul by God.

For us, then, love has a sacred purpose. It is to develop the power of another soul. Marriage is to lead people Godwards; that is its purpose. In it, love is the instrument of God's design. These two joined here at the altar, the ring that holds them, God's blessing solemnly given as they start out on their new life; what has marriage to show for this? What does it mean, what do? How should marriage always be remembered but as the sacrament by which souls are to help souls? Marriage is to lead men by God's power, through God's will, to God himself. To the souls for whom God has destined marriage, there is no other way by which they may properly reach their home.

But men question us, how can there be heaven-made marriages when after all you do sometimes find incompatibility of temper? Sometimes they cannot really agree. Perhaps this merely means one soul of the two is blind. God gave each to the other. If you don't see how the other can help you, if you don't see how you can help him or her, yours is the fault. The divine purpose is evident and clear. You and I believe the word of Christ. We believe that this is God's world, that God created it, that God wisely governs it. We believe this is God's world, and now, knowing it to be so, we say to those in difficulty: 'Go on with your life. It is God who has brought your souls together that they may help each other.'

'Oh, but this one hurts me, makes me irritable, makes me impatient, leads me astray. This one is no help to me. This one is a daily temptation to me. To separate for the day is to gain a little peace; to come back is irksome. It begins all that difficulty again.'

That is just blindness. This other was meant to help you. God knows your blindness. God knew you had something to gain. Here's your chance; here's your opportunity. 'I see no chance.' You will, when death takes the other away; then you will realize what you could have done. You will wake up to it. You will see almost year by year the hurtful things you said or did, or the things you left undone – to help that other soul nearer to God's throne. This is no pagan world to please you. This is no place where men and women wander free of their will. Here it is God's world, and God's great will is over all. A man, if he wishes, can find the way of God, and, finding it, be big enough to live it, if he has love in his heart. Love will let him see.

But if there be no love between them, what then? Sometimes a girl will say: 'Do you know I am going to marry him?'

'Do you love him?'

'No, I can't honestly say I do, but he has asked me, and I am tired of home and the interference of these elders. Here is an escape. I am going to take it.'

'But you should not marry without love. It is not fair to him, even though he asked you. It is not fair to yourself. One day there may come a time when love will cross your path, and you will suddenly see it and know the torment of the difference as it goes.'

Love we believe to be God's gift to us of divining a soul that was meant for our soul. We call it love; it is only the will of God, drawing one nearer to the other. That is what God meant. They fit in as the notes of a harmony fit in, twin souls – that is, fashioned each for each by God. Of course, the world over, and growingly, there are souls whom God never leads that way. There are souls the world over that God has never meant should lift another soul in that fashion to himself. The way of love is a great way. But, you know, there is a strange paradox about love. Though it be so wonderful, it is wonderful because it has made its choice or chosen its beloved. Love has made its choice, and because it chooses one, that means to say it rejects the others. Though love is wonderful, love of its very nature is narrow in its choice. Love seeks, primarily, a single soul. Motherhood – which stands always as the great example of unselfishness – is yet in no ignoble way selfish. For at least it holds by the home. Here is the center of love for it. Sacrifice it will make willingly, yes; but for these who form its home. Here are its gods. Here does it find God himself gleaming in the heart of the husband, in the eyes of the child. So is this true also of the father. Even under stress of great emotion, etiquette denies to the father the right to express what he feels. Mothers may weep, but the fathers must hold back their tears. Yet fatherhood has, in its way, all the feelings of a mother, without any right apparently to express them. Its sorrows have such little relief. Yet, with all the greatness of the father's love, it is busy only with the wife and the children. It is a narrow garden that love tills.

There are other souls in the world for whom God has chosen neither the way of marriage nor of the cloister. Both in their way are narrow – the cloister and the home. In a way this narrowness has power, and again, it has weakness. But there are souls whom God calls to an almost wider life. Their scope is not merely some other fellow-being, wife or husband or child, but a wider world lies before them. It is said that sometimes selfishness keeps people unmarried. Sometimes a man, when his years are at their youth and fullness, grudges that he should halve his pay, knowing that life will be more austere for him, more poverty-stricken, if he carries another on his slender means. It may be that she, herself, refuses the burden of motherhood. She wants yet to have her fun in life. It is sometimes selfishness that makes them wait till the best years have gone by them, and then selfishness hardens and narrows them till they would not alter even if they could. Such a soul as finds its lonely path deliberately and selfishly will never find another who will wish to share it. As it has chosen, so it will remain.

But it is not always selfishness that dictates this narrow choice. Sometimes it is because something has happened to them, within, without – nobody quite knows what. Why haven't they married, folk ask. So likely they seemed for marriage, so eminently desirable, yet nothing has happened to them, and the years have gone by. Later in life they seem to have mean, pinched souls, till people almost despise them. They have missed romance. Ah, this is not always the true verdict! Sometimes they are the only ones that have kept their dreams unsullied. The others have married, have had their romance and their dreams and visions, and have talked of the laughter of children and the patter of the little feet on the stairs; but all this romance and these joys have been killed for them by domestic worries, rent and prices, and having to ask always more money of their man. But these others, some of them, have a romance to live by – though it be only memories of things they hoped might happen and never did. They waited, were lonely, and somehow were forgotten. Romance, dreams, possess these dreamers, and the others, practical people, found their way to life.

Sometimes it is due to neither one nor the other. There is no cause other than a deliberate will. It just happened to be God's call, for there is a place for them also in God's wide kingdom. God's kingdom is as beautiful as a great show of flowers – colors and scents, shape, height, all beset with difference: such a glorious show to your vision, beautiful because of the variety that you see – massed blossom on blossom, massed glories of shrub and bush, the little flowers nestling, the big ones spreading over them, and high above them, the flowering trees. God's world is as varied. This blessed Gardener chooses his plants as his wisdom directs him, placing them where he will. There are these souls that are called to neither marriage nor cloister, but to a vocation of their own, wider in a sense than the other, more unselfish, carrying perhaps never a reward this side of death. The others have a reward in the love the home engenders for them. These are the fairy godmothers of their surroundings, sharing their limited time and money with the younger folk who turn to them when they despair of their own homes. And some share not time nor money only but, what is more blessed, a silent sympathy. They are God's silent, eloquent ones, who listen to the grumbles of those who have none to whom they dare tell them at home. To unburden your troubles to others and to be met with: 'Oh, I know that. I have been through it myself,' is irritating – to find someone who claims his sorrow is as keen as yours. But these others are silent, they just listen and become almost the confessors of the community where they live. People will go to them, but don't always remember to return with gratitude. These unmarried, they listen and share, but they have no claim for any return.

Gratitude! What a stunted growth of soul those have who demand it! If it is not given, it should not be asked. But these souls listen and share with those who confide in them time and all they have to give, knowing that many will never come back to thank them! When they opened the window in the Ark the bird only came back when there was nowhere else for it to perch. When the waters covered the earth, it came back. It wanted somewhere to stay. Once the waters had gone down and the land appeared again, the bird had found its shelter. No one expects gratitude from the dumb creatures of God. And there are hearts like that in the world, to whom men, women, and children come back only when they need comfort; when that need is over, they pass them by almost with disdain. These grow at last lonely. Oh, they have lonely lives. Romance? No romance or dreams about it. Their last years are lonely. There is no one to care. God's ways are wonderful, and every soul, as God calls it, is destined to a way of its own. Some have the course of human companionship, others have the cloister, but there is no life lonelier than the soul's that has had to live through the world in single blessedness, unlimited by walls of cloister or of home, touching wider margins, yet on that account more alone.

But no soul need be lonely, no soul that believes in God. Said the

Master, as he went out to the garden, down the valley, up the hill, to the garden of his doom: 'I go alone,' he said, 'but not alone, for the Father is with me.' To us of the faith there need be no lonely lives. Souls, all souls, are divinely fashioned. God has cut their pathway through the valley, over the hills. God knows what he is about. God has created souls, destined them for their pathway in life, and he knows that some souls need human love to develop them. Were they to give it up, their lives would be maimed and stunted. Virginity would hurt them. They were not made for that. There are souls that God calls into the cloister. They have a life that must there be lived. Their talents there will find ample opportunity. There they will find a family that never dies. Others God calls to the way he went himself on earth – lonely, save for the younger friends, the friends to whom he was the master and father. He who cared for the growing world at his feet – flowers and little children and the sparrows – gave up all the life he loved when he went to his doom. Always God chooses noble ways. Let no man point a finger of scorn at any way of God. God knows what he is about. God gives to every soul a capacity, brings them souls that they can manage, whose lives they can refashion and send back remade. Fairy godmothers are these – the unselfish aunts and uncles of a younger world.

God calls us then. Our business is to listen uncomplaining, and to obey. One of the poets has said: 'Life is only a small house, but love is an open door!' Life is so narrow, so small, so petty – birth and death and the little narrow years between.

Life, even greatness in life as men count it, is itself imprisoned between this year and that. Birth, death, what narrow boundaries! life is but a small house, but love is an open door!' Greatness? Love is all man's greatness. He has none other than that. Love has elevated man. Love is the flame that has inspired him. To the apostles of Christ, love was an open door. If your life is narrow, you can yet find in it a greatness wider than the horizons that your eye may see. Though it seems to you petty and small and unworthy, do not believe merely this judgment of it. If it is petty and small, the fault lies with you. Love is an open door! Go out through that door and find the souls that await you, husband or wife or child, or a wider world. God gave you that world to deal with, to touch, to help, to inspire, to listen to, to hear its cries and help, not only by advice, but more often by sympathy. Eyes searching and a heart that finds! An open door! am the door,' he said, and truly, for God is love!

32 MUTUAL LOVE

ONE of the things most difficult for a priest to do, is to give advice. I suppose in every Catholic family there is some priest who is a friend; who knew the children when they were little children; who has watched them grow from age to age; who knows perhaps better than anyone else the strength of their character and its weakness; knows what they can stand and where they are most likely to fail. They will come to him, first with their childish troubles – to them as great and as over-powering as are the grown-up troubles to grown-up souls. They will come to him again when they have grown out of childhood and are beginning to realize the difficulties of grownup life.

As children, it seemed to them as though only children were naughty, as though grown-up people were always right. Then they reach a period in life in which at last they learn that children are never really naughty; that sin is something which exists almost altogether among grown-up folk. Youth has to reconstruct its world. When it comes to the threshold of manhood or womanhood, or that 'space of life between,' again it is troubled. Everything is more complicated, more difficult to deal with, because at that period of life the soul is for the first time seriously grappling with itself, fascinated by itself, studying itself, almost necessarily growing morbid in consequence of this most difficult period of all; for its problems are the problems of love, human or divine, or the problem of the life to be settled, realizing that this step is the great step. They will go back to the priest who knows them, that priest whom they have known all their lives, and ask his advice.

Indeed, all he can give is advice. They have their individual responsebility to God. The priest cannot order them, he cannot decide for them. It is they who must decide. Moreover, the advice that he gives them must depend largely on what they tell him; and not all they tell him is necessarily always true. It is as true as they can see it, but they have got to the age that does not see clearly, that cannot unravel the tangled skein of its own character. So they go to their friend, telling the trouble to him as they see it. So much escapes them yet he gives advice and judges also on other knowledge which he has. He can remember so many earlier scenes, fits of temper when he alone could be called in to settle matters, the child with a terrible will of its own. Remembering all, he can give his advice.

Then will come one of those questions that sounds at first so ridiculous. 'Do you think I am really in love?' Some find it perfectly easy to settle it for themselves. They know. Others hardly know at all. After all, there are people who are incapable of vehemence or of any real vehement desires. Love? Even love cannot sweep them off their feet. It does not seem in them to have that overwhelming feeling; their nature is more calculating, colder; it does not catch fire. Then there are others again.

As you watch them, as you reason with them, you realize that they have another type of character which is slow of growth; which needs marriage to stimulate its powers of affection; which is only able to love when it is drawn into neighborly contact and familiarity. Only in marriage will the fire of love spring up for them.

In dealing, as the priest must, with all sorts of types and characters, using what he can of the knowledge of the life that waits before him, of such books as he reads, obviously knowing nothing firsthand of married life, he must advise with secondhand materials, not personal experience. He may make mistakes. He can only say what he sees.

In the choice of love, then, there must be some fitness between the two. I suppose one would call it compatibility of temper. There must be at least, of course, a liking, and a liking which is exclusive of others. That at least is necessary for a start. There must be respect and reverence. Otherwise it would be foolishness to embark even momentarily on the perilous waters of life. Otherwise there will be many long years of suffering, unless there is reverence each for the other kept always. Unless love lift soul to soul to a level of equality, esteem, and respect, love cannot last. And confidence of course. Each soul must have confidence in the other. Otherwise it is not worthwhile starting out together on any joint adventure, either in business or in love. No partnership is possible without mutual confidence.

But out of all this material will come a subtle sympathy which is for some the dawn of love. As Elias put the dry wood on the altar and then called the fire down from heaven, and the fire came down on the altar and set the dry wood ablaze, so with these materials for the divine fire involved in the sacrament of matrimony in the prayers of the Church, these souls will be set ablaze.

Love for each other, therefore, though mutual, need not be equal. To be equal in love is not always possible. Some souls are bigger, greater than others. Love, then, should be mutual, not necessarily equal or in all alike.

And this mutual love between soul and soul, even though mutual,

will be vastly different in each. Men and women are different. God
made them so. They are equal, of course; they stand equal in God's
creation, but two souls cannot be wholly alike. Each has its character.
Each calls for something like, yet unlike, itself. Man seems to love
because he needs love, and a woman because she sees she is needed.
Each has a different point of view. Man gives because he must give, and
she takes the love that is given because it seems to, her that only thus
can she also give what she has to give. His, generous, yet almost
touched with selfishness; and hers, seeming selfish, yet generosity
itself.

Mutual then love is, fitting in each with the other; not equal, or at
least not quite the same. Each is frail, each is a frail human character.
Each has to realize that he or she is frail. There is no use pointing
scornfully at frailty or failure. All are failures; if not in action, at least in
thought. The Master, when he taught his disciples the gospel of
marriage, with its rights and duties, said that when a man looked upon
a woman with evil in his heart, that man had already committed adultery. So again when the woman who was in sin was brought before
him, he wrote in the dust: let him who is without sin, cast the first
stone,' and there was not one to accuse her. Outwardly, each was
respectable; within, each a sinner, each desperately frail. Seventy
times seven must I forgive my brethren. There is no end to forgiveness.
God forgives us anything when we are sorry. God has shown no end of
his forgiveness of us. We must have no other mercy than the unlimited
mercy of an infinite God: mercy – no end to forgiveness. You need
mercy. Give the mercy that you will some day need in return, not from
man, but the mercy you will need as you stand before God's throne.

Mutual, different, will be the love of men and women, and all their
ways different. How different are the pleasures of both! And the
woman must realize that the man is a boy always, and will take his
pleasures always as a boy. He must have his own circle of fellow-men.
That is his way of pleasure. That is how he escapes. Sports, games,
recreation – he is a boy again; living a boy's memories even to old age.
But her pleasures are friend ships and visiting those she loves; and
that is why when her children are little she has little pleasure away
from them or her home. When her children are grown up – she looks
for and lives again her motherhood with their children. That was one
of the tragedies of the war, shattering the hopes of so many mothers,
knowing that they would never have grandchildren, knowing it with
the tolling of the bell.

Duties rather than rights, you see, have to be considered in marriage.

You will have sorrow, that is the badge of all humanity, but never show that sorrow even for a moment. Sorrows are linked with human nature, so that each one should bear his sorrows, not talking of them or telling them to others, for sorrows bring with them gifts that joy cannot bring. There are sorrows in life, in the home. The woman is tired. She is a good housewife, tired with her long day's labor. Each day should bring a day's labor for a woman, and the mother too And the man coming back tired in the evening and perhaps finding no one at home, his money quickly spent, and then his friends forgetting him, comes home white and tired. Each must give; not waiting for the other to give – giving first. Give because you should give – considering not your rights, but your debts. Rights have a way of taking care of themselves. 'I owe it to myself?' The debt you owe to yourself you need never pay at all. Go without paying it, and pay the debts you owe to others. You will find yourself happier so.

You expect to be interested? Don't wait to be interested but interest others. Don't wait to tell your sorrows, but listen to those of others. Be always comforting. Give all to the one you love – that is how God has loved.

When the Church blesses a marriage ring, she reminds those to be married of what is marriage by this symbol of bondage: 'Bless, O Lord, this ring which we hallow in thy name; may she who wears it hold her loyalty and fidelity always to him whom she has now taken, and may they grow together in mutual love.' That means mutual giving and mutual forgiving, the mutual love which God blesses, which Christ taught, which the Church repeats again all through the ages to men and women alike. Each in some sense obeys the other; each is the master or mistress in his or her own way; each rules; each guides; each settles difficulties. Love is the same.

Purity, therefore, is asked of each equally, though perhaps harder for the man; but each is asked for purity because love needs it, for love is a consuming fire. Moreover, God meant that man out of human love should find a way to himself. 'Unless,' says St John, 'you love the man whom you see, how shall you love God, whom you shall never see till one day in heaven?' Human love is in itself something that should teach souls the way to God. Will you love right? Listen to love's language. Would you know what love of God means, how it entrances men? Then know the language of human love first. It will teach you also the doctrine of the spiritual life. 'A great sacrament,' says St Paul. The sacrament of Christian marriage is magnificent, really divinely great. You feel God's own splendor shining through it. That is the way it should be seen. What a pity that it is not always so! Love means it to be unselfish. Love is unselfishness. Marriage is based on love.

33 LOVE'S EXPRESSION

IN ONE of those long quarrels that have been drawn out between the Catholic Church and some of those outside her borders, one of the points in dispute has been the origin of the world. There are all sorts of scientific theses, suggestions, sup-positions, as to how the world began. Of the theories them-selves, only a scientist, I suppose, is competent to speak, but there is one condition that the Catholic Church insists upon in all such explanations of the origin of the world. However it began, it was God who began it. We give the origin of the world to a divine creative act. God made the world; and we say that the Catholic Church insists upon this truth, not merely from the point of view of abstract reasoning or because it is something Catholic philosophers have considered proven, but because apart from this it has a very practical bearing upon human life. In the government, direction, and inspiration of human souls, the Church considers the remembrance of it a matter of grave importance. God created the world, and therefore (the Catholic Church argues) the world in itself, since it is divinely created and divinely planned, is good.

Behind the origins of all things is God working, and what follows naturally follows the action of God, and therefore is in a line of goodness. Man, however he began, was created by God, and man in himself was made good by God. In the Scriptures we are told that God looked out on the world which he had created and saw that it was good. 'God made us,' said the Psalmist, 'and not we ourselves,' and that saying is meant not simply to put us in our right place as a portion of a larger world or to see ourselves as creatures of the great Creator, but also to show us that our human nature is intimately related to the divine.

God made us, and as God looked out on the world (so we are taught by Scripture) and saw that man was good, he also saw that it was not good for man to be alone, and so he created for him a helpmate. Man was created after all the world was done. In the Scriptures, you must not look, indeed, for scientific but religious teaching. Morality is taught us there by divine in-spiration, the truths of faith, and the laws by which we are to live. Now Scripture tells us that it is God's judgment on man that it is not good for man to be alone. Because of this judgment, God provided him with a helpmate; and as on every other living thing, wheresoever it is placed in the scale of creation, so on man

God laid the command to increase and multiply. God created the world; the world in itself therefore is good, having a divine origin, fulfilling a divine purpose, working out a divine plan. God not only created man and gave him a law, whereby normally he is enriched in the development of his own character by the way of marriage, but he also inserted love to enable man the better to achieve his command, to lead men to the fulfillment of what he wished from them. It was, then, with the purpose of providing them with what should unite them one to another, that he gave them love. Just as in the Blessed Trinity the Holy Ghost proceeds from the Father and the Son as the spirit of love, just as the oneness of the Trinity is achieved by the love which is the Spirit of God, so in a lesser fashion God has gathered the units of mankind into one through love. To love is a divine command, and it has a divine motive governing it.

God laid on man a command to express externally the love that he had inserted in man's heart. This expression of love has a divine origin, is something that we must judge with reverence. 'You,' says St Paul, 'are God's workmanship.' We have been fashioned by the hands of God. So the Catholic Church, as she looks out on humanity, insists upon that belief in the divine origin of man, namely, that he is divinely created, because she wishes ever to keep alive in human hearts man's reverence for man. Moreover, she also wishes us to remember that whatever follows directly from a divine action must be good in itself.

Not only was this teaching given in the Old Testament, bringing to a people that had been degraded a revelation of high notions with which to inspire their lives, but when Christ our Lord came, wearing the vesture of human flesh and blood, he came to show man how it was possible to see matter in the light of the spirit; how it was possible by our ideas, by our wisdom, by our true understanding, to rob matter of its grossness and its evil, to lift it up somehow and to give it wings. The whole teaching of the New Testament is to bring that home to man Good men naturally tend to be puritans. They tend always to denounce everything dangerous as wrong. Our Lord would not have us accept that spirit. Things may bring evil, but that does not say that they are evil. It is for man to see them truly, sanely, with the eyes of purity, with the eyes of a child. So he laid down his great doctrine that it is open to the spirit to lift matter heavenwards, and that this elevation of mind is the purpose of the law of increase and growth. This is its purpose. This is why he inserted in man's heart love, to justify what else might seem repulsive, to lead men to what else, I suppose, they would never, or but seldom, have been induced to do.

God has his own way or persuasion; God has his own way of leading man where he would have him go. To spiritualize this desire and hunger, our Blessed Lord taught mankind his doctrine of the sacrament of marriage, pledging, giving, joining these 'two into one flesh'. Utterly fearless in the words he uses, this strong teacher, knowing the needs, knowing the passions of man, says that these human actions are the expression of human love; that they are not, or they need not be, the mere emotions of the animal nature of man. They can be justified to the spirit by human love.

There are laws and limits to this sacramental teaching, but they are wide enough to satisfy man. There are words and actions divinely planned, divinely purposed, sacred, and to be looked on with reverence, to be realized as an ideal. Not of mere animal origin are they. The Church will have none of that. They are not the mere growth or development of nature, as though nature stood outside the governance of God. He made it, and he gave it its own laws and character, otherwise it could not achieve what he wanted the world to do. God deals with man in his wisdom and then reveals to man his action and his motive and then teaches man to look at these from his point of view. Man is still able to spoil this, as he can spoil everything. Man is endowed with free will. Man is able, therefore, to take her whom God gave him as a helpmate, and use her as an inspiration to complete and enrich the character with which he started out in life; but man is also able always to degrade his use of her, able to exploit her for evil purposes of his own.

You have only to walk through a modern city and look at the flaming advertisements, at the flaunting billboards, to see how man can exploit every evil that may lurk and linger in the hearts of men – a kiss, a caress, something of God's own purposing, something God fashioned for high destinies of his own, degraded, exploited, to appeal not to man's highest nature, but deliberately to appeal to what the designers of these know is lowest in man. Books and plays, everything has been used to appeal to our instincts which can be degraded, as everything else can be degraded. Man can barter sacred things for wealth and power, can buy and sell them. Man can degrade the high purposes of God. But these need not be degraded. They should not be degraded. They should be looked at with clean eyes. They should be looked at with eyes that remember that from God's hands men come and to God's hands they go.

The expression of love is no mere movement of physical instinct. It is an action which should be justified by love. It is matter which can be relieved of grossness by the spirit, as you can see a solid block of stone relieved of its heaviness by an artist and fashioned to express some noble hope or dream. So, too, man must always remember the divine origin of mankind. It must be remembered that this expression of human love is the command of God, the normal fulfillment of a nature with its own clamorous desires. God gave those desires to man from the beginning and God has his own means of answering man's clamorous desires. God gave him someone to help him towards the heights for which he made him.

God gave man, not merely love, but love's expression, to achieve a purpose, fruitful of what he wished done in the world. And God did all this that he might lead men nearer to himself. A noble purpose! God would have each man and wife see it so. A purpose of his own, this same expression of human love, though it is in a sense only a second-ary purpose. Even when the time comes in life that there can be no living result from it, even then love justifies it, so noble is love in the creating eyes of God. Thus, it is part of the Christian teaching that each should give and receive with unselfishness, whatsoever may seem the hardship to one or the other. Husband and wife must be unselfish here, as unselfish everywhere. They are gathered, they are placed together, their union made blessed, in order that each may help each. Man or wife must think not merely of themselves but how each could help the other, namely, by unselfish giving of all each has to give. Thus is it at times an unselfish achievement of a divine purpose, where each is thoughtful of what will hold the other nearer to God. Man and woman have their own natures, their own natural likings or dislikings, for human nature is as varied as men are themselves. Each must in this act be conscious of the other soul made one with it, and each must remember that his business is to bring the other nearer to God. How shall I help him or her? How shall I keep him from evil? How shall I help him nearer to God? I know him I know his strength and his weakness. What must I do? Remember, this act has a divine origin and a divine purpose; remembering that, you can be left to judge ade-quately what you should do.

One of our poets has sung in his praise of good women: 'What prayer, what priest, can stay the fury of the beast?' What can tame the animal character of man? Apart from faith, which after all works on man through human instruments, there is no other means to rest on for him than this very flame itself of the human heart lit by God, which men call love. The beast in man can be held captive by it. There are moments, indeed, when a poor agonized soul, beleaguered with its enemies, feeling almost on the very edge of a moral breakdown, yet led by the memory of the human love which it plighted at the altar, still can find its ultimate escape. A woman's courage and love, her undaunted laughter, ringing like a clarion in the great warfare of a man's soul, when the hosts of God seem almost routed in him, at times will drive back the beast within him and give him peace and relief.

It is a divine command, then, this expression of human love. Men of divine workmanship, have reverence for your own human hearts, remember that you have been fashioned by divine fingers. Remember that as you are, God made you, and you have a purpose to fulfill. There are still the untenanted thrones of the angels in heaven. These are the places still to be filled by faithful souls. You men and women have your own apostolic work to be fulfilled by you to raise children to these empty thrones. This work of divine destiny has been committed by God to you, has been revealed as a belief to you, and is made possible to you by the spirit of reverence when you see that men and women are greater than they seem. We are not the mere result of blind forces of nature, not something that is a little higher than the beasts, but something only a little lower than the angels. The Catholic Church alone in the world now, fearless and remembering, teaches this sacredness of man. These others that appeal to man would appeal to that which is lowest in him, that of which he soon grows tired. She appeals to that which is highest in him, noblest, that which can never die. The rest passes, age may quench it; this is never quenched, even by age. This is a flame lit by God's hands – God who is immortal. He will shelter the undying flame.

34 LOVE'S RESTRAINT

WE HAVE insisted that for us, love, like every other human emotion, is a rational emotion; that man is man wholly, and that his natural instincts are not merely like the instincts of an animal, but that they partake of man's own nature and are in some degree rational themselves. We must now remind you that it is part of our Christian faith that we inherit a fallen nature, by which we mean that we are born heirs to a human nature which is in a state of disorder. We are heirs to it, for original sin is no act of our own will.

As children we were taught to distinguish between actual sin, the sin of our own doing, and original sin, which is a sin we inherit. We must not think of it as an action, but rather as a state or condition in which we find ourselves born. It is not an act we do ourselves. We receive a nature which is in some sense wounded, in some sense set in disorder, and of that we are painfully aware.

You can see it for yourself in the various faculties that make up your human nature. You can think of your reason, that which argues, discusses, understands; of your will, which chooses and decides; and then of the series of emotions – love, desire, hatred, anger, joy, and the rest. In a perfectly ordered humanity, those various powers of man would be in perfect order or control. At the summit would be reason; then will, obedient to reason, choosing what reason urges it to choose; then the emotions, obeying in their turn the will. That is a man who is perfect. That is not you or I. We inherit a fallen nature, which means that for us all our emotions have broken loose from the will. The will itself has broken loose from reason, and reason no longer reflects perfectly the divine reason, that is to say, the law of God. Perfect man reaches a height of tranquil blessedness. Even philosophers have sometimes grown near it.

Those nearest perfection are the saints. They are saints because at weary last they reached some measure of perfection in that control. Beyond the saints is another, and you can see why we have such honor for God's blessed Mother. She began where the saints leave off. She was from the first moment of her conception free from that disorder of original sin. Her intelligence was unclouded, reflecting calmly the divine intelligence, not infinitely, but adequately, in her human nature; her will chose rightly and well. Her will dictated to her emotions. For us, emotions outrun the will. We are angry because we are moved by emotion to anger. Before the reason has had time to think, we hate out of prejudice or ignorance or irritation. When we have had time to think it over, we realize we have not done right. Emotions, then, are those lower powers, half spirit and half matter, all those passing moods of man We inherit a nature in which they have broken loose from the will that should dominate them, according to the dictates, as we call them, of right reason. Perfect man has all that in security. You and I are aiming to achieve, by God's grace, something of perfection. That is our ideal.

It has been fulfilled in our Master, Jesus Christ, whose un-sullied humanity is the model at which all should aim. These emotions, these powers, these faculties, these passing moods, come and go untrammeled with us. They should be obedient. But even when they are disobedient, they are still human. Our business, then, is to control them, because they are emotions of a fallen nature which has not wholly been remedied by baptism. Baptism gives us the power, through grace, to control them. We are thus not left an impossible problem to solve.

These emotions of ours may also err by excess. Good in them-selves, they may be excessive. Anger, for instance, is sometimes good. The world needs anger. The world often continues to allow evil because it isn't angry enough. Our Lord, with his knotted scourges driving people from the temple, was angry and rightly angry. Emotions we need, but not to excess. It is possible to be not angry enough or to be over-angry. We can fail also in excess of desire. We can fail because of excess in love. Not that you can love too much, if love be lawful to you, but there can yet be excess, not in love so much as in love's expression. You can be intemperate in your expression of love, as you can be intemperate in other ways. If, after hunger and thirst, you eat to satisfy hunger or drink to satisfy thirst, these acts are good because rightly proportioned; but men can eat too much or drink too much. Excess in the way in which they are satisfied is a sin, because it is intemperate.

What is intemperance? Pleasure beyond the purpose: eating merely because you like eating, and eating beyond all measure of your need. That, we say, is intemperance. We are also taught in the household of the faith that it is possible to be intemperate in the expression of love. Beyond all imaginable limit of need to human nature, to go beyond that in things even good and natural is to sin by excess. Or again, not merely in the expression of human love, but in the times of it; when for instance the violent expression of it might be hurtful to one or other of those involved in it. There are seasons in life when it would be wrong to allow it. There are times like sickness, again, when it would be wrong. Sometimes, unhappily, it would be wrong because there would be danger of dread disease from it. Prudence, in other words, must govern this as it must govern all other good actions. It must preside like a controlling mistress over the actions of man's moral self. Love should be prudent.

Here, then, we have to urge, as part of the teaching of the Church, that it is possible to do wrong in love. Though love be lawful, love can still be ill-used. Though there be in itself no limit to love, there may be a limit, indeed there must be, to its expression. Times, seasons, and other conditions must control it. Nature otherwise may very well have her revenge. I don't mean that whenever we do wrong we suffer physically for it. That is not true. Nor would I urge on you any such argument of fear. We follow Christ, our Master. We go his way because we love. You may with success for a while frighten people with threats of nature's punishments for evil, but hardly in the time of youth can you frighten with danger. Danger does not drive youth off from action. Danger adds one more attraction to a human command. These youths that seek speed are attracted by the very danger of it. There is a thrill and a stir in danger, especially, I fancy, in the days of one's youth. Old age is cautious. You expect it to be moved by threats of danger.

The Catholic Church lays down the doctrine of Christ. Christ urges the restraint of love by the human will. Christ teaches that there is a remedy against excess, and that this remedy is the restraint of human will. The Catholic Church believes that men are men. She cannot be persuaded that they are just blind animals; that they are simply at the mercy of desire. The Church judges men, however faulty, to have this rule, this governance, this reason over them. She believes men have will and reason and the grace of God over them, and so she bids men when they must restrain, to do so by human reason, by an act of their human character under the power and influence of divine grace. She does not allow that anyone should, when performing the full act of the external expression of human love, directly prevent its natural fulfillment. She does not consider it a humanly justifiable action to seek pleasure and escape the responsibility which the pleasure brings. The purpose justifies pleasure. To take the pleasure and prevent the purpose is to frustrate that which justifies what is done.

The Church looks on love as something higher than un-controllable passion. She urges on her children her fine ideal: that love is something which teaches men of God. She considers marriage to be a sacrament and declares that it brings to men and women the graces that they need, not merely the graces of patience, sympathy, and understanding, but the grace of self-restraint. People should have no fear or no expectation that one day the Church may change her mind on this matter of child-prevention. She has faced this problem before in the past. It is no modern problem; it always emerges when society reaches a pitch of physical comfort. It has always been the attempted escape of a cowardly age. I do not mean cowardly in the sense of faltering; I mean cowardly only in this way, that it is too accustomed to comfort to forgo it for a moral principle and that it is losing something of its austerity and its strength. Her teaching is clear. Her teaching cannot be altered. It is based upon the nature of things. It must always be wrong to frustrate the powers of nature in the sense of taking the pleasure and denying the purpose justifying the pleasure. Such an act becomes gravely wrong when the matter with which it is concerned is grave matter. Impurity must always be grave matter to man, who lives so close in his heart to a dreadful beast within.

Of course, it is true that you will find medical opinion divided on this question. Some will say that it is hurtful to the woman; that it is always the woman who pays; that if the man is satisfied by the act even when its complete result is prevented she is never; that her nerves are strained and obviously get no relief. It hardly matters whether medicine says it or not. We do not take our morals from medicine, from law, nor from government. You and I take our morals from Christ. We are grateful, as all Catholic people must be grateful, to that inheritance of fine Catholic doctors, whose influence in this matter is more than a priest can ever hope to have. We would urge all Catholic families that they have as their doctor one whose faith they know to be not only Catholic but an enlightened, instructed faith. We realize, we whose business lies not only with the sanctuary, but with the confessional, how a doctor has a far wider opportunity to give sane advice in this matter than a priest. He can help where he sees nature shrinking from its duty. He can exhort, out of his knowledge, out of the experience that he meets with day after day. Fine, skilful, experienced, kindly, sympathetic, he can speak with wife or husband on matters which they hardly dare broach each to each. He can take, and often does take, husband aside and wife aside, and tell them what it is wise for each to do. He can lift their thoughts to the high Christian ideal of human nature. He can deny that man must always seek and have gratification. He can deny that a man may not be both continent and healthy. Even our philosophers deny it.

Bernard Shaw here at least strikes a blow for continence, when he denies that a man must go wrong, denies that a youth cannot keep his youth unsullied. The Church believes that youth can pass unscathed the ambush of young days. For us, Christ's teaching stands, reaching us through the faith. We believe in man's power, not just as human power, but in man's power re-enforced with divine power to live up to Christ's teaching. Under this, all things are possible to man. Certain things are forbidden men, ruled out by the faith. Man is capable of holding on to the ways of Christ if he will patiently begin by learning what is right, what is wrong. Your nature will not necessarily teach you what is right or wrong, or will only teach you too late. You must go for instruction, if you are un-certain, and ask a priest or a Catholic doctor. You will get the right answer to what you ask.

'But,' men will say to you, 'we can tell you of hard cases.' Oh, you can tell no harder cases to the priest than the cases he already knows very well. 'What does he know of family life?' men sometimes ask, almost sneering. 'What does he know who has never tasted what it brings, its joys or hurts?' It is true that he has renounced these and yet, after all, he listens week by week to the open anguish of souls. He knows better than anyone the secrets of human hearts. He knows tales of anguish that are known only to those that feel them. They do not speak to others. They feel too deeply. They speak only to him. Hard cases? Why, surely. Over and over again a priest knows and realizes that some souls that come to the confessional and have followed the way of the Gospel are not just ordinary folk. They are heroes and heroines walking erect on the hills of God. There is nothing that better teaches a priest humility than the stories of anguish that he hears from human lips. Hard cases? 'Why should we suffer? We?' Suffering is the badge of our profession. What is our symbol but the cross? Hard cases? Why, yes, these things must be, to anyone who, anywhere, at any time, in any line of life, follows the way of Christ. Would you have it otherwise? Would you go through life with perfect ease, with never an inch of suffering? If you did, you would go dwarfed, maimed. You cannot get the full fragrance of sweet herbs until you have rubbed them. Then only the fragrance will exhale. You must burn your incense if you would notice the sweetness of its fragrance. You must pay for what you value dear. Everything that is worth anything is to be paid for, and the highest are paid for with the highest price. Hard? Yes, of course it is hard, but it is the way set by our Blessed Lord, and he will help you to follow where he leads.

'I love too much to restrain myself.' Love can always restrain itself, for love is strong. Passion, passion is weak and lacking restraint. Passion may be something that escapes you. That is the way of passion. Know it for what it is. It is something un-tamed, is passion, while love is strong enough to obey. But untamed things are no longer serviceable, because they are untamed; because they are wild. Love is not wild. Love is something that holds, something that restrains or inspires, something that will lead men to death. Men will die for that. Men have died for some fine hope like that. When your leaders spoke to your sons or brothers or lovers of democracy and liberty and justice, measured against those things did they think death great? 'We dare look death in the face,' said the youth of your nation, because they loved the country whence they came. That is love. Love is not this untamed, wild passion that can't be bridled and can't be put to love's service. Love in itself does no wrong. Christ for us is the supreme Lover. Love led him to death.

One of the poets of our time, praising the ordinary woman, speaks of her in those very simple terms:

'I stood by, in unflinching ignorance of man's duty,
      To do in darkness God's obscure command,
And thrusting by intelligible beauty,
      I followed what I could not understand,
Because I knew that that alone that passes understanding
      Must be true.'

To you it is given to know the mysteries of the kingdom of God. Never deny they were mysteries. Don't dread knowledge, but remember that here we do not and cannot know all. To you it is given, God's gift, to know you are the saviors of your people. You can be. Men will look back to you if you carry the great tradition of fatherhood or mother-hood to the generation about your knees. What you receive, are you handing on? You are the children of a great ancestry. What will your children's children say of you? That you were cowardly? That you let passion ride roughly over you? That you had forgotten the beauty, the high beauty, of love? No one knows. Men here keep their secrets, sometimes in the confessional they are silent when they know silence to be a base thing. Some tell us this, that our people do not confess this wrong they do. Hardly can a priest believe so evilly of them across whose lips have passed the flesh and blood of God. Love is the texture of our faith. Love brought it to us. We ourselves must bring it to love at last. Love divine, of course, is what we worship, but love human is only a mirrored image of the infinite love of God. If you will not love those that you see, but merely seek your own passion in them, you shall know nothing of the infinite love which is of God.

35 TWO IN ONE FLESH

WHEN Christ our Lord became man, he came to sanctify all the world. Not only was God made flesh, but through the blessings of the Incarnation flesh was to be lifted to the heights of God. Our Blessed Lord came, partly at any rate, to tell creation that it was the creation of God, so that it might take a nobler view of the world about it, esteem others more because of their divine origin, and give us also a greater respect for ourselves. It was prophesied long before he came that when he came all flesh should see the glory of God, which means to say that our Blessed Lord came that he might help men to see the goodness of the world they lived in, that he might take the hurt out of those things that were hurtful to human nature, and rob of their sting all the ministers of death! He came to teach each living soul that followed him to see life nobly, because it had been nobly planned.

In a vision to St Peter, he showed him just such a vision of the world. Henceforward, there should be no division between the clean and the unclean of creation, that division of the Old Law that forbade men to eat unclean things All things that God had made were blessed to the eye that was blessed. All things were clean to the eye that was clean: 'What God had made, let no man call common or unclean.' Such was the vision on the housetop, a vision of the grace that faith has to give to every soul alive. So he took bread in his hands and blessed it. Food had hurt mankind. Food is needed by man's nature, but man can be intemperate in food. He took bread and blessed and broke and gave, and ever since that moment he has sanctified all human meals. Banquets have hurt man often. This is the hallowing banquet that has made every meal sacred to the eyes of faith. He took the wine cup. Oh, what a deal of hurt the wine cup had done to human nature! What evils, what hurt, what degradation, ever since the days of the pagan! How he had worshipped it, worshipped its very intoxication, as though in some strange fashion it lifted men above the earth. They saw the grape growing, but its power over men was so extra-ordinary they could not believe that its power was really be-gotten of earth whence it sprang, and so they wove their story that it was a god who had brought it. Yet that myth of theirs couldn't rob it of its hurt. But he took the wine and he showed all men that they should see in it not merely the blood that he gave in his real presence, but a choice emblem of himself. Since that day man can see it as no longer hateful. It need not be hateful; no longer hurtful. 'I am the vine,' he said, 'you are the branches.'

Can't you look at all life in this mystic way? Can't you take the things that might easily hurt souls and lift them and see them nobler because of him? The noblest things, the finest things that the world has to give, or heaven for that matter, are the things also that are necessarily dangerous because they are great. Even the sacrament of his love may carry hurt to the unloving: 'He that eateth and drinketh unworthily, eateth and drinketh judgment to himself.' Hurt? He has robbed the world of the power of hurting humanity, if humanity will look at it through eyes that God has cleaned. 'Become as little children,' he said. There is no guile in the world to the clean eyes of a child. You see hurt. They see none. That is what he wanted us to learn, that the evils of the world are the evils we let hurt us. We need not allow any hurt to come.

He took human nature to his divinity, and from that moment he lifted human nature to a new height. He taught man that flesh was not something evil. That matter was evil had been taught by the pagan philosophers that had gone before him; austere teachers, noble leaders of men. They said that man could only become noble by suppressing his body. Christ said no; flesh was to be sanctified, not suppressed. His flesh was sanctified because it depended upon the spirit within. The body was fashioned by the hands of God, and the spirit of man dwelling in the body could mould it, fashion it after the model intended by God. That is the secret of the saints. They fashioned their body, molded it, controlled it. They were masters of themselves. Their bodies were not a hurt to them, but a help to them, once they were mastered, once they were under control. If you let anything escape your control, however helpful to man it may be, if you let it escape your control, what can it do but hurt?

God became man to lift man Godwards, to help man, somehow, to find God even in himself. He showed that the radiance of the spirit can dominate the flesh, helping it. He took the things of earth, bread and wine, and made them forever blessed to us; and he took human love, which is also a danger, and he made of that a blessed thing. He blessed the love of man and woman for he came of a woman and he was born in a human home. It was a home because a Mother was there, and the mother's husband, and he, the Mother's Child. A Holy Family. If you look back in the records of the paganism that was just before his coming, you can see evil in the family of those days.

To us now, the family is blessed, sacred, but to read the story of Rome is to read of the terrible power of the father of the family, an awful power. In Rome the father had the power of divorcing his wife and selling his children to slavery. The power of the father of the family brooded like a menace over the whole social life of Rome. The mother, the children, were his possessions absolutely. With these he could do as he would. The family was ruining mankind when Christ was born in its midst. He sanctified the family and renewed the beauty of family love. The love of mother for child has always been thought beautiful and the love of father for child beautiful, too. A more beautiful love than that he taught man. 'For this cause,' he said, 'a man shall leave father and mother, and shall cleave to his wife, and they shall be one flesh.' He had bidden his followers to leave father and mother. He had called them, he said, to a higher life, and he had said to his followers: 'You must come out of your father's home. You must leave your folk behind you, else you are not worthy of me, not worthy of my following, of my fellowship, not worthy till you step out of your home.' He said it not only of his own following, but of the love between woman and man. They also must leave their home. They must, else there will be danger. They must go out from their father's dwelling. They must live alone.

He gave husband and wife power over each other. He was lord of her. She was his queen. He set them in that strange world of his, that kingdom of heaven on earth. In that strange kingdom there were to be two monarchs and each of the two was to rule the other with absolute sway. He gave power to the husband over the wife, yet he was hers; power to the wife over the husband, yet she was his. All his love was for her, and for none other. All her love was to be for him. Round about them he built a garden wall; they were to be garden-enclosed, intimate, fragrant, dear. He built a wall about them, the power of each over the other. This is his concept of human love: 'A man shall cleave to his wife and they shall be one flesh.' Not two,' he adds, 'but one.'

He taught the power of each over the other, and of course the duty of each to the other, and of both to himself, soul and body, body and soul. In the old form of marriage ran the phrase: 'With this body I thee worship,' as though there was something sacred about it, and of course there is, or should be. It should be sacred, blessed, the reverence of love for the body of the beloved. This is the teaching of the Incarnation. It is something that he came to give mankind; a new relationship of marriage, of power and duty, and of love over all. His view of it is of an intimate, personal relationship, their mutual intimate knowledge and their love.

It should be a great help to peace that the intimate relationship of twin human souls is to be based on the fact that each knows the other. Why? Each should know the other that each may help the other. For that reason was woman created in the world. God made Eve that she might be Adam's helpmate. Helpmate in what? Surely in God. What other purpose have we here, we Christians? What other purpose is there in life; what fine, noble, ultimate purpose but God, God always and God only?

Husband and wife are for that – to help one another. Their intimate knowledge of each other should guard, protect, inspire one another. Knowing each other's defects, even, should show them how they can help. This will not demand grudging human service of them. This means it is a privilege to help. For the Son of Man did not come to be ministered unto; he came to minister. That is divine love; and human love has to follow the same road. The soul, too, must learn the ways, the customs, the courtesies of human love in order to develop divine love. Help one another, then, lifting one another Godward, be you husband or wife. Husbands, have you helped your wife Godwards? Remember, for that you were linked with her under the blessing of God. Wives, are you helping your husbands? Helping, not merely pointing out their evil, but helping them against their evil, not hurting, not hindering, but helping them nearer to God?

You see that this intimate relationship of man and woman in love and marriage can be either a very great help or a very great hindrance. It brings them so closely together. Through it they are so intimate, each to each, that it is easy to jar nature on nature, character on character. It is so easy not to help, but to hurt. In the beginning, the love ecstasy carries them for-ward, and then the fire of it dies down and real life has now to begin, real life that forbids all pretence. The bandage is lifted now from the blinded eyes of love. The two made one are so close together that naught serves but the truth. After a short while, all their memories have been told to each other, all the stories of each other's childhood have been learnt by heart. Each one knows the other almost to tiredness, knows all the other's stories and familiar witticisms, hearing them over and over again. They may come to dread like a nightmare, when they entertain their friends, those things repeated which they have heard told so often, heard till they are sick and tired of them. All the element of surprise, the unexpected, which brings us such laughter and joy in life, all that, it would seem, is ruled out from their lives after a while. They know each other well, almost too well. They know each other's pet phrases and they know each other's weaknesses, each other's vanities, each other's virtues to the extreme point. They can see each other's vanity being played up to by others. They know where the flattery is to lead. They may easily let themselves grow weary of each other, till life becomes dull, dreary, drab, with drudgery added to family responsibilities and cares.

Even in our relationship to God there comes a period like this. We have experience of it in prayer. At the beginning, there is a sort of love ecstasy, the wonderful beauty of the prayers of the child. There follow, more touching than a child's prayers even, the prayers of youth, threatened by danger, stirred by temptation, real, alive. The prayers of youth are beautiful, emotional, touched with the exquisite colors of the spring-time and then – well, you know what follows, the utter dreariness of prayer. All emotion gone, everything of that sort. If you pray, you just pray because you know you should. There is no pleasure in it. There is no stir or uplift. There is no vision of the glory or the beauty of God. It is just the will, holding for us obscurely now, the friendship of God, feeling nothing, though believing all things Something like that happens not only in man's love of God, but the love of man for man. There is a danger of it, anyhow. All men know it and recognize it. Every priest has heard it over and over again in the confessional. A soul grown tired, weary, dreary: 'Can I ever go on?'

There is this in every mingling of human love; there is this because they are not two, but one. Two in one flesh, human nature so intimate and so united yet so dangerously near its quarrel because made from the moment of marriage, one. It begins so joyously but the ecstasy of it passes. Unless it is based on something deeper than mere physical pleasure, the love that they call love will go. It isn't an animal passion, this thing our Lord is speaking about, a thing so blessed that he bids men leave their homes to find it. To him it is something which is not of the earth, but of the heavens: 'It was said of old that a man could give his wife a bill of divorce, but I say to you, No.' He is teaching the world a nobler way. He wants men to be more than men, to walk on the height of the hills where God is. The love he preaches is not mere passion; it is not of the earth! This love has wings. It lifts. It flies. It is something that carries men upwards. It stoops indeed only like the fairy prince who stooped over the sleeping beauty and wakened her from her slumbers to life again with a kiss. It is a love which is not just of the earth, but somehow touched with God's glory. A wonderful love, this, which Christ came to teach!

It is hard to explain such a view of love to someone who has never had the glory of our light, to whom these things have never come as a revelation, who are pagans in their outlook on marriage, who are easily reconciled to divorce, to whom love is but a thing that comes eagerly and is part of the joy of youth – something that they can conceive as not only begotten in the youth time, but lasting only with it, going when it goes. Not real, you say, just a dream, a romance, something that is not higher than earth but like one of those mirages which you see when you look across the level desert. For us love is nobler, finer, 'a mystery,' says St Paul. By which he means that it shows us the union between God and the soul, as intimate, as wonderful, as splendid as that. For St Paul it was a sacrament, because it showed forth the union between God and the soul. There we have something in common with him. The soul is after God's image. The soul was made for God. Real love, therefore, will always hold, but this other love that is begotten in the eyes and dies in the eyes, that love must pass. 'Fed by gazing, fancy dies in the cradle where it lies.' There must be something in love besides this. Spirit must be mated with spirit; spirit must be in love with spirit as well as flesh with flesh.

He came, did our Blessed Master, to take hurt out of hurtful things. He came to take that intimate relationship of husband and wife – one flesh indeed, 'not two but one' – and make it some-thing which should be always full of life. He transformed it into something which was divine and therefore unselfish, in which each thought of the other. Not the power given to each over the other was to be remembered so much as the duty that should be given to each by each. He showed love robbed of whatever might hurt it, showed it something that would ennoble mankind. But who is sufficient for these things? What human love is capable of these great heights? At the beginning of love, yes, then it is possible. Again it is possible here and there in moment of crisis, but on the long, level stretch, that dreary dull passage of the road, the difficult places, familiarity palls on human nature. 'I have said all I can say. I am tired and weary. How can I go on?'

Oh, that ghastly self-pity! 'I am the victim. "He" or "she" rides free. I am the slave. It is I that am serving. It is I that hold the home together, and no one but I.' Self-pity. Are you not his follower, and didn't he come for service? Don't you realize that service is noble. That is where you rule. That is how you are a queen. A queen is not someone that walks in majesty wearing her jewels. A queen is someone who serves her people, at their beck and call. A king that is worth his kingship is not someone that domineers, not someone who only rules. To rule only is absurd. God on his throne is our servant. God is at our beck and call. Speak and he hears you. Cry and he answers you. He lifts you as a man is wont to carry his little child. 'So,' he said to the prophet, 'have I carried you, O you children of Israel!' God ordains us to service, not self-pity. Let there be none of that which cheapens the heroism of mankind and dwarfs man to being a god merely in his own eyes. Let him be a servant in his own eyes, and glad to serve where love impels him. That is love, not of the flesh, but of the spirit, the love that Christ blessed by wearing human flesh.

36 THE UNBREAKABLE BOND

SOMETIMES we Catholics are asked by those outside the Church why it is that we forbid what seems so reasonable to them: the practice of divorce. We must remember in any answer that we ever make to them that our sole reason, really, is the word of Christ. We forbid it merely because he forbade it. We forbid it because we believe him to be God.

We can, of course, after we have realized that it is precisely his teaching, we can discover all sorts of other reasons which seem to our mind to justify his action. We can bring in the experience of mankind We can show, merely by pointing to the pages of history, that wherever divorce has entered – and it has come not infrequently in history – wherever it has been introduced, society has fallen. You could show this from the records of the past. You could show the little value of divorce as a social institution. You could show the hurt it has done to the child. You could bring all sorts of other arguments, based on experience or social science, but those are not our reasons. Our reasons are the words of Christ. He forbade it, and we, believing him to be God, who knows all things, knows human nature, planned the destiny of man, we are sure that his advice – indeed, not advice, but command – is of obligation on all men, that all who know it should follow it because he is God. He knew quite well, when he was laying down the doctrine that marriage could not be dissolved, that he was teaching something severe to human nature. He says himself: 'It was written of old,' referring to the legislation of Moses, 'it was written of old that a man could by a bill of divorce put away his wife, but I say to you, no.' He knew he was teaching a higher doctrine, something harder to mankind, but he did not merely teach it. We know it to be a principle of divine providence that God never compels any human being to do anything without giving him the power to do it. God is just. God does not say to man, 'Thou shalt do this,' and command him to do what is above him. If God lays an order, God gives power. If it is God's will, God wants it done. He won't leave it to mere erring humanity. He gives grace. He brought in more severe legislation, but he gave a sacrament to enable man to fulfill his law.

These people outside the faith who would introduce divorce, do so because they have denied the sacrament of marriage. It doesn't appear in their religious code. They retained, or they did for centuries, the mere blind law and denied the sacrament. They have found the observance of this law at last to be a thing impossible. Having denied the sacrament of marriage, of course it is impossible. Christ knew what he was about. He was giving something more austere than the world had known until his time: a single wife, an unbroken bond of marriage, unbreakable except by the fingers of death. And yet he knew man, for he had made him, and so he established that blessed sacrament of marriage whereby he gave men and women grace to fulfill the law that he laid down. He laid on men, then, the obligation of an unbreakable marriage, and he bade mankind go to the sacramental sources of grace and so live with the help of that.

Now we, looking at divorce after the event, can see the evil that it has wrought in the children of men. We can see, for instance, that because divorce has now been made popular, accessible, cheap, none need hesitate in choosing a helpmate. There is no need to trouble over the choice or to take care of it. If the partnership does not work, the partners can separate and begin again. It is only a passing engagement. It is something that finally doesn't matter to human life.

If you know when you have been given change at the counter that unless you look at it at the moment and report a mistake immediately, no errors will be acknowledged or corrected later, that no one will listen to your complaints or pay any attention to you, you are careful to count your change. It is now or not at all, so you take pains to see that you have been charged correctly. But supposing you knew that if you came back next day they would still listen to you and correct errors you asserted they had made? You would hardly trouble about counting at the time. If it is so easy to change later, why bother about being careful now? To introduce divorce is therefore to open a flood gate. A torrent will follow. 'Divorce must be allowed only when it is necessary.' But once established, it is an ever widening breach. Once possible for any reason, it will soon be made possible for many reasons.

And we know another result of it. We know quite well that if people know they have got to live together, whatever betide, they have in that fact a very potent reason for making up any quarrel they may have. Since they can't separate, they have thereby a powerful motive for peace. They must live side by side; the same walls must enclose them; since it is so, what is the use of quarrelling? Thus they will more easily find a way out of their strife. Men agree to be patient when they see that they can't alter something and that there is no better way of dealing with life. Any other way weakens man. Thus, if he can be sure of getting a divorce, he has little motive for trying to reconcile differences that must inevitably arise. He just drifts with the tide.

And again we know, for all men who have studied the society of our day tell us so, that divorce has made sin easy by making adultery easy. There is less motive for not indulging in it. If a couple do not get on, they can separate, and since adultery can but result in a new marriage, why not make a trial of it? The door is thus opened to all sorts of other crimes.

The Catholic Church, indeed, allows the possibility of separation. Supposing married people can't get on together; supposing that it is absolutely impossible for them to get along together; supposing they have tried their uttermost and best. Very well, it is a pity, and it is plain that they must live apart; but neither can remarry Isn't that hard? Yes, but the Church claims no power over the word of Christ. She has no power to modify his teaching. It is strange, isn't it, of a Christian to say to us: 'But surely you will alter the old ruling to meet the times and new demands.' Times? Demands? We live by eternity; his unbroken word is eternal. The heavens, the earth may pass. No word that he spoke shall pass. These words which we echo, he spoke.

Hard? You see, it is perpetually an appeal to sentiment. If any man attacks you on divorce, his argument is always sentimental. He will say to you: 'I know a case . . . ' 'A case,' mark you. Not your reason, he is not appealing to that. He is appealing to your heart. He is getting away from the principle. It is not the teaching of Christ that he is looking for, but merely a way to ease the difficulty of man. But you know that any principle is hard to live exactly. To be just, to be generous, to be always truthful – arc you asking these of us? Why surely. Christ did. 'But I shall lose by following justice, generosity, truthfulness.' Oh, yes, you will lose but you gain, you know, something even greater than you lose. You and I have got to live by faith.

Hard? 'I know a case . . .Do you expect the woman to be faithful? He is shut up in an asylum for the insane.' 'He is a criminal. Are you going to tie them together until death parts them?' Yes, Christ thinks even thus nobly of mankind. He thinks a woman's heart or a man's heart can bear even that strain. You see how wonderful in his eyes is human love. Indeed, lit with the divine grace of the sacrament, even such a love, constant, enduring, unselfish, is possible to mankind! It is not we who despise men; we lift them. We believe in their power to endure. We say that love is really enduring. It can be enduring to a heart that wills to think it so.

Hard? Why yes, it is hard, but to be always truthful, or always to behave like a gentleman in life, is hard: 'I know a case . . .' You are going to get hurt by it over and over again. Of course you are. People will just jostle you in the subways of life. They will just fight over your head for the first place. You can do what you like, of course, jostle as they do or be ready to be courteous in spite of all. Supposing you say: 'Well, I have my own idea of what a man should be like. I believe in trying to behave like a gentleman whatever betide.' Then you have a principle to go on and, if you suffer on its account, you know really you are conquering. Your principle is worth more to you than the inconvenience of being left behind. Your ideals are finer than those of the people who trample on you as they go by. They are just beasts fighting, but you walk serene like a man.

Hard? Why of course it is hard, and so is all of Christ's teaching. 'Blessed are the clean of heart.' That is hard. 'Blessed are the poor in spirit,' 'Blessed are the merciful,' 'Blessed are the meek,' 'Blessed are they that hunger and thirst after justice,' to hunger and thirst after justice, that is too hard. It is so easy to watch the little injustices of human life untroubled and to use your influence merely to get yourself out of difficulties. But blessed are they that hunger and thirst after the justice of God.

It is hard, this teaching on divorce, but it is Christ's word, and that is our comfort, and that, indeed, is the very root of all our faith. We have got no other motive than that in forbidding it, that it is his teaching. All the social arguments are arguments that pass. They are good arguments but they are not real arguments. They are the arguments brought in afterwards, to justify the doctrine to those that need to find an external justification of it. But for us, the words of Christ are enough. We can easily let all the rest go.

Again, the union of love is the oldest and strongest union that we know in the history of man. Yet the State claims all sorts of powers to deal with marriage. We answer: 'Yes, you have got a perfect right to deal with the civil effects of marriage. That is your power. You have a right to regulate all sorts of things dealing with that aspect of it, to legislate on them as you will, but not to touch the bond of marriage. It is older than you are. It will be there still when you have gone.'

Supposing, as it well may be, that barbarians one day burst over the civilization that we know; that the whole of it is brought down about our ears, as all other civilizations have been brought down, and that all our fine towers lie in ruins to be rediscovered centuries after. Yet we know surely that, even though our civilization passes, the family will abide. It seems so weak, this little group of father and mother and child, huddling together against the storm outside them, tyrannized by politics, assaulted by unclean passion, denounced as dull by wretched scribblers who earn pay and publicity but no respect by their pens, and yet it is older than they, more venerable. They will soon be forgotten and for always. If it be forgotten, it will return. It is the source of all our culture. Out of it came the State. Out of it grew the tribe, till the tribes settled and grew in the ways of culture, and built cities and made laws. But the family began this. The family will outlive it. It is older than they. If you go down among the pagans who have never been debased by an evil civilization, a civilization of an Industrial age, if you go to the pagans you will find, perhaps, polygamy. You will find that a man may have many wives, but that he has no wife that another man can take. You will never find the sanctity of marriage in that sense lost even among the pagans, unless they have been degraded by a civilization that has failed.

As a young man, a prince in the Basuto tribe of South Africa went to the Catholic missionary and asked to be instructed and received into the Church. The priest said to him. 'No, I can't take you.' 'Why?' 'You are drinking too heavily. You are not fit for the kingdom of God. You are just going the way of the beasts. Go your way. Don't come to me.' 'But I am a prince,' he said. 'Were you a king I would not have you. Not for you the kingdom of God.' However, he came back after a time and said to the priest: 'I have finished with drink,' and the priest said: 'Very well, now I will instruct you. We will begin.'

When the young man came to the end of his instruction he said to the priest: 'What am I to do? You know I have my wives. I can send away the rest of them but there are two I love above all the others. I think I love them both equally. Both are of noble lineage, both come of the houses of kings. I don't know which of them to choose. I can't choose now, so I must wait. God, I know, will show me a way to settle my perplexity. It is not my fault that it has come on me. He will show me a way out.'

Now these two women realized somehow that the prince wanted something and that one or the other of them stood in the way of his obtaining it. They were pagans, mark you, but they had felt something of what Catholicism meant to the man they loved. So, in the blind pagan way, they went out of the kraal in the royal village and wandered on the wide, rolling veldt, open, treeless, the sun overhead, the arching blue sky. There they prayed to the unknown God of the Christians that if they stood in the way of the man they loved, he would do what he willed with them. Let him take one or other of them in death. As they prayed, out of the sky came the lightning. One of them was struck dead there and then. The other came back and told her tale. Her husband became a Catholic. He is now the paramount chief, one of the great Catholics of that color which has a majesty of its own, and he is a Catholic by the grace of a woman who guessed, somehow, that here was a unique way to show love.

Savage? Compare that woman with the women whose lives you read of in your daily press. Do you think it was she who was the savage? You say, perhaps, that she had strange, old-fashioned ideas of love. Old-fashioned? Why, yes, eternal. She, though pagan, had some concept of love. To her it was something so great that under its impulse she would gladly die just to set a man in the way he should go. If the Christian women of our time, women of culture, of civilization, had half the delicacy of this savage, it would be a nobler world, less vulgar, less flaunting, less gross. Let them learn from this 'savage' the tenderness and the strength of love.

For us the word of Christ matters. It is his law. Other reasons for what he orders there are, but none of them matter compared with that reason which is higher than reason: the glory of the faith. For us that matters most and must matter. We accept marriage as an unbreakable bond. An unbreakable bond? We don't deny that to the people who chatter to us about freedom. We say: 'Yes, it is a bond, just as he said his teaching was a yoke and a burden.' There was never any pretence in the preaching of Christ. He didn't pretend that things were easier than they really were. When he taught his doctrine of the indissolubility of marriage, the apostles were frightened by it.

When he laid down his doctrine that henceforth no divorce was to be allowed, they said: 'Why then, it is better for a man not to marry than to venture into such a hard way,' and he said: 'For them that are called it is better, but not for all.' Not for all. It is a bond. It is a burden. It is a yoke. It is something laid on a man, something that binds him.

Yet a man can be bound and free. When you talk about a nation achieving its freedom, you mean that it now governs itself; you don't mean that it has no government at all. You mean that it has broken away from tyranny, and tyranny means that someone is ruling it without the justification of law. You mean that whoever has possessed himself of power is lawless, using force but not using law. A man should be free, and only that man is free who is of himself obedient to law. No man is free that denies all obedience, just as no man is free who obeys because he must. A free man is a man who walks upright and takes the law, justice, and truth – all those fine things that your fathers thought worth dying for – takes all those fine things and says: 'I will obey them because I should obey them. I will obey them without force or tyranny. I will obey the law.' Now that is freedom. A bondage, yes, but the bondage of free service.

Thus, too, does God's authority bless the free choice of a woman, of a man. Marriage consists of their free choice, and God's blessing on them and holding them by the bond of love. For us, the word of Christ suffices. When they question you about our doctrine, go back always to that. Let that be your answer. Will the Church ever change?' She cannot, for she cannot alter the teaching of Christ. She is here to explain it, and you and I are here to listen to it, and listening, to obey it. We know that his words are not the words of blind power but of a wise power directing the society of men. We know that those that follow him, though they be laughed at, jeered at, have created and continued the only society that will survive. We know we carry with us the healing of the nations. One day people will realize, centuries after, that, in the heart of a civilization that was corrupt, we kept our part sacred and because of it some remnant of our civilization endured. The ways of the others will be forgotten, or described in far-off days as unbelievable. We alone who follow Christ in a world of madness are safe, on his assurance, who knows all.

37 THE HOME FIRES

IT Is around the subject of the family and the home that the war of the Church with the world now centers. The war there has begun. What is this war? It is the defense by the Catholic Church of the sanctity of human love and marriage, of the sanctity of the home against its enemies, because the Catholic Church, with her divine mission, comes not merely to speak to men of divine things, but to show them that human things, through Christ in human nature, have been made divine.

We are all of us aware of these attacks made on the home. We have noticed for ourselves, those at least of us who are midway towards their century, how the whole conception of the home, of marriage, has vitally changed in public estimation, in the public press. Divorce, an older thing indeed than our time or our generation, has yet within our own memory been pushed forward with an impetus that increases year by year. Nor is it divorce only that has developed in momentum, but that which has always in human history immediately followed it: the practice of birth-control. Once marriage has been followed by divorce in human society, then immediately this further step has always been taken. It is nothing new, nothing fresh, nothing modern – to use a word that for some reason people think to be a compliment. The conjunction of the two is something that occurs regularly in human history. Divorce has always been followed by birth-control. You will also find in all human history that birth-control in turn is followed by open immorality. Those are the three notes which have echoed together in harmony. Their arrangement is inevitable. One follows the other. For it is seen that divorce bears hardly on the children, so an age of sentiment and emotion forbids the little ones. Henceforward, let no public stigma follow immorality; no public shame; let there be no children to go through their lifetime pointed at, begotten out of wedlock. That, men say, is now ended, since there are no children. Thus, to prevent hurt coming out of adultery, its results are removed Immorality follows. It is followed by no disadvantages. No one now need know about it. Round it is a hushed mystery of silence. Later it will be public, unashamed. Then, along with these, this also has always followed a vital attack upon moral education. Children must be brought to believe that there is no certain truth. These things are inevitable; they follow steadily upon the heels of divorce.

But for all that, you must not scorn your fellows in this generation. It is true that they have forgotten the teaching that was customary among them. They have lost all sense of dogmatic principle. But then no moral doctrine has been taught them. Every man has been told that he should be a law to himself. Ever since the Reformation, they have had that idea hammered into their minds. Its creed was the formula that there must be no Church with dogmatic utterances. Man needs only his human conscience and the written word of God. It sounded magnificent. It sounded as though men were breaking out of slavery. What it meant really was the dissolution of all society. Every man a law unto himself. Then there can be no teaching outside of him greater than himself. No Church of Christ can tell him what he must believe or what to do. That has been the fundamental idea of Protestantism. It has ruined all notion of a definite teaching of Christ. So do not blame the people of your own generation. They are going where they have been led.

The only difference between this age and its elders is that it is fearless where they were hampered by prejudice. These are more logical, they are carrying out unashamed what their fathers covered in their hearts but didn't dare believe. Hence, we have about us a pagan generation. But Protestantism must breed paganism, it must breed eventually a creed that denies all creeds. It must demand that no law of Christ should be imposed imperially. Its faith is the faith of the rebel, and a rebel has no lot or part with Christ. He gave the law. He taught the law. He loved the law. Law is the way of Christ. What we witness in the present generation outside the Catholic Church is the inevitable result of the new Renaissance paganism; the inevitable result of Protestantism, namely, the destruction of all law, of all authority, and the individual left entirely to himself.

To meet this ill, the Catholic Church comes with a remedy. It is not her remedy, but the remedy of Christ. First, she lays down definite principles on the subject of the home, of marriage, of the relationship of child and parent, of the relationship of parent and child. She lays down certain definite obligations which are not of her making, for of herself she imposes nothing. She does but carry the message of Christ. She lays down her law, which is his law. She teaches merely what she has been taught. Christ, our Lord, spoke often of marriage. His first miracle was at a marriage feast when he turned water into wine. It is a subject which is often to be found in his parables: 'The kingdom of God is like to a marriage feast.' For him, evidently, there was something sacred in the relationship of woman and man It is not guesswork to suppose this, for in each of the four Gospels we are given his teaching on the sanctity of marriage, on the unbroken bond of marriage, that 'they two shall be but one flesh'. He laid down the law for us on this as on other subjects, and the Church does but echo it. What is revealed to us is the law of Christ, God Incarnate; he who knew man, whose hands had fashioned man, who knew therefore what was for man's good.

But people say to us: 'But those principles are impossible. No human power can obey them. You are asking too much of men.' They say to the Catholic Church: 'What do you know of love and marriage, who forbid it to your priests? What do you know of the capacity of human nature to keep these rules of yours, you who know nothing of the lot of human kind?' They say that the law of Christ is impossible for human nature. But of course it is impossible for human nature. That is exactly why Christ came. He came not only with a law, but a sacrament. He came not only to teach, but to help. He came not only to say: 'Thus shalt thou live. This is forbidden you.' He came to give to human nature a divine aid to carry out the new commands. Thus he gave men a sacrament instituted for the family. Now this sacrament supposes that human nature is not capable of itself of the high things of Christ. But then we are not left to unassisted human nature. You must remember, when you hear men denouncing Catholic teaching as narrow or impossible, that the Catholic teaching on marriage is incomplete without the Catholic doctrine on the sacrament of marriage. The two fit in, one with the other. They are needed to explain each other.

The law of Christ is not complete without Christ's sacraments. Thus Protestants, having abolished the sacrament of matrimony, find that the way of matrimony which Christ taught is impossible for man. Our Lord began with human nature. Here in this sacrament he supposes human love. People say to us again: 'Your doctrine of marriage is impossible. It is wicked. It would link together reluctant people.' But we are not in favor of linking reluctant people. We wish to change their reluctance. The Church echoes the voice of Christ. He came not to destroy, but to perfect human nature. He supposes a human love. If you find a generation which hardly cares about the sanctity of human love, is merely interested in human passion, thinks of marriage as a thing that comes and goes, builds it on choice or fancy, reconciles men to it or bids them separate because the two who have come together say their natures are incompatible, they are looking at it as though it were merely a contract, as though it were a mere business relation. In all our theory of it, we suppose as its basis human love. Christ supposes that, builds his fabric of marriage and the family on that solid, flaming foundation: love and marriage and the sacrament, and the Catholic home.

For the Church, the ideal of the Catholic home is something which is no less sacred than the life of the cloister. It is a life which the Holy Family chose for its own. Those three, one supremely good, and the others only less so, those three whom we follow as our great leaders, were joined in a Holy Family; not a cloister, but a home. The Catholic home should be built as care-fully as the cloister. The vocation to it studied as carefully, as prayerfully, as the vocation to the cloister, for it is a state made sacred with a sacrament, whereas there is no sacrament consecrating religious life. Just as the Catholic home as an ideal is something sacred, so those that enter it should view it through holy eyes. Just as the cloister is built, arranged, adorned, to enable the individual religious to live his life more easily, so, in Catholic concept, should be the Catholic home. There should be in it emblems of religion, especially the figure of the Crucified; that supreme emblem of unselfishness should adorn the walls of the home and be set over the marriage bed. There should be figures of the saints, prayer books, Catholic books, Catholic newspapers, holy water. People may laugh at these things. They may say: 'But we have parted with all that. That is no longer possible. Why will you force on us the superstitions of an older age?' We say: 'Well, has it changed for the better? What is your married life like after all? Have you now found happiness? Has the world found happiness by removing these sacred things? Is the married life easier because they have forgotten the Holy Family? Is married life easier with Nazareth forgot?'

'Holy water and the other old-fashioned gadgets, what have these to do with us?' Well, their purpose is to remind you of the sanctity of the room where you live, to see it as a shrine of human love and affection; to enable you to realize the spiritual side of its responsibilities, its pain, its joy, birth and death and childhood, gathered within its four single walls. You see, the Catholic ideal is something which you cannot despise in practice without losing all the beauty the home has to bring you, for the Catholic ideal is ruined only by selfishness. These symbols help to peace and unity. Selfishness is the individual against the group. I for myself, whoever I am in the family, mother or father or child. I for myself. Family? That is forgotten. My own rights, not my duties. Not others. Myself.

Ideals are always ruined by selfishness. They must needs be. An ideal lifts a man. Selfishness must drag him down. Those emblems of the faith have then their own purpose: to remind each member of the family that there is a holy purpose behind it, that they are to help one another to God. Wife and husband are united for a blessed purpose, namely, that each may lead the other nearer to the ways of God. A child is given them, that a child may be led nearer to the Father over them. The child should be got ready for his ultimate home. Now selfishness wrecks this. What is the trouble in our time but selfishness? The old are selfish and the young are selfish. Neither is to be acquitted of blame.

Now here is a queer thing People say now: 'What a blessed thing is frankness! How wonderful at last to say what we mean! In the old days they did things roundabout. They weren't openhearted. Now we say what we mean.' But they don't. For instance, they hate being questioned, the young by the old, or the old by the young. 'Let's be frank,' they say, yet they hate someone to say to them: 'Where were you last night?' 'Frank, not afraid. Utterly fearless.' These are the things they prate about. 'Let us put all our cards on the table, and let us talk quite openly, above board.' But they hate frankness where it unveils them, so they curtain it about. Interference, they call the questioning, these people that preach frankness; somehow, we wonder if it is because they are ashamed of what they are doing and won't be frank Anyhow, selfishness is really at the bottom of the trouble on both sides.

Of course, there are homes that are real places of sanctity. There are homes which are homes, indeed. There are mothers and fathers and children who somehow make a success of family life against all the laughter of the world. There are quiet homes, full of joy and happiness, radiant. There are mothers of many children, whose home is a blessed success, and whose children, like pigeons, come homing to them long after they have left their home. Authority? Oh, yes, authority, but somehow made romantic; lit, somehow, with the flame of love. A mother can hold them and a father can hold them. Impossible? It is not impossible in a Catholic home.

You know, you owe it to the world, you of America, to re-build the home. Divorce is older than your time, I know, and birth-control began outside your borders, but you have practiced it and preached it more widely than all the world. You, don't you lead the world? Aren't your fashions the world's fashions? Aren't you the nation of progress? Don't men look to you, bow to you, and say that you hold the scepter and the gold of the world? What will you do for it, you that are leaders? It carries responsibility, don't you think? Doesn't it mean something to have the foremost place in the world? Those that broke the home knew how to break it, they alone have the power to build it again from the beginning. You have that power. What we called a 'house,' you called a 'home'. You spoke of one of your cities as 'The City of Homes'. You and the home! It was you that sang that song that is undying wherever our common speech has gone. Men gather in loneliness in far places under the quiet stirring of the stars and sing it; men in ships, bored with their life on the sea, have whistled it one to another in the watches of the night; pioneers and adventurers sing it; exiles have hummed it; your song which is 'Home, Sweet Home'. It is your song. You sang the beauties of home as no one, I suppose, has ever sung them. Surely, you can find a home for home.

Do you remember after your Civil War was done, an English admirer wrote to Robert Lee, to offer him an estate in England, wanting to do something for him, for who could not admire the heroism, the exquisite courtesy of the man? But he wrote back: 'I only want a quiet home in the woods,' he said. 'A quiet home in the woods.' It is the old American ideal, the ideal of your fathers, a thing they fashioned wherever they went – a log cabin or whatever it might be. They had some such ideal as that. They had an ideal of a home, of some shrine that was sacred. Amongst you it still survives. No one can look on these great cities as America. They are indeed the places where is shown the splendor of your great architecture. But they are not homes, they are not you. All the while there are all sorts of people pouring in at your ports, who are not your people, so that the life here that men see is not your life. But beyond these cities there are wide plains and homes elsewhere, real homes, where the faith lingers, where men love and are not ashamed of love; where they look upon love as something enduring; where a child is welcomed, and no one forbids. Even in the city places, love still lingers under the ashes. The fire still burns. Under the ashes it burns.

But the home of today must be a new home. That is the trouble of it. The old ways won't do. It must be something new with a new fashion about it, for the old ways are impossible – at least I suppose they are – with modern life. The common prayer of the house, the prayers of the children, heard by father and mother, the family together at home every night. What home in this city could you enter in the evening and be sure of finding the family there? Do you know any such home? There must be a few homes like this still left; yet they are not typical. On the whole, I suppose, those old ways are finished with. Nothing can ever bring them back again.

Moreover, in our time the many unmarried, the bachelors and

spinsters, have introduced a new element into city life. Thus, in the organization of modern society, new forms of social life must be formed and met. So there has always to be something new in the world. You can't bring back the old fashions. That is not a matter of great concern. There are new forms to be invented. Who shall invent them but you? You were adventurers always. You are never afraid. Just as you tear down an old mansion and rebuild something more glorious in its place, can't you do it with the home? Can't you show the way to the modern world that will always follow you, imagining all you do is something greater than their own, holding some secret of your progress and success? Can't you fashion some new way of home under the faith, you of the New World that have it? Can't you rebuild it again?

You had a Revolution, and out of the ashes of the cities and the homes that were charred, you rebuilt the nation. You had your Civil War and you destroyed a civilization and remade it more wonderful than the age that had gone before it. Now here again, this is what men ask of you, those of the household of the faith; they say, pointing to your nation: 'What you do, the world will do after you. Now give us a leadership here. Show us the new way of the home, under life's new conditions: human love blessed again by faith.' Today ashes are on your brow. Under the ashes with which your brow is marked, was once a flame. If you could stir the spent ashes, they could be re-illumined, not now from beneath, but from above. With God helping, you may do such a blessed thing, not for your people only, but for the whole wide world. You can bring into fashion again the Catholic home, with its wonderful piety and its wonderful warmth of love; a home with God set in its midst. You can do it. Perhaps no one but you can do it. Perhaps, if you don't do it, the thing for many generations will not be done. Others may come after you and show the way. Don't leave it to them. Do it while you have the power of leadership. Show the world, you that see it, the beauty of the home.

38   THROUGH CHRIST TO GOD

WE HAVE tried to look at the sanctity of our Catholic world as centering around the home, and, indeed, to remember that that home is for us not merely that which shelters our spiritual life, but that which gives it its energy and vigor. We want to realize that the world as God made it has centered around the home, and that, as God made it, the unity of the home comes, humanly speaking, from love, and even divinely speaking, from human love lifted to a higher plane than it could itself achieve.

It is through the family, bound up with family life, and creating one by one the family feasts, that our Blessed Lord gave us the sacraments. The family begins with the sacraments and all the various stages of family life are marked by sacraments. It is the way in which our Blessed Lord has deigned to build up the home. In all those relations which must exist between the various parts of the family, our Lord has given us his own tender teaching, clear and strong. The relationship of husband and wife, a relationship that is founded on a spirit of unselfishness, or loyalty, of exclusive love. He has laid down for us the rule that governs it. Again, the relationship of father and mother to their children he taught us, a relationship which demands from the parents a sense of their responsibility for the child, bodily, intellectually, morally, spiritually, an obligation of guidance, of care, of correction; and, from the child, the realization of the duty of obedience and honor; they seeing to it that as far as is possible the child shall be fitly prepared for life; the child striving to avail itself of what is done for it. Again, he repeated the old commandment that fixed the relationship of children to parents, whom they should love, honor, and obey. So, too, he dealt with the relationship of the family to that circle of acquaintances that works for the family: that there shall be side by side with the work that is lawfully demanded an adequate return for labor, and that a sense of brotherhood should never be forgotten, which bridges and includes, howsoever divergent and different may be the type, every character and class.

If you would understand something of the new spirit that our Lord came to bring into the world, take the Epistle of St. Paul to Philemon, the shortest of the books of the New Testament, and read the injunctions that St Paul there lays down for Philemon to guide his dealings with his newly-baptized slave. The slave had run away from his master and had come to St Paul. St Paul had received him into Christianity, and was sending him back to his Christian master. 'You are now,' he says, 'still master and servant, but you are also a brother, and that sense of brotherhood must run through the whole of your relationship, each to each;' one commanding, one serving, and yet both common brothers of the Father of us all. They were brethren not only between themselves, but fellow-brethren of Christ. Lastly, of course, our Lord has left us the teaching that should govern the mutual relationship of the children between each other.

It stands to reason that all these high ideals are difficult to human nature. They demand from human nature two things which human nature itself finds hardest to give. They ask, first, unselfishness, and we are all naturally selfish. Naturally, we seek our own convenience and comfort, and, especially, we look at life from our own personal point of view. We see everything as it affects us. We are full of self-pity. We are continually measuring the actions or characters of others by the effect these actions or characters have on us. We are naturally selfish. And again, we are inconstant. We are creatures of moods. We take up work, and then after a while, when enthusiasm has in some way or other been quenched, we get tired of it and lay it aside. We think of something else. We invent numberless excuses for giving it up, by dressing up our self-fancy or pride lest we should see ourselves as we really are. We have innumerable reasons to suggest to ourselves why we should put it aside in order to take up something new, something even more valuable. We are naturally inconstant. Whatever work we take up, we are bound, after a while, to meet drudgery in it. There is inevitably at last a sameness in it, a certain amount of monotony in it, and our tendency, when we come to such a period in our work, is to give it up. It is true of all duties. It is no less true of the duties of the home. So this is the second thing that is asked of us. First, unselfishness, and secondly, a constant loyalty, a persistent constancy, doing what we have to do continuously and without complaint.

Life outside has its interruptions; life within the family must normally continue along the same line. That is the dreariness of it, for we need change. We feel that we must break out from the home life. It is so easy to be full of conversation, of amusement, when you are dealing with people whom you seldom meet; but at home, to be alive, to be amusing, to be full of new subjects of conversation – that is a demand upon human nature to which human nature with growing feebleness responds. Perhaps it is difficult always to be interesting and interested, yet it is much more difficult when we are continuously meeting the same people, as we must at home; when there is steady monotony in life; when the same persistent stories have to be endlessly listened to; where you know almost inevitably what will follow next. You know inevitably this story leads on to another story, and you must sit and listen to the same things over and over again. You need desperately both unselfishness and a persistent constancy - the two things hardest of all to the human nature which we share.

But in this our Lord has taught us, as he has taught us in everything, the way we should look at human life. When he was to be taken out of her life, he bade his Mother see himself in John, the Beloved Disciple. 'Behold thy son.' She was a mother. She was to take all the world under her mantle. She was to be a mother to every human soul. She, with her marvelous greatness and majesty, with the width of her heart and character, its firmness, its fire, how shall she take humanity – dull, dreary, simple, so petty, so small, so mean – how shall this great-hearted Mother gather to herself all human kind? One way alone would make it possible: in each one to ford her Son. We were each to be for her another Christ. She was to find him in us. She could easily be a mother if she could find Christ in every soul. What he gave to her, he gave to us as our vision: to find him in each with whom we live. How are these things possible? They are difficult to human nature. How are they possible? He has told us: by grace we can find him in every soul.

The way of Christ is a hard way, because a high way. He lifts us up to incredible ideals. He teaches us patience, to which our human spirit is hostile. He bids us be meek and gentle, we that by nature are proud. He bids us serve, we who by nature want to set everyone in order. He bids us be pure, we whose passions run riot of themselves. He bids us hold together through human love, when naturally men tend after a while to drift asunder. He asked of us everything which seems contrary to our nature, and yet he promised a power, a gift, an insight so that what seems impossible could yet be done. His remedy is always the same remedy. Why should we love our neighbor? Because of the good we see in him? Oh, no. It may easily happen that we see no good in some of our neighbors, that we cannot honestly discover anything in their character that can really appeal to us or attract us. Why should we love people? Have we got somehow to invent or fasten on to them some goodness that we cannot honestly find? Am I to take up the records of all criminals and say: 'Oh well, there must be something good in them.'

We are not obliged to love one another for the sake of the other; only to love them for God's sake. We are not asked to see good in them or to pretend that there is a good in them that we cannot honestly see. It is not that. He has set us an unfailing remedy, something which depends not upon what we can discover, but upon something that we know by faith. He has built the family on this basis, on his word that we find another Christ in every soul we meet. 'Because you did it to the least of my brethren, you did it to me.' He has told us that he takes whatever we do to all the world as done personally to himself. Whatever we do, he takes as done to himself. And just as he lays down that law, or if you like, that vision, by which we can regulate and sustain all those wonderful Christian ideals of charity and patience and meekness and gentleness in our ordinary external life, so even more he would gather us around himself in the family, not for each other's sake, but for his. Children must honor their parents. It sometimes might happen that they find in their parents little to honor and nothing to inspire. You are not asked to honor your parents for their own sakes. You are asked to honor them for his. 'Why should I? They are always interfering.' It is not at them you are to look; it is at Christ. You have got to look for him in them. Somehow, you must pierce that outward veil that hides all human flesh; you must pierce that veil that hides all the world from us, or that shows the world and hides the hidden God.

We are taught, therefore, to deal so with all our fellows because we find God in them. True as this is of all the world, it must be truer of the family, those that God out of his own destiny and fate has brought into such intimate relation with ourselves. We find God only by looking for Christ. Once when he was preaching someone bore him the tidings that his Mother and his brethren were without, and he said, pointing to his disciples: 'This is my mother. These are my brethren.' Christ took all his disciples into the family circle of his own home. The Pasch was a family feast, and he shared it with his family, the disciples, in that upper room. We are the family of Christ, and, contrariwise, we must find Christ in our family if we would hold steadily to the observance of these high duties to which we are called. He is the center. He is that which supports the whole family Withdraw Christ, and the family will fall apart. Will fall apart? Has fallen apart. It has lost its unity, its center, lost everything since men have forgotten God. They have forgotten divine things and divine teaching, and of course they have drifted to the evils that we see in our time besetting family life. They have denied religion, and inevitably, one by one, the links are broken that hold the home together. One by one the members of the family have drifted apart. The children have drifted from their parents. The parents have drifted from each other. The whole family circle is separating because the center on which the whole family is held together is gone.

God is our family. God is our home. God alone can gather again together the children of men. The sacraments, the feasts of the family, hold the family together, each sacrament in turn. Marriage gathers, is the beginning of the family, blesses it. By it the two, now one, go out to their life and their work. Baptism blesses the fruit of the family, that which promises a continuance of it, the fulfillment of the command of God. The sacraments, one by one, do their good in this way of Christ. Confirmation strengthens the child when it first becomes aware of life's difficulties, the temptations without and temptations growing within, needing grace to meet them and finding it here. The child realizes the difficulties of childhood, learns at least that is has got a will of its own, that its parents have been set over it, and that the Spirit of God is coming within it to make it strong enough to obey. Weakness disobeys, of course. To disobey is the sign of weakness. The weak cannot control their will. They break away. For us to obey, in our age, in the midst of a generation that knows not how to obey, for us to obey and be docile can only come through the grace of God in confirmation. Moreover, to hold the family together, to carry them through life, we have the banquet of the family, beginning with First Communion of each child, with the whole family assembled. This is one of the great family feasts. On that day each gives a present to the child. The child is a center. Oh, no; Christ is the center of that home. He has come for the first time to the child. It is now more than ever an intimately united family 'All ye are one,' says St Paul to us, 'that partake of one bread.' Here is the Bread that has gathered them all into one. Confession, too, has its place. For here is healing of the family. There must be, I suppose, with poor human nature, there must be at times quarrels, failures of justice, failures of charity, of peace. By the power of his blood in the words of absolution, these evils are blotted out, washed clean.

How shall you establish unity? Not one with another, but each of you with God. That is the concept. How shall the family hold together? How shall they hold hands all through life? Not by holding to each other, but by holding to Christ. Let him be the center, so always shall the family be held in one. Distance cannot scatter it, if it is held together in Christ our Lord, remembered in the sacrament of his body and blood, remembered in Mass, remembered in prayer. There, parents in Christ can gather daily a scattered family, holding all of their children by the hands of God. Not holding each other, not resting on each other, but all of them resting on God. We need unselfishness for this holding hands with God, but he will teach us unselfishness. We need constancy, loyalty. Where else shall we receive them but from the eternal, unchanging God? He will give them to us. Through Christ our Lord we shall find them. It is with this blessing that husband and wife go out of the church when they have been wed. 'Through Christ our Lord.' Loyalty, unselfishness till death, all the years ahead of them! Is it possible? Not to man, but to God.

He came himself out of a holy family. He, too, found himself in that narrow home of a mother's heart. He was the center of that family. He is to be the center of all families. Parents, children, and those that work and serve for them, shall find in him a constant home. He will gather them; he will hold them; he will establish them and keep the fire ever burning on the hearth which is the center of the home, on which in older days the family fire was lit. They gathered around the fire in the winter-time; in the summer they scattered. Here it is always winter, in the bleak wastes of man's duty, in the wind-swept heath of human life. We need a center, somewhere, where we can gather. We need a hearth, a home, a fire to keep even human love warm. 'I am the light,' he said. 'I am the fire. I am the door' that keeps out the cold, the outside world. He is the center. He should be, he can be. He is our home.

Part Five: The Last Things

39 WE ARE TRAVELERS

IF YOU were to try to summarize the teaching of our Blessed Lord, and if, for that purpose, you made yourself familiar with that record of his life and teaching, which we call the New Testament, you would find in it many phrases which might serve this purpose, many to keep by you to help you in your life. Certainly you would realize that what was evident in his life as of supreme importance was not so much what he did, but how he looked at what he did and at what was done to him. Indeed, in some respects his life was an ordinary life in its exterior. There were astonishing things in it, miracles, his very self, but the ordinary measure of his life was simple enough. The criticism made of him by the Pharisees was that he was a glutton and a wine-bibber; that he went out to dinner with the publicans and sinners. And yet, he looked at life strongly. Hence his meekness, his patience, his practical confidence in God! It is his attitude to what happened to him that stamps his character on the New Testament, and the same character can be seen in every follower of his. It is not what we do, but how we take things done to us, that seems especially to prove our right to call ourselves his disciples. It is not the external life, but the way we look at that life that matters. We Christians should take things differently from others. Our attitude to life should be different.

Now one phrase can be taken to show this, a phrase which seems to describe this attitude of the Christian. It is that expression of the life about him, wherein it is said that we are pilgrims, travelers; that we have no lasting city here; that we have no home. We are urged to live, remembering that we are pilgrims, travelers. This will help you to explain your life to yourself. As you look at your life, perhaps it seems unsatisfactory. It has no apparent continual growth in an orderly progressive fashion True, for life is not really a growing-up but a journey. You are a traveler, rather than a growing child. The Christian is building up no permanent achievement; he takes a journey to life eternal. People are disappointed because they do not understand this. This life is not a business; it is a journey. Things will not fit in comfortably if you are trying to live the life of a Christian! For if you are travelling, the whole secret of a happy journey is to remember always that you are a traveler. Otherwise, you will find people and places pulling at your heartstrings. It is so easy to settle down somewhere and then, when you move on, find you have left half your heart behind you.

You are being driven by the relentless hand of God. You do not realize that you are being driven along and you try to settle down. This means infinite pain and great dissatisfaction. You are a traveler; you must not settle down. You meet people and come into contact with them and then you never meet them again. The secret that we discover after a while is to remember that we may not meet them again, and to remain heart-whole. All life is like that. These places and people cannot but have their influence; yet so often we are torn apart from them, by physical distance or some break of sympathy, or death. It is so easy to find oneself left to mourn and to feel torn asunder. This is natural. But supposing all the time we had known that we were just journeying, and had remembered that here was not the end, we should not so easily have been hurt by life.

Again, death unites us. If we had remembered this, we should not so easily have been hurt by life; it is life that holds us at arm's length and sets up misunderstandings. But there is no misunderstanding between you and your dead. Misunderstandings are conditions only of this travelling life. We are travelers.

This explains these inevitable drawbacks. It explains God's action, his relentless action, always driving us. It seems that our life is restless. It must be. We are driven, at last, to our home. All that we learn as to how best to journey, we have to apply to life. Thus we shall realize that no place, no person, where we settle down, can be loved or longed for, without having in the back of our mind the consciousness of our withdrawal from it one day. At first you travel with a great many things, and, on each new journey you take, something is jettisoned. There is so much in life that you can do without. We learn to leave things behind us. Above all, we learn never to forget that our home life is outside time altogether. Unless we remember what is the end of all our journeying – what it is and to whom it is – we shall so easily get muddled and confused. Nothing here really matters, whether we have it or lose it – be it a book that seems to be a lifelong comfort and then one day palls on us, or be it a helper in our spiritual life who comes in to help us and then goes out again. We find him comforting, inspiring; then he drops out of life. We had thought that we should have him until we died!

Yet what you lose you will find again. Or what has been of use has already served its purpose. You must realize that nothing but God is of permanent value. Even good things may one day fail.

There must be people to whom the sacraments once upon a time meant a great deal. Then their conditions of life, near to church, with frequent services, made religion easy and comfort able to them. Now perhaps they find that the outer manifestations of spiritual life are denied them. Distance or ill-health makes the sacraments almost impossible. But God is still theirs. Him they have not lost. Life is so easy until something goes wrong. Learn to do without things. You are on a journey. If you journey well, you will certainly reach home. It is for the guidance of our attitude to life that we should always remember that we are only pilgrims. The secret of a happy and holy life lies in remembering that.

40 DEATH

IT IS the repeated cry of Don Quixote, whenever faced with a perplexing difficulty, that there is a remedy for everything but death. All else can be solved: only death is beyond our cure. It is this that strikes everyone, the finality of death, its unfathomable mysteries, its inevitableness. All else can be warded off with skill and persistence and high courage. But against death nothing can prevail. For that reason men do not discuss it. It hardly is a safe discussion. You can hardly discuss the problem of sunrise or sunset, hardly dispute about the fall of the leaves. Death is much too definite to be argued about. When you have mentioned its name you have said all there is to say about it. No, not quite all; for though death is quite clear, everything that precedes it and follows it is obscure. 'It is appointed unto man once to die.' That is about all one can be sure of, the rest is hidden from us: time, method, and result.

We very naturally dread and dislike the idea of its approach. Is it wrong? Should not a Christian 'desire to be dissolved and to be one, with Christ'? Is not death, to one who believes in God and a future life, a blessed release? Should it not be longed for? Yet we do not find in our hearts any such longing. Is it wrong? Even if it be wrong, perhaps, do we see how it can be helped? Certainly it would not be honest to say that we want to die when we do not. Before answering this question, let us remember that in some moods other people have an exactly opposite trouble. A priest in the confessional will sometimes hear this self-accusation from a penitent: 'I have wished I were dead.' Evidently, under the stress of misery of some kind, they have had a hatred of life and a desire to end all by leaving it. In such a mood is it that the poor suicide can see death only as the door of hope into a new world. At least he probably does not think of the new life; he is only anxious to be rid of the old.

The canon against self-murder is God's refusal to accept anyone's haste to be out of life; so that cowardly desire for life's ending has to be balanced against the idea that a Christian ought to desire death. We can say that in some sense a Christian should desire to die, and in some sense it is wrong for him to desire it. This juxtaposition of opposite ideas about the desire for death will help us to see our way through the difficulty. On the one hand, we guess that a Christian ought to want to die, yet we cannot honestly say we have any such idea; on the other, people who passionately desire death, feel convinced they ought not to desire it and confess it as a fault. We feel we ought to desire it, we feel we ought not to; who shall unriddle this?

The simplest way to unriddle most things is to leave them alone. Begin at the other end. Start by remembering that your life is a gift to you from God. That is certain. Well, because it is God's gift to you, you ought to think highly of it and value it. It is to be used, like all God's other gifts, in his love and service. It is a talent, and therefore, if not used to the full, will be requited against us at the judgment day. Now does that help you? It shows you at once that you ought not, from God's point of view, to desire to die, to desire to end God's gift. 'The night cometh wherein no man can work;' we ought to be in no hurry for the daylight to end. We ought to labor at the work he has given us to do, and we need life to be able to labor at it. If, then, we have this gift of God, is it surprising that we do not want to give it up? Can it be wrong of us if we have to say honestly that we do not want to give it up? It seems, indeed, that it is the only thing we can say, namely, that we want to keep this gift of God, our life, and enjoy it, and use it to the full.

But the saints? That does not seem to be their view. Wait a minute. Supposing we take the saints; cannot we be sure of this, that all they wanted was to do God's will? We can be sure of that. When, then, they spoke of their 'desire to be with Christ,' they meant that they loved God and wished to see him face to face, that they found by contrast that earthly life did not content them, was inadequate to their desires, inspired them with nobler hopes of a finer world. All they wanted was to do God's will; but they did not find that this life satisfied them. The same is true of all of us. We often feel that we would like to be spared to see this or that finished, we pray that this or that person may be allowed to live for the sake of the work he is doing, or the family or the friends who depend on him; we ask to be allowed to live because life is sweet to us, is full of interest, beauty, love. Why not, indeed? To wish to live is politeness to God for what he has given us; gratitude, an appreciation of his kindness. Yet all the while we are willing to accept his divine will, who knows better our needs and chances. We enjoy what he gives, yet are desirous only of what his will determined. At times we long for the peace and joy that will follow on life's ending; at times we are thrilled by its present pleasures. Neither is wrong, so long as beneath our desire comes acceptance of his will: 'My soul is sorrowful even unto death... Father, if it be possible, let this chalice pass; nevertheless, not my will but thine be done.' A dread of death is

compatible with perfect love. At the prime of life his body cried out
against its ending, but the greatness of the soul triumphed in its
acceptance of God's will.

We dread death for the same reason that children dislike going to
bed; we are happy, and want to retain our happiness. To go to bed
seemed such a waste of time when other people were remaining up; to
die seems hard on us when other people remain alive. We disliked
going to our solitary bedroom when we could hear all the laughter
below us and the clatter of dishes down-stairs. It seemed unfair. So
again we feel we have the right to happiness and yet do not always
possess happiness. What do we mean by this happiness that we all
pursue? It lies in so many different things. We are always chasing it.
We sometimes find it. Even then we are troubled for fear it should not
last. We must seek it. We cannot help ourselves. The pleasure-seeker,
of course, is after it; but no less in pursuit of it comes the man with a
sense of duty. He gives up pleasure, he tells you, and devotes himself to
live laborious days. But he knows that he ought to do this. It is not, of
course, that he loves pleasure less, but that he loves duty more. The
moral contentment and ease of conscience is not the prime motive of
his action, but the one sufficiently present to him to make his heroic
resolve constitute his happiness. The emaciated saint who seeks
penance and solitude does indeed enjoy these things quite truly. To
take penance sourly is no way of the saints. Even the Saviour of the
world did not face his Passion grimly. The temptation to reluctance he
fought and quelled in the Garden, and rose in the strength of his
triumph, a man, erect and free. We must think of him going radiantly
through it, joy shining in his eyes, love supporting his pains ('greater
love than this hath no man'), and despite the pains that love caused
him, by some subtle paradox, these in no wise diminished the pleasure
that love brought. It is true to say 'greater joy than this no man hath,
than that he should be able to lay down his life for his friends.'

The Loneliness of Death

The great effect produced in the soul by sin is an intense feeling of
loneliness, brought about by the very offence against God, for by the
fact of sin the deep consciousness of the intimate union between him
and ourselves can no longer be experienced. After all, no one can be
blind to the traditional reverence that we have for the divine Spirit
that governs the race. All men, since historic knowledge and memory
begin, have realized this Sovereign of the universe to be the most
intimate and familiar being to every human child. In our fear, our

success, in the moments when the beauty of things has come home to us, we have turned instinctively, not to address some one without, but the Spirit within. However far we go back, that is instinctive to man Sin, therefore, which breaks this bond, cannot but impress on the soul its loss; and since death is the penalty that God has attached to sin, it would seem natural that the terror of death should come precisely along the same line of loneliness. This, too, has been the age-long attitude to death taken by the race. Just as it has always slunk away to hide after its sin, so it has faced death as the great solitude. Even in prehistoric days this view of death impressed the mind of man. As far back as we can trace his life and habits, we find that he buried his dead with their most treasured possessions, something laid by the loved one's side to allow some semblance of companionship, of treasured gift, to break in on his loneliness. So, too, were wife and slave buried with their lord lest he should be lonely in death's great silence.

Indeed, solitary as life can become, death must be yet more solitary. Life comes to us as members of a family, as units in a great social organization, but death must leave us alone to ourselves. From the love that springs between two, the child is born; thus others herald it into the light, but it goes out from the light alone. Death works that change at least: whatever other rest or peace it will one day bring us, that loneliness is always its portion. It is the very pathos of a deathbed that the long shadows of the loneliness of the tomb are already being cast upon the soul; the voice of the dying person has to travel seemingly along endless cloisters before it can reach our ear; we have to stoop to catch the whisper of their failing breath; the constant chafing of the loved one's hands, the soothing pressure, is evidently only very slowly felt, perceived, and realized. It seems as though the soul had already retreated from the outposts of its dominions, and had shrunk back in fear to the keep, the citadel, the last strong place where alone it may hope to baffle the advancing foe. The communications are almost severed; only by the merest and most uncertain rallies does it still hold parley with its friends, who watch, hoping to hear the last request, the final farewell, the ultimate human recognition.

Yet, despite all this loneliness and solitude and aloofness, the souls of the just are never quite lonely in death. We gave, indeed, as our reason for supposing that death would be lonely, that it was the result of sin; and sin, we explained, meant cutting apart the two intimate things – my soul and God. But with the just there is never such severance: God and the just are always one. When other friends have to say to us, 'Farewell,' he says: 'Welcome, come ye blessed of my Father.' Nay,

because of my loneliness he clings closer to my soul, and in the
sustaining Viaticum hastens to guide me through the shadows of the
valley of death. The sacrament of Communion is given me for the
purpose of strength that springs from the nearness of his presence,
and never is that presence more required than when I go out alone
from life into the doors of death. For me, then, the vision of faith will
light up that valley, that I may see upon the Mil the crowded forms of
those who come to bid me enter into joy. I die, indeed, alone, but only
that I may pass into the company of the elect of God. The prayers that
are said about the bed of death repeat the thought that there is a
welcome beyond, and that I shall not be left lonely in the dread
moment when most I need the assistance of others, their comradeship,
their supporting affection. Freely, then, I shall face whatever befalls,
conscious of that hand held in mine, trusting in his own blessed words
that I shall not be left forsaken, but that to the end of the world he shall
be with me always.

41 JUDGMENT

PERHAPS for many the terrors of death are as nothing compared with the terrors of judgment, for all that affrights us in death is found far more fully in the awful moment that succeeds it. The loneliness of death that is its chiefest horror, its most overwhelming fear – that utter separation from our life and from that part of us, our bodies, which we have come to regard as so particularly ourselves – is followed by a still more bitter separation, a more cruel divorce: for our judgment must be solitary, isolated, alone. Even the saints can do little for us, for the judgment must be righteous and just, and this means assuredly that God cannot go out of his path of justice because of the pleading even of those whom he holds dear. What else, indeed, is the judgment, as far as we can grasp it, but the naked setting of our soul as it is now at this moment in the sight of God? He knows absolutely the state of my whole being. He knows what I do not – whether I am worthy of love or hatred. To me that blinding vision may be a tremendous revelation, a rolling back of all sorts of hidden curtains with which I had shrouded my soul from my own gaze: all the little deceptions that I had practiced on myself, the little ways in which I had hoodwinked my conscience and pretended to myself that I did not really think that in certain things I had done there was any great sin. Many times I had salved the conscience-pricks of my heart by distinctions and devices; now, in a flash, these are all laid bare.

Nay, so lonely shall I be, that even the very judge may be none other than myself. To the Son, indeed, is given all judgment; he must apportion the praise and blame, the reward or punishment. Yet in that moment, when the veils of ignorance and conceit are torn from my eyes, I must become awfully conscious of the pageant of my life. I can need no external voice to point out to me the evils of my life, for the loud cry of conscience itself will be the sole decisive voice required. The scenes through which we have lived will return to our remembrance and we shall be face to face with our lives. In the accounts of many of those who have gone so close to the doors of death as almost to have had a sight of what takes place beyond them, we are repeatedly told that they have seen then the whole forgotten vision of their lives. The whole past record has filed before them as though they sat as spectators in some theatre and watched the acting out in dumb show of every detail of another's tragedy or comedy.

From manhood back through the dim reaches of childhood the vision sped; nothing was omitted or passed by, the whole appeared as it had been. Would there be any need than this for further judgment? Would not the soul itself sum up by its own loathing and distaste what it thought of this record? Deserted, therefore, even by oneself, one's pride, one's conceit, one's fond hopes that all was well – oh, the biting, piercing loneliness of that utter isolation!

Yet even so is there consolation for us. There will be One who will be to us, then, a comfort, a refuge, a hope. The very figure of the Judge will be itself the sole sight that will give us any gleam of brightness in so horrid a scene. The five great wounds – will not their light illuminate even the dark corners of the stricken soul and give it hope in the weary waste of its bitter isolation? Through him will all our good actions take on an infinite value. The comfort that he himself has given in his own wonderful description of that day is found in the gracious text: 'Inasmuch as you did it to the least of my brethren, you did it to me.' Whatever good we have done will have its reward from him. The great doctrine of the unity of all Christians into a sacred body, of which Christ is the Head, will give, even in the horrors of that moment, a supreme relief. All the devotion that I have shown to the saints will there have been gathered up and regarded as devotion to him; for, to a Catholic, reverence for the saints is only exhibited because they are his friends, so that in reality (as we hold) those who have shown them reverence have really been showing reverence to Christ. The kindnesses of life, the little deeds we have done for others, will be remembered for our reward. Thus, through the terrors and horrors of the awful judgment there will always be the light lit by friendship; the unswerving love that we have shown to him who is ever faithful will not be forgotten. There can be no loneliness so long as he is there.

42 HELL

WE HAVE our Blessed Lord's own words for it that hell is 'everlasting punishment,' and it is of more concern to know what our Lord taught than to be able to make it fit in with our own preconceived notions of his mercy or his power. It is perfectly true that boundless mercy seems at first to imply that everything must be forgivable, indeed, in the end forgiven; but we have such difficulty in picturing to our imagination what is meant by eternity, that no mere man can understand what is meant by 'in the end'. Again, mercy is a virtue and not mere foolishness, for sometimes on earth we see mistaken kindness which is more disastrous than many crimes. But after all, discussions about hell, however interesting, are likely to be without result and are certainly of no consequence, since it is sufficient for us to know that our Lord explicitly taught the existence of a state of eternal punishment. On that we must take our stand. If Christ revealed it, we must accept it, whether we can justify it or not. But did he teach it? How can we be certain that the phrase bears the meaning that we put on it? Of course, we cannot be certain unless we have an infallible guide to interpret Scripture for us, so that here as elsewhere we have either to leave the question undecided or find some authority to tell us exactly what our Lord did mean.

Moreover, remember who it is that tells us of this terrible place: 'These shall go into everlasting punishment and the just into life everlasting' (Matt. 25: 46). Now the speaker of these words is the kindest and the gentlest of the sons of men. Cannot we be sure that if anyone was sympathetic, not likely to view life narrowly, not harsh to sinners, it was he? If anyone thinks it incongruous for a God of mercy to punish sins forever, and prides himself on so thinking, he would hardly claim to be more understanding than Christ. Yet it is precisely Christ who tells us of it. We have it not from the apostles, but from Christ. But he is never unkind to sinners. No, perhaps not; but he had a perfect hatred of sin. Kind to the sinner, he was full of anger to the sinner who thought he was a saint. He loathed sin with the force of his whole being; the vicarious contagion of it beat him to the ground in the Garden; his purity of heart and love of his Father made it revolting to him, though he would pardon it at once to the sinner who was contrite and realized the foulness of his sin. Sinners he loved; sin he hated. Does that help us to get a glimpse of the way in which he could accept and teach the doctrine of hell? Suppose we could really understand the meanness and awfulness of sin, would that help us to understand the inevitableness of hell? Can we hope to be able to reconcile our imagination to 'everlasting punishment' so long as we are unable properly and fully to grasp the evil of sin?

But do people really commit sin knowingly? Well, anyone who sins in indeliberate ignorance certainly will never be condemned to hell for it. All that the Catholic Church has ever taught is this: those who die in hatred of God, having sinned gravely and knowing the gravity of their sin (unless their ignorance itself be gravely culpable), will be punished everlastingly. To say that none die like this is beside the point, for who of us by human knowledge can answer whether they do or not? For us there are only two things to be said: first, we accept the doctrine for the one and only reason that we are taught it by Christ; secondly, we should not forget this teaching of our Lord, for it is never safe, honest, or manly to ignore the truth. We need not often call in the use of fear to help us, since the love of God must chiefly lead us; but love itself needs the instinct of fear and reverence, else it becomes mere emotion or passion, and misses the austerity of strength.

Hell is the most terrible of the Christian mysteries. The progression of loneliness in sin and death and judgment reaches to the furthest limits of possibility in the awful loneliness of hell. It has all the horrors of eternal solitary confinement; that is the real torment of hell, though there are others. Dante and others before and after him have imagined for themselves a place of torture; they have set to work to describe what, in the most frenzied of human thoughts, such a life must be; they have bidden to their assistance all the known and unknown horrors that the most morbid imagination can suppose. The effect has been at times, not terrible at all, but revolting; these writers who can imagine nothing save physical pain have often succeeded merely in giving one the idea that God gloated over the writhing bodies of his children. Very often the harm done by some so-called pious books is incalculable; the harrowing details even suggest that the authors themselves have taken pleasure in describing these tortures. But all these accounts, whether by canonized writers or not, count for nothing, since they know no more of that afterlife than we; they know only, as do we, that the real punishment of it is the loss of God. Our Lord himself used the word 'fire,' so that this must, therefore, represent the best possible description of the torment of the damned. But no one can suppose that he can fully understand what was meant: the precise significance of the phrase is beyond us.

This, then, is all that we know, namely, that the essential pain of hell is the loss of God to the soul, which at length knows what God means. Here, on earth, it is perfectly possible to go through life in more or less comfort while the thought of God is wholly absent from the soul; it is sometimes the easiest way, to forget and ignore God. But death brings with it a knowledge of things that our philosophy here ignores. It brings to the soul a knowledge of God and a realization that our nature was created for him as the purpose of its existence. Hence, the punishment of hell is the utter and eternal and conscious frustration of the soul's crying need. It is as though in a flash we had at last understood what everything in life was for, discovered the meaning of everything that had befallen us, found the solution to all the perplexities that had worried us – and then realized that our own previous ideas, and the practice that had followed them, had resulted in our complete inability to make use of life: a perfect nightmare in which one knew the use of everything, but could use nothing to its purpose. This torment, then, can come only to those who have died in revolt against God – not those who seemingly die in sin, for in the last ebb of consciousness who knows what mercies God has in store? But if any such pass out from here hating God, in revolt against him, then, flung out as they are into eternity, they must remain forever hating and losing, and conscious of their incalculable loss.

Am I worried over this? Does it come to me as opposed to the idea that the New Testament gives me of the character and ways of God? Then, assuredly, there is this much to be granted, that I can never hope to adjust in abstract method the justice and mercy of God in perfect balance. I can never hope to understand, still less explain to others, how hell is compatible with the Crucifixion I may, indeed, see how the one does necessitate the other, how love alone could build up hell, but that is but a fleeting vision which never wholly satisfies. I must be prepared, at any rate, to go through life unable to answer the questionings of my own soul, clinging only to his divine revelation and gladly confident in his mercy towards all the children of men. If I have so much compassion on the most guilty wretch on earth that I cannot in my heart wish him so terrible an end, then God, whose love is infinite, must be still less willing to see men in such straits. Indeed, is not Calvary a sign of the extremes to which he would go in order to safeguard man from it? In the case of my own soul, of which alone I have real knowledge, I see that he has continuously restrained me by grace from the edges of the pit. For others, then, I am full of hope. But for myself? The thought of hell should not be often in my mind, for, please God, I have no need of fear to lead me to his side. In times of overwhelming temptation, perhaps once or twice in a lifetime, I shall need to think of hell; but in my daily trials let me rather, though reverent and believing in his word, try the path of love.

43 PURGATORY

WHAT a very little we know about our future life! As Catholics we are taught less about it than many other religious bodies; we have no minute details given us such as Spiritualists so dogmatically teach. We do not accept any of their elaborate descriptions, since they are largely and manifestly colored by the imagination of the particular teacher and no less by the limits of his imagination. All who speak must use human language and even Catholic saints and poets are not immune from this law. The revelations of the one, the dreams of the other, are interesting and suggestive, but not very helpful. They lead us no nearer to the truth than we were before.

The Catholic Church teaches very simply, both of heaven and hell, that the joys of the one and the pains of the other are beyond description, since the first means the vision of an infinite God, and the second the loss of that vision, both in terms not of time but of eternity. We cannot imagine either one or the other; we had far better leave them both alone and make no efforts to guess their implications beyond the facts of the possession of God as heaven and the loss of God as hell. Though our understanding of purgatory is not hedged about with the same difficulties, since it is neither eternal nor deals with the vision or loss of an infinite God, it is, nevertheless, almost as mysterious to us as the others are, because God has chosen to reveal very little about it. We have hardly any conception of what it means, except in general outline. We know of course, as the name which we give it implies, that it is a place or state of cleansing, through which pass only those souls who have been judged worthy of heaven, but yet are not worthy of immediate entrance into it. God is so absolutely perfect, the vision of God is so overwhelming, sin even in its least form is so terribly disfiguring, the divine justice must be so devouring, that to go straight into heaven must be reserved for the soul that is wholly cleansed both from the guilt of sin and from its due expiation; only so can it attain the blessed vision of God. Purgatory is the name we give, then, to that process of purgation whereby guilt and expiation are consummated together and the soul is made fit to see God face to face. Cleansing implies some pain, submission to some process of destruction; expiation also implies suffering, the payment of a debt, the giving back of what has been withheld.

Yet purgatory is a place of joy and not of sorrow. The souls in the process of their cleansing are not in perfect peace; they yearn for and desire the vision that lies ahead of them, and therefore remain serenely in that process, gladly accepting what they know to be the only means of reaching their goal. The suffering is a joyous suffering, dictated by justice, accepted by love, and known to be required by God's glory. Yet God has softened even this for us by a wonderful disposition of his mercy. He has made it possible for us on earth to shoulder something of the pains they suffer who are in purgatory; he has extended the claims and desires of friendship till they affect even the life hereafter. To our friends on earth we are always eager to offer our services if in any way it is possible for us to relieve them of any trouble, putting ourselves out gladly in order to put them at their ease. God has mercifully allowed us, by a sheer act of his good will, to bear all the burdens of the dead. We can pray for them, that their process of purgation may be swifter; we can, as members of one mystic body of Christ, pass on to them the indulgences we gain; above all, we can offer for them patiently and in courageous silence our aches and pains, our disappointments, the drudgery of our work and profession, the sting of the weather, the normal and abnormal sufferings of human life. The thought of our dead is not only pitiful, but bracing. In memory of them we are touched to tears, yet our tears are wiped from our eyes, and our moaning is hushed to silence, for the silence will help them more than moaning. We can offer for them all life's ills.

I must not think, therefore, that my dear dead are in anguish. No doubt they are restless and eager for their release, but only as a lover might be restless who did not find himself fit to meet his beloved. He would wish, indeed, that his time for approach might be hastened; but he would be far from wishing to enter straight into that presence without being fitted for it. For love, too, makes its demands upon us; love, too, has its ceremonies more rigorously enforced than the ceremonies of court or altar. The suffering soul is certain of its ultimate reward, the sight of God. It has no feeling of fear, no anxiety as to whether or not it shall in the end be able, as its time approaches, to leave the purifying fire and draw near to the presence of God; surely, then, must its joy, the reward of the perfect knowledge of its Maker, already have overflowed into the soul. Hence there is pathos, but not rebuke, when it turns itself to beg the supplication of my prayers. It is established in the way, but it cannot now help itself. It is certain of its release, but it cannot, in any way that we know of, hasten the time of it; in that regard it is left entirely in our hands, at our mercy. It is, as St Thomas reminds us, the supreme expression of friendship that the friend bears the sufferings of his friend. If we could take upon our shoulders the pain of all our friends, surely they would always be at peace. Here, then, that course is open to us, and we can truly save them from their penalties. They are waiting – not impatiently – for they cannot cry out against the will of God; but it is in my power to help them. Let me see to it that this is done, and the law of love obeyed.

Prayers for the Dead

The communion of saints is a most comforting doctrine, for it links together the living and the dead. We believe so intensely in the life beyond, that for us death does not make the huge difference that others would have us suppose. Those who have crossed over to that other life are themselves alive. We call it life, and a real life we believe it to be. For us Catholics, indeed, there is no such thing as death in the sense that it means the absolute cutting off of all regard for the life that is this side of eternity. We ask the prayers of those whom we know to be beloved of God, nor does it much matter whether they be alive or dead, since we suppose them always to remain human enough to be interested in human things Even when they have put off mortality, mortality must have forever a meaning to them. Hence it is that we ask the good to pray for us when we meet them in our life here; and when we learn that they have gone over into the fuller and ampler life that is above, we do not say that then they cannot be asked to help us, but rather that their prayers are far more likely to have weight with God, and that they will be more interested in our welfare. Hence it is that the Catholic Church has always advocated prayers to the saints; just because the saints are dead, why should we cease to beg their intercessions? So is it with those who are in purgatory.

I prayed for them when they were alive; in their troubles, in their day of trial, I remembered them before God; and now that they are still in a state of trial why should I put aside their claims on me? How do I know that my prayers can be of any avail to the dead? How do I know that when they were alive, my prayers were of any use to them? I trusted in the mercy of God and followed the practice of Christian tradition; so now I trust in God's compassion and adopt the Christian inheritance.

Let me consider, then, that belief in purgatory and in prayers for the dead allows me the privilege of friendship continued beyond the grave. Surely it is part of the blessedness of friendship that a friend bears as much as possible of his friend's troubles. Indeed, the way that love best expresses itself is not in the external signs of affection, though these be sweet, but more especially if in sorrow I can by some loss to myself relieve my friends of their pain. The mother is most pleased when by denying herself she can give an extra treat to her child; the friend, when he can halve his friend's trouble and by his sympathy double his joy. It is one of the great gladnesses of my love when I can at the cost of my own ease purchase for my friends some consolation. Thus, as our Blessed Lord proclaimed, no greater love could be expressed than that a man laid down his life for his friend, for this meant the very last extremity of sacrifice taken joyously to save the life of those whom he has loved. Love, therefore, can at its best express itself in no other way so well, or with such pleasure to him who makes the sacrifice, as by obtaining relief for another by means of our own discomfort. After all, we should consider that when someone has given us his affection, we can never make any repayment; it is a thing so valuable because so sacred, that we have a debt of gratitude that is a debt always; consequently, we are glad of the little opportunities afforded us, not of repaying (for this is impossible), but for acknowledging our indebtedness; for even to acknowledge is to make both of us realize how great the thing is that has happened. The very largeness of the debt is recognized, and by being recognized is best returned.

Now it is just this that prayers for the dead imply. They make us see that friendship is, as Scripture made us aware, stronger than death. It has a hold so firm that it lasts beyond the grave. The mortmain for the mediaeval lawyers was the clutch that the dying hand never relaxed, and in the same fashion we hold that the dead do not let go of us; death does not part, but unites us. By our prayers we can help our friends that are dead; and more, it is not prayers only, but everything borne patiently for the dead can be offered up for them that their time of purgation may be shortened. I cannot tell for certain whether God has accepted my pains for theirs, but I am assured that, if he judges fit, what I have suffered may be taken as for them. Just as the whole Christian inheritance supposes that vicarious suffering is part of the divine plan, so that our Blessed Lord could take upon himself the sufferings of the whole world, so in a lesser way we know that God does allow the children to suffer for their fathers' sins, the innocent to make expiation for the guilty. Certain indulgences, that is, certain penalties of the older penitential code which I can now satisfy by the saying of certain prayers or by doing certain pious exercises of charity, can also be offered up for the dead. The advantage of all this is that life with all its troubles becomes a thing easily borne with. Gently I become resigned to the will of God which I cannot change; I offer my own daily annoyances and anxieties in satisfaction for the sins of my dead friends, and by my loving sacrifices speed them into the Presence. The fascination of life can be thus renounced for love, human in its origin, but divine in its consummation.

44 HEAVEN

HERE on earth, we are always lonely, nor can the best of us avoid that feeling, for we were made for friendship, human and divine, such as here can never be wholly realized or perfectly satisfied. To its full realization there are innumerable barriers which we cannot remove. We look forward to the meeting of friends and we find that often there is something that comes between us, not indeed in the sense that we disagree, but that the very limits of our being prevent that utter absorption of the lover in the loved one, which instinctively we yearn after. Despite our eagerness and their sympathy, we are conscious that absolute oneness is impossible. The presence of those we love is enjoyed, but it fails to satisfy the longing of our heart; the very limits of space and time seem often to put us apart. Hither and thither we run, turning to this friend or that, glad that we are still responsive to the call of affection; yet this very energy of our nature, which never is sated, tells that it was made for things that are better able to fill our hearts. Our hearts, indeed, were made for God, and they can never rest until they rest in him From the existence of this desire for friendship alone, one could prove the need of man for intimate union with God; one could show that nature itself pro-claims the idea of love as the only thing that can finally satisfy us.

To rest in God eternally is the supreme joy of heaven. Indeed, heaven has no meaning but that. As of heaven, so of hell, poets, artists, and saints have told us many things; they have described under various allegories both the delights of the one and the pains of the other; they have let loose the rein to their imagination and have conjured up scenes of surpassing loveliness or grim and awful suffering. The harmonies of music, the appeal of color, the delicious charms of perfume and taste, have all been laid under contribution in order to express as energetically as possible the wonderful joy of heaven; but we know that these are in reality but the imaginings of those who are endeavoring to depict truth, but know that they are incapable of doing so. They would not pretend that they were doing more than putting into sensible form things that lie outside the range of the senses; for, after all, the joy of heaven is no other thing than to see and know God. To stand face to face before him and know him even as we are known, to be able to detect line by line the features of his divine beauty, to trace the splendor   of that divine life which from all eternity has sufficed for God's perfect happiness, to study unendingly that marvelous harmony of justice and mercy, strength and tenderness, love and wisdom – the anticipation of doing this must always fascinate man's reason, for knowledge will not stop till it has passed to love.

It was spoken truly that it is not good for man to be alone. Here are we always in exile, weary strangers, sojourners who have come as yet to no abiding city; here we seem as though, like Dante, we wake to find ourselves in a dark wood. Yet, as to travelers there comes cheeringly the gleam of a distant light that streams in the dark from some cottage window and makes glad the path, gives elasticity to the steps, and hastens into regular rhythm the swinging pace, so must the thought of that true home encourage our progress here on earth. We should have the feeling of loneliness that comes on all wanderers in exile. The very joys of life, that might otherwise distract our thoughts from heavenly things, should appear now in their real significance, as foretastes of that everlasting joy sprung from everlasting life. Human love and the delights of friendship, out of which are built the memories that endure, are also to be treasured up as hints of what shall be hereafter. Heaven, then, is simply the vision of God. True knowledge, unveiling for us the sacred beauty, must drive the heart to love; over it, while it gazes on God, must break and sweep the fullest tide of rapture, a divine espousal, a union so intimate that the limits of our personality must be strained to the breaking-point. Yet it is not that we shall enter into all joy, but that all joy will enter into us.

It is a curious thing that our Lord usually uses the word heaven when he is talking of the earth. It figures in such an expression as the 'kingdom of heaven,' and this means almost always the Church which he came to found here below. In the Pater Noster, indeed, he speaks of heaven as the place where the Father dwells, but his chosen phrase when he is describing the joyous reward of the just is 'life everlasting' (Matt. 25: 46). Now, it is to be noted that in that passage our Lord speaks of hell as 'everlasting punishment,' but he does not speak of heaven as 'everlasting reward'. Thus, we are given a more detailed description of heaven than of the other place; hell is represented to us merely negatively, whereas heaven is set before us as 'everlasting life'.

We often speak of people that we meet or people of public character as having 'vitality,' or life in an exceptional way; and we mean by that particularly that these people radiate round them an energy or activity. Their coming into a room or on to a platform makes a difference to all present and creates an interest out of proportion to anything they have said or done. It is rather what they are than what they do that makes them exceptional. They can talk platitudes or do simple things, yet these are at once charged with new meaning and have a greater impressiveness merely because of the person from whom they come. But in saying this, we are describing the results of this vitality and are not touching its cause at all. What does it mean in itself? What would we say of these people themselves? Their vitality seems to be due to their greater consciousness of life, they are more awake than their fellows, they touch life at more points, are more responsive, more sensitive to everything around them, see what others miss. 'That fellow,' we say of some man, 'is only half awake,' and we mean by this, that about him things are happening which are lost on him because he is not on the look-out for them. On the contrary, those who abound with vitality have an eagerness that makes them go out to meet circumstances halfway.

Whatever happens near them they notice; their eyes are open; they are essentially awake. Hence it is, too, that they awaken others. Briefly, then, vitality means intense consciousness of life. Man is charged with life in proportion to his awareness of life; he gives out what he has first stored up.

When, then, our Lord speaks of heaven as 'everlasting life,' we conclude that those in glory are alive because they are intensely conscious of life; they have vitality because they are awake. What are they awake to? They 'live unto God,' they are awake to him and he is very life: 'I am who am.' God is life, and heaven is defined as life everlasting because it means that a soul there is brought into touch with God in a particularly intimate way. But how can we be nearer to God than we are at present on earth? God is everywhere and in everything; therefore he is within and close to us. Can he ever come closer? No; he cannot. Heaven does not therefore mean that God is closer to us, only that we then see how close he is. He could not be nearer than now, but here we are blind. Even the best must be blind to his nearness, since no man can see God and live.

'When did we see thee naked and cold and hungry and thirsty?' is the puzzled question our Lord puts on the lips of the good as well as of the evil; note that they ask when it was that they saw him Of course, that they never did. They believed him to be present in his brethren. They could not see that he was in the poor. Not sight, but faith, on earth; not faith, but sight, in heaven. That is the essential act of heaven, whence follow all its joys. Heaven, then, consists in a vision or an awareness of the life about one, and the life about one is God. It will therefore be a place intensely, eternally, alive. No question there of dullness or boredom, since souls see before them all truth and goodness and beauty, since all their powers find their fitting functions, since every desire is endlessly active and endlessly fulfilled. That vision, that awareness of life, that face-to-face consciousness of God, will be essentially the same for all; yet in the measure in which we have looked for God here, by some infinite rule of proportion, in that measure we shall find him in heaven. We shall know him wholly and essentially, all of us who get there, yet not all equally comprehend him. Our search and love for him here will determine our finding and our love above. So heaven is begun on earth, though none of us shall understand this till our earth days are finished and 'we know even as we are known'.

The Beatific Vision

In his teaching as to how this vision is achieved, St Thomas proves the richness of his intelligence. The glory of heaven, the essence of its joy for me, will be to know God even as I am known. The intimate acquaintance God has of my whole nature, his deep comprehension of my passing thoughts, his perfect and subtle understanding of my strength, will be somehow paralleled by my own true knowledge of him But how is this to be done? How am I, a creature, to get into my limited reason a perfect idea of the Infinite? Whatever I do know, comes to me by means of an idea; that is, I obtain my knowledge of things not by directly taking them into my mind, but by seizing in them the essential constituent of their being and formulating it in a sort of mental word or definition. The result is a kind of mental picture which contains the barest elements of what I am understanding Hence, the perfection of my knowledge of anything depends entirely upon the adequacy of my idea of it. Now it is evident that by no manner of means can any idea represent God adequately. He cannot be cramped into any human idea. Hence, it would seem that I could never see God as he is.

Then at once St Thomas points out the way the difficulty is overcome. It is really simple, but overpowering. No idea can perfectly represent God. Then God must himself take the place of the idea. No longer shall my ideas in heaven be, as here on earth, the mere fabrication of my own intelligence, but, in the case of the vision of God, it is he himself who enters familiarly into my intelligence and so impresses himself upon it that he becomes part of its very mechanism. So intimate is he with its texture that it is he who is its light and its informant. In other words, and to repeat, my idea of God in heaven is not as my idea of God on earth. Here I have seized it for myself, and have fashioned, from what I have been told and what I have read, an idea of what he is in himself. I have gathered together notions of a self-existing Being, who is just, wise, truthful, powerful, loving, merciful, etc. I have got more or less vague impressions (even though I cannot properly express them) as to what wisdom, justice, mercy, etc., mean. These I lump together and form for myself, under the light of faith and reason, an idea of God. But in heaven there will be no such process. God is at once in himself our idea. Hence, the souls in bliss see him adequately, fully, wholly, for they see him by means of himself without symbol, sign, representation, but with his single and immediate presence.

I shall in heaven see my Maker, yet not lose my own individual being. I shall be absorbed in him, see him steadily face to face. All the veils that at present hide him from me shall be rent asunder, every separating influence, every reflecting mirror or darkened glass (lest his glory dazzle my weak sight), shall be ruthlessly cast aside, and in the absolute contemplation of himself shall my happiness find its complete satisfaction. He shall be one with me; yet without his strong, overwhelming Being making me cease to be myself. He shall live in me; yet shall I myself live. It is all a very great wonder – this perfect knowledge, complete, adequate, obtained by no act of mine, but by the infusion into my soul of himself. As St Augustine noted it: 'Not we shall enter into all joy, but all joy shall enter into us.' Nor can this end in mere wonder, for there is to follow, consequent upon such a vision, the utmost rapture of love. The heart will itself break out into perfect songs of love. But it is the vision itself by which the soul attains perfection. The apprehension is an act of intelligence, a seeing, be-holding of God. Oh, how careful must I be of that frail, faltering reason which must one day be possessed by God! How clean must be that temple which God shall one day enter in! How guarded must it be from the profane defiling of evil thoughts, how ceaselessly defended from evil assaults! Here I must prepare for that ultimate embrace.

Epilogue: Salve Regina

Hail Holy Queen!

SINCE the days when our Lady walked the earth until our own day, there have always been shrines in Christendom where her power and her love were made manifest. Devotion to her is something which is tangled with the very roots of Christianity itself. When our first parents were driven out of the Garden of Paradise, before the gates were shut on them, God promised that he would send a Redeemer, someone to set right that mischief which had just been done, and he promised not only a Redeemer, but that the Redeemer should come through a woman; that she should be someone of power and should crush the serpent's head. And so, in the fullness of time, when the mystery of the redemption was due for its fulfillment, God sent, as he had promised, a Redeemer and a woman. In the mystery of the world's fall were found a woman, an angel of darkness, a tree, a man through whose action all the world was cursed; once more, in the mystery of redemption, were found again a woman, an angel – this time an angel of light – a tree, a Man who should set right that older mischief.

Again, in the redemption as at the beginning, the whole race was involved. By God's decree, its will was implicated in the will of our first parents. In Adam's deliberate sin all human wills were involved – the will of every soul from the beginning to the end. Here too, again, in this mystery of the Incarnation and redemption, the will of him who was to redeem mankind was to include not his will only, but as well, the will of all mankind. Our Lord redeemed us by his will to obey his Father. Adam had cursed us by his will to disobey. Will, human will, was needed to set right what human will had undone. 'I come to do the will of him that sent me.' 'I have finished the work thou gavest me to do.' Sin is disobedience and malice; redemption could only come through obedience and love.

But God demanded for the world's redemption not only the will of his Son, but the will of the woman through whom redemption was to come. He demanded her consent to the redemption; her assent to his request. When the angel came – that other angel of light – he asked of her whether she would accept the motherhood. That she would accept it, God foreknew. God dwells in eternity. Right from the beginning, before the gates had shut on our parents, closing paradise to them, long before, God had foretold what he would do. He knew what was to be accomplished; yet he knew that it would rest upon the acceptance, the consent of her who was to be the Mother of his Son. Hence he prepared her for that moment. God does not see, as you and I see, things happening one after another, a life unfolding. We only read it by turning over page after page. To God it is all visible, present – the end and the beginning God sees you, and not now, only; God sees you as you will be in that mysterious eternity. Where in it, God only knows. God saw his Mother from the beginning, saw her whom he was to make his Mother. God in eternity, above all time, from the first instant of her conception, knew her as his Mother, and so, from the first instant of her conception, he preserved her immaculate. So from the beginning he prepared her will, prepared her for the moment when the offer would be made her. Would she accept the motherhood of God? You say: 'But surely, anyone would accept so great a prerogative? Surely, any woman the world over would accept a message like that?' Yet if she could realize the awfulness of redemption, realize what was to happen to the Son, realize the greatness of it, then the better the woman, the more would she shrink from it. For that reason he was preparing her will to say yes to his request. 'Let it be done unto me according to thy word.'

Thus was she immaculate from the first instant, and thence forward endowed with grace after grace. We know, indeed (for this is our blessed comfort), that God gives none of us a work that we cannot do. A mother, a father, may say: 'But I cannot manage my children'. That cannot be true. If God calls you to be father or mother, God gives you the grace to fulfill your vocation. He must; he is just. God is also merciful. Both as just and as merciful, he would not ask of you what you could not do. If God calls some boy from the hills of Italy to wear the triple crown, the boy might answer: 'But I am not great enough for this awful office. I have not wisdom enough to direct the Church of God.' That cannot be true. What God chooses is well chosen. Whoever is set to do a work can do it. It is God who will set him there. He has only to rely upon God and all will be well with him God gives everyone the power to fulfill his vocation, however full of peril, however dreadful with power.

This is his Mother. What an awful dignity! Yet he must have given her every grace to fit her for it. Is anyone fit to be God's Mother? Not of herself indeed; but he made her fit. So when the angel came he saluted her: 'Full of grace!' Grace is God's heavenly benediction, God's holiness shared. 'Full of grace!' is the salutation of the angel. She has been filled with grace for her work, her vocation, God's purpose to be fulfilled in her. Thus was she fitted to become God's Mother. After the Annunciation and for the rest of her life, as her responsibilities grew always greater, so more and more grace was poured into her heart. Grace, why? What is grace for? What is it to do? It is to make man submit to God, to make man surrender to the divine will. Would you know whether you are good? Have you grace? Do you share holiness? Well, answer me this: are you doing God's will and doing it easily? Do you surrender without a murmur, joyously, out of love? That is what God's Mother did. That was her fullness of grace. That was why in her grace kept on increasing always. She grew more full of grace as the horizon of her responsibilities grew larger, received a fuller, fuller measure of grace. But God filled her with grace that she might be responsive to his will, do what he wanted, do it gladly – 'Thy will done on earth as it is done in heaven.' Holiness was hers. Grace was given her. We cry therefore: Hail, Holy Queen!

Do you see what was and is her royal prerogative? Do you see why she is a Queen? She is Queen because of her holiness, because God has flooded her with grace, because God has endowed her with goodness, his goodness. God has done this. For that is whence goodness only comes – not from man, but from God. Our Lady's goodness is not the achievement of her own will. Ah, no! We have been taught long ago that we cannot even mention the Holy Name unless God's grace be given us. Whatever is good in man is a blessed gift of God. She is holy – God's gift to her. But why did God make her holy? For his own purposes, for his own sake. He made her holy because she was to be the Mother of his Son. Here was someone from whom was to be born, in his human nature, the eternal Son of God. He was God's wisdom, God's holiness. He was equal in holiness, wisdom, and power, with the Father. Out of the womb of this Mother was God-made-man to be born. And so he made her holy. He gave her the grace of goodness for his own sake. Yes, but for another sake as well – hers, and mine! 'Behold thy mother!' He was thinking of her, not merely as someone who was to receive grace, but who was to shower grace. He was filling her with grace because she was to be a Queen. When a king summons someone to share with him his royal dignity, lifts her – a king always lifts – lifts the partner to be on a throne by him, he gives her her royal dignity, her majesty, her power. This one whom God summoned as a Queen, she is a Queen for the sake of the King that calls her, but she is also a Queen for the sake of the subjects over whom she is to rule. 'All generations shall call me blessed.' She knew this not only of the generation to whom she spoke, but of all generations – ours; you and me. She is Queen, she rules, she gives.

She is a Queen because of her holiness. You reverence holiness. You cannot help reverencing it; you cannot help holding it in honor. Why else do you reverence the innocence of a child? Why do you feel that it is something greater than you are – unspoiled, pure? Some old man or old woman, battered by life, poor, lonely – but you see them haunt the church; you see their lips in prayer; you see them riveted to the presence of God in the Blessed Sacrament. You say, at least to yourself: 'That is a saint.' You are in trouble. You say to them: 'Well, would you mind saying a prayer for me?' You reverence them. What have they got? Nothing, but holiness; the rest, whatever they had, is gone; their beauty, if they had any, is fled from them; poverty-stricken, sad, lonely, but holy. That is enough. That lifts them. That makes you reverence them.

She, full of grace, growing in grace, she is our Queen. Holiness puts her there. Holiness? That is her scepter, her crown, her dower. Hail, Holy Queen! That is what we say to her. We salute her as a Queen because of her holiness. We come to her, we her subjects, because it was promised that she should crush the serpent's head. What is the Lourdes statue but a Queen standing erect crushing the serpent's head? 'Queen?' you say, 'But she has put her hands together. That is not the way of a queen. We put our hands together because we are humble. We put our hands together because we pray. Queens hold out their hands. That is the way of power, the way of majesty.' At Lourdes, our Lady's hands are together, to symbolize holiness, goodness, prayer; her relationship to God. Even to look at her lifted Bernadette up. The mother of Bernadette, when she came and saw her child in ecstasy, cried: 'That is not my child.' She could not recognize her. There was something shining and splendid. Ah, not her child? It was true. That which she saw in the child's face was none of her mothering. That was a gift, a blessed gift of God. In that she was God's child only. Thus, too, is our Lady also our Queen; that is how we are her subjects.

Hail, Holy Queen! Have you heard it? That haunting chant in the grotto, away off where the river runs cold? Have you heard that echoing chant? 'Ave!' The salutation of the angel, caught up by lips that tremble with hope, with pain? Have you heard it echoing through the great church built to her honor; heard it out in the open when Jesus of Nazareth comes passing by; heard it from children and from those grown to manhood or womanhood, crying for themselves, for others:

'Ave, hail Mary,' saluting her surely as a Queen; heard it in the darkness as they wander carrying their lights in and out of the trees; heard it on those hot nights under the stars? It is the cry not only of those that are gathered there, sick and well, grown and children, but from the pilgrims from all our world. Age after age you could have heard it shouted and sobbed and lisped by men, women, children, fulfilling her prophecy, proclaiming her a Queen. Ave! Hail, Holy Queen.'

May that blessed Mother, his Queen as well as Mother, guard our goodness, cry to her Son to fill us with greater goodness – we in our misery, poverty, sorrow, pain, broken hearted. Who in our distress will protect us? The great men of the world, what can they do to right our troubles? Scheme after scheme has been tried, and the experts have failed. Who shall look after us? Hail, Holy Queen! Will she lift from us our troubles? It does not matter. She will do something finer. She will make us carry our troubles. She will give us a princely spirit. We can defy whatever may come. Dare you ask her that sorrow should be lifted from you? Dare you ask her, Mother of Sorrows who stands in memory watching her Son die? Dare you ask that she would stoop to your weakness? Shall you not ask rather that she lift you to her strength? Dare you? Surely you dare. She is your Queen. He gave her to you. She will understand you. She is good. Do not believe them when they say that only a sinner can understand sin. No one who sins can understand it. Only God knows it, because God never sins.

His Mother, our Queen, we hail her. You hear it, the appeal to the Mother? Let it be your appeal too. Ask her, in the name of the Son she begot, that she would give us greater goodness, increase our holiness, such as God has already given us, that she would increase that. All the grace she had was from him. Through him was she full of grace. He did that for her. He did it. 'He that is mighty hath done great things for me, and holy is his name.'

Mother of Mercy

Our Blessed Lady is a Queen because of her holiness. It was the greatness of her holiness that has made her supreme in our world. It is also because of her holiness, because of her goodness, that she is merciful. Goodness is always merciful; real goodness is always full of mercy. God, who is infinitely good, is infinitely merciful. He is merciful because he is good. Because he is great, mercy is a prerogative of God, a special quality. Great people are merciful. It is the little people who are unkind. The great official is nearly always touched with humanity.

It is the little official, because he is little, who is lacking in mercy. He is too full of his brief authority. He thinks not of those that come to him, but of himself. And, just as goodness is always merciful, so our Lady because she is good, holy, cannot help but be merciful. Indeed, we say of her that she is the Mother of Mercy. He, the All-merciful, was her Child.

If you think of her as a Mother, with this Child growing up with her, you know surely that she had great sympathy with her Child. He was more her Child than any other child is the child of its mother. In her case there was no human instrument of his birth other than herself. The Child was all hers and no one else's; hers wholly and of no one else but her, so that her sympathy with her Child was even deeper, from a natural point of view, than the ordinary sympathy of a mother with the child she loves. As she watched this Child growing up, it is not difficult to imagine her sympathy with him in his childish joys; her pleasure in seeing his happiness; her pleasure in him as he grew up. Sometimes mothers almost tire you with their tales of the wonders of their children. To this mother, worshipping her Child, watching him, and remembering (St Luke repeatedly says of her, 'the Mother pondered,' that is, thought over, remembered, stored in her memory this or that occurrence), must have come an absorbing interest in him. She was full of him and all he meant to her. She watched him; she took plea-sure, I suppose, in the gossip of the village about him, his beauty, his charm of character, his kindness. Are you not sure that they must have spoken of him pleasingly as of one who was always generous and kind, always eager to be of help and service to anyone he met? As a Child, so a Man, always infinitely good, infinitely full of mercy.

Then later, as she watched him in his agony and pain, and as she watched him dying, what was most evident was his in-credible mercy: 'Father, forgive them' – driving nails in his hands and feet – 'Father, forgive them, they know not what they do.' 'Know not?' The mercy of him! So as she watched him, her sympathy, because, he was all hers and God's, grew all the greater; she was touched even beyond the days of her early motherhood, touched with his pain and suffering, hurt by the jeering of the mob, hurt when she saw his bodily suffering, his frail human body wincing under its pain, hurt when she heard that ghastly cry of his: 'My God, My God, why hast thou forsaken me?' In the most bitter of all moments, with her heart full of sympathy for him and all he suffered, we were put in that dear Son's place: 'Mother, behold thy Son!' John indeed first, but in John all of us were set as her sons. The whole of the sympathy she had had for her Child was now transferred to us, to human nature, to all human nature in his place. As she had sympathized with him, so now she was to sympathize with us. And as she was moved by his joys, so ours now were to move her. She had been touched by his sorrows; she was now to be touched by the sorrows of all mankind. Ah, not in heaven – she is beyond the touch of all sorrow there. No sorrow enters heaven's gates. But on earth she saw and felt all sorrow; in the sorrows of St John she sympathized in the sorrows of all human nature. Though she is not sorrowful in heaven, she is merciful. If anyone is merciful, it is she.

But what do you mean by 'merciful'? Do you mean foolishly kind? Some think that they are merciful when they are bitterly unmerciful; think that they are kind to their children when they let them behave as they please. That is not mercy. Mercy is not idle sympathy in an emotional sense, feeling kindly towards someone. Mercy sometimes has to be severe, strong. The hands of a nurse dealing with her patient are merciful hands, not less merciful because they are firm! The poison may have to be pressed out of the wound. It looks unkind; he winces under her action. She presses the wound to expel the unclean matter. It must be expelled, by strong pressure if there be no other way. To be tender, compassionate, full of mercy, is the very profession of the nurse, yet that must not undo her firmness. A doctor, again, has strong hands, and merciful, because of the very strength of them. His cutting of human flesh is mercy. Mercy must be wise.

Now she, God's Mother, was herself the recipient of God's mercy. She knew what mercy meant. When she chanted her Magnificat she spoke of 'his mercy from generation to generation'. She spoke of his kindness to Israel, 'mindful of his mercy'. Israel had been treated with mercy, and yet Israel had been broken and scattered, Israel had been in captivity. Still a remnant had been redeemed, brought back, led home. That was God's mercy. She realized that it was God's mercy that dealt with her. God's mercy made her a mother, his Mother. God's mercy led her through all her ways. Some of her ways were joyous ways and some of them full of pain. Yet, in all of them was God's mercy. She knew that all her sorrows came to her from him. When the Child left her, her question showed she knew this: 'Son, why hast thou done this?' 'Thou?' He had done it. She had not lost him. He had run way without a word. 'Why hast thou done this? Thy father and I have sought thee sorrowing.' That is how she saw all her life. When she followed that Son up to Calvary, she knew that God was doing or allowing whatever happened. She knew that. To her, with her supernatural outlook, with her seeing of God everywhere, in everything, to her not far from God at any time, all her world was evidently governed by God. All the pain and anguish of her Son were part of God's deliberate intention. Deliberate. That is how she saw her world. God behind it all.

That is how we have to see it. Deliberate. Remember that word. All our life governed by God deliberately. All our anguish, all our pain – that is God's doing. God, at least, has allowed it. When you cry out to God in your suffering, do not imagine that your suffering shows that God has forgotten you. God is merciful. Always must we see life so. What? See God's mercy in everything? Yes, for God is merciful. Everything God does must be done mercifully. God cannot lay aside his mercy. His very justice is guided by mercy. Mercy is above all his works. You must not say to yourself only: 'God is merciful. You must say: 'Everything God does to me is done out of mercy.' It was mercy that made him deal with the children of Israel as he did. Cruel? Ah, no. It looked cruel. Mercy, that is his method, always his method. That is what his Mother had to learn. As she watched her Son, God's Son, dealt with, she had to say to herself: 'Mercy is behind it all.' Not mere justice, the naked sword of justice – but mercy, for all God's justice is tempered by mercy.

That is what Lourdes can do for our world in its anxiety and distress. God is dealing with us now in his infinite mercy. If we do not learn that in our own time, we must learn in his. We shall need to remember his discipline. God first scourged us with war. What did we learn from it? You would think man would learn something from that hard lesson. You would think that ruined homes and hearts would have taught mankind the dreadfulness of selfishness. You would have thought that such a terrible scourge, the most ghastly war since man walked the earth, you would have thought that it would have taught the nations something. They learnt nothing by it. Then he tested them with prosperity. What have they learned? It is not just this nation or that nation that failed to profit and grow wise. We watch now a world crisis, because it was a world that would not learn. God punished us? No, do not call it punishment. God is merciful. God is teaching us what, else, we would not learn. Is he teaching us? That is, are we learning? Are we learning what we should learn – above all the need of discipline? If we will not impose it on ourselves, God will impose it because he is merciful; because it is a thing we must learn. If we are to be saved at all, we can only be saved by discipline. After war, and again in prosperity, men laid it aside. What did they do in their days of wealth but give themselves whatever they wanted? Thrift? A hard day coming? They would have laughed at you had you told them that. 'What does it matter?' they cried, 'this is life. Let us have a good time! Let us enjoy our-selves!' Poor foolish children. God's mercy will deal with them. They must learn. God will teach us, for we are God's children. You would not have a mother let her child grow up selfishly, if she could help it. You would not have a father leave his boy to grow willful, when he could control him You would say of them that if they did this they did not love their children. God is love, God is full of an infinite mercy, so God must deal with his world. He is going to re-fashion his world. It will not learn of itself? Then he will teach it.

Age has to learn that lesson. You that are old, go down to the grotto in your time of trouble, go down there. You will see a rock, harsh as rocks are, unlovely. She stood in a rock and shed about her something of mercy and peace. It was a rock as they saw it, harsh, forbidding, but where she stood roses came. Harsh, unlovely, that rock as our life is. Yet where she stands, roses blossom out of the rock. The water, the bitter cold water, turned to healing when she came. Is not that Lourdes' endless miracle? He said, you remember: 'Go, tell what you have seen. The blind see.' Because their eyes are opened? Oh, no. He left them blind, but in their soul they saw. How quiet the blind are! How gentle the blind are! We, with our eyes, miss the world's beauty. They that are blind, if they have learned the lesson, truly see. It is 'the lame who walk'. It is 'the deaf who hear'. This is his lesson. She can teach it. Mother of Mercy, hail!

Ah, in youth, that is when we need discipline, but it is hard to impose it on ourselves when we are young. We have come out of school, we have gone out into business, and we found another world where the things that were sacred are no longer sacred; where their stories hurt us, at first; where all they have to teach is to throw away discipline. 'What! You believe in hell, and all that nonsense? Don't be so foolish. You are young. Take life as you find it.' Discipline thrown to the winds. Plays, pictures, books, what do they teach you? To throw aside discipline. They only teach you to unlearn.

God will teach you. Learn now. Youth, middle age, old; learn not to be bitter. Go to the grotto: 'Mother of Mercy, hail!' She that had to watch sorrow, she is not speaking to you as someone who does not know what sorrow was. He was all her Child, and she had to watch him going through torments. Let where she is be your home. In talking to her, you are talking to a Mother who knows all sorrows: 'Mother of Mercy, hail!' Teach me to see God's mercy in all that happens to me. The world of crisis will not alter because of your prayers, but you will. The world will still be harsh, forbidding, unlovely, but, for you, roses will bloom in the rock. The waters of life will be bitter cold to you, ah, but there will be healing for you at the grotto: 'Mother of Mercy, hail!'

Our Life, Our Sweetness, and Our Hope!

Because our Blessed Lady is holy, she is merciful. Mercy is one of the inevitable effects of holiness or goodness. But what, exactly, do we mean when we say of her, or of anyone, that she is holy or good? If you were asked how you would tell whether someone was good or holy, perhaps at first you might have some difficulty in describing exactly what you meant. You would remember, however, that our Blessed Lord in his teaching was determined that we should truly understand what goodness really was. He was at pains to point out to us what goodness was not. Goodness is not to be judged by what we do. It is quite possible for us individually to be thought good by other people and yet really not to have goodness. It is possible for us to misjudge those around us; to be ourselves misjudged. Thus, our Blessed Lord thundered against those who imagined that you could tell human goodness by human action. You remember, again, how determined St Paul is that we shall not misunderstand the Gospel of Christ. He is determined that we should realize that the following of Christ is not in external good actions (these should be, these should follow, but they are not the essence), that it is possible for people, apparently, to live good lives and yet not have goodness; apparently to break no law and yet to have no holiness at all. Our Lord was asked: 'What is the first and the greatest commandment?' and our Lord's answer was: 'There is but one. Thou shalt love the Lord thy God.' In his teaching, goodness is not in doing things, but in the reason why we do them; not what but why.

Are we good because we say prayers? Certainly not. Are we good because we go to the sacraments? That is no absolute test. It is possible to do all sorts of good things and yet not to do them out of the love of God; thus are they empty of goodness. It is not what you do only that matters; it is why you do it. It is not the thing; it is the motive. That is one of the great points of our Lord's teaching. St Paul echoes it: 'Though I were to give all that I possess to the poor and have not charity, it profiteth me nothing.' Goodness is not to be shown in action, but in the relationship of the soul with God. As Christians, what alone gives supernatural life to us is that relationship of love between our souls and God. If you wish to be a saint, to make your life good and holy, what you have most to be sure about is that you are right with

God; and not to trouble about your actions in themselves. Some actions are good actions, some are evil actions, but what makes them good is the attitude to God of the soul that does them; only if I love God, what I do is good. That is the sanctity that our Lord would preach to us. Get your soul right with God, then all you do, so long as you observe the law of God, all you do is full of supernatural life; without it, all you do is dead.

There is the danger of routine. There is the danger of human respect. I must do what others do about me. There is the fear that, if I do not, others will think ill of me, or wonder what is amiss with me. Now that is not religion. Love of God is the only one commandment, the one essential life-giving principle. The love of God! If we have that, supernaturally, we live; but that even of itself is not enough, not complete. We need to know him. Or, perhaps more truly, we only really love God when we know God as he is. And so in our Lord's teaching faith comes to complete love.

Why do we bother about our creeds? People say to us outside the faith: 'But we are all going the same way; we are all worshipping the same God. What does it matter about this creed of yours?' Oh, it matters vitally. If I believe aright, then I know God as he really is. If my faith is wrong, perhaps I have only a caricature of God in my mind, but God as he really is – I do not know. It is possible for us to have false ideas about people and to get fond of them, till one day suddenly they do something that shows us that we had a false estimation of them. We thought them better than they were, or worse, it may be. Our idea of them was inaccurate, untrue. Faith comes to give us an exact knowledge of God. People say faith does not matter. But St Paul says the knowledge it gives us is 'most excellent,' and that all other knowledge is not worth anything at all compared with this. I shall love, and love truly when I know God properly; faith gives me a right knowledge of God.

Why do we love God so little? Because we know him so little. He is love; he is infinite beauty. If we really knew God, our hearts would inevitably love God. We could not help it. Thus in heaven, where God's beauty is shown, the saints cannot help themselves. They must love him. They see his beauty unveiled. For us it is hidden. Faith is but the light of God showing us something of him through the veil that shields his beauty. Faith teaches me about God, and because now I know God, I can find all life lit with splendor . That is the reward of faith, the effect of faith – to give us a noble view of life. Faith shows you the unchanging things. Faith helps you to be patient with anybody, everybody, because what you do, if you do it to the least of his brethren, you do it to him. You find it hard to deal with people fairly because such a one is attractive, and such a one is very difficult to get on with, always grumbling, always complaining, never satisfied. But if you live your faith, you are not thinking of that all the time. You remember to say to yourself of each: 'This is another Christ. He has told me that what I do to these is done to him, and so I serve them. Not for their sakes, for his sake.' Faith, you see, can give us a wonderful world. You find someone difficult, and you say to yourself: 'Now, I am going to look on him as Christ,' and I am justified in so doing because Christ is going to take all I do to that one as done to him. And so I become patient, perhaps, or forbearing, or forgiving. Faith makes for us a very wonderful world. To us sometimes the lives of the saints seem hard and difficult, but to the saints life was wonderful. They were in love, in love with God. Their world was a wonderful world. It was full of God at every point in it. They despised no one. How could they? Why, everyone was made and loved by God. If these were good enough for God, they were good enough for them. That was their judgment. About them were not saints only. People were cruel to them, harsh to them. That did not trouble them. Each was someone to whom they were to behave patiently for they were sure somewhere, hiding in that disguise, was God.

And so out of their love and faith, came hope. They were perfectly secure in their world. What troubles us is the menace of uncertainty. What will happen tomorrow? It is hard enough today. I am all right for the moment, but what will happen next year? What will tomorrow bring? We need hope, and hope rests on God. Not on human beings; not on the state of business. We have something much more secure than either, for this is God's world. You may be in poverty. Perhaps. But you are in God's hands, and really does the rest matter? In God's hands, that is enough. Thus, faith sweetens life for you; and hope makes you independent of the circumstances of life. You are sure of God. If you are sure of God, you are sure of all that really matters. God's power is holding you, God's love is enfolding you – you feel perfectly secure. Nothing can disturb you. Only those who have no religion should be the disturbed.

Our Lady had her love of God, her deep love of God. The woman in the crowd praised his Mother because she was his Mother. 'Blessed is the womb that bore thee.' 'No, blessed are they that hear the Word of God and keep it.' He praised rather her faith, that she knew and obeyed God. St Luke loves to use the word 'ponder' about our Blessed Lady. He is so often telling us that 'the Mother kept these things in her heart'.

There she is, in all that happens, even in perplexity, knowing God, loving God. All she had was faith. She had nothing more than faith. Faith, as you and I have! She had no teaching given her by which to live other than faith, but how it sweetened all her life for her, and how she loved God, and how out of her faith and love she had hope and trust, undaunted! She was valiant! The others scattered under the threat of death, she remained. It was her courage that gave all the others courage.

You must have noticed that in the Passion all the men behaved badly. All of them failed, except St John, but St John was kept alive by her own blessed courage. It was the women who were faithful, not the men, and they were of her company, and it was she who held them together. Though the world shook and though the darkness covered him, she stood unmoved. When the darkness lifted, she was found still standing under the Cross – her faith, her love, her hope undaunted. She lived without fear. What she had in herself she can give us. If we keep ourselves in her company, she can radiate her love and faith and hope to us. Out of love she can give life, supernatural life, to all our living. Through her faith, our own faith finds life sweetened at every turn.

'Our life, our sweetness, our hope!' Not merely should we come devoutly to the sacraments. Holding by her, you can make your sacramental life true and rich. There will be no danger of mere routine in your sacramental devotion; there will be no danger of mere human respect and of dependence on other people's judgment; not if you hold by her and keep the thought of her by you when you come to the Communion rail. If we think of her love of him and her faith in him, then is our own faith in him and love made sure. Do I really believe? That is the thought that sometimes comes, perhaps to everyone. Do I really believe? Do I believe, really, in the Blessed Sacrament? Do I really believe that this is God's world; that God is in charge of everything; that all that happens really comes because God lets it happen, and that God is really kind and loving when he lets all these dreadful things happen in our world? If we hold by her, we shall believe. Just think of her life and what she had to live through and how she still believed in God, believed in him as she stood on Calvary. There was a God over her who could, but did not, interfere. A God? Her faith in him saved her from growing bitter, or from crying out against God allowing such misery. Her faith, her hope were perfectly secure.

And so for us, too, prayer to her can lift us above these troubles. That is the business of prayer. We do not pray to our Lady to call attention to ourselves, to call her attention to us. We do not say our Rosary in order that we may remind her that we exist. What we say our Rosary for is to remind ourselves that she exists. Prayer is lifting up, not pulling down. It is not pulling God down to my will; it is lifting my will up to God – that is prayer. It is not to make God agree with me, but to make me agree with God's dealings with me.

When our Lady appeared to Bernadette, she held her Rosary in her fingers. She did not say the Rosary. She did not pray to herself. But through her fingers passed all the Rosaries said by all souls the world over, passed through her fingers to her Son. And as you say your Rosary in her grotto, while you look at her, you see life as it is, its joys and its sorrows and the glories that come at last. You see life real, stark – not just a Mother playing with her Child, and the whole world full of happiness and joy; you see the Mother losing the Child in life, you see her losing him in death. You see him emptied of God, apparently. You see life real, but you see it with a hope beyond itself. You see that behind sorrow comes happiness again. Life begins in happiness and it ends in glory. The sorrows fall between. The Rosary is the prayer of Lourdes, the prayer of healing, because it shows you someone who was not healed; because it shows you sorrow that was not staunched by miracle; sorrow that was carried to the grave. Prayer gives our life its value. We speak of her as 'our life, our sweetness, and our hope'. If we pray to her and try to think what her life was like, it helps us also to see life as it really is; not as it appears, but as it really is; that is, God's power over it; God's power in everything that comes. 'May it be done unto me according to thy word.' That is her prayer. Keep it. Say it to yourselves. That will tide you through every crisis.

'Thy will be done. Do with me according to thy word.' Are you content? Can you dare say that to God, surely meaning it? If you can, nothing can ever disturb you in life again. If you can kneel down, and keeping her by you in your memory, say to God: 'May it be done unto me according to thy word'; if you can reach these heights that she reached, you also will share her valiancy. You can go through life and nothing can make you afraid. If you can say to others as she said: 'Whatever he shall say to you, do ye;' trusting him absolutely, sure that he will uphold you, then you also have found the secret of life. You live. You are afraid of nothing. The earth cannot hurt you, nor the sky above.

Have you poverty? Then it makes you nearer to her life and his life. Afraid of poverty, and you call yourself a follower of Christ? 'Follow me,' he called to us. Well, to follow him, is that to meet poverty, or not? Are you nearer to him in your days of comfort or your days of poverty?

To which has Christ called us? Which is the way of Christ? 'But,' you say, 'these times are hard.' Yes, they are hard and our ways seem cast in evil places. Are they evil? Is it evil to be as Christ was? Is that really evil? Then what does our religion mean to us? What is Christianity? What does it all mean? If we are afraid of what St Paul calls 'the fellowship of his suffering,' if we are afraid to be a fellow with Christ in what he went through, it is foolish for us to talk of the love of God. We do not love God; we love comfort, we love ourselves; we love ten thousand petty things. But God we do not love. 'May it be done unto me according to thy word.' If we keep with her, and, as we say our Rosary, think of her, we shall share something of her greatness. She will be for us life, sweetness, hope! Poverty will be sweetened, will make life keener to us. In spite of it and life's uncertainty, we shall hope.

She was great, and she was great because of her absolute reliance upon an unchanging love about her; an island stationed in a vast sea. All about her the vast ocean of God's love, and there was she in its midst, like some island in the tropic seas, rich, smiling, radiant. If we keep by her, she will share her life with us, that life begotten of the love of God. She will share her sweetness with us; for if our faith be real, it can sweeten all life for us. With her we shall learn to hope. She saw the Crucifixion. She hoped in the Resurrection. She saw it – her hope fulfilled She can do the same for us, make us hope on beyond our crises. Not that God will give us back prosperity, but he will give us the greatness not to care. Would you like to have that greatness, or are you afraid of it? We are human, we cry for sympathy. We are afraid. Yet, if we are devout to her, she will beat that fear from us, lift us above it to life, and sweetness, and unbroken hope.

To Thee Do We Cry, Poor Banished Children of Eve

Whatever has happened to us through the blessings brought on us by the Incarnation, nothing ever will undo, nothing ever can undo, that heritage that comes to us from our mother, Eve. When she, with Adam, had been driven from the Garden, he called her Eve, by which he meant that she was, so Scripture says, to be the mother of all living. From her we descend and inherit. What we inherit from her is our banishment from out of that garden of delight. We inherit from her a life of banishment, a life in a land which lies under a curse. When God drove them forth from the Garden and set at the entrance an angel with a flaming sword, turning, says Scripture, every way; when God drove our parents out into that world beyond the Garden, he drove them into a world which he had made harsh and terrible to them. It was a new life for them, not that first life of ease and happiness, but a life of labor and toil. The very land itself would be unkind to them. Out of the land would come brambles and weeds, and man himself would have to till the soil, and he could only till it with difficulty, with the sweat of his brow. And on womanhood God laid the travail of birth, and on womanhood, too, he laid the yoke of obedience. That is God's curse on a race that had disobeyed, and so for all time, until time ends, from all time, the earth will be like that for man, a place of hardship, of labor and toil, man winning for a while a living here and there, but having always to wage war against the earth he lives on, out of which once he came. If man were to relax his efforts, the world in which he lives would very soon demolish all he has done. Here is your great city, and you know perfectly well that unless the men in it were up and doing, your very city would tumble about your ears. What so frail as the grass? And yet if you did but relax your labor, the grass would soon come back in your streets. What so simple as the clinging growth of nature, but if she were allowed, with her tendrils she would force a way in between not only the bricks, but the plaster that links and divides the blocks of concrete. She would find a way to topple down your towers. Man lives on an earth which is hostile and is always full of discontent. And because man has memories of a garden where once everything was at ease and nature answered in plenty to the least effort of man, because of those dim racial memories and because of his nobler hopes, because man was not made for this life but another, man is always not only discontented, but striving to establish himself more comfortably on earth. Cursed is the earth he treads on; cursed, hostile to him. But, though he has been told that he must labor always with the sweat of his brow, man refuses to accept this as final and strives by ingenuity to labor, if one can say it, without toil. He will invent; he will discover a tool, a machine, something on the back of which he can load the weight of his own labor. Thus has he been able to sit with folded arms and watch the machine move and save him from toil.

This is a cursed world, but man is always striving to protect himself against the curse. Sickness? Is sickness our burden? Well, man will set himself to defeat sickness. He will discover remedies, he will prescribe treatment, he will wage, in his own turn, an unending war against disease. Pain? Oh, well, he will protect you against pain. He will still that throbbing pain that hurts you. He has discovered a way of dealing with pain. The pain is there, but he can make you unconscious of it. Man at war with those things that themselves war against man. Death?

Well he will defer it, he will push it away, hold it off from him. In his heart, he thinks one day he will conquer even death.

This is a world accursed for the plaguing man. But man refuses to admit defeat. He considers that he is here to hold at bay all the dreadful forces against him. He will live in comfort; he will live in pleasure; he will live, as far as he can, without toil. This is right! Would you not say man is right to have such aims, such purposes? Is not he driven irresistibly by the very intelligence that was given him, to protect himself against this hostile world? Right? Yes, no doubt, only he will never wholly succeed in this crusade of his. He is right to struggle, only he cannot win. That is all. He will struggle, yet the hostile earth will catch him up. He has conquered disease. Oh, has he? Wait! A new disease will come, a new disease that is more terrible than the others he has defeated. He conquers, but only for a while. Something else comes back on him His very ingenuity, his intelligence, his cleverness, in the end seem themselves to defeat him Man will live at peace. Will he? And what about the dreadful engines of war? Man has conquered the world, but only to use his mastership that one branch of humanity may be able to defeat some other branch of humanity. He will make himself comfortable. He will gather the world's wealth of produce. Ah, yes, but only by starving his neighbor. This no doubt does make for happiness but only if you think of yourselves and not of the world at large. But even then you will find that you have over-reached yourself, for you need to sell and you cannot trade with an impoverished world. We are a brother-hood. Within this brotherhood no man can shed his responsibilities to the whole, to the others. You can gather the wealth of the world, and only to starve. That has always been true since the world began. It is no new symptom of humanity, this suicide of selfishness. It is just the result of the accursed world man lives in. When God curses, he curses well. This is a spoiled world; this a place of banishment. Here there is no Garden of Paradise. Here man is in difficulty always, difficulty with his bodily life, difficulty with his soul.

You could, perhaps, endure a hostile world unmoved if you felt in your soul, secure and certain Will it not suffice to be devout? Will this not save me, protect me? There will come a time in your very devotion when the charm and beauty of your prayers will fail. You are devout. You would serve God earnestly. You will be at your Mass and sacraments daily and make your daily visits to our Lord in his Eucharist. Tell me, they give you pleasure? Oh, you will tell me, I think they should. Yes, but do they? You come and you say your prayers. Did your mind wander? Do you always find comfort when you come? Well, you will answer, other people do. But do they? If you could listen to the tale of almost everyone that comes to the confessional, you would find that even the spiritual life carries with it drudgery, so that in one sense there are times when little comfort or consolation reaches the soul in distress. Then there is sin, and all of us are sinners. Further is the physical discomfort of life. Thus there is the emptiness of our spiritual life, in so far as we go to it looking for comfort, and, secondly, there is the mortification and humiliation of repeated and repeated sin.

'To thee do we cry, poor banished children of Eve.' In these distresses of ours we turn to the Mother of God. And what do we expect from God's Blessed Mother when we turn to her, overwhelmed with our sense of banishment in the hostile world we live in – hostile to the body that enfolds us, hostile (or is it our own spirit that is hostile?) to the consolations even of prayer? What do we expect God's Mother to do for us? She loved God. She was obedient to the divine commands She followed God's way. And what did she gain? Is her life, because of her goodness, protected from distress? Did she go through her life untouched with sorrow or toil? Pain, is she free of pain, that Mother? She goes through life, and what does she meet with from good people and from evil people? What is her gain out of life? Joseph finds her with child, and she never enlightens him as to the manner of its coming to pass. She does not defend herself. That is not her way. She knows what is in St Joseph's mind. He is minded to put her away. She says nothing. She expects nothing of comfort. This is a hostile world. She comes to Bethlehem, carrying the Child within her. There is no room for her in the inn. No room for God's Blessed Mother! You see? Even for her this is a hostile world. Even for her there is little resting place. Moreover, immediately, the Child's life is threatened. She must go off into Egypt. This is God's world, and this is God's Mother, and with her is the Divine Child, yet the earth is still hostile for her, even for her. She lives her life. We do not know her circumstances, whether she was really poor, or whether the carpenter's shop carried them quietly along. We do not know. We only see her from time to time, and the real circumstances of Nazareth are hidden from us. We only know that she tasted sorrow and bitterness. We know in the end she had to watch her own Son die, hear him in his dying jeered at, see him in agony, with his spirit veiled in darkness and with God withdrawn. She had to outlive her Son. As she grew old, she was unable to do anything. She had to lay her activities aside. We know that much about her. Even God's Mother, or shall we say, all the more because she is God's

Mother, she must suffer. Here she has no home: 'Attend and see. Is there any sorrow like my sorrow? Is there grief like mine?' She challenges the world, she, the most obedient, the most loving, the most innocent of creatures; she challenges us that our sorrows do not match with hers.

A hostile world, cursed by God. This is the world we live in. Now, go to her and kneel at her knees. She will teach you. The Mother and the Child at her knee has been always the broad base of education. That is where all human teaching begins. Now ask her, and she will speak to you out of her own experience. Go to her with your troubles, whatever they be, and she will tell you, ah, of deeper troubles, to put yours in the true proportion, to help you to see your life as you should. Suffering have you? Yes; now look at her suffering. Poverty have you? Well it looks as though her life, at least at times, was desolately poor. Half a rock and half a ruin, that is where her Child was born. Tell her of your sorrows, and she will only answer you perhaps with a happy smile: 'I also had my sorrows.' Perhaps your complaining will die down, for it may be that she will tell you not only of what she suffered, but of that which came first. To her, first, was the good news told: 'Thou shalt conceive, and he that shall be born of thee shall be the Holy One, the Son of God.' That was her comfort. She knew that first. She had all her suffering, but here was a blessed thing to be remembered. She is the Mother; she carries the Child. She has the Child with her always. She suffered banishment as we all do, poor banished children of Eve. She also was Eve's child. She, too, paid the penalty, not by her sin, but by all sin's dread consequences; sorrow, pain, loneliness, death. She suffered all that. So she will teach you, teach you to bear your burden for the same reason she bore hers.

Here is banishment. We have no abiding city. There is nothing lasting, nothing that will inevitably survive. You may say: 'But my condition seems fairly established.' Maybe! It may be that you will be left like that always, but please admit that at least it is uncertain. Be ready for it, if that which supports you goes. Human love, perhaps, you counted on that: stronger than you, someone to shelter you to the end, or someone younger than you, on whom you relied for everything; yet they go before you. The world is cursed by God.

Go to her and she will give you no other remedy than a remedy within. She will give you courage, share it with you, rising out of the same source as her own courage came. She carried the good news. God was with her. We can say: am in a place of banishment where God also dwells.' Never loneliness then, where God is your companion; never death while you hold by the undying God. To remember that is what she can do for us. She can make us hold by prayer long after prayer is apparently ended, long after it has given us any comfort. We do not need comfort. We do not need the consolations of God but the God of consolations. He it is that matters. No gift (less than God himself) will content us. You feel no pleasure in prayer. You do not come for pleasure, I hope. You come to give something to God that you owe him. Is not that enough? You have done your duty by praying. It is the duty he wants of you, its discipline, obedience, service, submission: he does not promise comfort, but courage, not ease but the following of the Cross!

'May it be done unto me according to thy word.' That is her gift – not the taking away of trouble, but giving man the heart of courage to meet his trouble. She will teach us that, for she also is a child of Eve. She lived her years of banishment, yet she walked with courage. She lost no hope. It is true that there is a great difference between her and us. She had no sin, and we are sinners, but yet her Son seemed most to love enemies that were reconciled to him. He spoke of greater joy for the angels of God over a sinner doing penance. By telling us of his joy, he gave us hope. If you are really devout to God's Blessed Mother, this much can be promised you. You will have courage to the end; and that is the only fine thing man has – courage in all his adventures; courage in faith; courage in hope; courage in love. Courage, which gives us power to surmount anything and everything. Shall we take courage by saying that the world will get better, that our evil days will pass? Who knows, who dares to make that prophecy? Nobody knows. Let us prepare for the worst, for we have God with us. Why should we be afraid?

Having nothing, possessing all things – we that have God.

Mourning and weeping in this Valley of Tears

Not only did our Blessed Lord become man, but he chose a way of manhood that was of itself hard and difficult. This was not forced on him. He deliberately chose it. That is the beauty of the Incarnation. We must never think of him as forced, compelled to do what he did. He is absolute power, even as a Child lying in a manger. He has absolute power, even when being dragged through the streets. We must never think of his suffering as though it were something which was put on him by others against his will. He had all the many ways of human life to choose from. He chose the way of hardship He need not have gone that way. He could have redeemed mankind by the mere act of his

incarnation. Obedience, love, that is what God's justice demanded –
infinite obedience, infinite love. The least action of our Blessed Lord
would have been sufficient to have redeemed all mankind. He was God,
and his least action was an action of infinite obedience and love of his
Father. His suffering was not imposed on him by divine justice, but it
was deliberately chosen. He chose it and so fulfilled the richest way of
generosity. The justice of God would have been content with the least;
that would satisfy it; the generosity of God would be content only with
the most it could give: 'Greater love than this no man hath, that he lay
down his life.' He is going to do the greatest; he is going to lay down his
life for mankind, but deliberately, of set purpose, knowing what he has
chosen. He could have chosen an easy way, a comfortable way. He
could have chosen a way protected from evil and hurt. That is not the
way he did choose. He chose deliberately a way of sorrow, and then he
says to us: 'Follow me.' But he does not mean by that so much, in our
case, that we should deliberately choose sorrow – he loves us too
much to leave it to the choice of our own will. He will give sorrow. He
will give us a hard life, and in proportion to his love, that is, in
proportion to the respect he has for the depth and capacity of our love,
in that proportion he will give us hardship He will set us in places of
difficulty and sorrow. He will not leave our sorrows to our choosing All
that he asks of us is acceptance of his choice. He chooses; we are not
asked to choose. We are asked to accept what he gives us, and he
knows exactly how to treat us according to the greatness of our power
of endurance. No one is tried beyond his power. No one is accurate
who says: 'I am asked to bear too much.' God knows what you can
bear, and God will never test you beyond your power of endurance. He
will test your power of endurance. But why does he test us? Surely
already he knows? He tests us to bring out our best capacity, not
himself to know it. What does he ask of us? Acceptance, that is all.

Now, is that possible to mankind? Well, we do know this, that we do
meet people who are spoiled by suffering. We do meet people who are
made bitter by it, almost in a frenzy. We do come on people who
because of it have thrown all religion to the winds, who cannot
persuade themselves that there can really be a God, since he could not,
without interfering, watch the world suffer so. This is the problem of
suffering that disturbs mankind. If you think, one by one, of the
religions that come up and linger and disappear, you will find that they
are nearly all connected with sorrow. Christian Scientists, the
Spiritists, what are they? They are trying, by reason, to find some way
out of sorrow. They will not accept it as part of the human lot. You

could say of this problem that the touchstone of all human character is the way it reacts upon the idea of suffering in itself and others. Man can be ennobled by suffering, can be made greater by suffering; but man can be made bitter and narrow and small by it. What makes this difference in human character? There is only one word, love. Love can make sorrow acceptable – not pleasant, but bearable. With lack of love, sorrow can hardly be borne. It is possible out of love to bear suffering. We know not only that this is possible, but that it is done by everyone every day. They must take upon themselves daily some form at least of inconvenience, if they really love someone else. They will do things they dislike doing because they are asked to do them or asked to relieve someone of whom they are fond, of some trouble or pain – mothers, fathers, lovers, friends. How does love express itself, except by taking on itself something to the ease of another. Love it is that makes sorrow and trouble bearable the world over by everyone.

Of the hundreds, thousands, that go year by year to Lourdes, how many of them, do you think, come back physically healed? So few that you will find their names in headlines. Some, no doubt, are better and stronger, because of their prayers and pilgrimage, but those are not the miracles that are most widely spread. The miracle of Lourdes is the miracle by which they are sent back unaltered in body, but altered in soul. The miracles of Lourdes are the miracles of souls lifted to bear suffering, because of the one motive that almost alone makes suffering bearable. What moves them is what has moved you whenever you have borne pain happily. Love! Through the Mother, the love of the Son has come to them and through love for him, peace. That is her gift. For herself she asked nothing in her lifetime. She asked no respite and she, as far as we know, got none. She never asked for any miracle in her own behalf. The greatest of all miracles was done in her when her Child was born. That travail was saved her, but all other sufferings were hers. In Cana of Galilee she asked a miracle of him, and he did the miracle, not for herself, but to save the shame of the host that gave the banquet. For others she asked, not for herself. She knew, perhaps, what that beginning of miracles would do, not only in that household, but to the guests. St John says, speaking of that miracle and its ending: 'And his disciples believed in him.' Perhaps the Mother knew that, but the miracle was not for her, it was for others. She was big enough in the greatness of her soul to bear whatever would be given her; and what she had in this way of courage she will share with us, if we ask her.

By her blessed goodness and through her blessed prayer, she can gain for you the courage, whatever it be that you need, now, today, to deal with your burden. Whatever it is that is really pressing hard on you, she will give you a motive for bearing it without complaint. That is what she can do for you. No one will notice this miracle as men notice the others that startle their imagination. But you will know it by the happiness that survives.

You want a motive? She will choose a motive for you. Have you any dead? Have you any that perhaps at this moment are waiting, being cleansed from their sins, cleansed in those fires of purgatory which set right the disturbed balance of divine justice? Well, you can offer your suffering for them; and the more God asks you to suffer, the more he loves you, and the more he gives you an opportunity to show your love of them and him. He will not spare you suffering because he loves you. He will give you suffering, will let it come on you from others, from human sin, human folly, ill health, a thousand ways. Well, offer it for the dead, for your dead. Or perhaps you know some soul that has wandered, the scandal of someone near and dear to you? Well, you can offer your distress and pain for that. If the pain or sorrow or trouble grows greater, thank God that he is allowing you the greater share in setting straight someone you loved. Or you can offer it for your country, with its distress and its burden. Perhaps your land is burdened because no one will carry its cross. Perhaps God is searching in our hearts for the love of the land that has made us. Perhaps we could carry the troubles of our people from shore to shore. Perhaps we could carry the burdens of the poor. Perhaps we can do little else for them. Perhaps we have little enough as it is to share with them. Well, that we can share, their sufferings by our own. The Mother of Wisdom, the Seat of Wisdom, she will be ingenious in discovering for us motives that will give us the power through the grace of God to go on, to bear unruffled whatever be our lot. We are human. We naturally shrink from suffering. Yet, by a settled habit of the will, we can bow ourselves to accept it. Happy, though not taking pleasure in it. That is possible; by the grace of God, she will do that for us.

This, then, is the valley of tears. Down in the valley, with the mists that lie in the valley, what do you see, really, of life in the valley? There are clouds and shadows in the valley. They darken the horizon of the valley. But there is light on the hills. On the hills is God. Here for us, just a valley, shut in, a narrow horizon, the mists gathering – the mist of tears. But the light of God can set in those tears a rainbow, framed and quiet, all the world shining with the many-colored bow of God reflected in the broken tears of man. That is the miracle that she can help us to achieve in ourselves by God's grace. We are not forbidden to feel sorrow. He said: 'Blessed are they that mourn,' they that are mourning and weeping in the valley. He said they were blessed. Why blessed? 'For they shall be comforted,' he said. Oh, what a blessing will our sorrow one day bring us, that we shall be comforted by God! Who can know the depths of God's dear comforts? St Paul says: 'Measured against them, the sorrows of this life are not worth counting.' He knew, for he had suffered, but he hoped and had at one moment tasted what was in store.

Mourning and weeping in the valley of tears. Blessed, yet are ye, according to your mourning and your crying, according to the depth of your sorrow, for the greater your sorrow, the more will you share in the depths of the comforts of God.

Most Gracious Advocate!
It may seem strange, at first, that we should speak of our Blessed Lady as our advocate, someone who champions our cause, someone who will defend us at the judgment seat of God. It may seem strange because even God's Blessed Mother cannot love us as God loves us, God, who being infinite, has for us infinite love. God loves us. That is almost the first principle of our religion, almost the first point of doctrine that our Lord came to teach. His first revelation was the fatherhood of God. Thus, in the Sermon on the Mount, God's care for us individually was the very basis of the new spirit that our Lord came to reveal. Certainly, by the Old Testament as well as by the New Testament, we are assured over and over again of God's love for mankind.

Indeed, there is something almost gracious in the very way in which the creation of man himself is described to us. God had completed the other works of creation and then he paused and took counsel, Father and Son and Holy Spirit, and spoke in a new way of compassion: let us make man after our own image and likeness.' Is there not a certain graciousness in the wording of that story, of mankind being made after God's image and likeness? Because of it, God cannot help but love man always, everywhere. God cannot hold off his love from his likeness. His love is infinite and eternal. Having loved his own, he must love them to the end. Thus, through the whole story of God's dealings with man, we find God visiting mankind. So much was he in love with man that, long before the Incarnation, he would visit mankind under one form or another. He would speak with man. He spoke, so Scripture tells us, with Moses, as a friend speaks with a friend. He visited mankind as a man, as a light, a cloud, a voice. And then the Incarnation: in contrast to those passing visits of God with man, St John tells us that he became flesh and dwelt amongst us. He is pursuing man with his love. Formerly he paid merely a few scanty visits. Now he dwells amongst us, a long sojourn, dwells until at last the earth breaks and the end of all shall come. All through his life on earth we have again the same idea of God's love for man made manifest. The very life of our Blessed Lord, his miracles, his sermons, and again, the Agony, the Passion, the Death, the Resurrection, the Eucharist, the Church, what are all these but so many manifestations of God's love for man?

Now, despite all this mercy, it is true that one day man will come to be judged by God. True that all judgment is given to the Son, that our Blessed Lord, who came on earth and walked on earth, who knew man, for he made him, is to judge mankind individually and last of all, mankind in the mass, the great pageant of man. But, though he is our Judge, he will not cease to be merciful. Mercy is above all his works. Yet, as we read the scriptures, or hear them read to us in Advent, it seems as though awfulness is the note of the world's end, when the stars are to fall from heaven and the moon stumble in her flight; when men will be withering away for fear of what is to come on them; when the waves will raise themselves and break over the land. Yet in that description of the awfulness of the Last Judgment, our Lord suddenly says: 'When you see the fig tree and notice the tips of its branches softening, you know that summer is nigh; so when this awful judgment shall come on the world, look up, lift up your heads, for your redemption is nearer than you believed.' Here is the description of the awful majesty of God, our Judge – and yet our Blessed Lord, when he describes it, cannot leave us, in his infinite mercy, with that mere sense of fear. He bids us see in it summer, bids us know that summer is nigh. The fragrance of summer, its glory, splendor, color, warmth, and sunshine; awfulness, but summer is nigh. Our redemption is at hand. Everywhere, our Lord, even as the Judge of mankind, shows himself to us as full of love and mercy. His power is shrouded in tenderness; his threats are full of hope.

Why then do we speak of our Lady as the advocate of man? What need have we of advocacy, we who have so dear a Redeemer? What need have we of anyone to plead for us? Will not the wounds in his hands and feet and side plead for us?

Yes, but there is another principle to be remembered on which God seemingly has always acted. God deals with his creation in a way of his own. He deals with the lower through the higher. Here is God's wonderful world, and the more we know about it, of its construction, of the laws that govern it, the more wonderful does it show itself to be, and the God who made it, the more wonderful still. All that science has taught us (and we are grateful for what it has taught us) has only shown us a more wonderfully created world, and shown us therefore how much more wonderful God is than even we dreamed.

In this wonderful world of his, God acts in persistent fashion. He uses the higher to develop the lower. He will use what we call the animal kingdom to develop that growing kingdom of lesser value, the kingdom of vegetation, of floral growth, the flowers. These are developed in large measure because the insects pass from one to another carrying on their wings that which gives fruitfulness to the flowers to which they go. God uses the animal kingdom to increase and fertilize the lower kingdom. So too God uses man to develop his world. Man not only by his ingenuity has protected himself in the long years against the inclemency of the weather, but by this development, man has, without knowing it, been God's instrument in developing the lower world. All the rich fruits of man's labor have been brought out of the soil. Marble – the sun would not have shone on it and shown its dazzling beauty had not man dug it and cut and polished it and let it be illumined with the light. Diamonds, rubies, emeralds, would never have sparkled in the sun had not man cut them from their rock or dug for them; cut them and polished them and let them shine. The gold that crowns the sovereigns has been fashioned and rescued by the toil of man The very flowers that you love, that captivate you, that are so delicate and so fragrant, are not the wild flowers. Man has taken care of them and developed them, made them more varied, given them new beauties. That is God's way of dealing with his world. You go out to the countryside, and you say: 'How beautiful God has made it.' Oh, wait. Did God make it like that, or was it not man who leveled the meadows, and planted and yet forbade the straggling trees? Who made the beauty of the world we know? Virgin forests there are, but who has seen them? There are great stretches still of natural beauty, and how few of them, at least, do we ordinary folk see? God uses man to develop the beauty, not of the town only, not of the cities only, but even of that far-stretched countryside.

God uses man, and in mankind God uses the higher to develop the lower. How else would children learn? Parents guide them, train them, teach them. In mankind the more intelligent illuminate the less intelligent; the great discoverers, the great singers, the masters of music, the great leaders, have taught our race and inspired it. They have invented the arts of mankind. God gives us visions of loveliness, but, until an artist comes who shows us how lovely they are, we remain blind to them. God teaches lower minds by the higher minds. So, too, when God came to deal with man to redeem him, he repeats his older fashion. He chooses apostles and sends them out. Cannot man know God of himself? He does not. That is all. God teaches. Faith cometh by hearing. The apostles are scattered the world over. Says the sectary, the heretic: 'I will go to God directly.' We answer that is not God's way, that is all. God comes to us indirectly. God gives us the faith, not within, but without. He gives us the Spirit by which we believe his word when it is told us; but it has to be told us, revealed. We are not God, that we should know it of ourselves. We do not know it unless it be taught us. This is God's way.

This great order of God's, this fashion of dealing with creation, we did not choose it, but God chose it. There it is. So above man, come the angelic host, who are God's messengers to us (the very word, angel, means messenger). God governs us, God rules us, God illumines us by the angels, that higher creation above us that leads us. We have our guardian angel who walks and whispers by our side. We boast sometimes to ourselves how clever we are! Well, clever, but only by listening to the words that are spoken by him that God has assigned to us. You say as you look back: 'But now I see that I nearly failed.' He kept you. It was not you that saved yourself. It was he. All about us are these angelic presences. You hear, as the Mass enters into the Eucharistic Prayer, you hear the priest calling them, summoning them; he bids you see them crowding around the altar – thrones, dominations, principalities, powers, the vast angelic host through whom God governs mankind. It is the teaching of Scripture that each nation has its angel, guiding it in its trials and glories; comforting it in its depths of degradation, never leaving it, interceding for it always, guiding it to its greatness. We are guided by these spirits of God. Perhaps, as the blade of grass pushes up from the soil, angelic fingers draw it upwards. What are the colors of the spring-time but the cloaks of angels as they pass?

At the summit of creation stands God's Blessed Mother. The angels stooped to her. 'Hail, full of grace,' said the angel. She was greater than he. If you look in the Old Testament you will find that when the angels came to the prophets these were terrified. Ezechiel lay on the ground in terror. 'Stand upon thy feet,' said the angel, 'and I will speak to thee.' Not groveling, 'stand upon thy feet'. When St Gabriel comes, his words terrify the Virgin, but not his presence. Of him she is not afraid. He is God's messenger. She is his Queen. The angel speaks to her in deference. Queen of the Angels, we call her, for she is set above them.

She is the very peak and summit of all creation. So, because of God's way of dealing, all that comes up must pass through her to him. All that comes down again passes through her to all of us.

Most Gracious Advocate! That is her position at the height of created things. All that comes up – all the prayers the world over, whether they who pray them believe in her or whether they do not – must pass up in orderly fashion through all these stages of creation, until, passing through her, it reaches God at last. And when he scatters his benediction, falling like the gentle dew from heaven, it comes through her hands to mankind. Most Gracious Advocate! This does not mean that we ask her to pass our prayers to God and she passes on our request because we ask her. It must go her way: she must offer it to her Son. These words mean that we remind ourselves for our comfort that she is the highest of all creation, ransomed creation; and that all things pass from her to God.

'Behold thy son,' he said to her. We are her children, whether we know her name or not; whether we call her Mother or would thrust her from our prayers and devotions; everything must go through her. That is our hope. Our prayers are so poor, so feeble, so unwise, so indiscreet, but passing through her, they reach God; their faults cleansed, lessened; and so, too, God's blessings reach us through her, the awfulness of his glory shrouded a little that we should not grow blind.

Most Gracious Advocate! She will be there, because that is exactly her business, to carry what we give to the throne of God; to shed down upon us God's gracious blessings. She stands, for God has so placed her, between ourselves and him. It is not that God does not love us. It is only that God's love has chosen that way of dispensing his favors, of receiving what we have to give; that God, of his love and mercy, has given us this blessed hope that one of our race should stand at the head of all creation, one for whom, as with us, God died; that she should stand there praying his mercy for us, giving him our poor feeble prayers.

'Turn then, most gracious advocate, thine eyes of mercy towards us. Pray for us now, and at the hour of our death. Amen.'

Turn then Thine Eyes of Mercy towards Us!
Mercy, in its absolute sense, is the prerogative of God, but mercy in some sense or other is the prerogative of all those that love God. To love God is to be merciful. Moreover, mercy is not only God's prerogative, but the way, the net, by which human souls are caught by

God – by which he captures them and holds them and draws them to himself. Mercy is God's answer to the sinfulness of man. We, as human beings, are sinners, all of us. We shall always be sinners. We shall be sinners to the end. The saints were sinners who knew that they were sinners. A saint is not someone who is free from sin. There was only one of ransomed humanity that was free from sin. The saints, howsoever glorious, went to confession and made their acts of contrition. Indeed, the greater the saint, the more was he conscious of whatever was wrong in his life. To love God is to recognize sin more carefully and to measure it more accurately. We may sometimes be discouraged when we think of our own failings and shortcomings, at least the dreadful repetition of them. But we shall never be so discontented with ourselves as were the saints. We shall never reach their pitch of discontent, because we are not saints.

To hear people talk, you would imagine that they were discouraged because they knew themselves to be sinners. But is not that foolish? They say, or at least imply: 'I should feel more courage if I thought that I had been better.' Can you imagine anything so foolish as that? We can not really suppose that the saints imagined themselves to be holy. They were saints. They never thought that at all. A saint is someone who is dreadfully conscious of his own shortcomings That is all he knows; he is not aware of the goodness of his life. He is a saint. If we ever do get better, grow in holiness, we shall never realize it. All we shall know will be our own sinfulness; the holier we are the worse must we think ourselves.

Our Lady knew what sin meant far better than we because she loved God more. The better you are at anything, the more you realize any mistakes you make in it. The greater the musician, the more he knows how far short he falls from what he should do. We perhaps, in proportion to the littleness of our knowledge, say of a thing: 'But that is magnificent!' If we only knew more, we should realize how far it was from being magnificent. The greater the artist, the more discontented he is with his artistry. The better you are at any business in life, the more you realize how much better you should be, could be, or at least, how far short you fall from the ideal. And so, too, with goodness. If we really loved God, we should realize the wickedness of sin. We would realize not just the wickedness of sin, in general, but the wickedness of our own sin. To grow in holiness would be to grow in disesteem of self. There is no courage to be got from any impression I may have that I am getting better; or, if I did have courage on that account, it would be vanity, no true basis of courage at all.

What then is the basis of courage? The infinite mercy of God. That is God's answer to our failure. We are sinners, and God forgives us. That is God's answer to sin. God's answer is mercy, not excuse. To forgive a person is to recognize that what he has done is wrong. You do not forgive people who have done nothing against you; they would not be asking your forgiveness. You only forgive those that have done things against you. God forgives, but he does not excuse, mankind. When our Lord walked the earth, no one could have been so compassionate and tender as he was, but he never excused anybody from his wrongdoing. To excuse is foolishness; that is the folly of our modern doctors of error who say under the impression they are being helpful: 'Oh, well, I knew you did not mean it.' Is not that foolish? Of course you meant it. There is no comfort to be got out of a lie. If we had not meant it, of course, it would not have been wrong; but we did wrong and our own conscience is troubled with remorse. We know we did mean it. Now God never excuses man. He forgives man, which is a better thing for us. God cannot pander to our vanity; God is truth. God sees our folly and crime much more clearly than we ever can. God knows we are far worse than we ever could think of ourselves to be. No excuse can he make for us. Forgiveness is his way of dealing with man, the sinner You know that he taught this to us. He said we must never return evil for evil, railing for railing, but, contrariwise, blessing. We must do good to those that do ill to us. God never preaches what he does not practice. God deals kindly with those that have gone wrong. God, when we are in sin, God will still bear with us tenderly. He has charge of us and keeps us in life. God is merciful because he cannot help being merciful. He is that by the very force of his nature, its goodness, infinite goodness. Just is he, but merciful as well.

God's answer, then, to our sin is forgiveness; but he does ask of us on our side, sorrow, real sorrow. Now this is not a matter of emotion but of fixity of will. God asks sorrow. He does not ask that we should feel sorrow as an emotion, that we should be touched by our memory of the things wherein we have done wrong. God asks instead a good will from us. Fear, too, he asks – not that fear of God that keeps us away from him, but the fear of God that drives us to him. Reverence, respect, humility, that sort of fear, the fear that makes us conscious of our own wretchedness and also gives us the desire to go to him for support. Not merely should we be conscious of failure; not merely know ourselves to be sinners – that need not be sorrow; it may be just hurt vanity. Not just: 'I am sorry.' 'Why?' 'Oh, well, I thought I was better, and I find I am not. I thought I had got, over that rather humiliating series of temptations. I thought I had got out of it; that I was stronger; that I would not fall back. But I have fallen, so I am sorry.' That is not sorrow in the supernatural sense of the word. That is just hurt vanity. There is nothing fine or noble about that. That is just the reaction of hurt feelings. That is not religion. Sorrow includes fear and the going to God for help against the morrow. Sorrow implies consciousness that I am utterly wretched in my spiritual life, that, considering all he has done for me, I am a complete failure. Are you conscious of this? Very well, then, for you the only thing is to go at once to God. I am so wretched, I am so weak, I am so feeble, that I am driven back on God. Magdalen did not forget her sin; she knew how dreadful had been her life. She saw the selfishness of it, the passion of it. She saw how she had squandered the rich endowment of affection that God had bestowed on her. She knew all that, and she knew it so well that she knew her only comfort and consolation could be God. There was nothing else left. Man had failed her. Her own heart failed her. Nothing was left but God. It is the growing consciousness that you are being slowly driven into a corner, but knowing, too, that the corner is God; that beneath us are the everlasting arms.

Sorrow, then, is asked on our part, a sorrow that is based on fear, but of which the motive is love. Love is a mother. Love gathers and enfolds and caresses. Love inspires. Fear, of itself, might keep you down. Love gives you wings, lifts you up. Love is religion. 'Thou shalt love the Lord, thy God.' You shall also fear him because love itself enshrines the idea of reverence. You do not love unless you have reverence. Without it, what men call love is mere passion. It is not real love. You can give it a shorter name – but not the name of love. Love is reverence. Love is respect. This is true of our love of man and true of our love of God. There must be fear in our relationship to God, but love too, and a love which conquers and at last casts out servile fear. The fear of a son for his father, that will remain, but not the fear of the slave for his lord. For us, then, fear and love of God are essential to give us the true motive for contrition. Over it all the thought of God's infinite mercy.

When he created the world we are told that the Spirit of God brooded over it – the Spirit of God which is the love God bears himself, eternal, divine. This divine presence, the Spirit of God, the unchanging love of God which could never alter or diminish or dry up, broods still over the world. God shares his mercy with those that most love him, they having the larger share. And so God's Blessed Mother is the most merciful of all created beings, though perhaps, seeing the cost of sin, had she followed human judgments, she would have had least mercy on us sinners – we who brought about that dreadful thing.

You know, we have our moods, and everything is colored by the particular mood we find ourselves in. If you are angry, the most innocent person who does the most innocent thing may find your anger blazing out against him. He is not the real culprit, but he will be the victim of the resentment you feel against someone else. Or perhaps you are impatient, and not merely with the thing or person that happens to have made you impatient, but with everybody and everything that comes upon you in such a mood. Or, contrariwise, you are happy. Then how generous you are to people to whom normally you would not have been generous. But you are in the mood to be happy. Something has happened to make you happy; and all the world is now seen through very different eyes. It is a new world, for all the world is full of joy. Everyone you meet benefits by your mood of brimming happiness. God's Blessed Mother, her eternal mood is a mood of mercy, and she looks out on everything with merciful eyes. She is merciful to man-kind because mankind has been given to her by him alone who could give it. He gave us to her: 'Mother, behold thy son, behold thy children. Mother, these I give you in my last bequest.' He gave us to her and we belong to her, and so as she looks on us as her children, she sees us in him, sees him in us: we profit through her love of him. Merciful she is always to all men. She in love with her Son, is for his sake in love with us.

Merciful she had to be. Peter came and spoke with her, Peter, who had publicly apostatized; he came to her and she welcomed him. Does not she know what he has done? She knows. Why then is St Peter welcome? Because she is the Mother of Mercy; because Peter is her child, her wayward child. Do you think the mother loves the wayward child any less than she loves the others? The wayward children seem to be most loved in this topsy-turvy world of ours. Ah, but this is true also of that other world. There is more joy before the angels of heaven upon a sinner doing penance than upon the just who need it not. What a strange, odd world, the world of God! Well, into that strange world enters his Mother. She loves God, so she must love as God loves. She must forgive everyone. Thus it came about that she sat with the disciples and talked to them. I think it was then that she told them all about him as a little Child. They were thinking of themselves and their failure and they were angry because they had so badly failed. He had warned them beforehand that they would fail him. Yet he had given them every possible reason for being faithful to him, and still they had failed him. Now they come back to the Mother, and all they can think of is themselves. She knows this is not the way for them to become contrite. No sorrow lies that way. They must not be allowed to think of themselves, they must think of him I think it was then that she told them all about his babyhood and childhood, and told them of the angel coming to her. Only from her own lips could they have heard that. This was the time. Their thoughts must be taken away from themselves, otherwise, they would be crushed. Why not? For they had gone back on him, so blessed, so merciful, so kind, so patient. Men, they were hardly men at all – they were broken. But the bruised reed, ah, no, it must not be broken; it must be brought to stand up again: the flax must be fanned again to fire. They must forget, forget themselves and remember him. Then it was that she told them the story that St Luke later was to write down. It was then that she told them of the chant of the Magnificat, and told them of the losing and the finding of the Child, and all those early chapters of the Gospel. She told it to them then to bring them courage, to bring them back to him, to make them depend more thoroughly upon him.

Because she forgave and welcomed Peter, she will forgive and welcome us. He sinned. Who could measure the depth of his sin? We are sinners; ah, but at least we never saw the tenderness of him against whom we sinned. We never saw the most comely of the sons of men. We never heard the music of that voice of his, its pathos; we never heard him calling: 'Come follow me.' We never saw the miracles, never tasted of his glory on the Mount. We never watched the Heart show so marvelously its compassion. We never saw him touch the sick and call back even the dead. We never saw it. He saw it and apostatized. We cannot measure sin against sin. We only know that she must forgive where he forgives, and there is no limit to his forgiveness. God is infinite in all he is and does.

'Turn, then, thine eyes of mercy towards us!' Help us to see the wretchedness of our souls. Help us to see it and be humbled, but not discouraged by it. Help us to see, not that only, but the love of thy Son for us. Help us to see that what he asks of us is love for love. Do thou, O Mother of Mercy, lead us by the happy way of contrite sorrow, to peace within and to himself!

Turn, then, Most Gracious Advocate, thine eyes of mercy towards us. Always merciful shalt thou be to us who so lovest thy Son! Help us to be sorry for our sins, and to love him, and lead us at last to himself.

After this, our Exile, Show unto us the Blessed Fruit of Thy Womb, Jesus!
Here on earth we are in exile. Here on earth we have no real home.

This life is not life, really. The true life is a life which does not end. We were not really made for this life. We are too big for it. We were really made for another life, a life which will give us a better chance to use all our powers, such as we possess. That other life will give to everyone the fullest possible chance to use every gift of God he has.

Here we are pilgrims, strangers. We seek a city, and the city we seek is not to be found here. If you wanted to sum up in one single word the true attitude to life that we should have, the true attitude that our Lord wishes us to have, you could use that one word, pilgrim or traveler. That is the New Testament idea of the way in which we should look at life. Here we are just travelers, pilgrims, and it is as travelers and pilgrims we should behave.

Our Lord's attitude to life was of someone not of the world, though in it; not attached to the world; not concerning himself with the things of the world. The beauty of our Lord's character is his perfect freedom and independence. Nothing can ever happen to him that will disturb him. He walks through the world perfectly free. No one can really take from him anything No one could take even his life away. That was because all things lay under his will. But, altogether apart from that, our Lord was outside the reach of man, and when he gathered people to follow him, that was the very idea he gave them in his very words: 'Follow me.' You see them already on the march. They are travelers. They are pilgrims. They are followers. It is indeed not a command, but a counsel that they should leave behind all things to follow him. But all must follow him We see him then as the leader of a pilgrimage, a great traveler. So when someone says to him. 'But my father is dead. Let me go bury my father and then I shall follow you,' he answers: 'Let the dead bury their dead. Come thou and follow.' Again we see the picture of our Lord marching onwards, his disciples being indeed his followers. He strides ahead down the roadway and we all are to follow.

The whole Christian conception of life is that, to sit loose to life. We should rest heavily upon nothing, because everything one day will fail us. If you lean heavily on anything, and it is knocked from under you, you lose your balance. That is, in our experience, surely true of everything in life. So it becomes us to remember that here on earth we are travelers. If you have ever travelled at all, you know that the secret of good travelling is always to remember that you are a traveler; that you are not at home. As you travel, you cannot travel without some discomfort. It is very easy to allow yourself to be put out by your discomforts of travelling. Because you are travelling, you have not everything by you. You have not everything at your hand. To be sick when you are on a journey is a nuisance to you. It is a nuisance always to be ill, but much more so on a journey. At home you can rest quietly. You have everything at hand about you. You have your own things and you know where they are kept. But on a journey there are discomforts, inevitably so on a journey. You can never properly unpack. You can never spread your things round about you. You live half unpacked. Even when you stay somewhere, resting, you do not want to take everything out of your luggage. There are numberless other discomforts, and, unless you say to yourself resolutely all the time: 'I am on a journey, and this is a price I must pay for travelling,' you will be miserable as you go from place to place.

On a journey, there is a sense of unsettlement; everything has more or less to be improvised. You have got to make the best of what you have. You cannot allow yourself to think over desires and seek to satisfy them. When you are settled at the end of the journey you can do that. But while you are on a journey, to a large extent, you have to lay your desires aside.

You know there are two ways of getting through life more or less happily. One is to have your desires: 'First I want this, and then I want that, and again there is a third thing that I want' – to spend your life trying to get them. That is one way, and a very insecure way it is. There is another way of living here happily, and that is by saying: 'Well, what have I? I must make the most of what I have. These at least I can enjoy.' To do this is to go through life using the things that are at hand. Especially is this true on a journey. Because we are all of us travelers and pilgrims, we have to take life like that. It is always unsettled. You think now that when you have got to a certain stage in your life you will be able to settle down. But never! There is always something happening to you. Right till old age, you are on the march And you know how easily old people are put out. They have their regular regime. Everything follows by rule. If a day is disturbed for them, if they have to do things at a different time of day, or to do things differently than usual, all their day is thrown out for them. But that is life, it is always suffering unsettlement.

We say now as we look back thirty years ago: 'Ah, those were happy days, when people lived much more evenly and quietly; when they lived always in the same house where their fathers had lived before them; when they settled somewhere definitely, and everyone knew what district they came from. Men seldom moved aside. Life moved pleasantly and evenly.' But they never really were like that to those who lived in them. By contrast to us, they seem even and quiet days.

Every generation looks back and says: 'Ah, but the old people were more steady.' Well, they did not think so They thought that life even then was full of change and alteration. If you read their books, they thought their times stirring. Speed may grow faster as the years heap up, but unsettlement and change are the very conditions of our life. It cannot happen otherwise. We live in fluid conditions. We are creatures of time. Here we are pilgrims. We have no abiding city. We are on a journey and we pass.

And again, another secret of the good traveler is never to lose his heart on the way. It is so very easy on a journey. You meet people, you see perhaps a good deal of them, and at first it breaks your heart to leave them when the end of the journey comes. And then, as you get more accustomed to travel, you get more accustomed to remind yourself when friendships are forming: 'Now, I must not forget that this is a travel, a journey. We meet but we shall separate; it will then be all over and done.' You see a country, a place that charms you, and you say: 'Well, now, I would like to stay here a little while.' Stay, but remember you are on a journey. Do not dig yourself in too securely. You must leave one day and pass on.

Now all this is true of our life. Here it does not do to settle down too absolutely to life. Something will happen, and your heart will be broken. Enjoy what you have, what you see, but do not have any lust to own all you see. Enjoy? It is a dreadful thing to discover that there are people who cannot enjoy a thing without burning to own it. How sad to have that greed! They see some-thing beautiful. They are not content with seeing and remembering. They want to own. Are not there men and women the world over who are buying pictures for the pleasure, not of enjoying them, but of owning them? That is paltry. That is just a lust to possess, to own, to say: 'It is mine.' Poor people indeed they must be who cannot enjoy what they do not possess. Better it is surely to enjoy all that your eye lights on, but not to want to own it. These others would buy the sunset if they could. But to see the beauty of the sunset and to cherish it in your memory is to have unceasing joy. To see a wide stretch of country and to enjoy gazing at it and to let it haunt your memory, that is a blessedness! To get endless pleasure, not from possession, but from mere sight and the memory of sight, is to be well stored with wealth, to be rich. To walk down a picture gallery and see a picture that attracts you – whether artists consider it good or bad does not trouble you; you like it, it gives you pleasure – is to be able to carry that pleasure with you always. Those who can do this are free.

You know how children act when you take them out walking, and you go through the woods in the summer or spring. They pull the wild flowers and carry them, and after a while in their hot hands the flowers die, and they are tired of carrying the flowers and throw them aside – well, we are like children. We gather and own and possess. We heap up things for the mere joy of possession till we grow tired of them, burdened by them. How poor! How paltry! That is hardly the way of Christ. The way that he set is the way of a traveler, someone on a journey. Enjoy things, but do not want to have them. Learn not to envy, learn to do without.

You take your children along the seashore, and they gather the shells till their pockets are heavy with these beautiful treasures, and then they ask you to carry them. They have got more than they can carry. We are all children like that. We heap up our treasures, till they are a care, a burden, a menace to our peace.

Do you remember how our Blessed Lord speaks of the need of seeking only those treasures which no thief can get at? Fancy possessing things that must always put you in terror of losing; the menace that someone might break in and steal them! There is trouble enough in the world in every man's life without adding to our own trouble by the burdens of the treasures we house. To collect beyond our need is only adding to life's troubles. What our Lord suggests to us is a much freer, happier way of life. To enjoy what we have and let the rest go by us; to be master of our lives, and not to allow things to master it for us; to be able to get along with as little as may be; to need little; to cut down our desires. Our Blessed Lord does not say that we must give up everything, but that we must be free from everything. We must be able to get on with the least possible amount in our life.

That, at least, was the way he went. He had not even anywhere to lay his head! He does not ask that of us, but think of the freedom it gave him. He came and went as it pleased him; he took the life he found. They say that those that have begun to wander find it dreadful to live again in one place. There is something strangely, unbelievably attractive in the free wild world, in life in that world. The Arab, with the desert around him, feels the freedom of it. Men of civilized cities are caught by the attraction of the desert, its absolute freedom, its width, its openness, its far horizon. In it they feel free. Spiritually, that is where we should be; we can be so by remembering that we are travelers, but again to remember that we have a home: 'We seek a city.' We are not just wandering; we are wandering, seeking a city. Somewhere a home awaits us.

Now what makes a home? What is your home? Is it the house you live in? Is it not people that make a home? You look back to your childhood, and you say: 'That was my home.' Yet you can go back to the house now, if it is standing, and feel that it is not your home. There is a certain romance still about it, a romance if you go inside the door. Stories keep starting up from the rooms, from the staircase, the attic. Old dead memories come drifting back. Ghosts of the dead walk. The garden brings back so much to you, and the bushes in it round which you played, where you hid from the wild red Indians of your imagination. It all comes back to you as a living thing. But, despite this, it is not a home now to you. It is empty now of all that really made it home. You go back, but after a while it is with dreariness that you see it. The people have gone. It is people that made it home for you – our family, our friends, our lovers – fashion our home.

Here, then, we are pilgrims, travelers. Death comes to us, touches this one and that. Out of our great pilgrimage they pass. Death calls them, this one and that one. Older than we, younger. Those that might deceive us into thinking this our home dwindle year by year. Year by year there are more on the other side and less on this side that hold us. There they seem gathering and waiting for us. They never fall out of the group that passes over. They dwell there, abide.

That is home. And the center of the home? 'We seek a city whose maker and builder is God.' 'After this our exile, show unto us the blessed fruit of thy womb.'

After this, our exile. It is through that vision we should try to look at death. Oh, no doubt, when it comes, death will be something frightening. King Death, we say, for it has a majesty, a terror of its own. Death is strange and difficult and frightening because it is uncertain; the lot that lies for us on the other side. Who shall know? Death must always be disconcerting, for 'no man knoweth whether he be worthy of love or hatred'. Judgment – who dares foretell his judgment? It is the awful uncertainty of death that is the dreadfulness of it. Yet there is an element in it of home-coming. Through that gateway, though it be awful and dreadful, you must go to your home.

There are hills, sometimes, that men climb, steep and rocky, with their tops covered with snow; and sometimes to reach the summit, which has been split by ancient land convulsions, the climber must go into the rock through darkness, where the only light is the light that straggles in from the entrance of the cave. There are boulders in front of you. At first you do not see your way at all. It is dark and uncertain, but you must go that way now to reach the summit and find the air and light of day. There is nothing else but to dare that dark cavern and the heavy stones in it that trip you as you grope your way. It is terrible, but it is your only escape. Half frightened, not knowing what is coming next, and feeling your way with your stick to make sure there is no hole in front of you, you must go onwards. It is your only way out to the light. Such is the dark cavern of death.

'After this, our exile, show unto us the blessed fruit of thy womb.' That is her business. She showed him mortal to mortality. She shall show him immortal to immortal men. She brought him forth in his first birth; she shall bring us forth in that second birth of ours to the vision of the fruit of her womb. God gave us him through her, and the gifts of God are without repentance. God never goes back on his gifts. He shall give the Son to us again through the Mother. She will lead us to himself.

'After this, our exile.' She knew that life was an exile. She longed for home. She knew that she was only a traveler. As a traveler in a strange place, she brought forth her Child. As a traveler, she fled away to Egypt. She stayed in Egypt as a stranger. As a traveler out of Egypt, again she came. She went to Nazareth and journeyed to Jerusalem, and lost him and found him, and he taught her that life was full of coming and going. 'You cannot expect to have me always with you. You cannot expect that. I must be about my Father's business. You must be content with that assurance.' Every mother has got to learn that, not to be master of her child. He and she, boy and girl, must leave her. They have their life to live, their independence, their own home one day to form. Our Lady had to learn that, to learn that she was a traveler. Each stage would be passed and over. He was to leave her one day. She has only a respite of years, and then he goes out from her, and she but slowly follows. She is there on the edge of the crowd. She is a pilgrim; though she is his Mother; she is a stranger. Is not this God's world? Yes, but she must journey on.

And then he dies and she lives on. He comes back from the dead and she sees him. He ascends into heaven, ah, then her heart was nearer to breaking than when he died. How the sunshine must have gone from her life when he went out of it. All her happiness, we might suspect, would have left her. All? Not all. There was Mass, there was the Son again, as John, the Beloved Disciple, took her to his own, as he recited the liturgy and broke bread at dawn. She received again into her bosom the Son that had dwelt there. But then he left her, morning by morning, when Communion was done; and she, that poor and lonely Mother, was only again a traveler, a pilgrim. Even she. Then old age grew on her. She was indeed but a pilgrim, a traveler. Earth was no home for her. Earth was exile for her. For her of all people, this earth, with all its beauty, was but a place of exile. She was shut out from home.

And then her homecoming; the Assumption, we call it. Human love, divine love, mingled in perfect order. Her happiness, as she came home. Home? Why, that could be no home, for she had never visited it, had not come out of it. It is people who make the home. That was home to her, where her Son was. Home for her; home for us: we follow her, we are exiles with her: 'After this, our exile, show us the blessed fruit of thy womb.'

We must seek a city. We must remember that here we are travelers and pilgrims. Here we have no home, but we seek a city whose builder and maker is God. No, it is finer than that, even. God is not merely the builder and maker, God is the city itself. We shall dwell in God.

Dear Blessed Mother! Here we are in exile, with its discomforts, with its unsettlement, with its change. Mother, grant that we who taste the bitterness of exile may not lose in the end the sight of him; that we and those dear to us may be gathered where you stand, and be received and led by you to the vision of the blessed fruit of thy womb. As we have lived here as exiles, shall we find ourselves there at home. The vision of God is proportionate to the desire for God on earth. As you have longed for him, so you shall find him. If you have longed for him less ardently, you shall find less of his overflowing fullness when you come to him. If you have longed for him greatly, he will fill all your longing; all your yearning will he satisfy.

Blessed are they that hunger and thirst after this home of theirs. They shall have their fill.

O Clement, O Loving, O Sweet Virgin Mary!
St John tells us in his Gospel that on one occasion among the many questions that were put to him by the crowd that doubted, there was one question that they asked him° 'How is it that thou, being man, should make thyself God?' We, knowing better than they knew, would rather reverse the question, 'Why dost thou, being God, make thyself man?' and his answer, as we know, would have been immediate and instant. He made himself man that he might hold man's love. He came to make man love God, to solve that difficulty of man's imagination. How is man, who is so moved only by the things he sees and hears, or, at least, is most stirred by them, how is man with this imagination of his, ever to love the infinite God, a Spirit invisible, not to be seen in this life by him alive? How can man ever love God? Our Lord came to show

us God Incarnate, that through him we might have some better imagination of God and so love him with true love.

One of the apostles, even at the Last Supper, made to him what is a very natural request: 'Show us the Father.' Just give us one glimpse of God, and after that the whole spiritual life will be easy. 'He that seeth me,' was the answer, 'seeth the Father.' The nearest we shall ever get to God on earth is Christ. It is God, but shut in by human nature. Still, if we know Christ, we at least have some idea of what God is like – though he is infinitely more wonderful, infinitely more kind and tender, infinitely more just and awful than he could show himself. Christ multiplied by infinity, that is God.

He came wanting men's love, and endeavoring to hold men's love; and he came, not because he needed love, but because he desired it. To love because you need the love of those you love is one way; to love because you desire their love is higher and better. To love because you need their love in answer to yours is to love only as long as your need is; to love because you desire their love, is to love as long as you live. God loves us, not needing our love, but desiring it. God came to bring us captive, to conquer mankind, for you conquer in life not your foes only, you conquer not by force only, you conquer friends and you conquer by love. That is Christ's conquest. Those are the captives he led after him into the kingdom of his Father; captives made conquest of by love. But the first conquest that he made by love was the conquest of his Mother.

Before Joseph knew, she knew that he was coming. Before even John the Baptist had leapt in his mother's womb; before John's mother, Elizabeth, had saluted in her cousin the Lord of Glory, already she knew. Before the shepherds came heralding; before the kings had come out of the east, she knew; knew who he was and what he came for. This had been wrought in her by the miracle of his conception. She knew, and by her knowledge she was led captive to him; like all his captives she was led by faith and hope and love.

Do not imagine that in her life she had more than faith to go by. She had but faith. She had no higher gift. She believed on the Word that was spoken to her; she believed because of that.

You may think, yourself, that it was easy for her to believe. Well, in a sense, yes, it was easy, because of that miracle that had been done her; because, without human instrument, in her heart she felt the quickening of another life. Easy, because when he came forth at Christmastime, he came forth as through the tomb, without opening of doors. He passed through this first tomb that held him, and that was a miracle she could not but know. And yet, for her, faith in a sense must have been much harder – to believe that this One was God who depended on her for his breath. She had to say, 'Fiat,' let it be, before he came, before in her eyes there shone the light of motherhood. She had to give leave to Omnipotence before it came on earth, dwarfed in childhood. God waited on her word. This was God, whom she herself had to care for and protect. This was God that had to be safeguarded by flight into Egypt. Were not all our difficulties of faith, or almost all, hers ten times over? God, that she fed at her breast? God, that she carried? God, that slept while she went about her duty, cleaning the home? This God, that was subject to her in Nazareth? This God, whom she saw in agony, bereft of the divine presence, seemingly, in the darkness of Calvary? This was God by whose death she watched? She believed in him in spite of all that, and she had perfect confidence in him. Confidence, when he perplexed her by his sayings, by his actions, by what she could not understand.

She had perfect hope in him even when she saw the failure of all his dreams; when she saw that great audience that had gathered once about him dwindle, all the people leave him, and his own disciples go from him. She hoped even when she saw that little band gradually growing smaller. She had still to have perfect hope when she saw him lying dead in her arms. She had hope beyond that of the apostles. They had lost hope. Some of them had gone out of Jerusalem. They had lost hope in him. He that had seemed so wonderful was dead. They had hoped that this was the Messias. Now they all lost hope. But she hoped on.

She had to love him, and again, you might say: 'But that was easy! She saw how perfectly lovable he was.' True, and yet he treated her in a way that hurt her, and she knew that he knew she was going to be hurt. The losing of the Child – there was no losing. He went deliberately, and he went without saying a word. He could have softened the blow of his going by just telling her beforehand. 'I must be about my Father's business.' He might have said it before he left her, but he did not. He just left her in darkness. Yet she loved him even when he treated her with apparent harshness. She loved God even when God seemed harsh to her Child. She still loved God when God seemed to have abandoned him, left him to be the sport and the mockery of men. She loved God when she saw her Child hanging on the Cross, heard him crying, crying because he was thirsty, crying because God's presence seemed withdrawn; loved God when she heard the crowd jeering and no answer coming from heaven – heaven dumb and silent, yet she loved.

Ah, in our day people treated with harshness question: 'Is there a God? Can there be a God who saw all this terrific slaughter and never interfered?' Do not you think men now are questioning out in the cold when they have no home, no heat, no comfort: 'Can there be a God that lets us suffer so?' But their suffering, she challenges it. 'Look and see, is there suffering like my suffering?' and yet she went on, not only believing and hoping, but loving to the end.

Because of that, she has been given power over us. She is our Queen and our Mother; our Queen because our Mother; our Queen because we were given to her by her Son. We put up then our prayer to her: 'O clement, O loving, O sweet Virgin, be thou a Mother to us.' Clement, because it is the prerogative of royalty to show clemency to rebels that submit. It is her very grace as Queen of mankind that gives her that blessed prerogative of mercy. She is clement, has clemency, forgives. She is loving, or, as the prayer says in Latin, *pia*, dutiful. She loves God because of his command. She is also his Mother, and so she loves God with a mother's love, a sheltering love. It is the love he compared to his own. 'Even if the mother forget, I will not forget,' as though that were the very extreme comparison. Even if the mother forget, not God. She had that mother's love for God, and for love of him she loves us, and so her love is unchanging. She loves us, not for ourselves. How could she? She loves us for his sake. She must love us to the end. She loves God. She is God's Mother, and she is our Mother, too. That is her sweetness. She has the prerogative of pity. Does not all love begin in pity? The old romantic love of the knight for the maiden, the love of woman for man – is not pity always the dawn of love's sunshine? Does not love grow out of that, the love of the mother for the child? At the back of all love is pity. O clement, O loving, O sweet Virgin Mary! O her royal, her loving, her pitiful heart!

And at Lourdes, is she not all these, clement, loving, sweet. Clement. Do you remember that when she appeared in the grotto, she moved Bernadette to cry out: 'Penitence, penitence'? The sight of the Blessed Mother, the blinding purity, the white garment, the blue sash about her waist, the very purity of her gesture, her look – Bernadette cried out: 'Penitence, penitence.' And our Lady said to her: 'I do not promise to make you happy in this world, but in the next.' And when Bernadette came to die, in her mind were the sins of all people, and that was what she prayed for, that all men might be forgiven. This was the Immaculate Conception; this was our fallen nature's solitary boast. She was sinless; man was sinful. What are the cures at Lourdes but the clemency, the gifts of a Queen? She is there not only as a Queen, but as God's Mother. She is there loving God. She is there helping people to love him. It was her very demand almost from the beginning. 'I will have processions in this place.' Of what? Processions of the Blessed Sacrament. She is there not to exalt herself, but to exalt her Son. They tell us that the miracles are most often wrought when the priest carries the Blessed Sacrament down amongst the people. For us, devotion to God's Mother does not lead us away from God's honor, but to it. However we exalt her, he that made her is greater still.

When Bernadette lay dying, the memory of Lourdes came back to her. 'I desire Thy Cross, O God Almost the last words that she spoke were these. The Mother had passed, it was the Son she remembered, and he came, as always, carrying his Cross.

Clement, loving, sweet. Ah, the tenderness of her at Lourdes! Ask those that have been there. They will tell you of the tenderness of grace, of the delicacy of the miracles that are wrought there, of the dreadfulness of human disease and pain and suffering, but also of the gentle way she gives her mercy to each.

And so, when Bernadette lay dying – you know when you lie dying, it is those things that have bitten deepest into your memory that will come back to you. In the war, when a man was wounded into semi-consciousness, he remembered his mother, not his wife; it was childhood's days that came back. In the shock of death, if you listen, stoop over and listen to the dying; they talk of their childhood; not of yesterday, but many days before. Bernadette dying had forgotten where she was and what she was doing; she remembered only the grotto that she had not seen since the last vision on the feast of Mount Carmel when our Lady came back and never said a word and she herself left to become a nun at Nevers. She remembered the grotto so when a nun stooped over her and said to her: 'I will ask the Immaculate Mother to console you.' 'Not console,' she answered, 'not console. Ask her to give me strength and patience.' That is what she wanted, not comfort – courage, strength, patience. She was going the way of human pain.

Sweetness. What sort of sweetness, do you think, was hers? When they use that word, sweet, of her, are they thinking of some sweet fragrance or the echoing of sweet music? Or is it honey, that is sweet to the taste? Is it the sweetness of the clean air when you leave the city and go to the heights above it? Is it the sweetness of fresh water tumbling down from the hills? Is it the sweetness of a happy-tempered child that fascinates you? Is it the sweetness of someone going at his or her own sweet will? Well, all of it, I suppose; we would say of her that she is sweetness in every way. Fragrant, for we call her the Rose of Sharon; we name her the Lily of the Valley, the lily of our valley, this poor valley of tears. Sweet, as though it were the echo of music! What is she but the echo of God's Word, the Word that was begotten of her, that was fashioned of her. She is but an echo of the Word of God. Sweetness as of honey! It is said of her in Scripture that she has the sweetness of the winds passing over beds of aromatic spices. Every poetical device is used to help out the feebleness of our imagination about her; to help us to understand what she is meant for in our life. Sweet in her temper, surely; going God's way after her own sweet will.

O clement, O loving, O sweet Virgin Mary! Surely you, her faithful people, have every right to call her so. Ask her, you that have been faithful to her, ask her to be clement to you and yours. Remember, she is your Queen, the Virgin most powerful. 'Hail, Holy Queen.'

Because she is God's Mother, she is loving, she is the Mother of Mercy! The Mother of the all-merciful One. Ask her then for mercy; submit to her. Ask her to win you mercy, all of you, and yours, from her Son. Mother of Mercy, hail!

Ask her, too, to be to you a Mother 'Show thyself a Mother.' She knows your needs. She will mother you now and at the hour of your death.

'Turn then, most gracious advocate, thine eyes of mercy towards us, and after this, our exile . . .' Now in these days you know verily this is an exile, you who live in these hard days. Before, you might have forgotten, in your happiness and prosperity, might have thought that this was a place worth living in, thought that the world was a world in which your every dream might any day come true. For every comfort seemed yours, every desire within the range of fulfillment, nothing seemed likely to be denied to you. You gathered the wealth of the world. But now you find the world an exile. You realize this is banishment. You know that everything must one day fail you. You know that this is never your home. Remember, when you leave it, your exile is over. Remember, death means you go home. You are children, working or playing in your school hours; at last come the holidays, and the cry of home: 'At the hour of death, call me.' That is our prayer. Call me. 'Leaving all things, they followed him.' That is all death is. It is another call from God.

Turn then, most gracious advocate, thine eyes of mercy towards us, and after this, our exile, show unto us the blessed fruit of thy womb. O clement, O loving, O sweet Virgin Mary!

APPENDIX: Sources

The selections in the *Bede Jarrett Anthology* have been taken from the
following works:

Living Temples, Burns & Oates Ltd., London, 1919.
The Space of Life Between, Sheed and Ward, London, 1930.
No Abiding City, Blackfriars, London, 1956.
The Homiletic and Pastoral Review, Vol. xxxiv, 1933; Vol. xxxiv, 1933-4,
    Wagner and Company, New York.
The Abiding Presence of the Holy Ghost in the Soul, Newman Bookshop,
    Westminster, Maryland, 1943.
Lourdes Interpreted by the Salve Regina, Newman Bookshop, West-minster,
    Maryland, 1945.
Meditations for Layfolk, Catholic Truth Society, London, 1946.
The House of Gold, Blackfriars, London, 1954.

Chapter 1: *Space of Life Between*, pp. 17-25; *Meditations for Layfolk*, pp. 12-13.
Chapter 2: *Meditations for Layfolk*, pp. 4-5; 32-43
Chapter 3: *Meditations for Layfolk*, pp. 18-23; 26-31; *House of Gold*, pp. 209-
    38; *Homiletic and Pastoral*, Vol. xxxiv, pp. 260-5.
Chapter 4: *Meditations for Layfolk*, pp. 44-51; *Space of Life Between*, pp. 86-
    101; *House of Gold*, pp. 238-42; *Homiletic and Pastoral*, Vol. xxxiv, pp. 936-
    1049.
Chapter 5: *Meditations for Layfolk*, pp. 58-61; 152-3; 156-65.
Chapter 6: *Meditations for Layfolk*, pp. 224-35; 238-49; 188-9.
Chapter 7: *Meditations for Layfolk*, pp. 6-7; 16-17; 60-1.
Chapter 8: *No Abiding City*, pp. 20-5; *Meditations for Layfolk*, pp. 82-3; *Space of
    Life Between*, pp. 106-13.
Chapter 9: *No Abiding City*, pp. 47-55
Chapter 10: *Abiding Presence of the Holy Ghost*, pp. 30-53.
Chapter 11: Abiding Presence of the Holy Ghost, pp. 54-79.
Chapter 12: Abiding Presence of the Holy Ghost, pp. 80-118.
Chapter 13: *Homiletic and Pastoral*, Vol. xxxiv, pp. 43-7
Chapter 14: *Meditations for Layfolk*, pp. 270-I; Space of Life Between, pp. 175-
    8.
Chapter 15: *Meditations for Layfolk*, pp. 216-17; 220-3.
Chapter 16: *Meditations for Layfolk*, pp. 280-3.
Chapter 17: *No Abiding City*, pp. 63-7; *Meditations for Layfolk*, pp. 218-19.
Chapter 18: *Homiletic and Pastoral*, VOL XXXIVB, pp. 474-9; 715-20;
    Meditations for Layfolk, pp. 62-3.
Chapter 19: *Meditations for Layfolk*, pp. 208-15.
Chapter 20: *Space of Life Between*, pp. 191-4; *Meditations for Layfolk*, pp. 90-1;

130 – I.

Chapter 21: *Meditations for Layfolk*, pp. 276-7; *No Abiding City*, pp. 33-9.

Chapter 22: *No Abiding City*, pp. 14-19; 40-6; *Meditations for. Layfolk*, pp. 204-5; 206-7.

Chapter 23: *Space of Life Between*, pp. 138-41; *Meditations for Layfolk*, pp. 300-1; *No Abiding City*, pp. 5-8.

Chapter 24: *Meditations for Layfolk*, pp. 142-9; 266-7.

Chapter 25: *Meditations for Layfolk*, pp. 168-9; *Homiletic and Pastoral*, Vol. xxxiv, pp. 128-33; *No Abiding City*, pp. 26-32.

Chapter 26: *Space of Life Between*, pp. 35-41; 66-9; 74-7; *Meditations for Layfolk*, pp. 12o-1.

Chapter 27: *Meditations for Layfolk*, pp. 172-81; 194-5; *Homiletic and Pastoral*, Vol. XXXIVB, pp. 1050-5; *No Abiding City*, pp. 56-62.

Chapter 28: *Meditations for Layfolk*, pp. 264-5.

Chapter 29: *House of Gold*, pp. 91-101.

Chapter 30: *House of Gold*, pp. 115-24.

Chapter 31: *House of Gold*, pp. 125-35.

Chapter 32: *House of Gold*, pp. 136-42.

Chapter 33: *House of Gold*, pp. 143-50.

Chapter 34: *House of Gold*, pp. 151-60.

Chapter 35: *House of Gold*, pp. 67-79.

Chapter 36: *House of Gold*, pp. 80-90.

Chapter 37: *House of Gold*, pp. 55-66.

Chapter 38: *House of Gold*, pp. 230-40.

Chapter 39: *No Abiding City*, pp. 1-4.

Chapter 40: *Space of Life Between*, pp. 160-4; *Meditations for Layfolk*, pp. 64-5.

Chapter 41: *Meditations for Layfolk*, pp. 68-9.

Chapter 42: *Space of Life Between*, pp. 151-4; *Meditations for Layfolk*, pp. 74-5-

Chapter 43: *Space of Life Between*, pp. 155-9; *Meditations for Layfolk*, pp. 56-7.

Chapter 44: *Meditations for Layfolk*, pp. 72-3; 80-1; *Space of Life Between*, pp. 146-50.

Epilogue: *Lourdes Interpreted by the Salve*

CPSIA information can be obtained at www.ICGtesting.com
Printed in the USA
LVOW01s2125130114

369235LV00032B/1691/P